Forecasting Methods for Management

Forecasting Methods for Management

SPYROS MAKRIDAKIS
The European Institute of Business Administration (INSEAD)

STEVEN C. WHEELWRIGHT
Graduate School of Business Administration, Harvard University

FIFTH EDITION

JOHN WILEY & SONS
New York · Chichester · Brisbane · Toronto · Singapore

To our children

Aris and Petros

and Marianne, Michael, Melinda, Kristen,
Matthew, and Spencer

Library of Congress Cataloging in Publication Data:

Makridakis, Spyros G.
   Forecasting methods for management.

   Includes index.
   1. Economic forecasting.   2. Economic forecasting —
   methodology   3. Business forecasting.   I. Wheelwright,
Steven C.   II. Title.
ISBN 0-471-60063-6

Printed in the United States of America

10 9 8 7 6 5 4 3 2 1

PREFACE TO THE FIFTH EDITION

When the first edition of *Forecasting Methods for Management* was published in 1973, only a handful of books on forecasting were available. Those books tended to be mathematical and to provide in-depth coverage of only a few forecasting techniques. We wanted to present an overview of a broad range of forecasting techniques that would help managers understand the strengths and weaknesses of those techniques without requiring them to have a substantial background in quantitative methods. Since then, this book has been translated into half a dozen languages and has established itself as the best-selling management book in the field.

During the past twenty years the forecasting field has expanded significantly; more than 200 books have been published in English alone. At least twenty of those have imitated the format, coverage, style, and intent of the earlier editions of this book. We have accepted the challenge they present to improve our coverage and to meet the needs of managers more effectively. Substantially different from the first four, this fifth edition reflects the newest developments in the forecasting field and the expressed needs of managers.

In recent years the scope of forecasting has expanded well beyond its technical aspects, encompassing a much broader set of planning, decision-making, and managing issues. In addition, the optimistic expectations of the 1960s that the forecasting accuracy problem would be solved have been tempered as experience has scaled down grandiose expectations to more attainable objectives. This fifth edition seeks to address this broader set of managerial concerns through down-to-earth descriptions of forecasting, its possibilities and limitations, and its role in the management process.

Most managers are not directly concerned with forecasting's theoretical aspects. Few have the time or inclination to study the details of every possible method. They need a book that covers a wide range of forecasting approaches and tools and accurately describes their essential characteristics and their application in practice.

To be most helpful to management, a forecasting book must deal with the forecasting function in the organization, as well as the many available techniques and their applications. This function includes such activities as data acquisition, data audits, links with formal planning procedures and other management systems, maintenance of existing applications, and identification and implementation of new applications. Management needs guidelines to carry out these functions and to assign responsibility for them in the corporate organization.

Finally, one of the primary needs of management in the 1990s is to deal with an increasingly uncertain environment, one very dissimilar to that of the 1960s, the decade when most of the widely used statistical methods of forecasting were developed. During the 1960s most of the industrial world witnessed unprecedented economic stability and growth accompanied by relatively modest inflation and unemployment rates, whereas the economically turbulent 1970s were marked by major recessions, oil shocks, and stagflation with high unemployment rates, low productivity improvements, and economic and political turmoil. Although the environment in which the manager had to act seemed to improve on some of these dimensions in the second half of the 1980s, no one believed the world would return to the relative economic stability of the 1960s. Instead, most saw competitive pressures increasing as new technologies and global competition led to shorter product life cycles, tough trade-offs, and the need for more focus. What was needed were new methodologies to handle such uncertainties and diverse demands and to complement the more traditional quantitative techniques of the preceding decade.

In this book we hope to provide the materials with which managers can build a solid foundation to cope with the challenges of the 1990s. Like each of the previous editions, the fifth edition represents a major revision and includes several new chapters. Two of those chapters (Chapters 3 and 11) address the need for realism in effective business forecasting. They focus on helping managers (1) assess what can and cannot be predicted (and the factors that determine that), (2) understand why explaining the past (and assuming its continuation) often gives only limited help in forecasting, and (3) make choices from a range of methods and variety of models. A third addition (Chapter 16) explores the advantages of integrating judgmental and quantitative methods. Chapters 19, 20, and 21 examine forecasting application issues that are specific to the time horizon—short, medium, or long term. In addition, the judgmental aspects of forecasting have been given prominence (Chapters 12 and 13) as they are of critical importance to real life forecasting. Finally, a new section about new product forecasting and the challenge it presents to management has been added to Chapter 21.

The book is organized into four parts, reflecting the collective experience built up by managers since the fourth edition appeared five years ago. Part

A introduces the various forecasting methods currently available. The importance of forecasting and its role in improving future-oriented decision making are also discussed. The establishment of realistic expectations as to what forecasting can and cannot achieve is discussed and the limits to predictability are described.

Part B presents the full range of available quantitative forecasting methods. These include smoothing, decomposition, autoregressive-moving average, regression, econometric models, and several newer approaches, such as vector autoregressive and ARARMA methods. The chapters in Part B describe in detail the major quantitative methods in each category (smoothing, decomposition, and so on) and present examples of their usage.

Part C deals with management judgement in forecasting. We begin by discussing the difference between explaining the past and predicting the future, a point that is central to forecasting accuracy. The next two chapters deal with judgmental biases. The following chapter discusses monitoring approaches, which can help management determine rapidly when fundamental changes are taking place. The next two chapters present guidelines for selecting appropriate forecasting methods and integrating judgmental and quantitative forecasts. The final chapter describes technological and environmental forecasting techniques.

Part D describes forecasting applications, beginning with a discussion of the use of forecasting in business organizations. The data for this chapter come from recent surveys among forecasting users and our own experience over two decades with a variety of business organizations. The next three chapters describe a full range of forecasting applications for short-, medium-, and long-term time horizons. A chapter follows on support tools for applying forecasting, and a final chapter addresses the question of achieving the most from forecasting resources on an ongoing basis.

To keep this volume to a manageable length we had to make trade-offs between technical completeness in the discussion of individual forecasting methods and coverage of a wide range of implementation guidelines and experiences in the application examples. Other authors have concentrated on describing individual techniques in more detail, and we have listed their work under "Selected References for Further Study" at the end of each chapter.

The challenge to the manager and the forecaster is to improve forecasting accuracy and its contribution to planning and decision making. We hope this fifth edition will continue the tradition of earlier editions and contribute to this progress in a significant way.

This work has benefited significantly from comments and suggestions from numerous practitioners and academics. We express our thanks to them for those contributions. Especially helpful were the detailed reviews provided by Scott Armstrong, Ev Gardner, Robin Hogarth, and Jim Seabloom. We would also like to thank Michelle Bainbridge for her invaluable help in editing and proofreading the manuscript, and Romayne Ponleithner for her superb editorial contribution.

Fontainebleau, France   SPYROS MAKRIDAKIS
Boston, Massachusetts   STEVEN C. WHEELWRIGHT
March 1989

CONTENTS

PART A

THE ROLE AND IMPORTANCE OF FORECASTING IN MANAGEMENT

CHAPTER 1

FORECASTING AND MANAGEMENT: AN INTRODUCTION

Just as Molière's character was surprised to learn that he had been speaking prose all his life, most people are surprised to learn that most of the decisions they make involve forecasting. In fact, apart from decisions dealing with historical evaluations, all others are directed toward future events and require forecasts of circumstances surrounding that future environment. This is true for simple personal decisions, such as the time to arise in the morning; for more important personal ones, such as when and how to invest savings; and for critical, complex decisions affecting an entire organization, such as whether to build a new factory. To reach a decision on building a factory, forecasts concerning future demand, technological innovations, cost, prices, competitors' plans, labor, legislation, and many other factors are needed.

Most forecasting required for decision making is handled judgmentally in an intuitive fashion, often without explicitly separating the task of forecasting from that of decision making. This is true even within large organizations. The authors' experience and studies indicate that relatively few companies use forecasting extensively on a regular basis, although the evidence supporting its value, in small organizations as well as in large ones, is straightforward and unequivocal. Unaided, subjective judgments clearly are not as accurate and effective as more systematic, explicit approaches to forecasting. As we will see later, techniques ranging from simple naive procedures to sophisticated quantitative methods and from simple judgmental methods to complex qualitative ones are available. This book covers the full range of those techniques, illustrating their strengths and weaknesses and suggesting guidelines for selecting and applying individual methods.

Since the early 1960s, commitment to forecasting in organizations of all types has grown steadily. Several factors have stimulated interest in forecasting. Important benefits can be gained from systematizing and addressing

3

explicitly the task of forecasting. Unlike many volumes on the topic, however, this one will try also to present a pragmatic view of forecasting. Problems of forecasting errors and the limitations of forecasting methods (and the situations to which they apply) will be discussed candidly. A tenet of the authors is that recognizing what forecasting can and cannot do is often as important as obtaining the forecasts themselves. Knowing and understanding these limits helps the decision maker develop realistic expectations regarding the decision situation and can help those seeking better solutions and improved techniques in handling forecasting situations.

The next section of this chapter explores some of the limits of forecasting in predicting and dealing with future environments and situations. The two following sections address two fundamental elements of any forecasting approach—the identification of patterns within past experience and the discovery of relationships among key factors or variables. We conclude this chapter with a discussion of forecasting methods currently in use and the need for management to be realistic in its expectations of forecasting.

THE LIMITS OF PREDICTABILITY

Over the past few years, considerable criticism has been voiced in regard to the inability of forecasters to warn of forthcoming events and changes. Furthermore, forecasting users often have been disappointed because of large forecasting errors that have caused planning and decision making to go awry. It is interesting to note, however, that as the complaints about forecasting have increased, so have the number of requests for and the interest in obtaining additional forecasts. Upon reflection, this is not surprising, because when there is little uncertainty in the environment and things turn out largely as expected, there is much less need for formal forecasts, whereas in a turbulent environment with high uncertainty, the need for such forecasts is great.

No doubt many of the criticisms of forecasting have been well founded. Unexpected developments, predicted events that never materialize, large forecasting errors, and mistakes in the timing and intensity of predicted changes are just a few of the problems commonly cited. However, users of forecasting must share the blame, because, like those seeking advice from fortune-tellers or astrologers, their expectations have often been unrealistic, particularly with regard to error-free forecasts. Explicit systematic forecasting approaches can provide substantial benefits when used properly, but it is illusory to believe that omniscient powers are plumbed by such approaches.

To understand the advantages and limitations of forecasting, it is most important to recognize that all types and forms of forecasting techniques are extrapolative in nature. (To be technically correct, this term ought to include *interpolation*, that is, predicting within the existing data, which can be thought of as a special case of extrapolation.) When historical quantitative data are available, the forecasting methods used are called quantitative. Otherwise they are generally referred to as qualitative/technological or judgmental/subjective methods.

It is unfortunate but true that users of quantitative forecasting techniques have no simple, reliable way to predict what will happen when established patterns or relationships change. Because quantitative methods base their forecasts on extrapolations from past patterns and interrelationships, they work well *only* when the future is similar to the past or when changes (by chance) happen to cancel out.

When quantitative techniques do not work well, human judgment with an appropriate degree of help and structure is the only alternative for predicting the impact of the change. However, since judgmental methods also base their forecasts on the observation of existing trends, changes in those trends, and the magnitude of future change, they too are subject to a number of shortcomings. The advantage, however, of human-based forecasting approaches is that they can identify systematic change more quickly and interpret better the effect of such change on the future. Weighted against this is the fact that we all have vested interests that often override good (objective) judgment; our desire for a specific outcome or event colors our view of what is the most likely outcome.

In spite of these shortcomings, some forecasters develop a reputation for being extremely successful. It is useful to recognize some of the ways in which "experienced" forecasters are able to develop what appear to be extremely successful track records. To put this question in proper perspective, however, it is important to state at the outset that the authors are not aware of any published evidence that any individual forecaster or forecasting method has been consistently and significantly more accurate than any other. This does not mean that some forecasters have not become better known than others or that some have not earned more money and fame than others. In this respect, some have been extremely successful.

If the records of a variety of forecasters are examined (as a number of individuals, economic forecasting models, and organizations have been recently), it is clear that some are more successful (accurate) than others, at least for short periods of time. However, from a predictive point of view, the evidence is equally clear that there is no way of knowing a priori who or which method will be more accurate. The accuracy of forecasts does not correlate with the fame of the forecasters, their background, their experiences, or their past records. Although we might wish it otherwise, recognizing this basic fact is fundamental to understanding the advantages and limitations of various approaches to forecasting, and thus to developing expectations that can be helpful in planning and decision making.

In spite of the foregoing statement, you may consider your own knowledge and experience somewhat at odds with the notion of being unable to identify who will do the best job of forecasting in the future. There are some characteristics that can help in selecting the forecasters and forecasting methods that have the highest probability of providing the information desired in a given situation. However, picking from the group the one that will consistently perform best is not possible, at least not on the basis of the empirical evidence currently available. Because those selling forecasting methods and forecasts would like potential customers to to think otherwise, it is useful to understand some of the selection techniques that can make a professional forecaster look especially effective in a given environment.

MAKING FORECASTS (AND FORECASTERS) LOOK GOOD

As an illustration of how consistent success can appear to be undeniable, consider the forecasters who might claim they have a model that can predict all of the recessions from now until the year 2000. Furthermore, suppose those forecasters could show published evidence that they have predicted all nine recessions since World War II. This would be impressive indeed. Actually, it would be very simple to achieve such a record simply by predicting every year that there would be a recession the following year. With this approach, one would have predicted all nine post–World War II recessions. (The forecaster, of course, would not tell you about the recessions he or she predicted that did not occur.) As a practical matter, someone with even modest experience in analyzing recessions probably would be somewhat more sophisticated and yet almost as accurate. For instance, if one were to predict no recession the first, second, or third year following the preceding recession and then predict a recession in the fourth year, fifth year, and so on until one actually occurred, that forecaster's record would be over 85% correct. That is, this scheme would have predicted all the post-1944 recessions except the 1982–1983 recession, which happened less than three years after the previous one. Predicting eight of the nine post–World War II recessions would not be a bad record.

After the stock marked crash of October 19, 1987, some forecasters became famous for predicting the crash (*Business Week*, November 30, 1987). This is not surprising. Today there are about 800 newsletters offering stock-picking advice. In addition, thousands of experts work in the research department of brokerage houses or give advice on stocks. Since their advice covers the entire range of future possibilities, some of their forecasts will undoubtedly come close to reality. The test of good foresight is not whether one predicted a single event by chance but whether one's performance was consistently above average. Few forecasters have achieved such consistent performance. As the *Business Week* article points out, the great majority of gurus who had predicted previous turns of the market did not forecast the crash of October 19. Some of them gave advice (like buying on margin) that ruined the clients who followed such advice.

The same is true of those who predict recessions, or even depressions. Stock market sages who predict a downturn—and there are always some who do—occasionally turn out to be right, but to our knowledge, no forecaster has predicted all the recessions correctly. Furthermore, none of the predictions about major recessions or depressions that have been made since the 1950s have been correct, as we know. Currently popular is the book *The Great Depression of 1990*. Its author, Dr. Rawi Batra, claims a wide range of accurate predictions. However, when he was asked why he had not predicted the October 19 crash (in which he lost $2000 from his own investments in mutual funds), he answered, "I can't call every turn."

Batra's book is not the first to predict a serious recession or depression, or even the end of the world (see end of chapter for references). Although the predictive or scientific value of such books is zero, people seem to buy them because of curiosity mixed with fear, in the hope that by reading such a book they may avoid the negative consequences of the impending calamity.

Many other tools can be used by "successful" forecasters. One is simply to predict a continuation of a basic trend (pattern). For example, a number of forecasters, particularly in Europe, profited considerably during the 1970s by using a model that predicted continued increases in the price of gold. For many years their forecasts were correct and they and their clients made millions of dollars. In early 1978, one of these services (with a $2000 annual subscription price) was predicting that the price of gold would exceed $1000 per ounce by the middle of 1979. At that time, gold was selling for about $700 per ounce. Many people in Europe "invested" (speculated?) on the basis of those forecasts. Generally they felt that they could trust their forecasting source since it had been correct for many years and in the process had brought them considerable wealth. As we know, the price fell. The faithful bought more in order to average their losses and gain aditional returns when the price, according to the forecast, would eventually return to and exceed the $1000 level. Many buyers lost considerable sums because the price of gold has remained around $450 per ounce since 1980. When inflation and holding fees are considered, the value of gold purchased in 1980 had dropped by over 75% in 1988. The same story has been repeated for a number of other commodities and the stock market in general, when experts were predicting an increase in the price of stocks and such an increase was taking place. Perhaps the major lesson is that it is not difficult to predict the continuation of an established pattern or relationship. What is difficult is to predict accurately a change in such a pattern or relationship and the timing, intensity, and consequences of that change. In our opinion, this is the real test of the "success" of a forecaster's record.

Another approach to improving a forecaster's record is to make predictions that are general or conditional. The likelihood that such forecasts will be correct is extremely high, but they may have very limited usefulness. For example, predicting that the price of a barrel of oil will exceed $50 by the end of this century has a high probability of being correct, but it is not very beneficial to most decision makers. Another example of largely useless predictions is "If A and/or B and/or C occur, then the economy will recover from the recession and the inflation rate will drop." When such forecasts are sufficiently general and conditional, they can seldom be proved wrong (although, again, this accuracy is at the expense of usefulness).

Still another way that forecasters have learned to improve their "success" record is by the use of self-fulfilling prophecies. For example, if sufficient numbers of people believe a forecast that predicts a drop in the stock market, such a drop may occur as a result of actions they take following that forecast. A variation of this "sure bet" approach to building credibility as a forecaster is to make numerous predictions in a broad range of fields, and then highlight (after the fact) those that turn out to be correct. It is much like playing roulette: occasionally a jackpot is won, but not because the player has a good prediction method; it is simply a matter of luck and probability. If a sufficient number play roulette, some, by chance, will end the night with large gains. However, the majority of those playing will end up with losses. These are the laws of probability at work.

Without overstating the case, we hope that our perspective is becoming clear. Forecasters (and their methods) do not possess crystal balls. Understanding the limitations of forecasting and setting realistic expectations as to future performance are central to making effective use of forecasts in decision making. On a more positive note, some aspects of forecasting clearly can add value to the job of management. The focus of this book is on how such value can best be added. Two basic ways in which that occurs are described in the next two sections of this chapter—the identification of basic patterns and the discovery of relationships among important variables.

IDENTIFYING PATTERNS

Suppose you live on Long Island and work in New York City. Further, suppose you commute daily by driving the 25 miles between your home and your office. When there is no traffic, the trip takes you about half an hour but, alas, on weekday mornings it takes much longer. One of the forecasting problems you face is when to leave your house in order to arrive at your office by 9.00 A.M. While it is not a disaster if you arrive a few minutes late, you do not want to make a habit of it nor do you want to be more than 15 minutes late, since that would put you behind schedule for the entire day. But since you are not a "morning person," you don't want to get out of bed any earlier than you have to.

How do you estimate how long it will take you to drive to work? Well, since you do it every day, you have a good idea of how long it takes on average. You usually need one hour and five minutes door to door, but there are exceptions. Mondays, for instance, take much longer. Many people who live in the city during the week spend their weekends in the suburbs, which means that more people drive into the city on Monday mornings. These Monday drives might take up to half an hour longer. Also, Fridays tend to take somewhat less time as it seems some people decide to spend a long weekend at home. There have been Fridays you've made the trip to the city in three-quarters of an hour. Tuesdays through Thursdays are normal days with fewer variations.

You remember 22 years ago when you first started working and the traffic was much lighter. Even on Mondays it took less than an hour to commute to work and there were days when it took only 35 minutes. But then, as more people moved to the suburbs and as traffic increased, the commuting time increased as well.

You also remember that traffic decreased at the end of 1973 as the oil embargo began and the gas prices jumped and supplies shrank. During this period more people took the train or carpooled. However, when gasoline became more plentiful and prices decreased (in real terms), the pre-1973 traffic pattern began to return.

You make your estimates on the basis of this experience (information). Usually you are correct in your estimates, but there are days when random events, such as accidents, lengthen your commute time.

The foregoing example can be used as a reference point in identifying and defining the basic task of forecasting—gathering and analyzing repeated observations. The difference between purely judgmental and quantitative forecasting lies in the method by which the information is observed and recorded. If it is recorded directly in your memory and then used intuitively (implicitly) for prediction purposes, the forecast is referred to as judgmental. If it is recorded in some external (explicit) location, such as figures recorded in a notebook, and then some forecasting method is used to process that information systematically, that forecast is referred to as quantitative. Combinations of judgmental and quantitative approaches are also very common.

One major dimension in which judgmental and quantitative techniques differ is their accuracy. Numerical data and statistical methods can provide precise and objective answers, which in many cases can be very important. In others, as in the driving example, accuracy might not be so important. This difference raises the question as to whether more accurate predictions can be obtained from quantitative methods than from judgmental methods. In some instances the answer is yes; in others it is no. As we will see in subsequent sections, understanding the circumstances under which each general class of methods performs best is one key to effective forecasting for decision making.

Generally speaking, in repetitive situations where the data can be systematically collected, quantitative methods do provide more accurate forecasts. Unfortunately the human mind does not process information in a precise, consistent manner, and human memory is often faulty in recalling information and data. However, it is important to remember that both human judgment and quantitative methods work on the same basic principle—the identification of existing patterns or relationships. The differences lie in the methods by which information is recorded and processed in preparing predictions.

One useful way of approaching the identificaiton of past patterns and their extrapolation into the future is to treat them as comprising four elements: *seasonality, trend, cyclicality*, and *randomness*. In the earlier example of commuting to work, seasonality is reflected in the fact that more people drive on Monday mornings and fewer drive on Friday mornings than on average. The trend is reflected in the gradual increase in traffic (and thus longer commute times) as the population in the suburbs increased. The cycle is reflected at the time of the energy crisis when traffic decreased but then reverted to normal levels (that is, the trend) later on. Finally, an accident slowing traffic on a particular day is one form of randomness.

A major advantage of quantitative methods is their ability to identify these elements of seasonality, trend, cyclicality, and randomness in an efficient and fairly objective manner. Subsequently, each of the first three elements—seasonality, trend, and cyclicality—can be extrapolated to prepare more accurate forecasts. By definition, randomness cannot be predicted, but once it has been isolated, its magnitude can be estimated and used to determine the extent of variation likely between actual and predicted results. In other words, randomness can help us determine the extent of uncertainty in our future predictions.

In judgmental methods, the elements of seasonality, trend, and cyclicality are inferred through experience gained from repeated observations. However, because of the way the human memory functions and the brain processes information, judgmental methods do not do as well as quantitative methods in identifying seasonality, trend, and cyclicality in situations such as the commuting example, where ample data exist and where established patterns remain constant (or change slowly) over a long period of time.

DISCOVERING RELATIONSHIPS

Returning to the commuting example for a moment we note that several factors affect the amount of traffic and therefore the time it takes to travel to work on weekday mornings. For instance, when snow is falling, the traffic moves much more slowly and the drive takes much longer. Usually the heavier the snowfall, the slower the traffic. Furthermore, even when the snow stops, traffic continues to move at a slower rate because the snow that has accumulated narrows the highways and prevents the traffic from flowing smoothly. If a car breaks down, the traffic almost always slows down to stop-and-go, and the chances of breakdowns increase during cold weather. Moreover, city streets become congested because parked cars hinder snow removal. The result is that during and after heavy snowfalls the commute might take more than two hours.

Other factors may affect traffic. A strike on the Long Island Railroad causes many of those who normally take the train to drive to work. The result is a substantial increase in traffic and huge traffic jams. At other times when a highway or bridge is under repair, those remaining open must carry the extra traffic diverted to them. On the other hand, when bridge tolls are increased, the number of cars seems to decrease, at least temporarily. The same seems to be true when gasoline prices increase.

All of these factors affect daily commute times, and through experience you can gain a pretty good idea of their impact. While some are very noticeable (for example, snowfall or rail strikes), others are more difficult to identify and their impact is harder to determine. Discovering existing relationships, such as how much a rail strike will increase traffic and thus commute time, requires repeated observations, just as identifying patterns does. Such observations can be made in a purely judgmental fashion or through one of the available quantitative methods.

The principle used in discovering relationships is similar for both judgmental and quantitative approaches. The relationship between the item to be forecast and one or more of the factors that influence that item is identified and used for prediction purposes. For instance, it might be determined that a rail strike adds 30 minutes to the commute time; four inches of snowfall adds 20 minutes to the commute time, and eight inches adds an extra hour.

Business forecasting situations are often very similar to the commuting example. They require forecasts that can be obtained through the identification and extrapolation of established patterns or existing relationships. For instance, sales of product A may be forecast after identifying the seasonality of demand (some products sell better in the summer than in the winter and vice versa), the trend (whether sales are increasing, remaining constant, or decreasing over time), the cyclicality (reflecting how revenues are affected by the level of economic activity), and the extent to which randomness affects sales. In addition, accurate forecasting requires the identification of key relationships such as those between advertising or promotions and sales volume, the influence of increases or decreases in prices and revenues, and the way in which competitors' actions are reflected in the demand for the company's products. In the terminology of the forecasting world, identification of past patterns generally is associated with time series—that is, patterns that are directly related to the passage of time—whereas identification of relationships generally is associated with causal impacts, where a change in one factor directly affects the item under consideration.

REALISM IN FORECASTING

Forecasting in the frictionless physical and natural world is perfect. We can estimate with a high degree of accuracy the high tide or the exact timing of sunrise tomorrow or a year from now. Similarly, the position of a spacecraft traveling toward Mars can be estimated within a few meters. Some people believe that a similar degree of accuracy can be achieved in forecasting in the economic or business spheres. This is not, unfortunately, the case. In the previous section we indicated that forecasting depends on identifying and extrapolating established patterns or relationships. The frictionless physical world, however, where patterns are perfect and relationships exact, is nothing like the economic or business world, where considerable randomness exists. Furthermore, the patterns and relationships in economics and business change, sometimes dramatically. In addition, people's actions can and do influence future events. A forecast can, therefore, become a self-fulfilling or self-defeating prophecy that changes established patterns or relationships. For these reasons economics forecasting is characterized by less accuracy than in the natural sciences.

Managers and other forecasting users must realize and accept the limitations of forecasting and the uncertainty associated with all forms of predictions; otherwise, unexpected results and unpleasant surprises may await them. Forecasting is not crystal-balling. Instead, established patterns or relationships are identified and these patterns extrapolated or interpolated in an optimal manner in order to forecast. As long as these patterns or relationships do not change, forecasting will be accurate. However, there is no way of telling whether these patterns or relationships will change during the period of forecasting. As a matter of fact, we know that patterns and relationships do change—sometimes too often.

In this book we clearly spell out the advantages and limitations of forecasting, what can and cannot be predicted, and the full extent of uncertainty associated with any form of prediction in the economic and business worlds. This, in our opinion, is a critical aspect of planning and developing appropriate strategies capable of dealing realistically with future uncertainty.

FORECASTING METHODS CURRENTLY IN USE

Although many different classification schemes could be used in considering major approaches to forecasting, the one we have found most useful divides those methods into three major categories: judgmental, quantitative, and technological, as summarized in Table 1-1. Each major approach includes several types of methods, many individual techniques and variations of each technique.

Judgmental methods are the methods most commonly used in business and government organizations. Such forecasts are most often made as individual judgments or by committee agreements or decisions. While most large organizations do use some quantitative methods and a few technological methods on a continuing basis, our experience suggests that the vast majority of forecasting needs are addressed through judgmental methods.

The second category—*quantitative methods*—is the type on which the majority of the forecasting literature has been focused. There are three subcategories of these methods. *Time-series methods* seek to identify historical patterns (using time as a reference) and then forecast using a time-based extrapolation of those patterns. *Explanatory methods* seek to identify the relationships that led to (caused) observed outcomes in the past and then forecast by applying those relationships to the future. *Monitoring methods*, which are not yet in widespread use, seek to identify changes in patterns and relationships. They are used primarily to indicate when extrapolation of past patterns or relationships is not appropriate.

The third category—*technological methods*—addresses long-term issues of a technological, societal, economic, or political nature. The four subcategories here are extrapolative (using historical patterns and relationships as a basis for forecasts), analogy-based (using historical and other analogies to make forecasts), expert-based, and normative-based (using objectives, goals, and desired outcomes as a basis for forecasting, thereby influencing future events).

Table 1-1 Classification of Forecasting Methods, Fields of Their Development, and Areas of Applications

Column groups:
- **Field in Which Method Was Developed:** Statistics; Operations Research; Economics; Psychology; Long-Range Planning; Practice; Marketing
- **Major Area of Business Application:** Production Planning; Production Scheduling; Inventories; Material Requirements; Personnel Scheduling; Personnel Planning; Sales — Aggregate (Short Term, Medium Term, Long Term); Sales — Disaggregate (Short Term, Medium Term, Long Term); Pricing; Advertising and Promotion; Yearly Budgeting; New Products; R&D Projects; Capital Budgeting; Competitive Analysis; Strategy

Category	Forecasting Method	Chapter	Stat	Oper. Res.	Econ.	Psych.	Long-Range Plan.	Practice	Mktg	Prod. Plan.	Prod. Sched.	Invent.	Mat'l Req.	Pers. Sched.	Pers. Plan.	Agg. Short	Agg. Med.	Agg. Long	Disagg. Short	Disagg. Med.	Disagg. Long	Pricing	Advert. & Promo.	Yearly Budget.	New Prod.	R&D Proj.	Cap. Budget.	Compet. Anal.	Strategy
Time series	Naive	4						X		X	X	X	X	X	X				X			X							
Time series	Smoothing	5		X				X		X	X	X	X	X	X		X		X										
Time series	Decomposition	6			X					X	X			X	X					X				X					
Time series	Autoregressive moving average	7	X												X														
Explanatory	Vector autoregressive	7	X		X											X						X							
Explanatory	Regression	8, 9	X		X											X	X					X	X	X					
Explanatory	Econometrics	10	X		X											X	X					X	X	X					
	Monitoring approaches	14	X	X				X		X	X	X	X	X		X	X	X	X										
	New products forecasting	21	X						X							X		X							X	X		X	X
Individual	Individual judgment	12, 13				X		X		X	X			X		X	X					X	X	X	X	X	X	X	X
Individual	Decision rules	13				X						X	X	X						X									
	Sales force estimates	12						X	X		X								X					X					
Group	Juries of executive opinion	12						X	X								X					X	X	X	X	X	X	X	X
Group	Role playing	17				X																						X	

(Quantitative: Time series and Explanatory methods; Judgmental: Individual and Group methods.)

Technological	Aggregate	Anticipatory surveys	12
		Market research	12, 21
		Pilot programs and pre-market tests	21
	Extrapolative	Growth curves	17
		Time-independent comparisons	17
		Historical and other analogies	21
	Expert-based	Delphi	17
		Futurists	17
		Cross-impact matrices	17

15

OVERVIEW

The remainder of this book is organized around these three major categories of forecasting methods. Part B, consisting of seven chapters, starts with quantitative methods, in part because they are the group that has been studied most systematically and in part because they appear to hold the greatest promise in a broad range of decision-making situations. Part C deals with technological methods, and addresses a range of judgmental techniques. One reason for placing the judgmental category after the other two, even though it tends to be the more widely used, is that its limitations and advantages can be better understood after the categories of quantitative and technological approaches have been explored. In addition, while many judgmental methods are very simple, others are extremely complex and often can be used to integrate a variety of methods in a given situation.

The final chapters of this book, which make up Part D, deal with the practice of forecasting in today's organizations. Included is a survey of several recent articles regarding managers' and firms' experience with forecasting—which methods are most used and where, their performance, and the sequence in which they tend to be adopted. A discussion of research and experience in establishing and pursuing a forecasting function, including linking it with planning and budgeting processes, concludes that part.

Because forecasting approaches are so diverse, we encourage the reader to review Table 1-1 in some detail and to become familiar with the major categories and subcategories of methods. In addition to the short descriptions provided, Table 1-1 indicates the chapters in the book that cover those methods and the major fields of development and areas of application for the methods themselves.

SELECTED REFERENCES FOR FURTHER STUDY

Batra, R., 1987. *The Great Depression of 1990*, Simon and Schuster, New York.

Cleary, J. P., and H. Levenbach, 1982. *The Professional Forecaster*, Lifetime Learning Publications, Belmont, CA.

Gardner, S., and S. Makridakis (Eds.), 1988. "The Future of Forecasting," *International Journal of Forecasting*, 4, no. 3, special issue.

"Gurus Who Called the Crash—or Fell on Their Faces," *Business Week*, Nov. 30, 1987, pp. 92–100.

Makridakis, S., 1988. "Metaforecasting: Ways of Improving Forecasting Accuracy and Usefulness," *International Journal of Forecasting*, 4, no. 3, pp. 467–491.

Makridakis, S., S.C. Wheelwright and V.E. McGee, 1983. *Forecasting: Methods and Applications*, 2nd ed., Wiley, New York.

Makridakis, S. and S. C. Wheelwright (Eds.), 1987. *The Handbook of Forecasting: A Manager's Guide*, 2nd ed., Wiley, New York.
Willis, R. E., 1987. *A Guide to Forecasting for Planners and Managers*, Prentice-Hall, Englewood Cliffs, NJ.

CHAPTER 2

THE NEED FOR AND ROLE OF FORECASTING

Forecasting is important in a wide range of planning or decision-making situations. The preceding chapter outlined some fundamentals that underlie the preparation of forecasts and some of the limitations of forecasting. This chapter deals with planning and decision-making environments and the way in which forecasting techniques can be used in different circumstances.

This chapter is divided into three parts. The first addresses the requirements of planning and decision making for forecasting. These requirements are described from different perspectives to provide the reader with a better understanding of the range of situations to which systematic forecasting approaches can be applied. The second part outlines available methods and their match with decision-making requirements. Included in this material is a brief overview of the evolution of the forecasting field over the last few decades, which helps set the stage for understanding the characteristics of individual techniques. The final part of this chapter deals with assessing the options in any given situation and provides a general framework for matching available methods with situation requirements so as to identify the techniques most applicable to a given management problem.

THE ROLE OF FORECASTING IN PLANNING AND DECISION MAKING

In recent years increased emphasis has been placed on improving decision making in business and government. A key aspect of decision making is being able to predict the circumstances surrounding individual decision situations. Examining the diversity of requirements in planning and decision-making situations illustrates clearly why no single forecasting method or narrow set of methods can meet the needs of all decision-making situations.

One way to classify the need for forecasting in the management field is in terms of the functional areas to which those forecasts relate. Table 2-1 presents a summary of this type. Using the organizational unit, or function as one dimension and the time horizon for planning as the other, we will cite specific examples in which management finds forecasting a useful tool. It is instructive to examine some of these functional perspectives in more detail.

In marketing, a number of decisions can be improved significantly by basing them on reliable forecasts of market size and market characteristics. For example, a company that produces and sells major appliances (washing machines, television sets, and refrigerators) must be able to forecast what the demand will be for each of its products by geographic region and type of consumer. The marketing department can use these forecasts as it plans advertising, direct sales, and other promotional efforts. Marketing also requires forecasts of such things as market share, prices, and trends in new product development.

In production, a major need for forecasting is the area of product demand. This involves predicting both volumes and mix so the firm can plan its production schedule and inventories to best meet market requirements. Other areas of the production function that need forecasts include material requirements (purchasing and procurement), labor scheduling, equipment purchases, maintenance requirements, and plant capacity planning.

Finance and accounting are areas in which forecasting has proven especially valuable in recent years. These departments must forecast cash flows and the rates at which various expenses and revenues will occur if they are to maintain company liquidity and operating efficiency. In making such projections, it is often useful to predict each of the elements that make up the firm's net cash flow, so these can be used by other departments and functions throughout the organization. The finance and accounting functions must also forecast interest rates to support the acquisition of new capital, the collection of accounts receivable to help in planning working capital needs, and capital equipment expenditure rates to help balance the flow of funds in the organization.

Even the personnel department requires a number of forecasts in planning for human resources in the business. Workers must be hired and trained, and benefits must be provided that are competitive with those available in the firm's labor market. Furthermore, trends that affect such variables as labor turnover, retirement age, absenteeism, and tardiness need to be forecast as input for planning and decision making in this function.

Because the general management function is central to the successful operation of the firm, forecasts that can be used as the basis for decision making at this level are perhaps the most critical. Espiecally helpful here are forecasts of economic factors that can serve as a common background for all of the planning and decision making that go on in the various functions.

Table 2-1 Forecasting Needs for Management

	Time Horizon			
Organizational Unit	Immediate Term (Less than 1 Month)	Short Term (1 to 3 Months)	Medium Term (3 Months to 2 Years)	Long Term (2 Years or More)
Marketing	Sales of each product type, sales by geographic area, sales by customer, competition, prices, inventory levels	Total sales, product categories, major products, product groups, prices	Total sales, product categories, prices, general economic conditions	Total sales, major product categories, new product introduction, saturation points of existing products, customer preferences and tastes
Production	Demand of each product, plant loading	Total demands, demand of product categories and product groups, scheduling, employment level, costs	Costs, budget allocations, buying or ordering equipment and machinery, employment level	Costs, facility investments, expansion of plant and equipment, ordering of heavy machinery and equipment, demand of production facilities, new technologies
Inventory	Demand for each product's production, demand for material, demand for semifinished products, weather conditions	Demand for materials, demand for semifinished products, demand for products, possible strikes	Possible strikes in suppliers or transportation facilities	Total sales, expansion of warehouses

20

Finance and accounting	Sales revenue, production costs, inventory costs, leading indicators, cash inflows, cash outflows	Total demand, inventory levels, cash flows, short-term borrowing, prices	Budget allocations, cash flows	Total sales, investment selections, capital expenditure, allocations of resources, capital programs, cash flows
Purchasing	Production, cash availability, purchasing of supplies and materials	Demand for products, demand for materials, lead time for purchasing	Demand for products, demand for raw and other materials	Contracts for buying raw materials, customer preferences and tastes
R&D			New product introduction, R&D selections	Total sales, technological, social, political, and economic conditions of future, new product development
Top management		Total sales, sales breakdowns, pricing	Demand for sales, costs and other expenses, cash position, general economic conditions, control objectives	Total sales, costs and other expenses, social and economic trends, goals, objectives, and strategies, new products, pricing policies
Economic unit		Level of economic activity	General economic conditions, turning point in economy, level of economic activity	State and type of economy, level of economic activity, sales of industry

Table 2-1 (*Continued*)

Organizational Unit	Time Horizon			
	Immediate Term (Less than 1 Month)	Short Term (1 to 3 Months)	Medium Term (3 Months to 2 Years)	Long Term (2 Years or More)
Environmental unit			Available technologies	Areas of technological innovation, R&D selections, available technological opportunities
			Social attitudes	Social trends, tastes, areas of social concern
		Availability of money, interest rates	Fiscal and monetary policies	Trends in the rate of taxation, depreciation, and concept of free market
	Prices, sale promotions	Prices, advertising selection, sales promotions, new product introduction	New product development	Capital investment, new technologies, R&D selections of competitors
	Weather conditions	Weather conditions	Crops	General environmental constraints (pollution level, availability of raw materials, etc.)

Often top management refers to these as the "common assumptions" or "basic economic scenario" to be used in budgeting and other forms of planning. Projecting changes in prices, costs, growth rates, and so on are important elements in such a shared set of assumptions.

A number of other requirements for forecasts cut across multiple functional areas. For example, decisions related to capacity planning, to new product introduction, and to overall competitive advantage involve the preparation of forecasts that have data inputs from multiple functions. In addition, these forecasts can be used across functions in coordinating and integrating actions in these major decision categories.

The notion that planning and forecasting are different functions deserves special mention here. Forecasting is generally used to predict (describe) what will happen (for example, to sales demand, cash flows, or employment levels) given a set of circumstances (assumptions). Planning, on the other hand, involves the use of such forecasts to help make good decisions about the most attractive alternatives for the organization. Thus a forecast seeks to describe what will happen, whereas a plan is based on the notion that by taking certain actions now the decision maker can affect subsequent events in a given situation and thus influence the final results in the direction desired. For example, if a forecast shows that demand will fall in the next year, management may want to prepare a plan of action (such as to advertise the product) that will compensate for or reverse the predicted drop in demand. Generally speaking, forcasting and forecasts are inputs to the planning process.

An important point for managers to remember is the impact of the decisions they make on the forecast. That is, when action is taken, the forecast may need to be adjusted to reflect the impact of that action. If the forecast is not adjusted, it may become misleading if it is used as a basis for making other decisions. In addition, it will no longer be possible to evaluate the accuracy of that forecast because it no longer reflects the circumstances (assumptions) that existed when it was prepared.

CURRENT FORECASTING APPROACHES AND THEIR FIT WITH PLANNING AND DECISION-MAKING REQUIREMENTS

To understand the range of forecasting approaches currently available, a brief historical review is useful. Before the 1950s there was little or no systematic business forecasting. Although a handful of methodologies such as regression and time-series decomposition were available, their applications were limited to leading economics departments in academia and government agencies. Systematic, widespread application of such techniques was severely hampered by a lack of timely data and the tediousness of the required computations.

In the mid-1950s two major breakthroughs dramatically changed the forecasting field. The first was the introduction of a broad range of exponential smoothing techniques. At first these methods were employed rather timidly by the military, but then they gradually spread to business organizations. The greatest advantages of these methods, which were empirically based and practically oriented, were their simplicity in concept and their ease of computation. For the first time the door was opened to a group of methods of considerable practical value that could be used easily even with the mechanical calculators of that day. Although such methodology had significant appeal to the practitioners, most academics and professional forecasters thought that such simple methods could not be sufficiently accurate to deserve serious attention. It took almost 30 years before exponential smoothing methods—simple and unsophisticated as they may be—gained widespread adoption and it was recognized that they would often perform as well as much more sophisticated techniques. (See Makridakis et al., 1982; Makridakis, 1986. Also, it should be noted that Robert G. Brown, a leading developer and proponent of exponential smoothing methods, has for more than 30 years asserted that this is so.)

Although exponential smoothing methods are extremely easy to use, requiring only a few equations and relatively few calculations, in the 1950s they were difficult to apply on a grand scale. If forecasts were needed for several thousand items, an enormous amount of work was required to maintain data files, make the required computations, and simply transcribe the results. Fortunately, a second major breakthrough in the 1950s, the introduction of the computer, made it possible to use not only exponential smoothing but also a host of other forecasting methods on a much more continuous basis. Since that time the computer has revolutionized the applicability of forecasting in general, and exponential smoothing models have been widely used in business and the military.

Since the initial work on smoothing methods in the 1950s, a number of variations and extensions of such techniques have been developed. Most notable are those of Brown (1950), Holt (1952), and Winters (1960). More recent adaptations and modifications have made it possible to use smoothing methods in an even more mechanical and automated mode. These newest techniques do not even require the user to specify the parameter values for the exponential smoothing model; they are computed and updated in the computer.

Not long after smoothing methods began to gain attention in the mid-1950s, decomposition methods experienced a rise in popularity. Prominent in the group responsible for this was Shiskin (1957, 1961) at the Census Bureau of the U.S. government. (Shiskin developed the Census II package.) Although these decomposition methods had little statistical underpinning, they had significant intuitive appeal for practitioners in both government and business.

As computer power became cheaper and more widely available in the 1960s, the door opened for more statistically sophisticated forecasting methods. Such techniques as multiple regression and econometric models became practical and were used to quantify and test economic theory with quantitative data. Within a decade the field of econometrics-based forecasting had developed as a profession in its own right, and by the early 1980s it represented a market of several hundred million dollars per year in the United States alone.

During the 1950s and 1960s academicians were still searching for a unifying theory of forecasting. An approach that incorporated many of the elements of such a theory became a reality with the work of Box and Jenkins (1976). The Box–Jenkins methodology, as it became known, provided a systematic procedure for the analysis of time series that was sufficiently general to handle virtually all empirically observed time-series data patterns. The popularity of this method was boosted significantly when several comparative studies of forecasting methods done in the 1970s showed the Box–Jenkins approach to be at least as accurate as econometric approaches (see Armstrong, 1978).

Variations of the autoregressive/moving average (ARIMA) method developed by Box and Jenkins began to emerge in the mid-1970s. Complementing these variations were more efficient approaches for modeling and forecasting time-series situations. These modifications corrected some of the problems associated with the Box–Jenkins methodology, overcame some of the computational difficulties of Box–Jenkins, and aided in the interpretation of the results, which had previously been viewed primarily from a black box type of perspective. These new methods, which came from a variety of fields (statistics, engineering, practice), have taken the names of ARARMA models, Kalman filters, vector autoregressive models, and so on.

On the qualitative side, technological forecasting methods also gained in popularity during the 1960s and 1970s. Methods such as the Delphi approach and that of cross-impact matrices were used in a number of organizations. These approaches attempted to deal with long-term trends where the historical data and patterns necessary to apply statistical forecasting approaches were not available or did not apply. Concurrently, considerable effort was expended in the marketing field on the topics of new product and new market forecasting, areas where the lack of historical data was also a problem.

One of the most interesting developments in the field of forecasting in the late 1970s was the realization that forecasts were useless until applied for planning and decision-making purposes. Several studies pointed out that organizational problems frequently blocked the use of forecasts even when such forecasts could demonstrate highly accurate performance at the time. During the same period several studies identified the individual behavior characteristics that could block the use of "proven" forecasting techniques. These studies, often of a multidimensional psychological nature, indicated that management revisions of forecasts were often based on wishful thinking, biased illusions, and political influence rather than on objective reality (see Hogarth and Makridakis, 1981; Lawrence and Makridakis, 1988; Tyebee, 1987). By the early 1980s much more systematic analyses of judgmental methods and the advantages and limitations of the human mind as a forecasting tool were being developed (see Schnaars and Topol, 1987).

One conclusion of this brief historical review of forecasting is that a number of parallel approaches have been developed over the past 30 years. Several chapters of this book take those approaches and describe their present status, what they are able to do currently, and their major limitations. As the range of methods available in the late 1980s is considered, it becomes clear that some types of situations are generally covered much more effectively by these techniques than are others. Generally, the primary distinction is that of constancy in the pattern and relationships over time. Existing methods do fairly well when there is a significant level of constancy but not so well when established patterns or relationships change. (See Chapter 3 for more detailed coverage.)

It is important, therefore, to look at ways of forecasting when patterns or relationships change, and to measure the extent of uncertainty involved. Since such a topic is not considered in the forecasting literature, it will be discussed in detail throughout this book.

ASSESSING MANAGEMENT'S FORECASTING OPTIONS: MATCHING THE SITUATION WITH THE METHOD

Any manager concerned with the application of forecasting in his or her decision making knows the importance of selecting the appropriate forecasting technique. Table 1-1 is a first attempt to match the various forecasting methods to different applications. This topic will be considered further in the remainder of this section. Although each situation is different and each technique has somewhat different strengths and weaknesses, it is extremely helpful to identify the general characteristics of forecasting situations and to contrast those with the general characteristics of available forecasting methods. These two sets of characteristics or criteria can be used as a basic framework for matching specific needs with specific approaches. At this point it is useful to have these characteristics or criteria firmly in mind before proceeding to learn about individual approaches and methods.

Characterizing Forecasting Situations

The authors have identified six characteristics or dimensions of planning and decision-making situations that play an important role in determining the requirements that forecasting must accommodate and respond to in order to be effective.

1. *Time Horizon.* The period of time over which a decision will have an impact and for which the manager must plan clearly affects the selection of an appropriate forecasting method. Time horizons generally can be divided into immediate term (less than one month), short term (one to three months), medium term (three months to two years), and long term (two years or more). Although the exact length of time used to describe each of these four categories may vary by company and situation, some guidelines are necessary to ensure that the forecast will be appropriate for the planning horizon being addressed. For example, it would be inappropriate to extrapolate an increase in the growth rate over the past three months to predict sales ten years into the future.

2. *Level of Aggregate Detail.* Decision-making tasks in most corporations generally are subdivided for ease of handling according to the level of detail required. Thus a firm may have a corporate planning department that does aggregate planning, perhaps by product group and for the entire company, and at some other level in the organization, such as production planning, a department that plans on the basis of individual products and their individual styles. In selecting a forecasting technique for a specific situation, one must be aware of the level of detail that will be required for that forecast to be useful in making decisions. The corporate planning department would see little value in having a forecast by individual item in the company's product line; similarly, a production supervisor trying to schedule weekly production would find little value in a general estimate of total corporate sales. In general, the greater the level of detail (and frequency) that is required, the greater the need for an automated forecasting procedure, and vice versa.

3. *Number of Items.* In situations in which the decisions made concern hundreds or even thousands of products, companies often find it most effective to develop simple decision rules that can be applied mechanically to each item. The same general principle holds true in forecasting. When only a single item is being forecast, the procedure(s) used in preparing that forecast

can be much more detailed and complex than if hundreds or thousands of forecasts had to be prepared. Clearly, an inventory control manager with 10,000 products would not use the same method to meet forecasting requirements that the corporate economics staff would in its attempt to predict the general economy. The automation of the former must be much greater than that of the latter.

4. *Control versus Planning.* In control, management by exception is the general procedure. What is needed is some way to determine, as early as possible, when a process is out of control (that is, when the basic pattern has shifted). Thus a forecasting method in such situations should be able to recognize changes in basic patterns or relationships at an early stage. On the planning side, where it generally is assumed that existing patterns will continue in the future, the major emphasis is on identifying those patterns and extrapolating them into the future.

5. *Constancy.* Forecasting a situation that is constant over time is very different from forecasting one that is in a state of flux. In the stable situation a quantitative forecasting method can be adopted and checked periodically to reconfirm its appropriateness. In changing circumstances, however, what is needed is a method that can adapt continually to reflect the most recent results and the latest information.

6. *Existing Planning Procedures.* Instituting any forecasting method generally involves changes in the company's planning and decision-making procedures. As managers are well aware, there is built-in resistance to change in any organization. Often it is important in the effective application of forecasting methods to start with those that are most closely related to existing procedures and then to use an evolutionary approach to upgrading, improving, and enhancing these methods. In this way the changes can be made in a steplike fashion, rather than all at once.

Undoubtedly other characteristics exist that can be used to describe individual forecasting situations, but the authors have found these six to be particularly important. Once these six have been identified and understood for a specific situation, it is possible to consider the characteristics of the various forecasting methods in order to find a good fit between the method selected and the situation.

Characterizing Forecasting Methods

We have found six major factors that are important in describing forecasting methods. These reflect their inherent capabilities and adaptability.

1. *Time Horizon.*   Two aspects of the time horizon relate to individual forecasting methods. First is the span of time in the future for which different forecasting methods are best suited. Generally speaking, qualitative methods of forecasting are used more for longer term forecasts, whereas quantitative methods are used more with intermediate and shorter term situations. The second important aspect of the time horizon is the number of periods for which a forecast is desired. Some techniques are appropriate for forecasting only one or two periods in advance; others can be used for several periods. There are also approaches for combining forecasting horizons of different lengths.

2. *Pattern of Data.*   Underlying the majority of forecasting methods is an assumption as to the type of pattern(s) found in the data to be forecast: for example, some data series may contain a seasonal as well as a trend pattern; others may consist simply of an average (mean) value with random fluctuations around that; and still others might be cyclical. Because different forecasting methods vary in their ability to predict different types of patterns, it is important to match the presumed pattern(s) in the data with the appropriate technique.

3. *Cost.*   Generally three direct elements of cost are involved in the application of a forecasting procedure: development, data preparation, and actual operation. There are also opportunity costs in terms of other techniques that might have been applied. The variation in costs obviously affects the attractiveness of different methods for different situations.

4. *Accuracy.*   Closely related to the level of detail required in a forecast is the needed accuracy. For some decision situations, plus or minus 10% may be sufficient; in others, a variation of as little as 5% could spell disaster.

5. *Intuitive Appeal, Simplicity, and Ease of Application.*   One general principle in the application of scientific methods to management is that only methods that are understood get used over time by decision makers. This is particularly true in the area of forecasting. Managers will not base decisions for which they are responsible on forecasts they do not understand or in which they have no confidence. Thus, in addition to meeting the requirements of the situation, the forecasting technique must fit with the manager who will use the forecast.

6. *Availability of Computer Software.*   It is seldom possible to apply a given quantitative forecasting method unless appropriate computer programs exist. Such programs must be easy to use, well documented, and free of major "bugs," so managers can apply them and understand and interpret their results.

At least four key areas need to be considered by management as it assesses alternative forecasting methods for a specific situation. First is the item to be forecast. This requires studying the characteristics of the situation, paying particular attention to whether one is trying to predict the continuance of a historical pattern, the continuance of a basic relationship, or a turning point. Second is the interaction of the situation with the characteristics of available forecasting methods. Here the manager must be aware not only of values and costs but also of relative changes in value and costs when the level of accuracy changes. If a manager can use a more straightforward and less expensive forecasting method (as opposed to a more sophisticated and expensive one) and still achieve the required level of accuracy, he or she generally should do so.

A third consideration is the amount of historical data available. Since different methods (particularly quantitative methods) are based on historical information, the manager must consider the quantity of data at hand, the appropriateness of the data, and what it would cost to gather additional data. Often it is most effective to start with a simple forecasting method that does not require many data, and then, as the manager builds experience and gathers more data, increasingly sophisticated methods can be adopted.

Fourth, the manager must consider the time allowed for preparing the forecast. Although some forecasts may not be prepared for several weeks or even months after historical data have been gathered, others, particularly for short-term decision making, must be ready a few days after the data are available. Urgency and the amount of time allowed for data gathering therefore are factors in the selection of a forecasting method.

In selecting a forecasting method, it is important that the manager deal with each step of the process so that it will be understood and so that the limitations and capabilities of what is being done can be interpreted and judged. Generally, it is much wiser to apply a straightforward, simple approach initially and to upgrade gradually to more sophisticated methods if this proves beneficial and necessary. More will be said on this later.

Managers can incur an extremely high cost from a very unexpected source—the opportunity cost associated with a false sense of security induced by what appears (is perceived) to be an accurate forecast. Forecasting is not a substitute for management judgment in decision making; it is simply an aid to that process. Having watched a variety of managers deal with forecasts, we have concluded that those who are most pleased with its role and contribution are those who view it as a tool and not a crutch. Forecasting is not a substitute for prophecy that can eliminate future uncertainty. Instead, it is a systematic way of facing the future that can enhance and often improve unaided human judgment.

Finally, a strong finding reported in the forecasting literature needs to be recognized. In all cases when a selection decision as to the "best" forecasting method is unclear, it has been shown to be beneficial to hedge by using more than one forecasting method or forecaster and then combining their predictions. This has proved to be an extremely effective way of increasing forecasting accuracy and decreasing the variance in errors. Thus, when in doubt managers should combine (that is, average) multiple forecasts that come from a variety of independent sources.

SELECTED REFERENCES FOR FURTHER STUDY

Armstrong J. S., 1978. "Forecasting with Econometric Methods: Folklore versus Fact," *Journal of Business*, S1, pp. 549–600.

Box, G. E. P., and G. M. Jenkins, 1976. *Time Series Analysis: Forecasting and Control*, rev. ed., Holden-Day, San Francisco.

Brown, R. G., 1956. "Exponential Smoothing for Predicting Demand," presented at 10th National Meeting of the Operations Research Society of America, San Francisco, Nov. 16.

———, 1959. *Statistical Forecasting for Inventory Control*, McGraw-Hill, New York.

———, 1963. *Smoothing, Forecasting and Prediction*, Prentice-Hall, Englewood Cliffs, NJ.

Hogarth, R. M., and S. Makridakis, 1981. "Forecasting and Planning: An Evaluation," *Management Science*, 27, no. 1, pp. 115–138.

Holt, C. C., 1957. "Forecasting Seasonal, and Trends by Exponentially Weighted Moving Averages," Office of Naval Research, Research Memorandum 52.

Lawrence, M., and S. Makridakis, 1988. "Factors Affecting Judgmental Forecasting and Confidence Intervals," *Organizational Behavior and Human Decision Processes*, forthcoming.

Makridakis, S., 1986. "The Art and Science of Forecasting: An Assessment and Future Directions," *International Journal of Forecasting*, 2, no. 1, pp. 15–39.

Makridakis, S., et al., 1982. "The Accuracy of Extrapolation (Time Series) Methods: Results of a Forecasting Competition," *Journal of Forecasting*, 1, no. 2.

Mental, J. S., 1985. *Nonextrapolative Methods in Business Forecasting*, Quorum Books, Westport, CT.

Murdick, R. G., and D. M. Georgoff, 1986. "How to Choose the Best Technique—or Combination of Techniques—to Help Solve Your Particular Forecasting Dilemma," *Harvard Business Review*, Jan.–Feb., pp. 110–120.

Schnaars, S. P., and T. M. Topol, 1987. "The Use of Multiple Scenarios in Sales Forecasting," *International Journal of Forecasting*, 3, no. 3/4, pp. 405–420.

Shiskin, J., 1961. "Tests and Revisions of Bureau of the Census Methods of Seasonal Adjustments," Bureau of the Census, Technical Paper 5.

———, 1957. "Electronic Computers and Business Indicators," National Bureau of Economic Research, Occasional Paper 56.

Shiskin, J., A. H. Young, and Y. C. Musgrave. The X-11 Variant of the Census II Method Seasonal Adjustment Program, Bureau of the Census, Technical Paper 15.

Tyebee, T. T., 1987. "Behavioral Biases in New Product Forecasting," *International Journal of Forecasting*, 3, no. 3/4, pp. 393–404.

Winters, P. R., 1960. "Forecasting Sales by Exponentially Weighted Moving Averages," *Management Science*, April, pp. 324–342.

CHAPTER 3

WHAT CAN AND CANNOT BE PREDICTED*

In the previous chapter, we discussed the role of forecasting in planning and other future-oriented decision-making activities. As we have mentioned on several occasions, some events or situations can be predicted with a high degree of accuracy, while others are less predictable or completely unpredictable. In this chapter we will describe the extent of predictability of the various events or situations most often encountered in practical applications. We believe it is extremely important for decision makers and policy makers to be aware of the advantages of forecasting; it is equally important that they know its limitations.

THE PERCEPTIONS AND REALITY OF FORECASTING

The stock market crash of October 19th, 1987, caught a great number of investors by surprise. Obviously, many did not anticipate the crash. Believing the forecasts that the bull market would continue, they anticipated huge profits from increases in their stock portfolios. We do not pretend that we predicted the crash; however, we were not surprised by it. As will become clear from this chapter, predicting the direction of the stock market or of individual stocks is impossible. Stock market prices are cyclical (that is, they fluctuate widely around a long-term secular trend). For instance, before 1974 the Dow Jones Industrial Average reached 1300. Then it dropped to less than 800 in a period of a few months, a drop of 40%. Therefore, a similar drop of 40% should not be surprising. This means that the Dow Jones of 2800

*This chapter is based on S. Makridakis, 1988. "Metaforecasting: Ways of Improving Forecasting Accuracy and Usefulness," *International Journal of Forecasting*, 4, no. 3, pp. 467–491.

could drop below 1700 without surprising anyone, but people tend to forget what happened in the past (see Chapter 13). Similarly, they would like to believe in the prophetic abilities of someone or some method.

Stock market investors are not the only ones who get caught by surprise through erroneous beliefs in the accuracy of forecasting, and the uncertainty surrounding all predictions concerning events in the economic or business environment. Government officials and business people get surprised too. It is necessary, therefore, that we set the record straight. Repeating ourselves, it is extremely important not to have unrealistic expectations in terms of how accurately and with what degree of certainty the future can be predicted.

THE PREDICTABILITY OF THE FUTURE

As we indicated in Chapters 1 and 2, a prerequisite of any form of forecasting, whether judgmental or quantitative, is that a pattern or relationship exists concerning some event of interest. Such patterns or relationships have to be correctly identified and projected in order to forecast. When patterns or relationships do not exist, forecasting is not possible, although judgmental assessments based on similar past events can be made. Scientific progress has improved considerably our ability to predict future events, albeit unevenly, in various areas. In the physical domain, forecasting accuracy is perfect for all practical purposes. In other areas, notably in the economic or business field, predictability ranges from negligible to excellent.

In the physical domain, patterns are exact and relationships precise and, for practical purposes, they remain unchanged over time. This is not the case in the economic or business field, where patterns and relationships are intermixed with random noise and can change unpredictably over time. Two major causes of change in patterns or relationships are the capriciousness of human behavior (such as shifts in attitudes fueled by fashions or differences among individuals) and people's ability to influence future events by their actions (that is, the forecasts themselves can become self-fulfilling or self-defeating prophecies that change established patterns and relationships).

Table 3-1 summarizes the factors that influence predictability as well as the characteristics of patterns and relationships as a function of the events involved and the forecasting horizon. The longer the forecasting horizon, the greater the chance of a change in patterns or relationships, because (1) people's behavior or attitudes can change, (2) there is more time to use the forecasts to modify the future in order to achieve desired benefits, or (3) a fundamental change occurs in the environment, for example, a technological breakthrough. Furthermore, Table 3-1 lists some general factors that systematically influence predictability. These factors are briefly described below.

1. *Number of Items.*   The larger the number of items involved (all other things being equal), the more accurate the forecasts. Because of the statistical law of large numbers, the size of forecasting errors, and therefore the accuracy, decreases as the number of items being forecast increases, and vice versa. Thus it is more accurate to predict the number of telephone calls arriving at a switching station during a five-minute interval than the number of personal computers sold on a certain day.

2. *Homogeneity of Data.*   The more homogeneous the data (all other things being equal), the more accurate the forecasts, and vice versa. Thus, data referring to a single region can predict seasonality more accurately than data covering many regions with varying weather patterns. Similarly, sales of consumer goods to individual customers can be predicted more accurately than sales to both individual and industrial customers.

3. *Elasticity of Demand.*   The more inelastic demand (all other things being equal), the more accurate the forecasts. Thus, the demand for necessities can be forecast with a higher degree of accuracy than the demand for luxuries, and the demand for nondurable goods with a higher degree of accuracy than that for durables. Related to the elasticity of demand is the influence of business cycles. Such cycles have the least impact on inelastic demand and the greatest impact on elastic demand. People give food and other necessities priority over other purchases when their income is reduced, for example, during a recession.

4. *Competition.*   The greater the competition (all other things being equal), the more difficult it is to forecast, since competitiors can use the forecasts to change the course of future events and thus invalidate the forecasts.

SOURCES OF FORECASTING ERRORS AND FUTURE UNCERTAINTY

In the physical sciences the identification and verification of patterns or relationships are exact and objective. For all practical purposes, precision instruments reduce measurement errors to zero, and laboratory or controlled experimentation makes it possible to keep all factors constant, except the one being tested. Moreover, feedback is unambiguous. In the economic and business domains, however, measurement errors abound, laboratory-type experimentation is not possible, and feedback is infrequent and often unclear. Furthermore, because of the complexity of economic situations, the inconsistency of human behavior, the varying time lags between actions and outcomes, and other factors, forecasting errors much larger than those

Table 3-1 Extent or Ability to Forecast and the Factors Involved

Events or Situations that Can Be Forecasted for All Practical Purposes with a Perfect Degree of Accuracy	Forecasting Horizon	Events or Situations that Can Be Forecasted with a High Degree of Accuracy	Events or Situations that Can Be Forecasted with a Medium Degree of Accuracy	Events or Situations that Can Be Forecasted with a Low Degree of Accuracy	Highly Inaccurate Forecasting of Events or Situations	Unable to Forecast More Accurately than Utilizing the Most Recent Actual Values to Do So	Unable to Forecast More Accurately than Statistical Actuary Averages	Unable to Forecast at All
Physical events or phenomena (e.g., exact time of arrival of Halley's comet or its nearest distance to the earth; exact time of sunrise each day, month, or year from today; result of putting two atoms of hydrogen and one of oxygen together)	Short (up to 3 months)	Large numbers of items (products, customers, services) → (a) → Small numbers of items Highly aggregate → (b) → Single items	(a), (b)			Events determined by the collective actions of many individuals or organizations (attempting to maximize their benefits) when information is disseminated efficiently (e.g., stock and futures markets, exchange rates, prices of almost all raw materials and most finished products)	Unusual or infrequent events (e.g., a fire destroying one's home or a factory, a major car accident, the accidental death of a young, healthy person, an extremely severe snowstorm)	Unexpected or inconceivable events (e.g., growth and importance of computers for someone before 1950; oil crisis for a decision maker in the 1960s; fall of the Shah of Iran for a political analyst before 1970)
	Medium (3 months to 2 years)	Forecasting horizon close to 3 months → (c) → Forecasting horizon close to 2 years Inelastic demand → (d) → Elastic demand No competition → (e) → Strong competition						

Characteristics of patterns or relationships	Characteristics of patterns or relationships	Characteristics of patterns or relationships	Characteristics of patterns or relationships
Patterns or relationships do not change over time	Patterns or relationships change over time	Aggregate patterns (involving large numbers of cases or people exist; the larger the numbers involved, the more precise the pattern and vice versa)	Patterns or relationships do not exist, or they cannot be identified given today's knowledge
Events cannot be influenced by human actions	Events can be influenced by human actions	Patterns might change over time but usually do so slowly	
Patterns are exact	Patterns are not exact	Relationships are weak or nonexistent	
Relationships are precise	Relationships are not precise		

Characteristics of patterns or relationships

(a), (b), (c), (d), (e)
Long (2 years or more) ⟷

(f)
Forecasting horizon close to 2 years ⟷ Forecasting horizon of many years

(g)
Low degree of technological change ⟷ High degree of technological change

(h)
Strong barriers to entry ⟷ No barriers to entry

Patterns or relationships vary widely (ranging from those listed in the column on the left side to those listed in the three columns on the right), depending upon the factors specified observed in physical science are a fact of life. The size and the persistence of such errors depend upon the following.

Erroneous Identification of Patterns and Relationships.   An illusory pattern or relationship might be identified when none really exists. This can occur in both judgmental and statistical forecasting. In their quest to master and control the environment, people often glimpse illusory correlation, while statistical models based on a small number of observations (for example, with new products) can "identify" a pattern that is not maintained over a longer period. Similarly, a relationship between two variables might be spurious, existing only because a third factor causes both variables to move in the same direction. Alternatively, patterns or relationships that exist might be incorrectly identified or ignored because insufficient information is available, or because reality is too complex to be understood or modeled with a limited number of variables (see Einhorn and Hogarth, 1987). Illusory or inappropriate identification can cause serious and nonrandom forecasting errors, since the future could turn out to be very different from what was postulated by an erroneous pattern or relationship.

Inexact Patterns or Imprecise Relationships.   In the social sciences, for the reasons discussed, patterns are inexact and relationships are imprecise. Although an average pattern or relationship can be identified, fluctuations around such an average exist in almost all cases. The purpose of statistical modeling is to identify patterns or relationships in such a way as to make past fluctuations around the average as small and random as possible. Whether or not this is a good strategy is questionable (see below), but even if it is appropriate, it does not guarantee that future errors will be random or symmetric or that they will not exceed a certain magnitude.

Changing Patterns or Relationships.   In the social sciences, patterns or relationships are constantly changing over time in a way that is not predictable in the great majority of cases. Changes in patterns or relationships can cause large persistant errors whose magnitude cannot be known in advance. The size of such errors depends on the magnitude and duration of the change.

Table 3-1 summarizes the discussion so far by presenting the entire range of events or situations, the extent of their predictability, and the characteristics of patterns and relationships. In addition, it shows the importance of the time horizon and how it influences forecasting accuracy (the longer the horizon, the less accurate the forecast). Many events such as changes in stock and futures market prices, interest and exchange rates, and most raw material prices cannot be predicted more accurately than by extrapolating the current price. This means that no one (unless he or she possesses inside knowledge) can benefit from accurate forecasting of such events, because all known information is efficiently disseminated and used by great numbers of individuals or organizations, as soon as it becomes available, to maximize their benefits or minimize their losses. Although this evidence has been shown to hold true beyond any reasonable doubt, few people use it. In the stock market case, for instance, they act on "tips," seek the council of "gurus," and read numerous publications in an effort to beat the market. Similarly, some unusual or infrequent events cannot be predicted any better than "on the average." This information, although useful when a larger number of events are involved, is of little forecasting value for single cases. Thus, it makes no practical sense to attempt to predict when you will have your next car accident or how serious it will be. On the other hand, an insurance company can predict reasonably well how many car accidents its policyholders will have each day or each week. Finally, there are many new events which cannot be predicted.

Between the events or situations in the physical world and those just described are those whose predictability varies from very little to excellent (see Table 3-1). Most of those events belong in the business world. It is interesting, therefore, to consider further these in-between events.

Table 3-2 lists a range of events or areas that can be predicted and some that cannot in terms of forecasting horizons. In general, we can accurately predict (1) seasonality, (2) average relationships, in the short term, assuming no competitive actions or reactions, (3) average cyclical patterns, (4) emerging technological trends and their influence, (5) continuation of established trends, and (6) general tendencies. On the other hand, we cannot accurately predict special events, competitive actions or reactions, sales of new products, the start and depth of recessions, the duration and strength of booms, changes in trends, changes in relationships or attitudes, and technological innovations. In addition, Table 3-2 lists the implications of accurate and inaccurate forecasting.

Forecasting accuracy is greatly influenced, therefore, by changes in established patterns or relationships that can be classified, as shown in Table 3-3, in terms of the character of the change, the duration of that change, and whether or not it is a random occurrence or a systematic change. Random indicates that it cannot be predicted, whereas systematic suggests that it can be, although the understanding necessary to make such predictions may not yet be available. In considering the range of changes suggested by Table 3-3, two important aspects must be kept in mind. First, and perhaps most obvious, patterns and relationships can and do change. Second, however, because of inertia (momentum), even when a pattern or relationship does change, the outcome of such a change tends not to be immediate. A good example of this is when you apply pressure to the brakes in a car but the car

Table 3-2 Events or Areas that Can and Cannot Be Forecasted and their Implications

Time Horizon of Forecasting	Major Events or Areas that Can Be Forecasted with a Reasonable Degree of Accuracy	Major Benefits from Accurate Forecasting	Major Sources of Surprises or Unexpected Forecasting Errors	Problems or Difficulties Caused by Surprises and Unexpected Forecasting Errors
Short term (less than 3 months)	Seasonality in sales Effect of promotional and advertising actions Required level of inventories Impact of price changes Cash inflows and outflows Raw and other material requirements Work force, personnel needs	Improved customer satisfaction Better production or service scheduling Fewer inventories More effective advertising and promotion policies More effective pricing policies More profitable cash management Better material and personnel management	Special events (e.g., big snowstorm, a strike) Special competitive actions (e.g., advertising campaign or price decrease by competitor) Sales of new products	High inventories Underutilized workforce Lost sales, loss of market share Liquidity squeeze Opportunity losses Decreased profits or losses
Medium term (3 months to 2 years)	Average length of recovery and expansion of business cycle Average length of recession Average number of months between a change in the index of leading indicators and a change in the level	Better financial management Improved allocation of resources Reduced levels of inventories Improved profits or reduced losses Better competitive position	Booms continue longer than average or longer than expected Recessions shorter than average or unexpected Business climate and consumer attitudes different than expected Changes in relationships Sales of new products	Underutilization of personnel High inventories Lost sales Lost market share Serious financial problems Opportunity losses Decreased profits or losses

				Decreased long-term competitive position
Emerging (2 to 5 years)	of economic activity Theoretical effects of fiscal or monetary policies on economy Estimation of existing relationships Technological changes and their implications Changes in attitudes and their implications Demographic changes and their implications Economic and political realities Competitive environment Financial resources and requirements	More effective strategy formulation Introducing changes in the organization Identifying promising areas for capital investments, realizing, however, that competitors might have access to similarly accurate forecasts Promising R&D projects Improving (or maintaining) competitive position	Underestimating effects of emerging technologies and their implications on organizations or society Unwillingness to consider flattening or negative trends Unwillingness to accept possible effects of major environmental changes Assuming that fads will continue	Inability to introduce change Inability to harness advantages of new technologies, inability to deal with major environmental changes Loss of competitive advantage Losses from getting involved in fads whose demand dries out Opportunity losses

Table 3-2 *(Continued)*

Distant (5 to 15 years)	Established trends Some technological innovations Some demographic changes Basic economic, competitive, and financial realities	Building consensus Initiation of feasibility studies for promising R&D projects Establishing strategic directions	Overestimating applicability of new technologies (e.g., nuclear power, artificial intelligence) Overemphasizing ability of forecasting new technologies and their impact or usefulness	Losses from getting involved in unsuccessful projects involving untested technologies or projects
Far away (15 years or more)	General tendencies in: Technology Societal attitudes Economic environment Demography Political environment	General strategic directions	Inability to forecast major technological innovations and their impact on business or society (e.g., growth and importance of computers)	Wasting resources to make forecasts whose usefulness is dubious

Table 3-3 Classification of Future Events (with Examples) as a Way of Exploring the Entire Range of Future Uncertainties

Character of Change	Type and Duration of Change		
	Random Fluctuations	Systematic Changes	
		Temporary	Permanent
Normal	Machine breakdown	Seasonal fluctuations in demand for product A	Shift in consumer preferences (e.g., small cars)
Unusual	Big snowstorm	Recession	Three Mile Island nuclear accident
Unexpected	Fire burning down a hotel	Severe recession	Fall of the Shah of Iran
Inconceivable	Meteorite hitting earth and destroying all physical facilities of Company XYZ	Worldwide depression	All-out nuclear war that destroys civilization

does not stop immediately. Because of its speed (inertia), the car continues to move for some distance before stopping.

This concept of inertia is very important in most business and economic situations. Stopping advertising will not result in an immediate decline in sales. It usually takes some time, often serveral months, before the full impact of that type of change is felt. Similarly, if one looks at some major events of the 1970s or 1980s, such as the oil embargo and the quadrupling of oil prices, or the stock market crash of 1987, one recalls that the impact of those events was not felt immediately. It was almost a full year, for instance, after the oil crisis before the industrialized economies of the world slipped into a recession. As a result of inertia and subsequent response lags, established patterns can be extrapolated in the short term with some degree of accuracy.

Two other aspects of existing forecasting techniques should be kept in mind at this point. One is the role of forecasting in connection with management's desire to reduce uncertainty. Those using forecasting must develop realistic expectations as to what forecasting can and cannot do. One of the most frequently misunderstood aspects of forecasting methods is their relationship to uncertainty. Generally, managers believe (and thus often expect) that the more time and resources committed to forecasting, the lower their uncertainty should be. However, in many situations, simply spending more time and effort on forecasting has the opposite result—the very process of exploring the future through forecasting techniques may open up new possibilities and lead to the consideration of more rather than fewer alternatives. For the manager, this often means more uncertainty.

From this perspective a major purpose of forecasting is to enable decision makers and policy makers to understand the uncertainties of the future and to consider such uncertainties and their associated risks while planning and making future-oriented decisions. Planners and decision makers might consider, through careful forecasting, a wider range of options than they would have otherwise. For example, they might consider buying insurance against possible undesirable events not previously considered possible. Alternatively, guidelines might be developed to prevent the organization from venturing into situations involving extreme risks.

Second, forecasting can be a major benefit, even when traditional patterns and relationships are changing and methods that identify and extrapolate them are not particularly useful. Often this benefit comes simply from identifying systematic changes as they occur. This aspect of forecasting, generally referred to as *monitoring*, has begun to gain attention only recently. The purpose of monitoring is very similar to that of a radar system scanning the horizon. As long as nothing appears on the screen, the existing state (that is, clear skies) is assumed to be continuing. However, when the radar system picks up an object in the skies, it signals the need for more careful attention and perhaps a need for an alert that may necessitate a change of plans and decisions.

Monitoring methods in the forecasting field provide warning signals of impending changes so that forecasting users can evaluate their significance and develop appropriate responses. One reason why such monitoring methods have been receiving increased attention is that recent studies of human capabilities in forecasting suggest that when systematic change occurs in a cumulative, incremental fashion and it occurs in a number of variables in a parallel fashion, human judgment has extreme difficulty perceiving and interpreting such nonrandom change. Thus these changes can be best handled through quantitative monitoring techniques. (Some specific forms of these techniques will be explored in Chapter 14.)

Because systematic changes in established patterns and relationships degrade the performance of existing forecasting methods and can be extremely costly to an organization, some type of monitoring technique should be used as a complement to more traditional forecasting approaches in almost all situations. Even though monitoring techniques cannot detect systematic change until such change has actually begun to occur, much as an early warning system does, they can significantly speed management's recognition that such change is occurring and provide more lead time for responding to such change.

SELECTED REFERENCES FOR FURTHER STUDY

Armstrong, J. C., 1985. *Long-Range Forecasting: From Crystal Ball to Computer*, 2nd ed., Wiley-Interscience, New York.

Ascher, W., 1978. *Forecasting: An Appraisal for Policy Makers and Planners*, Johns Hopkins University Press, Baltimore, MD.

Berenson, C., and S. Schnaars, 1986. "Growth Market Forecasting Revisited," *California Management Review*, Summer, pp. 71–88.

Dawes, R.M., 1986. "Forecasting One's Own Preferences," *International Journal of Forecasting*, 2, pp. 5–14.

Einhorn, H. J., and R. M. Hogarth, 1986. "Decision Making: Going Forward in Reverse," *Harvard Business Review*, Jan.–Feb., pp. 66–70.

Fishoff, B., P. Slovic and S. Lichtenstein, 1977. "Knowing with Certainty: The Appropriateness of Extreme Confidence," *Journal of Experimental Psychology: Human Perception and Performance*, 3, no. 4, pp. 552–564.

Hogarth, R. M., and S. Makridakis, 1981. "Forecasting and Planning: An Evaluation," *Management Science*, 27, no. 2, pp. 115–138.

Lawrence, M., and S. Makridakis, 1988. "Factors Affecting Judgmental Forecasts and Confidence Intervals," *Organizational Behavior and Human Decision Processes*, forthcoming.

Makridakis, S., 1986. "The Art and Science of Forecasting: An Assessment and Future Directions," *International Journal of Forecasting*, 2, pp. 15–39.

Makridakis, S., and D. Heau, 1987. "The Evolution of Strategic Planning and Management," in W. R. King and D. I. Cleland (Eds), *Strategic Planning and Management Handbook*, Van Nostrand, Reinhold, New York, pp. 1–20.

Moriarty, M. M., and A. J. Adams, 1984. "Management Judgment Forecasts, Composite Forecasting Models, and Conditional Efficiency," *Journal of Marketing Research*, 21, Aug., pp. 239–250.

Porter, M., 1985. *Competitive Advantage: Creating and Sustaining Superior Performance*, Free Press, New York.

Schnaars, S. P., 1984. "Situational Factors Affecting Forecast Accuracy," *Journal of Marketing Research*, 21, Aug., pp. 290–297.

QUANTITATIVE FORECASTING METHODS

CHAPTER 4

INTRODUCTION TO QUANTITATIVE FORECASTING METHODS

A major concept introduced in Chapter 2 is that each situation for which a forecast is needed has certain generic characteristics, and each category of forecasting method has certain capabilities and limitations. A key task for management is finding a good match between a situation and a method *before* launching into the detailed steps of collecting data, applying the method, evaluating the results, and making modifications as needed to improve predictive performance.

In this chapter we introduce the measures and techniques that can be used to determine the capabilities and limitations of quantitative forecasting methods. We also discuss the terminology, vocabulary, and basic definitions that will be used. Although some of these definitions involve straightforward arithmetic, we have tried not to overcomplicate them with high-powered mathematics. We hope that these definitions are still consistent with what a staff specialist with several years in forecasting and statistics would accept as correct and consistent.

This chapter is divided into four parts. The first discusses the types of models represented by quantitative forecasting methods. Understanding the conceptual differences between the two major types—time series and explanatory—is a useful starting point in selecting a specific method.

The second deals with performance measures of accuracy. Here the basic notation that will be used in discussing quantitative forecasting methods is introduced. A range of accuracy measures is illustrated and discussed, and we conclude with a summary set of definitions that can be used in a wide range of forecasting situations.

The third part of the chapter builds on the standard measures of forecasting accuracy, exploring the degree of improvement attainable from sophisticated methods. Two key questions in any forecasting situation are: (1) how valuable is forecasting? and (2) is that value worth the cost? To help the reader find answers to these questions, the concept of using a simple naive method as a reference point is introduced. The simplest form of such a benchmark is to set future forecasts equal to the most recent actual observation. Referred to as Naive Forecast 1, this method is easy to apply. When its accuracy and cost (which is extremely low) are computed, it can be used as a standard against which other methods (presumably more accurate but also more costly) are evaluated. Naive Forecast 2, a second form of this naive approach, which is useful in dealing with data containing a seasonal component, is also introduced.

The final part of the chapter outlines the need for criteria that can complement, and must be balanced with, accuracy—the level of effort and resources required when a specific forecasting method is applied to a specific situation. Like most management situations, forecasting involves trade-offs, the most important of which is that between effort required (cost and ease of use) and results obtained (accuracy and understanding).

TYPES OF MODELS

The notion of a model has long been used by engineers and scientists to examine different processes and physical systems; for example, aerospace engineers generally develop a mock-up of new aircraft and use that model to examine certain characteristics of shape or size in various physical environments. The model becomes a way of experimenting with reality without actually having to invest in a full-scale operating unit.

Another model would be one that deals with a representation of a previously developed *procedure* or *process*, consisting of an abstraction (simplification) of the complexities of the procedure itself to a set of higher-level steps that can be used as a summary of its details. Such models often are developed in decision-making situations and represented graphically on a flowchart of some form. It is in this descriptive sense that we use the notion of a model of a forecasting technique.

A forecasting model consists of the procedures used by that technique in developing a forecast. Clearly, a wide range of models could be used, but for quantitative methods they fall into two fairly well-defined categories. By understanding the properties of each of these models (categories of methods), the manager can get a better grasp of the assumptions that underlie individual forecasting techniques and the pros and cons of using them in specific situations.

The first type of quantitative forecasting model, and perhaps the most common, is the *time-series model.* Two factors are important in a time-series model: the data series to be forecast (such as weekly supermarket sales) and the period of time to be used. A time-series model always assumes that some pattern or combination of patterns is recurring *over time.* Thus, by identifying and extrapolating that pattern, forecasts for subsequent time periods can be developed. The commuting time example developed in Chapter 1 falls into this category. Forecasting tomorrow's commuting time is related to the time it took to commute in the past several days or weeks.

In addition to the importance of the sequence of the periods as a variable in a time-series model, such a model assumes explicitly that the underlying pattern can be identified solely on the basis of historical data from that series. This means that the model will not be particularly helpful to the manager in predicting the impact of certain decisions he or she may make. Any forecasting method that uses a time-series model will give the same forecast for the next period, no matter what the manager's actions may be. Thus, a time-series model may be appropriate for forecasting environmental factors such as the general economy and level of employment or for forecasting activity levels, such as cost patterns, where individual decisions have little impact, but it will be inappropriate for forecasting monthly sales resulting from changes in pricing and advertising.

One advantage of time-series models is that the basic rules of accounting are oriented toward sequential time periods. This means that in most firms data are readily available on the basis of these time periods and can be used in the application of a time-series forecasting method.

Time-series forecasting treats the *system* as a black box and makes no attempt to discover the factors affecting its behavior. As shown in Figure 4-1, the system is simply viewed as an unknown generating process. (The system can be anything—a national economy, a company's sales, or a household.)

There are three main reasons for wanting to treat a system as a black box. First, the system may not be understood, and even if it is understood, it may be extremely difficult to measure the relationships assumed to govern its behavior. Second, the main concern may only be to predict what will happen, not to know why it happens. During the eighteenth, nineteenth, and twentieth centuries, for example, several scientists have been concerned with the magnitude of sunspots. Little was known originally about the reasons for the

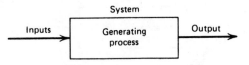

Figure 4-1   Time-Series Relationship.

sunspots or the sources of energy of the sun. This lack of knowledge, however, did not hinder investigators who collected and analyzed data about the frequency of sunspots. Schuster found a regular pattern in the magnitude of sunspots, and he and several others were able to predict their continuation through time-series analysis. Third, while it may be of little value to know why something happens as well as predicting what will happen, the cost of doing the former may be extremely high, while the cost of the latter—using a time-series method, for example—may be relatively low.

The second type of quantitative forecasting method is *explanatory* (see Figure 4-2). Under such methods any change in inputs will affect the output of the system in a predictable way, assuming the relationship is constant. The first task of forecasting is to find the relationship by observing the output of the system (either through time or by studying a cross section of similar systems) and relating that to the corresponding inputs. For example, one might seek to determine the relationships in a system in order to predict outputs such as gross national product, company sales, or household expenses. Such a process, if carried out correctly, will make it possible to estimate the type and extent of the relationship between the inputs and output. This relationship can be used to predict future states of the system, provided the inputs are known for those future states.

Basically, the explanatory method assumes that the value of a certain variable (the output) is a function of one or more other variables (the inputs). In a very narrow sense a time-series model could be called an explanatory model, since the actual values are assumed to be a function of the time period alone. The term "explanatory model", however, is generally reserved for models with variables other than time. An example would be an equation for predicting sales that bases its forecast on the values of price and advertising within the company and the industry; that is, the equation would state that sales are a function of these other variables.

The real strength of an explanatory model as a forecasting method is that a manager can develop a range of forecasts corresponding to a range of values for the different input variables. However, a drawback of these methods is that they require information on several variables in addition to the variable that is being forecast. As a result, their data requirements are much larger than those of a time-series model. In addition, since explanatory

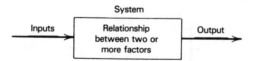

Figure 4-2 Explanatory or Causal Relationship.

models generally relate several factors, they usually take longer to develop and are more sensitive to changes in the underlying relationships than would be a time-series model. Furthermore, they require an estimation of future values of the input factors before the output variable can be forecast.

Quite often it is possible to forecast by using either explanatory or time-series methods. Economic activity, for example, can be forecast by discovering and measuring the relationship of the gross national product (GNP) to several factors that influence it, such as monetary and fiscal policies, inflation, capital spending, and imports and exports. This will require that the form and parameters be specified for the relationship

$$\text{GNP} = f(\text{monetary and fiscal policies, inflation, capital spending,}$$
$$\text{imports, exports})$$

where f means it is a function of, depends on, or is being influenced by.

The procedure for selecting an appropriate functional form of this causal equation and estimating its parameters will be discussed in detail later on. At this point it should be emphasized that according to this model, GNP depends on, or is determined by, the factors on the right-hand side of the equation. As these factors change, GNP will vary in the manner specified by the form of this model selected.

If the only purpose is to forecast future values of GNP without concern as to why a certain level of GNP will be realized, a time-series approach would be appropriate. It is known that the magnitude of GNP does not change drastically from one month to another, or even from one year to another. Thus the GNP of next month will depend on the GNP of the previous month and possibly that of the months before. On the basis of observation, GNP might be expressed as follows:

$$\text{GNP}_{t+1} = f(\text{GNP}_t, \text{GNP}_{t-1}, \text{GNP}_{t-2}, \text{GNP}_{t-3}, \dots)$$

where

$$
\begin{aligned}
\text{GNP}_t &= \text{GNP in the present month} \\
\text{GNP}_{t+1} &= \text{GNP in the next month (the forecast)} \\
\text{GNP}_{t-1} &= \text{GNP in the last month} \\
\text{GNP}_{t-2} &= \text{GNP two months ago}
\end{aligned}
$$

and so on.

This model is similar to the explanatory one except that the factors on the right-hand side are previous values of the left-hand side. This makes the job of forecasting easier once the specific form of the model is known, since unlike the explanatory model, this model requires no special input values. However, it is necessary with both models that the relationship between the left- and right-hand sides of the equation be discovered and measured so that it can be extrapolated in order to forecast.

Notation for Quantitative Forecasting Methods

In preparing a forecast with any quantitative method one begins with a number of *observed values, past data,* or *observations.* These observations may represent many things, from the actual number of units sold to the cost of producing each unit to the number of people employed. Because these observed values vary, they are generally represented by a *variable* such as X. A variable is simply the symbol of the value of some item. Thus X could be the number of washing machines sold in a month. The actual value of X would depend on the month in question, and for May we might have $X_5 = 320$ washing machines.

Because a variable that represents observations takes on different values depending on the *time period*, a way of identifying this period is also needed. This is usually done by assigning consecutive numbers to consecutive time periods. Thus the 24 months beginning with January 1988 and ending with December 1989 would be referred to as time periods 1, 2, 3, . . . , 24. Obviously the length of the period has to be defined at the outset. Depending on the situation, it might be defined as one day, one week, one month, one year, or some other span of time. Once the time periods have been established, the observed values can be referred to with the use of *subscripts*; for example, X_{10} would refer to the observed value in period 10 and X_{13} would refer to the observed value in period 13. One thing to keep in mind with regard to time periods is that the decision maker can decide arbitrarily which to call number 1. Subsequent periods then are given consecutive numbers.

Although X or some other symbol generally identifies the actual (historical) observed values of a variable, a different symbol is often used to represent the *forecast value* of that variable. In this book the symbols F_{t+1} or $\hat{X}_{t+1}$ will be used to denote the forecast value for time period $t + 1$. As a summary of the relation between observed values and forecast values in a time-series situation, consider Table 4-1.

The basic assumption underlying the use of any forecasting technique is that the actual value observed will be determined by some pattern plus some random influences. This can be written algebraically as

Table 4-1   Notation Used in Time-Series Forecasting

						Forecast Values								
Observed values	X_1	X_2	X_3	X_4	$\cdots$	X_{t-2}	X_{t-1}	X_t	F_{t+1}	F_{t+2}	F_{t+3}	$\cdots$	F_{t+m}
Period i	1	2	3	4	$\cdots$	$t-2$	$t-1$	t	$t+1$	$t+2$	$t+3$	$\cdots$	$t+m$
Estimated values	$\hat{X}_1$	$\hat{X}_2$	$\hat{X}_3$	$\hat{X}_4$	$\cdots$	$\hat{X}_{t-2}$	$\hat{X}_{t-1}$	$\hat{X}_t$	$\hat{X}_{t+1}$	$\hat{X}_{t+2}$	$\hat{X}_{t+3}$	$\cdots$	$\hat{X}_{t+m}$
	F_1	F_2	F_3	F_4	$\cdots$	F_{t-2}	F_{t-1}	F_t					
Error values	e_1	e_2	e_3	e_4	$\cdots$	e_{t-2}	e_{t-1}	e_t					
								Present					

$$actual = pattern + randomness$$

Because the economic or business world is not deterministic, randomness will always be present. This means that even when the average pattern of the underlying data has been identified, some deviation will exist between the forecast values and the values actually observed. A common goal in the application of forecasting techniques is to minimize these deviations or errors in the forecast. These errors are defined as the difference between the actual value and what was predicted. They can be written as

$$e_i = X_i - F_i$$

The subscript i indicates that it is the error of the time period i being examined. As shown in Table 4-1, an error value is associated with each observation for which there is both an actual and a predicted value. To simplify the manipulation of expressions involving the adding of many numbers, it is convenient to use a summation sign, $\sum$. The use of this sign and the elements of notation mentioned previously can be demonstrated using the information in Table 4-1: X_i is the actual sales value, $\hat{X}_i$ or F_i is the forecast value for sales, and e_i is the error, or the difference between actual (X_i) and forecast ($\hat{X}_i$) values of sales in time period i.

If one wants the sum of the errors and there are n observations, it can be obtained from

$$e_1 + e_2 + e_3 + \ldots + e_n = \sum_{i=1}^{n} e_i$$

The expression on the right-hand side can be read as "the sum of the error values, e_i, taken from $i = 1$ to $i = n$ (inclusive)."

MEASURING THE ACCURACY OF QUANTITATIVE FORECASTING METHODS

Using the notation outlined above, we can now turn our attention to what generally is the overriding criterion for selecting a forecasting method—accuracy. In many instances, the word *accuracy* refers to "goodness of fit," which in turn refers to how well the forecasting model is able to reproduce the data that are already known. In explanatory modeling, goodness-of-fit measures predominate. In time-series modeling, it is possible to use a sub-set of the known data to forecast the rest of the known data, enabling one to study the accuracy of the *forecasts* more directly. To the consumer of forecasts, it is the accuracy of the *future* forecast that is most important; how well a model fitted available historical data is of little or no value. Questions that are often asked are:

1. What additional accuracy can be achieved in a given situation through use of a formal forecasting technique? (How inaccurate will the forecasts be if they are based on a very simple or naive approach rather than on a more statistically sophisticated technique?)

2. For a given situation, how much improvement can be obtained in the accuracy of the forecasts? (How close can one come to achieving perfect forecasts?)

3. If the opportunity for achieving greater accuracy in a given situation is understood, how can that knowledge help in selecting the most appropriate forecasting technique?

These questions will be addressed throughout the next several chapters as individual forecasting methods are examined. At this point, it is useful to define a number of specific measures of accuracy that can be used with a wide variety of methods.

Table 4-2 presents a set of data that can be used to illustrate these measures of accuracy. The data in this table represent weekly sales (in thousands of dollars) for a supermarket over a 12-week period. As a starting point, the forecasts are very simple—the preceding week's actual sales (for example, $9,000 in week 1) are used as the forecast for the following week (that is, $9,000 is the forecast for week 2).

One measure of accuracy that can be calculated is the average error. Using the data of Table 4-2, if we simply add up the values of the errors and compute the average, we find that it is close to zero, since many of the positive errors have canceled out the negative errors (see column 4 in Table 4-2). To avoid this problem we can compute the absolute errors (disregarding the plus or minus sign) and look at what is commonly referred to as the mean absolute

Table 4-2 Weekly Supermarket Sales

(1) Week i	(2) Sales ($000) X_i	(3) Forecast F_i	(4) Error $X_i - F_i$	(5) Absolute Error $|X - F_i|$	(6) Absolute Percentage Error $\left|\dfrac{X_i - F_i}{X_i}\right| 100$	(7) Squared Error $(X_i - F_i)^2$
1	9	–	–	–	–	–
2	8	9	−1	1	12.5%	1
3	9	8	1	1	11.1	1
4	12	9	3	3	25.0	9
5	9	12	−3	3	33.3	9
6	12	9	3	3	25.0	9
7	11	12	−1	1	9.1	1
8	7	11	−4	4	57.1	16
9	13	7	6	6	46.2	36
10	9	13	−4	4	44.4	16
11	11	9	2	2	18.2	4
12	10	11	−1	1	10.0	1
Sum			1	29	291.9	103
Mean			0.091	2.64[a]	26.5[b]	9.36[c]

[a]Mean absolute deviation (MAD).
[b]Mean absolute percentage error (MAPE).
[c]Mean squared error (MSE).

57

deviation (MAD). (This is simply the average absolute error over several periods.) From column 5 in Table 4-2 we see that the value of the mean absolute deviation in this example is 2.64. This second measure is often preferred to that of the mean error.

Another accuracy measure is the mean absolute percentage error (MAPE). This is obtained by computing the absolute error for each time period, dividing the absolute error (column 5) by the corresponding actual value (column 1), and multiplying by 100%, then summing those and dividing by the number of values used (all 12 in this case), to get the mean absolute percentage error, or MAPE. As a percentage, this measure is a relative one, and thus it is sometimes preferred to the mean error or the MAD as an accuracy measure.

Still another measure of forecasting accuracy is the mean squared error (MSE), obtained by squaring each of the errors and computing the mean of those squared values. Column 7 in Table 4-2 shows that in the supermarket example the mean squared error has a value of 9.36. One of the differences between the mean absolute deviation (MAD) or the mean absolute percentage error (MAPE) and the mean squared error (MSE) is that the MSE penalizes a forecast much more for extreme deviations than it does for small ones. For example, in computing the mean absolute deviation, an error of 2 is counted only twice as much as an error of 1. In computing the mean squared error, however, an error of 2 is squared, which means that it counts four times as much as an error of 1. Thus adopting the criterion of minimizing the mean squared error implies that we would rather have several small deviations from the forecast value than one large deviation. Statisticians have long used a measure very similar in nature to the mean squared error—the standard deviation.

Using the notation introduced earlier, we can now summarize the equations representing these measures of accuracy:

1. *Mean error*

$$\text{ME} = \frac{\sum\limits_{i=1}^{n} e_i}{n}. \tag{4-1}$$

2. *Mean absolute deviation*

$$\text{MAD} = \frac{\sum\limits_{i=1}^{n} |e_i|}{n}. \tag{4-2}$$

3. *Mean squared error*

$$\text{MSE} = \frac{\sum_{i=1}^{n} e_i^2}{n}.$$

(4-3)

4. *Standard deviation of errors*

$$\text{SDE} = \sqrt{\frac{\sum e_i^2}{n-1}}.$$

(4-4)

5. *Percentage error*

$$\text{PE}_t = \frac{X_t - F_t}{X_t} 100.$$

(4-5)

6. *Mean percentage error*

$$\text{MPE} = \frac{\sum_{i=1}^{n} \text{PE}_i}{n}.$$

(4-6)

7. *Mean absolute percentage error*

$$\text{MAPE} = \frac{\sum_{i=1}^{n} |\text{PE}_i|}{n}.$$

(4-7)

NAIVE METHODS: A BENCHMARK FOR FORECASTING PERFORMANCE

As suggested in the previous sections of this chapter, there are many measures of forecasting accuracy, and different methods may perform quite differently on these measures. Some methods take considerably more effort and resources to apply than others. As a reference point for deciding whether that effort is worthwhile and a benchmark against which improvements can be compared, it is useful to define two very simple naive methods against which the performance of more sophisticated methods can be evaluated.

The first of these methods is referred to as *Naive Forecast 1*, or NF1. This method uses as a forecast the most recent information available concerning the actual value. Thus, if a forecast is being prepared for a time horizon of one period, the most recent actual value would be used as the forecast for the next period. This was the method used to obtain the forecasts shown for weekly supermarket sales in Table 4-2. The equation on which such an NF1 forecast is based is

$$F_{t+i} = X_t \qquad (4\text{-}8)$$

where

$$
\begin{aligned}
F_{t+1} &= \text{forecast for period } t + i \\
t &= \text{present period} \\
i &= \text{number of periods ahead being forecast} \\
X_t &= \text{latest actual value (for period } t)
\end{aligned}
$$

Naive Forecast 1 is known as a *random walk model* in statistics, and there are times when it is the best forecasting procedure. For example, studies have shown that the stock market, certain commodity futures markets, and currency exchange markets often behave like random walk models, which would make Equation (4-8) the most appropriate form of forecasting method. This implies that there are fluctuations in the data, but that turning points cannot be predicted.

The mean absolute percentage error (MAPE) of Naive Forecast 1 forecasts can be computed as shown in Table 4-2 for the supermarket sales data. The general form of this computation is as follows:

$$\text{NF1}_{\text{MAPE}} = \frac{\displaystyle\sum_{i=2}^{n} \left| \frac{X_i - X_{i-1}}{X_i} \right|}{n-1} \, 100 \qquad (4\text{-}9)$$

Only $n - 1$ terms are included in computing the MAPE of this naive forecast, since forecasting begins with period 2 rather than period 1. The difference between the MAPE obtained from a more formal method of forecasting and that obtained using NF1 provides a measure of the improvement attainable through use of that formal forecasting method. This type of comparison is much more useful than simply computing the MAPE of the formal method or the MSE, since it provides a basis for evaluating the relative accuracy of those results.

Types of Patterns in Time-Series Data

Before introducing Naive Forecast 2, let us look at the basic elements of pattern found so often in data series. There are four such elements or components: horizontal, seasonal, cyclical, and trend.

A *horizontal* pattern exists when there is no trend in the data. (Statistically, this is referred to as stationarity.) When such a pattern exists, the series generally is referred to as stationary, that is, it does not tend to increase or decrease over time in any systematic way. Thus it is just as likely that the next value of the series will be above the mean value as it is that it will be below it. Figure 4-3 shows a typical horizontal pattern for a variable.

The kind of situation that generally exhibits a horizontal pattern would include products with stable sales, the number of defective items that occur in a stable production process, and perhaps the sales of a company over fairly short time periods. The element of time is generally an important one in considering horizontal patterns, since in the short run even patterns that may exhibit a definite trend over several years might be assumed to be horizontal patterns for purposes of short-term forecasting.

A *seasonal* pattern exists when a series fluctuates according to some seasonal factor. The seasons may be the months or the four seasons of the year, but they could also be the hours of the day, the days of the week, or the days in a month. Seasonal patterns exist for a number of different reasons, varying from the way in which a firm has chosen to handle certain operations (internally caused seasons) to external factors such as the weather.

Items that typically follow seasonal patterns include the sales of soft drinks, heating oil, and other products conditional on the weather; the receipt of revenues at a utility company, which may depend on the pattern used in sending out the bills and the pay period in that community; and the number of new cars sold, which may depend on the timing of style changes and even tradition. Figure 4-4 illustrates a pattern in which the seasons correspond to the four calendar quarters of spring, summer, fall, and winter.

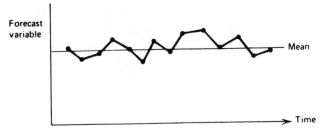

Figure 4-3 Horizontal Data Pattern.

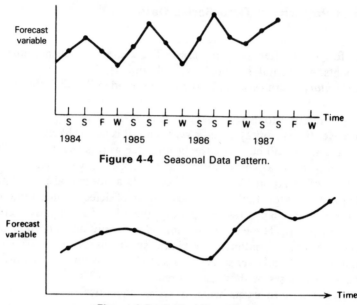

Figure 4-4 Seasonal Data Pattern.

Figure 4-5 Cyclical Data Pattern.

A *cyclical* pattern is similar to a seasonal pattern, but the length of a single cycle is generally longer than one year. Many series, such as the number of housing starts, the price of metals, the gross national product (GNP), and the sales of many companies, contain a cyclical pattern. Figure 4-5 illustrates a cyclical pattern. The cyclical pattern is a difficult one to predict, because it does not repeat itself at constant intervals of time, and its duration is not uniform.

A *trend* pattern exists when there is a general increase or decrease in the value of the variable over time. The sales of many companies, the gross national product, prices, and many other business and economic indicators follow a trend pattern like that shown in Figure 4-6 in their movements over time.

Although a number of other patterns can be found in specific series of data, the four we have discussed are the most important. They often can be found together or individually. In fact, some series actually combine a trend, a seasonal pattern, and a cyclical pattern in addition to the horizontal level, which is part of *all* series. Such combinations of patterns will be the primary focus of the chapter on decomposition methods.

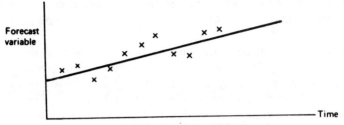

Figure 4-6 Trend Data Pattern.

A Naive Method Benchmark for Seasonal Data Series

When a data series contains a seasonal pattern, the benchmark method described as Naive Forecast 1 will not do very well, because it ignores that seasonal component. In such situations, a second naive method of forecasting has been found to be extremely useful as a basis for evaluating more formal forecasting methods. This method is referred to as *Naive Forecast 2*, or NF2. It goes beyond NF1 in that it considers the possibility of seasonality in the series. Since seasonality often accounts for a substantial percentage of the fluctuation in a series, this method can frequently be more accurate than NF1, yet it is still a very simple, straightforward approach. The procedure is to remove seasonality from the original data in order to obtain seasonally adjusted data. Once the seasonality has been removed, NF2 is comparable to NF1 in that it uses the most recent seasonally adjusted value as a forecast for the next seasonally adjusted value.

In practice, NF2 allows one to decide whether or not the improvement obtained from going beyond a seasonal adjustment of the data is worth the time and cost involved.

EFFORT AND RESOURCE REQUIREMENTS FOR FORECASTING

Several types of expenditures are required to apply quantitative forecasting methods successfully. Two of the most important are costs and the amount of effort required to use the method and its forecasts. Three different elements are involved in determining the cost of applying a specific method: development costs, the costs associated with data acquisition and storage, and the actual operation and maintenance costs.

Development costs include the resources required for defining the actual variable to be forecast and any independent variables that may be included in a causal model, gathering the initial data that can be used to identify the pattern needed for forecasting, determining the pattern in those data, and finally, establishing a procedure that can be used in making repetitive forecasts.

Storage requirement costs are generally affected by the number of observations needed to apply a forecasting technique and the number of variables involved. Generally speaking, a forecasting technique that employs an explanatory model is much more costly in terms of data storage than a technique that employs a time-series model.

Finally, operating costs depend largely on the amount of computer time required to make the computations for a single forecast and the frequency with which forecasts are made.

For one forecasting technique the major costs may be those associated with the developmental level. For another technique, the highest costs may be associated with data storage, and for a third, operating costs may be primary. Clearly, a naive forecasting technique such as that used by the supermarket manager for forecasting weekly sales requires some development costs, virtually no storage costs, and little in the way of operating and maintenance costs. On the other hand, causal models, which are often developed in the area of econometrics, may have substantial development costs and relatively modest amounts for data storage and usage costs.

In most situations the actual computation of the costs associated with a forecasting technique is not unusually difficult. What does create problems, however, is trading off these costs against the various levels of accuracy obtained. Often a deciding factor in choosing among methods is the ease with which they can be applied and maintained.

One major aspect of the applicability of a quantitative forecasting method is the time required to develop a working application of a given forecasting technique for a specific situation. If the appropriate data are not readily available, or if a computer system is not easily accessible for certain techniques, the development of the application can take several months. When this is the case, the manager is usually well advised to adopt initially a much less sophisticated technique and then follow an evolutionary approach in upgrading his or her use of forecasting.

A second aspect of applicability is the ease with which the manager can gain an understanding of the fundamental technical properties of the method and an *ability to interpret* the results. A great advantage of the simpler methods is the ease with which a manager can fully understand their assumptions and limitations and interpret their results. As much more advanced and sophisticated techniques are considered, the number of managers who can readily understand them and are willing to make the investment to do so decreases rapidly. Thus, few managers would find the most advanced techniques applicable on this criterion.

The need to consider the manager's understanding and confidence in any forecasting technique he or she applies cannot be overstressed. For forecasting to have value it must have an impact on the manager's method of making decisions, and this will happen only when the manager feels confident that the use of the forecast represents good judgment and is consistent with his or her activities as a manager.

SELECTED REFERENCES FOR FURTHER STUDY

Carbone, R., and S. Armstrong, 1982. "Evaluation of Extrapolative Forecasting Methods," *Journal of Forecasting*, 1, pp. 215–217.

Hanke, J. E., and A. G. Reitsch, 1981. *Business Forecasting*, Allyn and Bacon, Boston.

Levenbach, H., and J. P. Cleary, 1981. *The Beginning Forecaster*, Lifetime Learning Publications, Belmont, CA.

Mahmoud, E., 1987. "The Evaluation of Forecasts," in S. Makridakis and S. Wheelwright (Eds.), *The Handbook of Forecasting*, 2nd ed., Wiley, New York.

Schuster, R., 1906. "On the Periodicity of Sunspots," *Philosophical Transactions*, ser. A, 206, pp. 69–100.

CHAPTER 5

SMOOTHING METHODS

One problem business managers frequently face is that of preparing short-term forecasts for a large number of different items. A typical example would be the production manager who must schedule production on the basis of some forecast of demand for several hundred different products in a product line. In many of these situations it is not practical to develop and apply a sophisticated forecasting method for each item. What is needed is a technique that can be employed easily for each of many items and that will provide reasonably good forecasts over the short-term horizon in which they are needed.

In such situations managers frequently use a class of forecasting methods referred to as *smoothing methods*. With all methods of this type, historical data are used to obtain a "smoothed" value for the series. That smoothed value is then extrapolated to become the forecast for the future value of the series.

In this chapter two subclasses of smoothing methods will be described. The first, *averaging methods*, conforms to the conventional definition of an average—namely, equal weighting (or smoothing) of the number of values included in the average. The second, *exponential smoothing methods*, applies an unequal set of weights to past data. These weights decay in an exponential manner from the most recent data value to the most distant value.

The basic notion inherent in exponential smoothing is that there is some underlying pattern in the values of the variables to be forecast and that the historical observations of each variable represent the underlying pattern as well as random fluctuations. The goal of these forecasting methods is to distinguish between the random fluctuations and the basic underlying pattern by "smoothing" (averaging) the historical values. This amounts to eliminating the randomness found in the historical sequence and basing a forecast on the smoothed pattern of the data.

To understand better how moving averages and exponential smoothing can be used in practice, let us consider the situation faced by a manufacturer of knives and forks. For several months this company has kept a record of the demand for knives. To help schedule production, the production manager would like to use these observations to prepare a forecast of what the demand will be during the coming month.

SIMPLE MOVING AVERAGES

In Chapter 4 we saw how a manager might select a naive forecasting approach by simply taking the most recent observation and using it as a forecast for the coming period. If substantial randomness is contained in the series, a naive approach will produce forecasts that will vary considerably. To eliminate this randomness we might consider the use of some kind of average of recent observed values. The method of moving averages does this by taking a set of observed values, finding their average, and then using that average as a forecast for the coming period. The actual number of observations included in the average is specified by the manager and remains constant. The term *moving average* is used because as each new observation becomes available, a new average can be computed and used as a forecast.

For the manufacturer of knives and forks, Table 5-1 shows how the technique of moving averages can be applied with a three-month and a five-month average. In this table, column 4 is the three-month moving

Table 5-1 Forecasting the Demand for Knives One Month Ahead Using Moving Averages

(1) 1988 Month	(2) Time Period	(3) Observed Demand	(4) Forecast with a Three-Month Moving Average	(5) Forecast with a Five-Month Moving Average
January	1	2000		
February	2	1350		
March	3	1950		
April	4	1975	1767	
May	5	3100	1758	
June	6	1750	2342	2075
July	7	1550	2275	2025
August	8	1300	2133	2065
September	9	2200	1533	1935
October	10	2770	1683	1980
November	11	2350	2090	1915
December	12		2440	2034

average forecast based on the values of the three preceding months; for example, the forecast of 1767 for April 1988 is based on the average demand for periods 1, 2, and 3 (January, February, and March 1988). This three-month moving average value (the smoothed value) then becomes the forecast for the following month, period 4. The last figure in column 4 (2440) is the average for periods 9, 10, and 11 and serves as the forecast for December 1988, period 12.

Similarly, in column 5, the five-month average, the entry of 2075 for June represents the average (that is, the smoothed value) of the observed demand in periods 1 through 5 and is used as the forecast for period 6. The last entry in column 5 (2034) is the average for periods 7 through 11 and serves as the forecast for period 12.

An example of the performance of this method of forecasting is shown in Figure 5-1. On this graph are plotted the actual values of demand and the forecast values for the corresponding period based on a three-month and a five-month moving average. Two characteristics of moving averages are readily apparent in this figure. The first is that before any forecast can be prepared, the manager must have as many historical observations as are needed for the moving average. Thus it is not until the end of period 3 that a three-month moving average can be prepared to forecast period 4, and it is not until the end of period 5 that a five-month moving average can be computed as a forecast for period 6.

A second characteristic of moving averages is that the greater number of observations included in the moving average, the greater the smoothing effect on the forecast. Looking at the three-month moving average, we note that the

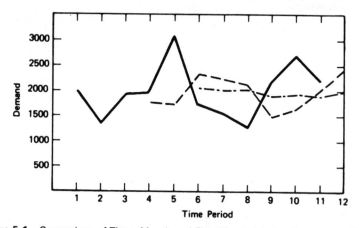

Figure 5-1 Comparison of Three-Month and Five-Month Moving Average Forecasts for Demand for Knives (from Table 5-1). ——— Actual Data; – – – Three-Month Moving Average Forecast; —·— Five-Month Moving Average Forecast.

smallest value is 1533 and the largest is 2440, a range of 907 (2440 − 1533). From the five-month moving average forecasts we can see that the smallest and largest values are 1915 and 2075, respectively. This represents a range of only 160. Thus, increasing the number of periods included in the moving average has a marked effect on the amount of smoothing done. If we desire a smoother value, either because we think the historical observations contain considerable randomness or because we think there is little change in the underlying pattern, a large number of observations should be used to compute the moving average forecast. On the other hand, if we feel that the underlying pattern in the data is changing (and we want to react to fluctuations more rapidly) or that there is little randomness in the observed values, a much smaller number of observations should be used to compute the moving average. Figure 5-1 shows the effect of increasing the number of terms in the moving average. (The larger the number, the greater the extent of smoothing, or the closer one gets to the average of all values.)

To determine whether the three-month or the five-month moving average is more appropriate for forecasting demand, it is useful to compute the error in both forecasts. Table 5-2 shows the error for each forecast and computes the mean absolute deviation and the mean squared error for comparative purposes. Both forms of error measurement indicate that the five-month moving average gives a better forecast than the three-month moving average when tested on the historical data. (Later in this chapter we use the same error measurements to compare the accuracy of moving averages with exponential smoothing for this particular example.)

For a better understanding of the technique of moving averages, it is necessary to look briefly at the mathematical representation of this method. In simple terms, the technique of forecasting with moving averages can be represented as follows:

$$F_{t+1} = S_t = \frac{X_t + X_{t-1} + \cdots + X_{t-N+1}}{N} = \frac{1}{N} \sum_{i=t-N+1}^{t} X_i \quad (5\text{-}1)$$

where

F_{t+1} = forecast for time $t + 1$
S_t = smoothed value at time t
X_i = actual value at time i
i = time period
N = number of values included in average

It can be seen from Equation (5-1) that in the method of moving averages, equal weight (or importance) is given to each of the last N values in the series,

Table 5-2 Comparison of Forecasting Errors for Moving Averages

Time Period	Observed Demand	Three-Month Moving Average				Five-Month Moving Average			
		Forecast Demand	Error	Absolute Error	Squared Error	Forecast Demand	Error	Absolute Error	Squared Error
1	2000								
2	1350								
3	1950								
4	1975	1767	+ 208	208	43,264				
5	3100	1758	+ 1342	1342	1,800,964				
6	1750	2342	− 592	592	350,464	2075	− 325	325	105,625
7	1550	2275	− 725	725	525,625	2025	− 475	475	225,625
8	1300	2133	− 833	833	693,889	2065	− 765	765	585,225
9	2200	1533	+ 667	667	448,889	1935	+ 265	265	70,225
10	2770	1683	+ 1087	1087	1,181,569	1980	− 790	790	624,100
11	2350	2090	+ 260	260	67,600	1915	+ 435	435	189,225
12		2440				2034			
Sum			+ 1414	5714	5,108,264[b]		− 1655	3055	1,800,025
Mean			+ 177	714[a]	638,533[b]		− 276	509[a]	300,004[b]

[a] Mean absolute deviation.
[b] Mean squared error.

but no weight is given to values observed before that time. It can also be seen that to compute the moving average, we must have the values of the last N observations. A somewhat shorter form of Equation (5-1) for calculating the moving average can be developed. The moving average forecast for period t is given by

$$F_t = \frac{X_{t-1} + X_{t-2} + \ldots + X_{t-N}}{N} \tag{5-2}$$

This means that once we have the forecast for the period t (that is, F), we can obtain the forecast for period $t + 1$ by adding X_t/N and subtracting X_{t-N}/N.

The value of F_{t+1} of Equation (5-1) can be alternatively found as

$$F_{t+1} = \frac{X_t}{N} - \frac{X_{t-N}}{N} + F_t \tag{5-3}$$

Written in this form, each new forecast based on a moving average is an adjustment of the preceding moving average forecast. It is also easy to see why the smoothing effect increases as N becomes larger: a much smaller adjustment is being made between each forecast.

SINGLE EXPONENTIAL SMOOTHING

At least two major limitations to the use of moving averages have prompted most forecasters to apply the method of exponential smoothing in its place. First, to compute a moving average forecast it is necessary to store at least N observed values, which takes up considerable space if a large number of items need to be forecast. Second, the method of moving averages gives equal weight to each of the last N observations and no weight at all to observations before period $(t - N)$.

A strong argument can be made that since the most recent observations contain the most current information about what will happen in the future, they should be given relatively more weight than the older observations. What we would like is a weighting scheme that would apply the most weight to the most recent observed values and decreasing weights to the older values. Exponential smoothing satisfies this requirement and eliminates the need for storing the historical values of the variable.

In principle, exponential smoothing operates in a manner analogous to that of moving averages by "smoothing" historical observations to eliminate randomness. The mathematical procedure for performing this smoothing, however, is somewhat different from that used in moving averages. The technique of exponential smoothing can be developed using Equation (5-3) to compute the moving average. Suppose we had available only the most recent observed value and the forecast made for the same period. In such a situation, Equation (5-3) might be modified so that in place of the observed value in period $(t - N)$ we could employ an approximate value. A reasonable estimate would be the forecast value from the preceding period. Thus Equation (5-3) could be modified to give

$$F_{t+1} = \frac{X_t}{N} - \frac{F_t}{N} + F_t \tag{5-4}$$

This equation can be written as

$$F_{t+1} = \frac{1}{N}X_t + \left(1 - \frac{1}{N}\right)F_t \tag{5-5}$$

What we now have is a forecast that weights the most recent observation with a weight of value $1/N$ and the most recent forecast with a weight of value $(1 - 1/N)$. If we substitute the symbol alpha in place of $1/N$, we have

$$F_{t+1} = \alpha X_t + (1 - \alpha)F_t \tag{5-6}$$

This equation is the general form used in computing a forecast by the method of exponential smoothing. Note that it immediately eliminates one of the problems associated with moving averages in that extensive historical data no longer need to be stored. Rather, only the most recent observation, the most recent forecast, and a value for α are required to prepare a new forecast. If Equation (5-6) is expanded by substituting the value for F_t, which is equal to $F_t = \alpha X_{t-1} + (1 - \alpha)F_{t-1}$, we have

$$\begin{aligned} F_{t+1} &= \alpha X_t + (1 - \alpha)[\alpha X_{t-1} + (1 - \alpha)F_{t-1}] \\ &= \alpha X_t + \alpha(1 - \alpha)X_{t-1} + (1 - \alpha)^2 F_{t-1} \end{aligned} \tag{5-7}$$

However,

$$F_{t-1} = \alpha X_{t-2} + (1 - \alpha)F_{t-2}.$$

If this substitution process is carried out even further, we obtain the relationship

$$F_{t+1} = \alpha X_t + \alpha(1 - \alpha)X_{t-1} + \alpha(1 - \alpha)^2 X_{t-2} + (1 - \alpha)^3 F_{t-2}$$

By further substituting the values of $T_{t-2}, F_{t-3}, \ldots$, we obtain the following:

$$F_{t+1} = \alpha X_t + \alpha(1 - \alpha)X_{t-1} + \alpha(1 - \alpha)^2 X_{t-2} + \alpha(1 - \alpha)^3 X_{t-3} +$$
$$\alpha(1 - \alpha)^4 X_{t-4} + \ldots \qquad (5\text{-}8)$$

From this equation it can be seen that exponential smoothing also overcomes another limitation of moving averages in that decreasing weights are given to the older observed values; that is, since α is a number between 0 and 1 [thus $(1 - \alpha)$ is also a number between 0 and 1], the weights α, $\alpha(1 - \alpha)$, $\alpha(1 - \alpha)^2$, etc. have exponentially decreasing values. Hence the name exponential smoothing.

An alternative way of writing Equation (5-6) can provide further insight into exponential smoothing. By rearranging terms in Equation (5-6) we can obtain

$$F_{t+1} = F_t + \alpha(X_t - F_t) \quad \text{or} \quad F_{t+1} = F_t + \alpha e_t \qquad (5\text{-}9)$$

In this form, the new forecast prepared by exponential smoothing is simply the old forecast plus α times the error in the old forecast, that is, the term $(X_t - F_t)$ is simply the error in that earlier forecast. In this form it is evident that when α has a value close to 1, the new forecast will include a substantial adjustment for any error that occurred in the preceding forecast. Conversely, when α is close to 0, the new forecast will not show much adjustment for the error from the previous forecast. Thus the effect of a large or small α is analogous to the effect of including a small or large number of observations in computing a moving average.

Using the example given earlier, in which the demand for knives was forecast, we can illustrate the various aspects of exponential smoothing. Table 5-3 shows the computed values of the forecast with values for α of 0.1, 0.5, and 0.9. The last three columns in this table can be computed with Equation (5-6) or Equation (5-9). The only point that must be remembered is that for the first period no previous forecast is available. In that case the value of the first data point (i.e., the observed demand for January) can be used as the first forecast. Thus, $F_2 = X_1 = 2000$. (The appendix to this chapter provides further discussion of initializing a smoothing method.) Thus the number 1935 in the $\alpha = 0.1$ column was obtained by taking 2000 (the preceding forecast) and adding to that $0.1(1350 - 2000)$. This gives the value of 1935, which can be used as the forecast for period 3.

The effect that the value of α has on the amount of smoothing done on

Table 5-3   Forecasting the Demand for Knives One Month Ahead Using Exponential Smoothing

Month	Time Period	Observed Demand	Exponentially Smoothed Forecasts		
			$\alpha = 0.1$	$\alpha = 0.5$	$\alpha = 0.9$
January	1	2000			
February	2	1350	2000	2000	2000
March	3	1950	1935	1675	1415
April	4	1975	1937	1813	1897
May	5	3100	1940	1894	1967
June	6	1750	2056	2497	2987
July	7	1550	2026	2123	1874
August	8	1300	1978	1837	1582
September	9	2200	1910	1568	1328
October	10	2775	1939	1884	2113
November	11	2350	2023	2330	2709
December	12		2056	2340	2386

previous observed values can be seen in Table 5-3 and in Figure 5-2. A large value of α (0.9) gives little smoothing in the forecast, whereas a small value of α (0.1) gives considerable smoothing.

Figure 5-2 indicates that a small value of α tends to produce forecasts that are more smoothed (that is, have less fluctuation) than larger values of α. However, to find the value of α that produces the best forecasts for the past data, we need to compute the mean squared error or the mean absolute deviation. This is done for the three values of α in Table 5-4, from which it

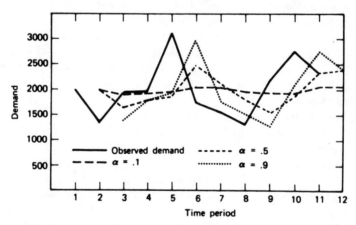

Figure 5-2   Comparison of Exponential Smoothing Forecasts. $\alpha = 0.1$, 0.5, and 0.9.

Table 5-4 Comparison of Forecasting Errors for Exponential Smoothing

Time Period	Observed Demand	Forecast with α = 0.1				Forecast with α = 0.5				Forecast with α = 0.9			
		Forecast Demand	Error	Absolute Error	Squared Error	Forecast Demand	Error	Absolute Error	Squared Error	Forecast Demand	Error	Absolute Error	Squared Error
1	2000												
2	1350	2000	−650	650	422,500	2000	−550	650	422,500	2000	−650	650	422,500
3	1950	1935	+15	15	225	1675	+275	275	75,625	1415	+535	535	286,225
4	1975	1937	+38	38	1,444	1813	+162	162	26,244	1897	+78	78	6,084
5	3100	1940	+1160	1160	1,345,600	1894	+1206	1206	1,454,436	1967	+1133	1133	1,283,689
6	1750	2056	−306	306	93,636	2497	−747	747	558,009	2987	−1237	1237	1,530,169
7	1550	2026	−476	476	226,576	2123	−573	573	328,329	1874	−324	324	104,976
8	1300	1978	−678	678	459,684	1837	−537	537	288,369	1582	−282	282	79,524
9	2200	1910	+290	290	84,100	1568	+632	632	399,424	1328	+872	872	760,384
10	2770	1939	+831	831	690,561	1884	+886	886	784,996	2113	+657	657	431,649
11	2350	2023	+327	327	106,929	2330	+20	20	400	2709	−359	359	128,881
12		2056				2340				2386			
	Sum		+551	4771	3,431,255		+674	5688	4,338,332		−423	6127	5,034,081
	Mean		+55	477[a]	343,126[b]		+67	569[a]	433,833[b]		−42	613[a]	503,408[b]

[a] Mean absolute deviation.
[b] Mean squared error.

75

can be seen that $\alpha = 0.1$ yields forecasts with smaller errors than do larger values of α. This is true for both the mean absolute deviation and the mean squared error. Since we have computed error measurements for moving averages as well as for exponential smoothing, we can now examine the relative accuracy of the two different methods.

If we compare the five-month moving average (which was found to be the better of the two moving averages computed) with the exponential smoothing forecasts with $\alpha = 0.1$ (the best of the three exponential smoothing procedures applied), we find that exponential smoothing gives only slightly better results than moving averages. However, the reduced data requirements associated with exponential smoothing and the intuitive appeal of weighting the most recent observations most heavily would lead most managers to select exponential smoothing over a moving average approach.

To use exponential smoothing, a manager need have only the most recent observed value, the most recent forecast, and a value for α. The use of single exponential smoothing is both easy and cheap, because computer programs can find the best value of α automatically. In addition, empirical evidence and experience among forecasting users have confirmed that exponential smoothing is an accurate, effective, and reliable method for a wide range of forecasting applications.

In the preceding sections we saw that simple smoothing techniques such as moving averages or exponential smoothing can be used effectively and inexpensively when the historical pattern of the data can be treated as horizontal. However, these techniques may not be effective in handling trends or seasonal patterns. Other forms of smoothing can be developed to deal with these situations.

In the next section we discuss a linear smoothing method that can be used effectively with data that exhibit a trend pattern. This method is inexpensive and can be applied easily to hundreds or even thousands of items.

LINEAR (HOLT'S) EXPONENTIAL SMOOTHING

The method of single exponential smoothing we examined in the previous section is theoretically appropriate when the data series contains a horizontal pattern (that is, it does not have a trend). If single exponential smoothing is used with a data series that contains a consistent trend, the forecasts will trail behind (lag) that trend. The method of linear exponential smoothing avoids this problem by explicitly recognizing and taking into account the presence of a trend.

Suppose we are asked to forecast the next value in the randomless series (with a constant trend of 3) 3, 6, 9, 12, 15, 18, 21, 24, 27, 30. As a first approach, we might use single exponential smoothing as outlined in the preceding section, obtaining the results shown in Table 5-5. (The best value of α is 1.0 since that minimizes the errors.) The errors for each of the initial nine forecasts have a value of 3.0.

These are the one-period-ahead forecasts. If the observed values continue to increase by 3 units per time period beyond period 10, and we forecast these periods using the most recent smoothed value, 27, the future error terms will also increase by 3 units with each time period.

Examining Table 5-5, we discover that the amount of the error in each time period, 3, is constant when there is trend in the data. Linear exponential smoothing recognizes this fact and uses it through Equation (5-10) to prepare a smoothed estimate of the trend in the data series:

$$T_t = \beta(S_t - S_{t-1}) + (1 - \beta)T_{t-1} \tag{5-10}$$

where

S_t = equivalent of single exponential smoothed value
β = smoothing coefficient, analogous to α
T_t = smoothed trend in data series

The basic principle underlying Equation (5-10) is the same as that of single exponential smoothing represented by Equation (5-6). The most recent trend, $(S_t - S_{t-1})^*$, is weighted by β and the last smoothed trend, T_{t-1}, is weighted by $(1 - \beta)$. The sum of these weighted values is the new smoothed trend value.

Linear exponential smoothing uses Equation (5-10) to obtain a smoothed value of the trend and combines this trend with the standard smoothing equation to obtain

$$S_t = \alpha X_t + (1 - \alpha)(S_{t-1} + T_{t-1}). \tag{5-11}$$

The only difference between this and the earlier form, Equation (5-6), is the additional term T_{t-1} that is added to S_{t-1} to adjust the smoothed values for the trend pattern in the data series.

As an illustration of linear exponential smoothing, Equations (5-10) and (5-11) can be applied to the data of Table 5-5. The best values of α and β are found by trying various combinations of values (between 0.0 and 1.0) and

---

* $S_t - S_{t-1}$ represents the trend in the data. This can be verified by subtracting any two successive values in column 3 of Table 5-5. The reason that $S_t - S_{t-1}$ gives the trend is that if the data have been smoothed to eliminate randomness, what remains is the pattern (trend in this case) in the data.

Table 5-5 Forecasting a Randomness Series with Trend Using Single Exponential Smoothing

Time Period	Observed Value	Forecast with $\alpha = 1.0$ Single Exponential Smoothing	Error
1	3		
2	6	3	3
3	9	6	3
4	12	9	3
5	15	12	3
6	18	15	3
7	21	18	3
8	24	21	3
9	27	24	3
10	30	30	3

choosing that set of values that minimizes the mean squared error or the mean absolute deviation. Because there is no randomness in the data of Table 5-5, the best values are found to be $\alpha = 1.0$ and $\beta = 1.0$. Using these values with Equations (5-10) and (5-11) gives for period 2

$$S_2 = \alpha X_2 + (1 - \alpha)(S_1 + T_1) = (1)X_2 + (0)(S_1 + T_1) = 6$$
$$T_2 = \beta(S_2 - S_1) + (1 - \beta)T_1 = (1)(6 - 3) + (0)(T_1) = 3$$

For period 3, the results are

$$S_3 = (1)X_3 + (0)(S_2 + T_2) = 9$$
$$T_3 = (1)(9 - 6) + (0)(3) = 3$$

Continuing these calculations for the intervening periods, the results for period 10 are

$$S_{10} = (1)X_{10} + (0)(S_9 + T_9) = 30$$
$$T_{10} = (1)(27 - 24) + (0)(27 + 3) = 3$$

It should be noted that the value of S is updated first, and then the trend T is updated. To use these smoothed series values S and the smoothed trend component T to prepare a forecast, we must add the trend component to the basic smoothed value for the number of periods ahead to be forecast. The general equation is

$$F_{t+m} = S_t + T_t m \qquad (5\text{-}12)$$

Thus, the forecast for period 11, which is one period ahead (that is, $m = 1$), using Equation (5-12) is

$$F_{11} = S_{10} + T_{10}(m) = 30 + 3(1) = 33.$$

Similarly, the forecasts for periods 12, 13, and 14 (2, 3, and 4 periods ahead, respectively) are

$$
\begin{aligned}
F_{12} &= 30 + 3(2) = 36 \\
F_{13} &= 30 + 3(3) = 39 \\
F_{14} &= 30 + 3(4) = 42
\end{aligned}
$$

This method does account for a linear trend and thus with a randomless series gives zero error when α and β have their optimal values. When the data series contains randomness, it is more difficult to determine the optimal α and β values, and the forecasting errors will not be zero, but the approach is exactly as illustrated above and simply makes repeated application of Equations (5-10), (5-11), and (5-12). For more details of how the method of linear, or Holt's, exponential smoothing can be applied, see the next section, which describes a similar method.

Just as Equation (5-9) provided a simpler, yet equivalent, way to apply simple exponential smoothing, by arithmetic substitution we can develop a set of three equations that are often easier to use than Equations (5-10) through (5-12) yet are completely equivalent. These are as follows:

$$S_t = S_{t-1} + T_{t-1} + \alpha e_t = F_t + \alpha e_t \qquad (5\text{-}13)$$

$$T_t = T_{t-1} + \alpha \beta e_t \qquad (5\text{-}14)$$

$$F_{t+m} = S_t + T_t m \qquad (5\text{-}15)$$

An example of using the equivalent of these equations instead of Equations (5-10), (5-11), and (5-12) will be used with damped trend exponential smoothing later in this chapter.

WINTERS' LINEAR AND SEASONAL EXPONENTIAL SMOOTHING

Another useful form of smoothing was developed by Winters in the early 1960s. This method produces results similar to those of linear exponential smoothing as we have discussed it, but it has the extra advantage of being capable of dealing with seasonal data in addition to data that have a trend.

Winters' linear and seasonal exponential smoothing is based on three equations, each of which smooths a factor associated with one of the three components of the pattern—randomness, trend, and seasonality. In this respect it is similar to linear exponential smoothing, which smooths for randomness and adjusts for trend. However, Winters' method includes an additional parameter to deal with seasonality. There are three basic smoothing equations involved in Winters' method. They are as follows:

$$S_t = \alpha \frac{X_t}{I_{t-L}} + (1 - \alpha)(S_{t-1} + T_{t-1}) \tag{5-16}$$

$$T_t = \beta(S_t - S_{t-1}) + (1 - \beta)T_{t-1} \tag{5-17}$$

$$I_t = \gamma \frac{X_t}{S_t} + (1 - \gamma)I_{t-L} \tag{5-18}$$

where

S = smoothed value of deseasonalized series
T = smoothed value of trend
I = smoothed value of seasonal factor
L = length of seasonality (e.g., number of months or quarters in a year)

The equation for I is comparable to a seasonal index. That index is found as the ratio of the current value of the series X_t, divided by the current smoothed value of the series S_t. If X_t is larger than S_t, the ratio will be greater than 1. If it is smaller than S_t, the ratio will be less than 1. To understand this method and the role of the seasonal index, I, it is important to realize that S_t is a smoothed (average) value of the series that includes trend but not seasonality. The data values X_t, on the other hand, do contain seasonality. Thus the ratio of X_t/S_t tells us something about the level of seasonality in the data. Remember that X_i is the actual data value which contains seasonality, while S_t is smoothed and does not. However, seasonality at each period is not perfect. It contains randomness. Thus it must be smoothed or averaged to eliminate such randomness.

To smooth this seasonality, the equation for I weights the newly computed seasonal factor (X_t/S_t) with γ and the most recent seasonal number corresponding to the same season I_{t-L} with $(1 - \gamma)$.

The equation for T_t smooths the trend since it weights the incremental trend $(S_t - S_{t-1})$ with β and the previous trend value T_{t-1} with $(1 - \beta)$. This is done in exactly the same way as in linear smoothing [see Equation (5-10)]. In Equation (5-16) for the smoothed value S_t, the first term is divided by the seasonal factor I_{t-L}. This is done to deseasonalize (eliminate seasonal fluctuations from) X_t. This adjustment can be illustrated by considering the case when T_{t-L} is greater than 1, which occurs when the value of I in period $T - L$ is greater than average in its seasonality. Dividing X_t by I_{t-L} gives a value that is smaller than the original value by a percentage just equal to the amount that the seasonality of period $t - L$ was greater than average. The opposite adjustment occurs when the seasonality factor is less than 1. The value I_{t-L} is used in these calculations because I_t cannot be calculated until S_t is known.

The forecast based on Winters' method is computed as

$$F_{t+m} = (S_t + T_t m)I_{t-L+m}. \tag{5-19}$$

The data of Tables 5-6, which are graphed in Figure 5-3, can be used to illustrate the application of Winters' method. Using parameter values of $\alpha = 0.20$, $\beta = 0.10$, and $\gamma = 0.05$, forecasts and related smoothed values are as shown in Table 5-7.

The computations involved in applying Winters' method to obtain the results in Table 5-6 can be illustrated for period 24 as follows. First, using Equation (5-19),

$$F_{24} = [S_{23} + T_{23}(1)]I_{20} = (709.56 + 17.4)0.90 = 654.03.$$

Then, using Equation (5-16),

$$S_{24} = (0.2)\frac{X_{24}}{I_{20}} + 0.8(S_{23} + T_{23})$$

$$= 0.2\frac{661}{0.90} + 0.8(709.56 + 17.40) = 728.06$$

while, using Equation (5-17),

$$T_{24} = 0.1(S_{24} - S_{23}) + 0.9T_{23}$$
$$= 0.1(728.06 - 709.56) + 0.9(17.40) = 17.51$$

Finally, using Equation (5-18),

$$I_{24} = 0.05\frac{X_{24}}{S_{24}} + 0.95I_{20}$$

$$= 0.05\frac{661}{728.06} + 0.95(0.9024) = 0.9027$$

Table 5-6   Quarterly Sales Data

Year	Quarter	Period	Sales ($000)
1982	1	1	362
	2	2	385
	3	3	432
	4	4	341
1983	1	5	382
	2	6	409
	3	7	498
	4	8	387
1984	1	9	473
	2	10	513
	3	11	582
	4	12	474
1985	1	13	544
	2	14	582
	3	15	681
	4	16	557
1986	1	17	628
	2	18	707
	3	19	773
	4	20	592
1987	1	21	627
	2	22	725
	3	23	854
	4	24	661

Forecasts for periods 25, 26, 27, and 28 can be obtained by varying the value of m and the seasonal indices:

$$F_{25} = [728.06 + 17.51(1)](1.01) = 753.0$$

$$F_{26} = [728.06 + 17.51(2)](1.07) = 816.5$$

$$F_{27} = [728.06 + 17.51(3)](1.18) = 921.1$$

$$F_{28} = [728.06 + 17.51(4)](0.90) = 718.3$$

One of the problems accompanying the use of Winters' method is determining the values for α, β, and γ that will minimize MSE or MAD. The approach for doing this is trial and error. The search for the best values is made by a grid approach where the results using different values for α, β and γ are compared to find the combination that minimizes MSE or MAD. With today's computers, finding the best values of α, β, and γ is no longer the

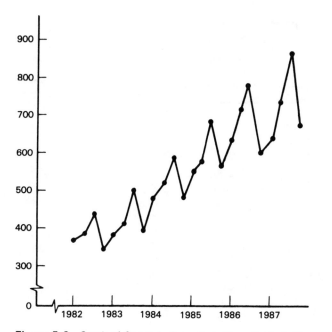

Figure 5-3 Graph of Quarterly Sales Data (from Table 5-6).

problem it used to be. It takes from a few nanoseconds to a couple of minutes, depending on the speed of the computer used and the amount of historical data available.

As was the case for Equations (5-9) and (5-15), by algebraic substitution we can develop an alternative, but completely equivalent set of equations for Winters' linear and seasonal exponential smoothing. These can be used in place of Equations (5-16) through (5-19). The four equations are as follows:

$$S_t = S_{t-1} + T_{t-1} + \alpha e_t / I_{t-l} \qquad (5\text{-}20)$$

$$T_t = T_{t-1} + \alpha \beta e_t / I_{t-l} \qquad (5\text{-}21)$$

$$I_t = I_{t-L} + \gamma (l - \alpha) e_t / S_t \qquad (5\text{-}22)$$

$$F_{t+m} = (S_t + T_t m) I_{t-L+m} \qquad (5\text{-}23)$$

USING LINEAR EXPONENTIAL SMOOTHING AFTER DESEASONALIZING A DATA SERIES

If a data series contains a seasonal pattern, there is an alternative to using Winters' smoothing method. This alternative consists of first deseasonalizing

Table 5-7 Application of Winters' Linear and Seasonal Exponential Smoothing to Seasonal Data (from Table 5-6)

Period	Actual Values X_t	Smoothed Deseasonalized Values S_t	Smoothed Seasonal Factors I_t		Smoothed Trend Values T_t	Forecast when $m = 1$
1	362.00		0.95 ⎫			
2	385.00		1.01 ⎬ Initial			
3	432.00		1.14 ⎱ values			
4	341.00		0.90 ⎭			
5	382.00	382.00	1.00		9.17	
6	409.00	394.05	1.07		14.70	424.79
7	498.00	411.62	1.18		14.99	481.10
8	387.00	427.39	0.90		15.07	383.53
9	473.00	448.17	1.01		15.64	444.32
10	513.00	467.08	1.07		15.97	495.53
11	582.00	485.20	1.18		16.18	569.34
12	474.00	506.52	0.90		16.70	450.90
13	544.00	526.64	1.01		17.04	526.75
14	582.00	543.74	1.07		17.04	581.68
15	681.00	564.08	1.18		17.37	661.55
16	557.00	588.78	0.90		18.11	523.98
17	628.00	610.11	1.01		18.43	611.79
18	707.00	634.99	1.07		19.07	672.48
19	773.00	654.15	1.18		19.08	772.49
20	592.00	669.65	0.90		18.72	608.19
21	627.00	674.96	1.01		17.38	694.66
22	725.00	689.13	1.07		17.06	742.26
23	854.00	709.56	1.18		17.40	834.08
24	661.00	728.06	0.90		17.51	654.03
25						753.03

the data series and then using linear exponential smoothing on that deseasonalized series.

For example, using the data of Table 5-6 we can find the seasonal indices for each one of the four quarters as follows:

Quarter	Seasonal Index
1	0.96
2	1.02
3	1.14
4	0.88

In the following chapter, the computation of these indices is discussed.

Using these seasonal indices, Table 5-8 shows the same data as Table 5-6, except that each sales value has been divided by the seasonal index (column 3). This gives the deseasonalized values shown in column 4. Having deseasonalized the data means that seasonality has been eliminated. Thus, a nonseasonal method can be applied to this deseasonalized data series to obtain forecasts. Working with the deseasonalized data of column 4 in Table 5-8, we use Holt's smoothing to find the forecast for period 20 as

$$F_{t+m} = S_t + T_t m$$
$$F_{20} = S_{19} + T_{19}(1) = 680.69 + 18.25 = 698.94$$

where $S_t = \alpha X'_t + (1 - \alpha)(S_{t-1} + T_{t-1})$ [see Equation (5-11)],

$$S_{19} = \alpha X_{19} + (1 - \alpha)(S_{18} + T_{18})$$
$$= 0.862(675.71) + 0.138(691.32 + 20.59) = 680.69.$$

(*Note*: The optimal value of α was previously found to be 0.862.) Similarly,

$$T_t = \beta(S_t - S_{t-1}) + (1 - \beta)T_{t-1} \text{ [see Equation (5-10)]}.$$

Thus,

$$T_{19} = \beta(S_{19} - S_{18}) + (1 - \beta)T_{18}$$
$$= 0.075(680.69 - 691.32) + 0.925(20.59) = 18.25.$$

(*Note*: The optimal value for β was found to be 0.075.)

Summing $680.69 + 18.25$ gives the forecast for period 20. This forecast of 698.94 (column 7 of Table 5-8) does not contain any seasonality. To reseasonalize this forecast (that is, add back the seasonality), we must multiply this deseasonalized forecast by the corresponding seasonal index for period 20. This index is 0.88 (column 3). The result is the seasonalized forecast for period 20:

$$F_{20} = 698.94(0.8755) = 611.90.$$

The forecast for periods 25, 26, 27, and 28 can be found in a similar way, except that m now takes on values of 1, 2, 3, and 4, respectively. The forecasts are 742.59, 806.98, 922.02, and 727.25. These are not too different from those found using Winters: exponential smoothing (Table 5-7). Those values were 753.0, 816.5, 921.1, and 718.3.

Table 5-8 Application of Holt's Linear Exponential Smoothing to the Deseasonalized Data of Table 5-6

(1) Period	(2) Actual Values X_t	(3) Seasonal Indices	(4) Deseasonalized Values X_t	(5) Smoothed Values S_t	(6) Smoothed Trend Values T_t	(7) Forecast When $m = 1$	(8) Forecast Reseasonalized
1	362.00	0.96	376.09	373.26	18.14		
2	385.00	1.02	378.19	380.00	17.29	391.40	398.45
3	432.00	1.14	377.63	380.33	16.01	397.29	454.49
4	341.00	0.88	389.51	390.45	15.57	396.35	346.99
5	382.00	0.96	396.87	398.13	14.98	406.02	390.81
6	409.00	1.02	401.76	403.32	14.25	413.11	420.55
7	498.00	1.14	435.32	432.88	15.39	417.57	477.69
8	387.00	0.88	442.05	442.91	14.99	448.27	392.45
9	473.00	0.96	491.41	486.80	17.16	457.90	440.74
10	513.00	1.02	503.92	503.93	17.16	503.96	513.04
11	582.00	1.14	508.75	510.45	16.36	521.08	596.11
12	474.00	0.88	541.43	539.42	17.30	526.80	461.20
13	544.00	0.96	565.17	564.01	17.85	556.72	535.86
14	582.00	1.02	571.70	573.10	17.19	581.86	592.35
15	681.00	1.14	595.29	594.60	17.52	590.29	675.28
16	557.00	0.88	636.23	632.92	19.08	612.12	535.89

86

17	628.00	0.96	652.44	652.38	19.11	652.00	627.57
18	707.00	1.02	694.49	691.32	20.59	671.49	683.59
19	773.00	1.14	675.71	680.69	18.25	711.92	814.42
20	592.00	0.88	676.21	679.34	16.78	698.94	611.90
21	627.00	0.96	651.40	657.55	13.89	696.12	670.04
22	725.00	1.02	712.17	706.57	16.52	671.44	683.54
23	854.00	1.14	746.52	743.29	18.04	723.09	827.20
24	661.00	0.88	755.03	755.90	17.63	761.33	666.52
25		0.96				773.53	742.59
26		1.02				$m = 2$, 791.16	806.98
27		1.14				$m = 3$, 806.79	922.02
28		0.88				$m = 4$, 826.42	727.25

DAMPED TREND EXPONENTIAL SMOOTHING

Another useful variation of exponential smoothing was introduced by Gardner and McKenzie in 1985. It differs from Holt's linear smoothing by dampening (diminishing) the linear trend being extrapolated as we move further into the future. Practically speaking, this makes a lot of sense since the majority of data series do not increase or decrease forever.

Damped trend smoothing includes the extra parameter ϕ (in addition to Holt's two parameters), which applies the optimal dampening by trying different values and choosing the one that minimizes MSE or MAD. The equations included in the damped smoothing are

$$S_t = \alpha X_t + (1 - \alpha)(S_{t-1} + T_{t-1})\phi \tag{5-24}$$

$$T_t = \beta(S_t - S_{t-1}) + (1 - \beta)T_{t-1}\phi \tag{5-25}$$

$$F_{t+m} = S_t + \sum_{i=1}^{m}\phi_i T_t \tag{5-26}$$

Alternatively, Equations (5-24), (5-25) and (5-26) can be expressed in terms of errors as follows:

$$e_t = X_t - F_t \tag{5-27}$$

$$S_t = S_{t-1} + \phi T_{t-1} + \alpha e_t \tag{5-28}$$

$$T_t = \phi T_{t-1} + \beta e_t. \tag{5-29}$$

The equation for forecasting is the same as Equation (5-26).

Table 5-9 shows the quarterly sales of a major car model produced by a U.S. manufacturer. (These data, although real, have been multiplied by a constant to ensure confidentiality.) Because the data are seasonal, we will not be able to use the method of damped smoothing unless the data are deseasonalized. To do so, we must first calculate the seasonal indices (see next chapter for details), which are the following:

Quarter	Seasonal Index
1	99.53
2	119.78
3	99.09
4	81.61

If the original car sales shown in Table 5-9 are divided by the seasonal indices, we obtain deseasonalized values (for example, the values for the first four

Table 5-9   Quarterly Sales of a Car Model

Year	Quarter	Period	Sales in Units[a]
1982	1	1	35,900.0
	2	2	26,366.7
	3	3	27,355.5
	4	4	32,022.2
1983	1	5	45,542.0
	2	6	83,199.9
	3	7	71,938.3
	4	8	82,745.6
1984	1	9	95,323.4
	2	10	125,129.7
	3	11	111,350.6
	4	12	90,339.5
1985	1	13	119,627.2
	2	14	151,519.7
	3	15	125,867.9
	4	16	101,979.1
1986	1	17	114,906.1
	2	18	123,040.7
	3	19	103,527.1
	4	20	68,679.1
1987	1	21	112,103.7
	2	22	84,926.0
	3	23	81,739.5
	4	24	71,612.1

[a] Values include a decimal because they have been multiplied by a constant to be disguised.

quarters (1982) will be 36,069.5, 22,012.6, 27,606.7, and 39,238, respectively). These values can be used to find the optimal values of α, β, and ϕ that minimize MSE. The optimal values of α, β, and ϕ then can be used to prepare the quarterly forecasts for 1988 and 1989.

By trying different values of α, β, and ϕ, we can fit alternative models to the historical data shown in Table 5-9 and find the MSE. Table 5-10, for instance, shows several values of α, β, and ϕ and the corresponding MSEs. Obviously, if we assume that the future will be similar to the past, the values of α, β, and ϕ that correspond to the smallest MSE will be chosen to forecast for 1988 and 1989. With the data of Table 5-9 these values are $\alpha = 0.277$, $\beta = 0.999$, and $\phi = 0.551$.

In addition to the optimal values of α, β, and γ we need the values of S_{24} and T_{24} to forecast for 1988 and 1989. These values are 79,303.5 and 5565.4, respectively. Thus, using Equation (5-26),

Table 5-10   Different Values of α, β, and ϕ and Corresponding MSE

α	β	ϕ	MSE
0.277	0.999	0.551	14,140.9 (smallest)
0.2	0.3	0.5	14,531.2
0.1	0.2	0.3	26,164.9
0.4	0.5	0.6	14,615.7
0.6	0.7	0.8	26,053.5
0.4	0.3	0.2	17,584.4
0.4	0.5	0.1	17,826.2

$$F_{24+1} = S_{24} + \phi T_{24}$$

$$F_{24+2} = S_{24} + \phi T_{24}\phi^2 T_{24} = F_{24+1} + \phi^2 T_{24}$$

$$F_{24+3} = S_{24} + \phi T_{24}\phi^2 T_{24} + \phi^3 T_{24} = F_{24+2} + \phi^3 T_{24}$$

$$F_{24+4} = F_{24+3} + \phi^4 T_{24}$$

$$F_{24+5} = F_{24+4} + \phi^5 T_{24}$$

$$F_{24+6} = F_{24+5} + \phi^6 T_{24}$$

$$F_{24+7} = F_{24+6} + \phi^7 T_{24}$$

$$F_{24+8} = F_{24+7} + \phi^8 T_{24}$$

Since $S_{24} = 79{,}303.5$ and $T_{24} = 5565.4$, the forecasts become

$$F_{25} = 79{,}303.5 + 0.551(5565.4) = 79{,}303.5 + 3{,}066.5 = 82{,}370.1$$

$$F_{26} = 82{,}370.1 + 0.551^2(5565.4) = 82{,}370.1 + 1{,}689.7 = 84{,}059.8$$

$$F_{27} = 84{,}059.8 + 0.551^3(5565.4) = 84{,}059.8 + 931.0 = 84{,}990.8$$

$$F_{28} = 84{,}990.8 + 0.551^4(5565.4) = 84{,}990.8 + 513.0 = 85{,}503.8$$

$$F_{29} = 85{,}503.8 + 0.551^5(5565.4) = 85{,}503.8 + 282.7 + 85{,}786.5$$

$$F_{30} = 85{,}786.5 + 0.551^6(5565.4) = 85{,}768.5 + 155.7 + 85{,}942.2$$

$$F_{31} = 85{,}942.2 + 0.551^7(5565.4) = 85{,}942.2 + 85.8 + 86{,}028.0$$

$$F_{32} = 86{,}028.0 + 0.551^8(5565.4) = 86{,}028.0 + 47.3 + 86{,}075.3$$

These forecasts must be reseasonalized by multiplying them by the corresponding seasonal indices. The final forecasts thus are given in Table 5-11.

Table 5-11   Final Forecasts for 1988 and 1989

Year	Quarter	Forecast Without Seasonalizing	Seasonal Index	Final Forecast
1988	1	82,370.1	0.9953	81,983
	2	84,059.8	1.1978	100,686.8
	3	84,990.8	0.9909	84,217.4
	4	85,503.8	0.8161	69,779.7
1989	1	85,786.5	0.9953	85,383.3
	2	85,942.2	1.1978	102,941.6
	3	86,028.0	0.9909	85,245.2
	4	86,075.3	0.8161	70,246.0

OTHER FORMS OF SMOOTHING

Although there are several other forms of smoothing, we have found that those presented so far are adequate for almost all situations found in business or governmental applications. Single exponential smoothing is usually appropriate for monthly data or when the trend in the data is weak or nonexistent. Holt's smoothing can be used successfully when there is a consistent and persistent trend in the data, as often happens with yearly data. Damped smoothing can be used when there is a trend in the data that does not persist over longer forecasting horizons. Winter's smoothing can be used when there is seasonality in the data in addition to a consistent trend. However, we have found that it is preferable to deseasonalize the data first, then to use single, Holt's, or damped smoothing, and finally to reseasonalize the forecasts. In the great majority of situations this procedure produces more accurate forecasts when there is seasonality in the data than when Winters' smoothing is used directly.

SELECTED REFERENCES FOR FURTHER STUDY

Brown, R. G., 1982. *Advanced Service Parts Inventory Control,* 2nd ed., Brown Materials Management Systems, Norwich, VT.

——, 1963. *Smoothing, Forecasting and Prediction,* McGraw-Hill, Englewood Cliffs, NJ.

Gardner, E. S., Jr., 1985. "Exponential Smoothing: The State of the Art" (with commentary), *Journal of Forecasting,* 4, pp. 1–38.

Gardner, E. S., Jr., and E. McKenzie, 1985. "Forecasting Trends in Time Series," *Management Science,* 31, pp. 1237–1246.

Gardner, E. S., Jr., and D. G. Dannenbring, 1980, "Forecasting with Exponential Smoothing: Some Guidelines for Model Selection," *Decision Science*, 11, pp. 370–383.

Makridakis, S., S. C. Wheelwright, and V. E. McGee, 1989. *Forecasting: Methods and Applications*, 3rd ed., Wiley, New York.

Makridakis, S., and S. C. Wheelwright (Eds.), 1987. *The Handbook of Forecasting: A Manager's Guide*, 2nd ed., Wiley, New York.

Montgomery, D. C., and L. A. Johnson, 1976. *Forecasting and Time-Series Analysis*, McGraw-Hill, New York.

Winters, P. R., 1960. "Forecasting Sales by Exponentially Weighted Moving Averages," *Management Science*, April, pp. 324–342.

APPENDIX: INITIAL VALUES FOR EXPONENTIAL SMOOTHING APPROACHES

The Need for Initialization

The reason why initial values for the exponential smoothing methods are needed can be seen by examining the equation of single exponential smoothing.

$$F_{t+1} = \alpha X_t + (1 - \alpha)F_t \qquad (5\text{-}30)$$

where

$$
\begin{aligned}
X_t &= \text{most recent actual value} \\
F_t &= \text{latest forecast} \\
F_{t+1} &= \text{forecast for next period} \\
\alpha &= \text{smoothing constant}
\end{aligned}
$$

When $t = 1$, Equation (5-30) becomes

$$F_2 = \alpha X_1 + (1 - \alpha)F_1 \qquad (5\text{-}31)$$

To obtain a value of F_2, F_1 must be known. The value of F_1 should have been

$$F_1 = \alpha X_0 = (1 - \alpha)F_0 \qquad (5\text{-}32)$$

Since X_0 does not exist, F_0 cannot be found, which creates the problem of an initial value for F, namely, F_1. This value is necessary because F_1 is needed to compute F_2 in Equation (5-31). However, under the present formulation F_1 cannot be found. Therefore some alternative approach is needed to estimate the initial value of F_1 in Equation (5-31). In an analogous way, initial values are needed for any type of exponential smoothing. The number and the type of values depend on the particular exponential smoothing approach being used.

If the data are seasonal, beginning values for the seasonal factors can be computed using one of the decomposition methods (see Chapter 6). If there are insufficient data to apply decomposition, the beginning seasonal factor values must be based on subjective estimates or the seasonal indices of similar products or situations. The average smoothed level S and trend T components can be estimated using one of the following approaches:

1. *Least Squares Estimates.* Initial values can be calculated using ordinary least squares (as described in Chapter 8). For instance, in single exponential smoothing S_1 can be found by averaging, say, 10 past values. In linear exponential smoothing S and T can be found by solving the equation for a straight line to obtain the intercept and the slope, and using these as starting parameter values. The same will hold true in damped smoothing. This is the most commonly used approach to initialization.

2. *Backforecasting.* This method is used by the Box–Jenkins methodology (see Chapter 7), but it also can be applied to exponential smoothing methods. It involves inverting the data series and starting the estimation procedure from the latest (most recent) value and finishing with the first (oldest) value. This will provide forecasts or parameter estimates for the beginning of the data, and these can be used as initial values when the data are forecast in the usual sequence, that is, from the oldest to the most recent.

3. *When Only Limited Data Exist.* Sometimes very few data exist on which to estimate starting values. Alternatively, the users might not think it important to start with precise initial values. In such cases models that do not require starting values may be attractive. For example, simple smoothing can be applied using

$$F_1 = X_1,$$

while in Holt's or damped smoothing the following initialization might suffice:

$$S_1 = X_1$$
$$T_1 = X_2 - X_1$$
$$e_1 = 0$$

Finally, in Winters' smoothing the corresponding values could be

$$S_1 = X'_1$$
$$T_1 = X'_2 - X'_1$$

where X'_1 and X'_2 are deseasonalized values of X_1 and X_2.

CHAPTER 6

DECOMPOSITION METHODS FOR TIME-SERIES FORECASTING

The forecasting methods outlined in the previous chapter are based on the concept that when an underlying pattern exists in a data series, that pattern can be distinguished from randomness by smoothing (averaging) the data values. The effect of this smoothing is to eliminate randomness, so the pattern can be projected into the future and used to forecast. Smoothing methods make no attempt to identify individual components of the basic underlying pattern. However, the overall pattern can be broken down, or decomposed, into subpatterns that identify each component of the time series separately. Such a decomposition can frequently facilitate forecasting and help the forecaster understand the behaviour of the series.

Decomposition methods identify three separate components of the basic underlying pattern that characterize economic and business series. These are the trend, cycle, and seasonal factors. The trend factor, which represents the long-run behavior of the data, can be increasing, decreasing, or unchanged. Often the trend can be approximated by a straight line, but an exponential, S-curve, or other long-term pattern may exist in certain situations. The cyclical factor represents the ups and downs caused by economic or industry-specific conditions. It is common to such series as the gross national product (GNP), the index of industrial production, the demand for housing, stock prices, interest rates, and most economic and business series. The cycle often follows the pattern of a wave, passing from a large to a small value and back again to a large value. The seasonal factor relates to periodic fluctuations of constant length and proportional depth that are caused by such things as temperature, rainfall, month of the year, timing of holidays, and corporate policies. The distinction between seasonality and cyclicality is that seasonality repeats itself at fixed intervals such as a year, a month, or a week, while cyclical factors have a longer duration that varies from cycle to cycle.

Decomposition assumes that the data consist of

$$\text{data} = \text{pattern} + \text{error}$$

and that the pattern is made up of trend, cycle, and seasonality,

$$\text{pattern} = \text{trend, cycle, and seasonality.}$$

In addition to the components of the pattern, an element of error or random-ness is also assumed to be present. This error is the difference between the combined effect of the three subpatterns of the series and the actual data.

Decomposition methods are among the oldest forecasting approaches. They were used in the beginning of this century by economists attempting to identify and control the business cycle. The basis of current decomposition methods was established in the 1920s when the concept of ratio to moving averages was introduced. Since that time, decomposition approaches have been used widely by both economists and managers.

There are several approaches to decomposing a time series, all of which aim to isolate each component of the series as accurately as possible. The basic concept in such separation is empirical and consists of removing first seasonality, then trend, and finally cycle. Any residual is assumed to be randomness, which although it cannot be predicted, can be identified. A number of theoretical weaknesses in the decomposition approach are trou-blesome from a pure statistical point of view, but practioners have largely ignored these weaknesses and have used the approach with considerable success.

The general mathematical representation of the decomposition approach is

$$X_t = f(S_t, T_t, C_t, R_t) \tag{6-1}$$

where

X_t = time-series value (actual data) at period t
S_t = seasonal component (or index) at period t
T_t = trend component at period t
C_t = cyclical component at period t
R_t = random component (or error) at period t

The specific functional relationship used to relate these four subpatterns can take a variety of forms. The most straightforward are additive (simply summing the four elements) and multiplicative (taking the product of the four elements). The multiplicative form is the one most commonly used; it will be the focus of this chapter. Practically all series in the economic and business domains consist of seasonality and cycle, which are proportional to the trend, and hence the multiplicative model is appropriate. The specific mathematical representation is

$$X_t = S_t \times T_t \times C_t \times R_t. \tag{6-2}$$

The remainder of this chapter is divided into three main parts. The first describes the major steps involved in separating the various subpatterns for a specific data series and preparing a forecast based on estimates for each of those subpatterns. While a set of sample data is used throughout this explanation of the individual steps, the second part of the chapter provides an in-depth example of decomposition and concludes with a summary of the procedure generally followed in such applications. The final part of the chapter considers some additional aspects of decomposition. An elaboration of the general procedure is described, and the use of percentage changes (differences) is explained.

MAJOR STEPS IN DECOMPOSITION

The basis of the decomposition method is intuitive and can be easily understood. Most important, however, it provides extremely useful, unique information for forecasting and monitoring purposes. To illustrate the method, we will use 12 years (1977 to 1988) of quarterly sales data of a French paper product (see Table 6-1). The graph of these data (Figure 6-1) exhibits some trend, considerable seasonality, and possibly other types of fluctuations. Decomposition can be used to identify these subpatterns in order to understand past fluctuations in sales and then to forecast future values.

Using decomposition, the data are expressed as $X = T \times C \times S \times R$, where X represents the actual observed values of Table 6-1, or the solid line of Figure 6-1. The purpose of decomposition is to identify T, C, and S (whatever remains will be R) by analyzing the original data X.

Trend and Seasonality

Suppose the first four quarters (that is, the four quarters of 1977) are summed and their average is computed. This gives

$$X_1 + X_2 + X_3 + X_4 = 3017.6 + 3043.54 + 2094.35 + 2809.84$$

$$= \frac{10{,}965.33}{4} = 2741.33.$$

The value of 2741.33 is the average of one whole year and, by definition, has

Table 6-1 Quantity Data for a French Paper Product and Moving Averages, 1977–1988

(1) Quarter (Season)	(2) Observation X	(3) Moving Average $T \times C$	(4) Ratio $S \times R \times 100$
1	3017.60		
2	3043.54		
3	2094.35	2741.334	76.399
4	2809.84	2805.632	100.150
5	3274.80	2835.569	115.490
6	3163.28	2840.558	111.361
7	2114.31	2894.240	73.052
8	3024.57	2907.411	104.030
9	3327.48	2989.961	111.288
10	3493.48	3071.367	113.744
11	2439.93	3187.921	76.537
12	3490.79	3277.322	106.514
13	3685.08	3319.258	111.021
14	3661.23	3303.883	110.816
15	2378.43	3296.073	72.159
16	3459.55	3337.209	103.666
17	3849.63	3347.198	115.010
18	3701.18	3413.185	108.438
19	2642.38	3444.678	76.709
20	3585.52	3501.936	102.387
21	4078.66	3553.405	114.782
22	3907.06	3597.425	108.607
23	2828.46	3723.421	75.695
24	4089.50	3788.657	107.941
25	4339.61	3849.043	112.745
26	4148.60	3873.540	107.101
27	2916.45	3872.325	75.315
28	4084.64	3848.029	106.149
29	4242.42	3810.274	111.342
30	3997.58	3801.414	105.160
31	2881.01	3789.311	76.030
32	4036.23	3818.788	105.694
33	4360.33	3909.526	111.531
34	4360.53	3982.320	109.497
35	3172.18	4029.203	78.730
36	4223.76	4111.740	102.724
37	4690.48	4195.228	111.805
38	4694.48	4237.770	110.777
39	3342.35	4326.237	77.258
40	4577.63	4394.982	104.156
41	4965.46	4477.872	110.889

Table 6-1   (*Continued*)

(1) Quarter (Season)	(2) Observation X	(3) Moving Average $T \times C$	(4) Ratio $S \times R \times 100$
42	5026.05	4509.818	111.447
43	3470.14	4496.895	77.167
44	4525.94	4570.210	99.031
45	5258.71	4611.094	114.045
46	5189.58	4642.750	111.778
47	3596.76	4481.667	80.255
48	3881.60		

no seasonality. (Seasonality refers to quarterly subperiods of a year in this situation.) Furthermore, the value of 2741.33 has little or no error or randomness, since randomness fluctuates around 0. Thus by adding values together, the randomness largely cancels itself, since both positive and negative fluctuations are combined.

Adding, therefore, as many values of X as the length of seasonality (four quarters in the year, or 12 months when seasonality is monthly) provides a set of values that include no seasonality and a minimum amount of randomness. That is, they include only trend and cycle ($T \times C$).

If the second through fifth quarters are summed and their mean is found, the result is

$$X_2 + X_3 + X_4 + X_5 = 3043.54 + 2094.35 + 2809.84 + 3274.80$$
$$= \frac{11,222.53}{4} = 2805.63.$$

As before, since 2805.63 is the mean of four quarters, it does not include seasonality and has little or no randomness. It consists of trend and cycle. The same process can be continued, dropping X_2 and including X_6 (the mean is 2835.57), dropping X_3 and including X_7, and so forth. Doing so for all the data gives a series of moving averages (called *moving* because one value is dropped and another is included) from the beginning to the end of the data of Table 6-1. The dotted line of Figure 6-1 shows a plot of these moving averages. It should be noted that these moving average values are placed opposite the third value used in their computation. (Thus, the moving average value placed next to quarter 3 is computed using quarters 1, 2, 3, and 4).

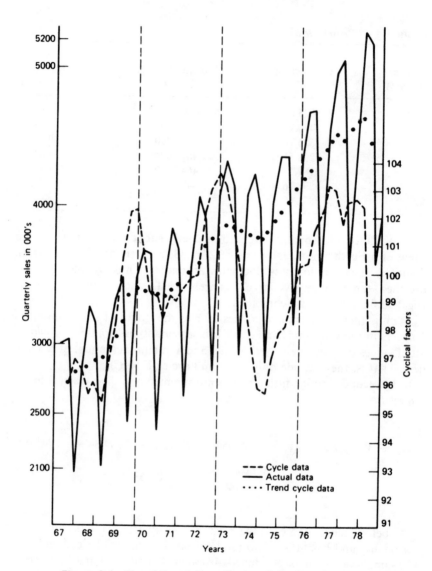

Figure 6-1 Plot of French Paper Product Sales (from Table 6-1).

These moving average values are relatively smooth (since they include no seasonality and little error or randomness) and give a much more precise picture of how the shipments of the paper product behave with regard to trend and cycle. Thus, it can be specified that

$$MA = T \times C \tag{6-3}$$

where MA is a moving average from the beginning to the end of the data. The value of such a moving average covers one complete set of seasons.

Seasonality and Randomness

Column 3 of Table 6-1 represents $T \times C$, and column 2, the original data, represents $T \times C \times S \times R$. If the values of column 2 are divided by those of column 3, the results are the ratios shown in column 4, as given by Equation (6-4):

$$\frac{X}{MA} = \frac{T \times C \times S \times R}{T \times C} = S \times R. \qquad (6\text{-}4)$$

As a set of data values, these ratios contain only seasonality and error or randomness. (By convention, these values have been multiplied by 100.) These ratios contain information needed in identifying the seasonality. If the value of a single ratio is above 100, it implies that the actual value X is larger than the moving average $T \times C$. But since X includes seasonality and randomness, and $T \times C$ does not, seasonality and randomness are higher for this quarter than on average. If the ratio is below 100, the opposite is true: seasonality and randomness are less than average.

Randomness. Equation (6-4) provides important information about the data. However, since error or randomness is something that cannot be controlled or explained, it would be helpful to eliminate randomness from Equation (6-4) in order to isolate the seasonality. This can be done by recalling that randomness refers to chance fluctuations, the absence of a pattern, or totally unexplainable variations. As such, random values, by definition, fluctuate around 0, and they have an average or mean of 0. Therefore, if several random value are summed, the result will be a value of 0, or close to 0.

Seasonality. In Table 6-2 the ratios taken from column 4 of Table 6-1 are arranged according to quarters (seasons) and years. Thus the second column gives the values of all first quarters, the third the values of all second quarters, and so on. This table also gives the average of all first, second, third and fourth quarters (112.72, 109.88, 76.28, and 103.86). Averaging all values of the same quarter for the years of 1977 to 1988 eliminates randomness, since randomness, by definition, fluctuates around zero. Thus the values of 112.72, 109.88, 76.28, and 103.86 represent seasonality only. In algebraic terms this is equivalent to

Table 6-2 French Paper Product, Seasonality. Uncentered Moving Averages

| Year | Ratios of Actual to Moving Averages by Quarter | | | |
	First	Second	Third	Fourth
1977			76.40	100.15
1978	115.49	111.36	73.05	104.03
1979	111.29	113.74	76.54	106.51
1980	111.02	110.82	72.16	103.67
1981	115.01	108.44	76.71	102.39
1982	114.78	108.61	75.70	107.94
1983	112.75	107.10	75.32	106.15
1984	111.34	105.16	76.03	105.69
1985	111.53	109.50	78.73	102.72
1986	111.81	110.78	77.26	104.16
1987	110.89	111.45	77.17	99.03
1988	114.84	111.78	80.26	

Mean or average of quarters

S	112.72	+	109.88	+	76.28	+	103.86	= 402.74
S (adjusted)	111.95	+	109.13	+	75.76	+	103.16	= 400

$$\frac{400}{402.74} = 0.9932$$

$$\overline{S \times R} = S \qquad\qquad (6\text{-}5)$$

where the overbar denotes averaging.

One could stop at this point, having captured the essence of the decomposition method. The trend-cycle values given by Equation (6-3) and the average seasonality shown in Equation (6-5) are basically all that are needed. Some refinements, however, are still possible, which could improve the benefits of decomposition. These improvements will be described below.

Adjusting the Seasonal Indices to Average 100. Adding the four seasonal factors of the averages of Table 6-2 does not give a value of 400. A simple adjustment is needed to make them have an average value of 100. If 400 is divided by the sum 402.74 (see Table 6-2), the result is 0.9932. Multiplying each of the unadjusted seasonal factors by 0.9932 gives values of 111.95, 109.13, 75.76, and 103.16. The sum of these four seasonal indices is now exactly equal to 400. This makes their meaning and interpretation clearer. For instance, the seasonal factor of 111.95 means that the first quarter

(January, February, and March) is 11.95% higher than the average for the year, and 75.76 means that the third quarter (July, August and September) is 24.24% below the average for the year.

Centered Moving Averages. In order to obtain $T \times C$ in Table 6-1, four data values were averaged. The first three columns of Table 6-2 are repeated in Table 6-3. When any four quarters are averaged, the result is a single value, their mean. Consequently, three values are lost. Thus, columns 3 of Tables 6-1 and 6-3 have three fewer values than the original data in the second column.

A problem that arises when four quarters are averaged is determining where to place their mean—opposite the second or third quarter in the average? As the average of four quarters, these values refer to the middle of the data, or halfway between the second and third quarters. The same is true for quarters 2 through 6, and so on. The average should be placed next to quarter 2.5, 3.5, and so on. The problem, however, is that, practically, this cannot be done, since the data are for quarters 1, 2, 3, 4, and the like, and not for half-quarters. This requires that the averages be placed half a period later (opposite periods 3, 4, etc.) in column 3. However, if two consecutive moving averages are themselves averaged (see column 4 in Table 6-3), this problem can be corrected. For instance, the average of the first four quarters

Table 6-3   French Paper Product, Centered Moving Average

(1)	(2)	(3)	(4)	(5)
		Uncentered Moving Average	Centered Moving Average	
	Observation			Ratio
Quarter	X	$T \times C$	$T \times C$	$S \times R \times 100$
1	3017.60			
2	3043.54	2741.334	2773.483	75.51
3	2094.35	2805.632	2820.600	99.62
4	2809.84	2835.569	2838.064	115.39
5	3274.80	2840.558	.	.
.	.	.	.	.
.	.	.	.	.
.	.	.	.	.
44	4525.94	4570.210	4590.652	98.59
45	5258.71	4611.094	4626.922	113.65
46	5189.58	4642.750	4562.210	113.75
47	3596.76	4481.667		
48	3881.60			

is 2741.334 and refers to quarter $2\frac{1}{2}$. The average of quarters 2 to 5 is 2805.632 and refers to quarter $3\frac{1}{2}$. The average of these two averages is 2773.483 and refers precisely to quarter 3 $[(2\frac{1}{2} + 3\frac{1}{2})/2 = 3]$. This average (2741.334 + 2805.632 divided by 2) is called the centered moving average since it is centered to period 3 exactly. It should be noted that the average of two numbers is one value which results in a series with one less observation. Thus, four values are missing in the forth column of Table 6-3—two at the beginning of the series and two at the end. Centered moving averages become necessary when the length of seasonality is even (as with quarterly data of four seasons, or monthly data of 12 months). However, when seasonality is odd (as with weekly data of seven days a week), no centered moving average is needed.

The ratios of the actual values divided by the centered moving average can now be used to compute the seasonal factors in a manner completely analogous to that illustrated previously. Table 6-4 shows these ratios and their related seasonal indices. The sum of these indices is 112.2 + 109.44 +

Table 6-4   French Paper Product, Adjusted Seasonal Factors, Centered Moving Averages

Year	Ratios of Actual to Centered Moving Averages by Quarter			
	First	Second	Third	Fourth
1977			75.51	99.62
1978	115.39	110.32	72.89	102.57
1979	109.79	111.63	75.48	105.84
1980	111.28	110.95	71.71	103.51
1981	113.89	107.94	76.88	101.64
1982	114.08	106.74	75.04	107.09
1983	112.39	107.12	75.55	106.67
1984	111.47	105.33	75.74	104.45
1985	110.50	108.86	77.93	101.69
1986	111.24	109.63	76.65	103.18
1987	110.49	111.61	76.54	98.59
1988	113.69	113.75		

Mean or average of quarters

S 112.20 + 109.44 + 75.37 + 103.17 = 400.18

S (adjusted)   112.15 + 109.39 + 75.34 + 103.12 = 400

$$\frac{400}{400.18} = 0.99955$$

75.37 + 103.17 = 400.18, very close to 400. This sum is closer to 400 (see Table 6-2) because the moving averages have been centered. It will be noted that the adjusted seasonal averages of Table 6-4 provide values very close to the seasonal indices of Table 6-4.

Medial Averages. Frequently, unusual events—a strike, bad weather, a war, a promotional campaign, a lawsuit—may have had a major impact on the historical data of the item being forecast. Including the influence of such unusual past events may materially affect the calculations of seasonality. To minimize this influence, a medial average can be calculated. A medial average is found by dropping the smallest and the largest of the ratios for each season (quarter). For instance, the smallest and the largest values for each quarter in Table 6-2 are given in Table 6-5.

If 110.89 and 115.49 are subtracted from the sum of all first quarters (that is, 1239.92), and the result is divided by nine (the number of years for which ratios remain), then the seasonal average is 112.619. Similarly, the medial averages for the other three quarters are 109.98, 76.289, and 103.941. The sum of these medial averages, 402.83, can be used to adjust the seasonal indices so they will sum to 400. This is shown in Table 6-6.

It would, of course, be possible, and more correct, to calculate the medial averages using the ratios found in Table 6-4 (that is, using the centered

Table 6-5   French Paper Product, Smallest and Largest Ratios without Using a Centered Moving Average

	Quarter			
	First	Second	Third	Fourth
Smallest ratio	110.89	105.16	72.16	99.03
Year	1987	1984	1980	1987
Largest ratio	115.49	113.74	80.26	107.94
Year	1978	1979	1988	1982

Table 6-6   Seasonal Index for Years 1977 through 1988

Quarter	Medial Average	Seasonal Index
1	112.619	111.828
2	109.980	109.208
3	76.289	75.753
4	103.941	103.211
Total	402.830	400.000

moving averages). The smallest and largest values for each quarter, the averages of the remaining quarters (that is, the medial average), and the seasonal indices are shown in Table 6-7.

Comparing the seasonal indices found in Table 6-7 with those computed in Tables 6-2, 6-4, or 6-6, we can see that the differences are small. This means that the basic procedure of ratio to moving averages suffices to separate the various components of a time series. The various refinements play a lesser role, although in some cases they may improve the estimation of seasonality, especially when there are large random fluctuations in the data.

Table 6-7 French Paper Product, Seasonal Factors, Smallest and Largest Values, Medial Averages, and Seasonal Indices using Centered Moving Averages

	Quarter			
	First	Second	Third	Fourth
1977			076.	100.
1978	115.	110.	073.	103.
1979	110.	112.	075.	106.
1980	111.	111.	072.	104.
1981	114.	108.	076.	102.
1982	114.	107.	075.	107.
1983	112.	107.	076.	107.
1984	111.	105.	076.	104.
1985	111.	109.	078.	102.
1986	111.	110.	077.	103.
1987	110.	112.	077.	099.
1988	114.	114.	000.	000.
Smallest value	110.	105.	072.	099.
Year	1979	1984	1980	1987
Largest value	115.	114.	078.	107.
Year	1978	1988	1985	1982

Quarter	Medial Average		Seasonal Index
1	112.11		112.03
2	109.42		109.35
3	75.50		75.45
4	103.24		103.17
Total	*400.27*		*400.00*

Separating the Cycle from the Trend

Equation (6-3) expresses the trend-cycle value of a data series. Although this is sufficient in the majority of cases, it is sometimes desirable to separate the trend from the cycle. This can be done by specifying a specific type of trend that best describes the data. For example, the trend might be linear or of some other form. For the data in Table 6-1, a linear function (straight line) appears to describe the trend adequately. The parameters a and b of this linear trend line can be estimated using simple regression (see Chapter 8) applied to the data of Table 6-1. (In this regression, the observed value is the dependent variable Y and the quarter is the independent variable X.) The values for a and b, the coefficients in the equation for the line, can be computed as

$$a = 2735.85$$
$$b = 38.96.$$

The equation for the line is

$$T_t = a + bt = 2735.85 + 38.96t \tag{6-6}$$

where a is a constant term and b is the trend (the amount by which sales increase each quarter).

For quarter 10 (that is, the second quarter of 1979) the linear trend value is

$$T_{10} = 2735.85 + 38.96(10) = 3125.45.$$

For quarters 20, 30 and 40 the corresponding trend values are

$$T_{20} = 2735.85 + 38.96(20) = 3515.05$$
$$T_{30} = 2735.85 + 38.96(30) = 3904.65$$
$$T_{40} = 2735.85 + 38.96(40) = 4294.25$$

If the trend T is divided into Equation (6-3), the result is a set of values for the cycle C:

$$\frac{MA}{T} = \frac{T \times C}{T} = C. \tag{6-7}$$

Thus, the cycle of periods 10, 20, 30, and 40 can be found by dividing the moving averages from Table 6-1 (or 6-3) by the corresponding trend values and multiplying by 100 to make them fluctuate around 100:

$$C_{10} = 3071.367/3125.45 = 98.2$$
$$C_{20} = 3501.936/3515.05 = 99.63$$
$$C_{30} = 3801.414/3904.65 = 97.36$$
$$C_{40} = 4394.982/4294.25 = 102.35.$$

The dashed line in Figure 6-1 represents the values of the cyclical indices for the French paper product data. As with the seasonal indices, the cyclical factors fluctuate around 100. If the cyclical value is below 100, it indicates that the level of economic activity for that quarter is below the average for all the years. A value above 100 indicates the opposite.

In summary, the decomposition method provides a means of isolating the various components of a time series. Equation (6-3) isolates the trend and the cycle, Equation (6-6) the trend, Equation (6-7) the cycle, Equation (6-4) the seasonality and randomness, and Equation (6-5) the seasonality. All of this is done with simple algebra. Decomposition methods are not only simple; they are highly intuitive and provide information about the position of the organization in its environment.

Isolating the Randomness in a Series

The only factor not yet isolated is the error or randomness. Remembering from Equation (6-2) that

$$X = S \times T \times C \times R$$

and from Equation (6-3) that

$$MA = T \times C$$

we can divide X by the corresponding seasonal index, obtaining

$$X' = \frac{S \times T \times C \times R}{S} = T \times C \times R$$

The randomness or error can be isolated using

$$\frac{X'}{MA} = \frac{T \times C \times R}{T \times C} = R. \tag{6-8}$$

Since by definition the error or randomness R is not predictable, isolating this factor is not of direct help in preparing a forecast using decomposition. However, it does provide useful information about the data series being analyzed. For example, if the average randomness in a series is computed, it can serve as a benchmark or reference point in evaluting other forecasting methods and estimating the size of the errors that might be anticipated from forecasts based on decomposition. Moreover, an estimate concerning the uncertainty in future forecasts can be made based on the amount of randomness that exists in past data.

PREPARING A FORECAST BASED ON THE DECOMPOSITION METHOD FOR TIME-SERIES ANALYSIS

Continuing with the example used in the preceding section, it is now possible to prepare a forecast based on the seasonal index, the trend, and the cyclical factors that have been identified. To illustrate how this is done, we can consider the preparation of a forecast for the first quater of 1989. Recall first that the basic relationship assumed was that

$$X = T \times C \times S \times R$$

In preparing the forecast, the last term, the randomness, cannot be projected. Therefore the relationship for forecasting is simply

$$X = T \times C \times S.$$

For the first quarter of 1989 (the 49th quarter), the trend forecast is

$$T_{49} = 2735.85 + 38.956(49) = 4644.694$$

The seasonal factor for the first quarter (see Table 6-7) is 112.03. Finally, the cyclical factor must be estimated, usually on the basis of judgment. Examining the cycle in Figure 6-1, we see that its value for period 48 was 98. Without more information we might use this value as an estimate of the cycle value for quarter 49. Thus, to complete this example, we estimate the cycle value to be 98. The forecast, then, is

$$F_{49} = T_{49} \times C_{49} \times S_{49} = 4644.694 \times \frac{98}{100} \times \frac{112.03}{100} = 5099.4.$$

Similarly, for the second quarter of 1989 (the 50th quarter), the trend is

$$T_{50} = 2735.85 + 38.956(50) = 4683.65$$

The corresponding seasonal index is 109.208, and the cyclical factor might be estimated to be 99. The forecast is

$$F_{50} = T_{50} \times C_{50} \times S_{50} = 4683.65 \times \frac{99}{100} \times \frac{109.35}{100} = 5073.8.$$

Similarly, the forecasts for quarters 51 and 52, assuming the cyclical factor to be 100, are

$$F_{51} = 3563.2$$

and

$$F_{52} = 4912.5.$$

A FURTHER ILLUSTRATION OF DECOMPOSITION

Table 6-8 and Figure 6-2 show monthly sales of a major car model manufactured in the United States between 1982 and 1987. The data are seasonal and exhibit a strong cycle and considerable randomness. Unfortunately, however, little information of direct use in forecasting is provided by looking at Figure 6-2. The trend and cycle are masked by the seasonality and randomness, and it is difficult to recognize patterns and to predict future values. This is the type of situation in which decomposition can be most useful.

Table 6-9 shows the simple and centered moving average values and their ratios. As before, these moving averages can be used as the basis for calculating the seasonal indices. The values of these indices, together with the seasonal factors and the information needed to compute them are given in Table 6-10.

Estimating the values of the trend cycle is of critical importance for management seeking to determine the stage of the business cycle that its firm (product, service, etc.) occupies currently. However, since a centered moving average of 12 periods has to be calculated, we loose six values of the trend cycles at the beginning and six at the end of the data (see Table 6-9). The missing values at the beginning present no special problem, but those at the end are extremely important because they are needed to forecast the trend cycle beyond period 72.

Table 6-11 illustrates an approach to overcome the problem of missing values. In this table, column 4 gives the deseasonalized data values. These are

Table 6-8 Monthly Sales of a Car Model (in Units)

Year	Period	Observation	Year	Period	Observation
1982	1	5987.7	1985	37	37239.5
	2	13104.9		38	33713.6
	3	16807.4		39	48674.1
	4	8265.4		40	66635.8
	5	12009.9		41	54846.9
	6	6091.4		42	30037.0
	7	5948.1		43	32842.0
	8	7970.4		44	46786.4
	9	13437.0		45	46239.5
	10	8769.1		46	27295.1
	11	12838.3		47	29695.1
	12	10414.8		48	44988.9
1983	13	12503.7	1986	49	44516.0
	14	13874.1		50	40712.3
	15	19164.2		51	29677.8
	16	23272.8		52	34840.7
	17	26069.1		53	43342.0
	18	33858.0		54	44858.0
	19	27498.8		55	33728.4
	20	22993.8		56	28708.6
	21	21445.7		57	41090.1
	22	28729.6		58	22364.2
	23	27837.0		59	19063.0
	24	26179.0		60	27251.9
1984	25	28044.4	1987	61	26106.2
	26	29770.4		62	43969.1
	27	37508.6		63	42028.4
	28	39435.8		64	35777.8
	29	46766.7		65	23155.6
	30	38927.2		66	25992.6
	31	39238.3		67	26948.1
	32	34993.8		68	29400.0
	33	37118.5		69	25391.4
	34	30745.7		70	24472.8
	35	30018.5		71	21512.1
	36	29575.3		72	25627.2

found by simply dividing the data $T \times C \times S \times R$ by the corresponding values of the seasonal indices. The result is a set of data without seasonality $[(T \times C \times S \times R)/S = T \times C \times R]$. From these deseasonalized data the randomness can be eliminated by averaging several data values—but not

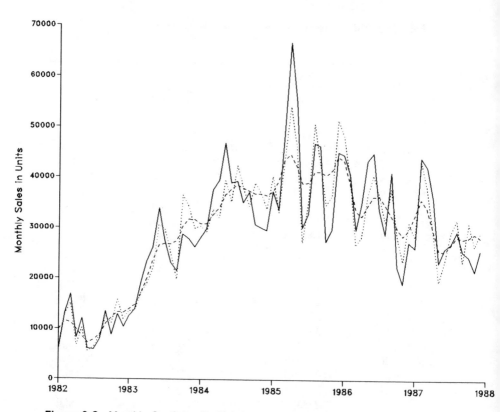

Figure 6-2 Monthly Car Sales (in Units). ──── original data; ···· seasonally adjusted data; ─ ─ ─ trend cycle.

necessarily 12. A 3 × 3 moving average is often used to eliminate the randomness from the deseasonalized data. This is done by taking first a three-period moving average of the deseasonalized data (see column 5) and then another three-period moving average of these three-month moving averages (see column 6). This eliminates the randomness from the data and gives a rather good picture of the trend-cycle component. Furthermore, the 3 × 3 moving average has only two values missing at the beginning and two at the end of the data series. As in the earlier example, the values missing at the beginning are of little importance, but those at the end are much more critical. However, two rather than six missing values are a substantial improvement. Furthermore, estimates for these two missing values can be found as follows.

After period 70, a switch from a 3 × 3 to a simple three-period moving average is made. The values averaged are 32,285.689 + 25,867.07 + 30,973.775 (periods 70, 71, and 72, respectively). Their average, 29,708.846,

Table 6-9 Monthly Car Sales, Centered Moving Averages

Period (Month)	Data	12-Month Moving Average[a]	12-Month Centered Moving Average[a]	Ratios[a]
1	5987.70			
2	13104.90			
3	16807.40			
4	8265.40			
5	12009.90			
6	6091.40			
7	5948.10	10137.03	10408.53	0.571
8	7970.40	10680.03	10712.08	0.744
9	13437.00	10744.13	10842.33	1.239
10	8769.10	10940.53	11565.84	0.758
11	12838.30	12191.15	12776.95	1.005
12	10414.80	13362.75	14519.69	0.717
13	12503.70	15676.64	16574.58	0.754
14	13874.10	17472.53	18098.50	0.767
15	19164.20	18724.48	19058.17	1.006
16	23272.80	19391.87	20223.56	1.151
17	26069.10	21055.24	21680.19	1.202
18	33858.00	22305.13	22961.98	1.475
19	27498.80	23618.82	24266.35	1.133
20	22993.80	24913.88	25576.22	0.899
21	21445.70	26238.57	27002.92	0.794
22	28729.60	27767.27	28440.73	1.010
23	27837.00	29114.19	29976.59	0.929
24	26179.00	30838.98	31050.20	0.843
25	28044.40	31261.42	31750.56	0.883
26	29770.40	32239.71	32739.71	0.909
27	37508.60	33239.71	33892.74	1.107
28	39435.80	34545.78	34629.78	1.139
29	46766.70	34713.79	34804.68	1.344
30	38927.20	34895.57	35037.09	1.111
31	39238.30	35178.60	35561.73	1.103
32	34993.80	35944.86	36109.16	0.969
33	37118.50	36273.46	36738.69	1.010
34	30745.70	37203.92	38337.26	0.802
35	30018.50	39470.59	39807.26	0.754
36	29575.30	40143.94	39773.51	0.744
37	37239.50	39403.09	39136.57	0.952

Table 6-9 *(Continued)*

Period (Month)	Data	12-Month Moving Average[a]	12-Month Centered Moving Average[a]	Ratios[a]
38	33713.60	38870.05	39361.42	0.857
39	48674.10	39852.78	40232.82	1.210
40	66635.80	40612.86	40469.09	1.647
41	54846.90	40325.32	40311.84	1.361
42	30037.00	40298.37	40940.60	0.734
43	32842.00	41582.83	41886.02	0.784
44	46786.40	42189.21	42480.82	1.101
45	46239.50	42772.43	41980.91	1.101
46	27295.10	41189.40	39864.61	0.685
47	29695.10	38539.81	38060.44	0.780
48	44988.90	37581.07	38198.61	1.178
49	44516.00	38816.15	38853.09	1.146
50	40712.30	38890.02	38136.77	1.068
51	29677.80	37383.54	37168.98	0.798
52	34840.70	36954.42	36748.97	0.948
53	43342.00	36543.51	36100.51	1.201
54	44858.00	35657.50	34918.46	1.285
55	33728.40	34179.42	33412.34	1.009
56	28708.60	32645.27	32780.97	0.876
57	41090.10	32916.67	33431.28	1.229
58	22364.20	33945.88	33984.93	0.658
59	19063.00	34023.97	33182.88	0.574
60	27251.90	32341.78	31555.72	0.864
61	26106.20	30769.66	30487.15	0.856
62	43969.10	30204.64	30233.45	1.454
63	42028.40	30262.26	29608.14	1.419
64	35777.80	28954.03	29041.89	1.232
65	23155.60	29129.74	29231.79	0.792
66	25992.60	29333.84	29266.14	0.888
67	26948.10	29198.45		
68	29400.00			
69	25391.40			
70	24472.80			
71	21512.10			
72	25627.20			

[a] Six values missing at the beginning and end of the series because of averaging.

114

Table 6-10 Monthly Car Sales, Seasonal Factors, Smallest and Largest Values, Medial Averages and Seasonal Indices

	Month											
	1	2	3	4	5	6	7	8	9	10	11	12
1982	0.00	0.00	0.00	0.00	0.00	0.00	0.57	0.74	1.24	0.76	1.00	0.72
1983	0.75	0.77	1.01	1.15	1.20	1.47	1.13	0.90	0.79	1.01	0.93	0.84
1984	0.88	0.91	1.11	1.14	1.34	1.11	1.10	0.97	1.01	0.80	0.75	0.74
1985	0.95	0.86	1.21	1.65	1.36	0.73	0.78	1.10	1.10	0.68	0.78	1.18
1986	1.15	1.07	0.80	0.95	1.20	1.28	1.01	0.88	1.23	0.66	0.57	0.86
1987	0.86	1.45	1.42	1.23	0.79	0.89	0.00	0.00	0.00	0.00	0.00	0.00
Smallest value	0.75	0.77	0.80	0.95	0.79	0.73	0.57	0.74	0.79	0.66	0.57	0.72
Year	1983	1983	1986	1986	1987	1985	1982	1982	1983	1986	1986	1982
Largest value	1.15	1.45	1.42	1.65	1.36	1.47	1.13	1.10	1.24	1.01	1.00	1.18
Year	1986	1987	1987	1985	1985	1982	1983	1985	1982	1983	1982	1985

4
110.

Table 6-11 Monthly Car Sales, Moving Averages

(1) Period (Month)	(2) Data $T \times C \times S \times R$	(3) Seasonal Index S	(4) Deseasonalized Data $\dfrac{T \times C \times S \times R}{S} = T \times C \times R$	(5) Three-Period Moving Average 3 MA	(6) Three-Period Moving Average of Moving Average, 3×3 MA	(7) Trend Cycle
1	5,987.7	0.9086855	6,589.409	—	—	10,337.048
2	13,104.9	0.9567188	13,697.756	11,757.	—	11,756.844
3	16,807.4	1.1217371	14,983.368	11,877.	11,370.	11,369.912
4	8,265.4	1.1890798	6,951.090	10,476.	9,889.	9,888.497
5	12,009.9	1.2651296	9,493.021	7,313.	8,270.	8,270.192
6	6,091.4	1.1088263	5,493.557	7,022.	7,020.	7,020.134
7	5,948.1	0.9781848	6,080.753	6,726.	7,538.	7,537.564
8	7,970.4	0.9265178	8,602.533	8,865.	8,762.	8,761.454
9	13,437.0	1.1280887	11,911.297	10,694.	10,844.	10,843.699
10	8,769.1	0.7580077	11,568.615	12,972.	12,288.	12,288.016
11	12,838.3	0.8316404	15,437.321	13,198.	13,366.	13,366.084
12	10,414.8	0.8273838	12,587.629	13,928.	13,581.	13,580.788
13	12,503.7	0.9086855	13,760.206	13,617.	14,220.	14,219.980
14	13,874.1	0.9567188	14,501.753	15,115.	15,262.	15,261.425
15	19,164.2	1.1217371	17,084.395	17,053.	17,085.	17,085.051
16	23,272.8	1.1890798	19,572.111	19,087.	19,904.	19,903.537
17	26,069.1	1.2651296	20,605.873	23,571.	23,025.	23,025.137
18	33,858.0	1.1088263	30,534.990	26,418.	25,937.	25,936.455
19	27,498.8	0.9781848	28,112.070	27,822.	26,073.	26,072.809
20	22,993.8	0.9265178	24,817.441	23,980.	26,980.	26,347.982
21	21,445.7	1.1280887	19,010.650	27,243.	27,117.	27,116.867

116

22	28,729.6	0.7580077	37,901.4?1	30,128.	30,570.	30,569.545
23	27,837.0	0.8316404	33,472.4?2	34,338.	32,153.	32,152.434
24	26,179.0	0.8273838	31,640.6?9	31,992.	32,512.	32,511.984
25	28,044.4	0.9086855	30,862.6?4	31,207.	31,668.	31,667.902
26	29,770.4	0.9567188	31,117.1?9	31,806.	31,862.	31,861.725
27	37,508.6	1.1217371	33,437.9?1	32,573.	32,967.	32,967.090
28	39,435.8	1.1890798	33,164.97	34,523.	34,059.	34,058.168
29	46,766.7	1.2651296	36,965.9?8	35,079.	35,666.	35,665.473
30	38,927.2	1.1088263	35,106.6?2	37,395.	36,713.	36,712.168
31	39,238.3	0.9781848	40,113.3?3	37,663.	37,329.	37,328.699
32	34,993.8	0.9265178	37,769.1?4	36,929.	37,223.	37,222.953
33	37,118.5	1.1280887	32,903.8?3	37,078.	36,842.	36,842.000
34	30,745.7	0.7580077	40,561.1?5	36,520.	37,022.	37,021.535
35	30,018.5	0.8316404	36,095.5?1	37,467.	37,198.	37,198.043
36	29,575.3	0.8273838	35,745.5?6	37,608.	37,466.	37,465.313
37	37,239.5	0.9086855	40,981.7?7	37,322.	38,267.	38,266.410
38	33,713.6	0.9567188	35,238.777	39,871.	40,694.	40,693.883
39	48,674.1	1.1217371	43,391.7?9	44,890.	44,119.	44,118.098
40	66,635.8	1.1890798	56,039.8?5	47,595.	44,882.	44,881.352
41	54,846.9	1.2651296	43,352.7?3	42,161.	41,476.	41,475.383
42	30,037.0	1.1088263	27,089.0?4	34,672.	37,962.	37,961.656
43	32,842.0	0.9781848	33,574.4?4	37,053.	37,804.	37,803.781
44	46,786.4	0.9265178	50,497.0?1	41,687.	40,413.	40,412.535
45	46,239.5	1.1280887	40,989.2?2	42,498.	40,585.	40,584.141
46	27,295.1	0.7580077	36,009.0?0	37,568.	40,699.	40,698.566
47	29,695.1	0.83164.4	35,706.6?0	42,030.	41,985.	41,984.742
48	44,988.9	0.8273838	54,374.8?7	46,357.	45,676.	45,675.098
49	44,516.0	0.9086855	48,989.4?5	48,639.	44,777.	44,776.219
50	40,712.3	0.9567188	42,554.0?4	39,334.	40,248.	40,247.445
51	29,677.8	1.1217371	26,457.0?2	32,771.	34,037.	34,036.184
52	34,840.7	1.1890798	29,300.557	30,006.	32,483.	32,482.236

Table 6-11 (Continued)

(1) Period (Month)	(2) Data $T \times C \times S \times R$	(3) Seasonal Index S	(4) Deseasonalized Data $\dfrac{T \times C \times S \times R}{S}$ $= T \times C \times R$	(5) Three-Period Moving Average 3 MA	(6) Three-Period Moving Average of Moving Average, 3×3 MA	(7) Trend Cycle
53	43,342.0	1.2651296	34,258.941	34,672.	33,692.	33,691.477
54	44,858.0	1.1088263	40,455.391	36,398.	35,459.	35,458.676
55	33,728.4	0.9781840	34,480.598	35,307.	35,223.	35,222.652
56	28,708.6	0.9265178	30,985.480	33,964.	33,858.	33,858.109
57	41,090.1	1.1280887	36,424.531	32,305.	31,962.	31,961.365
58	22,364.2	0.7580077	29,503.920	29,617.	30,125.	30,125.043
59	19,063.0	0.8316404	22,922.168	28,455.	28,756.	28,755.645
60	27,251.9	0.8273838	32,937.438	28,196.	30,842.	30,841.699
61	26,106.2	0.9086855	28,729.631	35,875.	33,819.	33,818.512
62	43,969.1	0.9567188	45,958.230	37,385.	37,033.	37,032.355
63	42,028.4	1.1217371	37,467.242	37,838.	34,614.	34,613.883
64	35,777.8	1.1890798	30,088.646	28,620.	30,134.	30,133.711
65	23,155.6	1.2651296	18,302.947	23,944.	25,221.	25,220.367
66	25,992.6	1.1088263	23,441.543	23,098.	24,872.	24,871.871
67	26,948.1	0.9781848	27,549.088	27,574.	25,978.	25,978.082
68	29,400.0	0.9265178	31,731.717	27,263.	27,893.	27,892.748
69	25,391.4	1.1280887	22,508.336	28,842.	27,664.	27,663.721
70	24,472.8	0.7580077	32,285.689	26,887.	28,479.	28,478.980
71	21,512.1	0.8316404	25,867.070	29,709.		29,708.846
72	25,627.2	0.8273838	30,973.775			29,035.333

118

is centered on period 71 and is the estimate of the trend cycle for this period (see column 6 of Table 6-11).

After period 71, a two-period moving average is calculated. The values averaged are 25,867.07 + 30,973.775, and the result, 28,420.4, must be centered between periods 71 and 72, that is 71.5. Thus, it is half a period late and should be adjusted accordingly. The latest trend-cycle value is 29,708.846 (period 71); the one before that is 28,478.98 (period 70). Therefore, the latest change in trend cycle is 1229.866, and half of that is 614.933. If this amount is added to 28,420.4, the trend cycle can be centered to period 72. The estimated value of the trend cycle for period 72 is thus 28,420.4 + 614.933 = 29,035.333 (see column 6 of Table 6-11).

Finally, in analyzing the car sales data, Figure 6-2 shows the seasonally adjusted values (dotted line) and the trend-cycle values (broken line) together with the actual values (solid line). This clearly illustrates how the amount of information known regarding the data series increases significantly as we go from the original data to the seasonally adjusted data and finally to the trend-cycle data. At this point, January 1988, the management of this car company is seriously concerned about the possibility that a recession in the car industry has already begun or is about to start. Furthermore, it worries about a recession in the U.S. economy that might start in 1988 or 1989. The information from decomposition showing the trend-cycles in their data can help management determine which stage of the business cycle its company has reached. By looking at Figure 6-2 one can see that the sales peaked in February 1987. Whether or not the recession has started cannot be answered as yet since temporary declines, not necessarily recessions, are possible. However, the trend cycles clearly show a flattening in car sales, of which management can become fully aware by looking at Figure 6-2 or Table 6-11. Decisions and actions need to be taken as new data become available and new information about the trend cycle is computed. In this sense the trend-cycle values are the equivalent of early warning signals that must be watched closely during unsettled periods.

SUMMARY OF THE STEPS IN DECOMPOSITION

The steps that must be followed in applying the decomposition method of forecasting in a management situation can now be summarized. The first three steps involve identification of the seasonal, trend, and cyclical factors. In the fourth and fifth steps these three factors are applied in forecasting.

1. Determine the seasonal factors. For example, if a full set of seasonal observations covers 12 periods, as with monthly data, start by computing the 12-month moving average and the centered 12-month moving

average for each value and the ratio of that value to the average. Then compute the medial average for each month and adjust it to get the seasonal index for each month.

2. Determine the trend factors. This requires fitting a trend line to the data. If a linear trend is assumed, either a graphic approach or simple regression can be used to obtain a and b for the straigh line $Y = a + bt$.

3. Determine the cyclical factors. Since the moving averages eliminate the seasonal pattern and the randomness, what is left is the trend and the cycle. Thus, the cyclical factors can be determined by dividing the moving average value by the trend value for each observation.

4. Get more estimates of the trend-cycle values. Start with the deseasonalized data and compute a 3×3 moving average to reduce the number of trend cycles lost at the beginning and the end of the data. Then obtain estimates for the missing trend-cycle values at the end of the data.

5. Prepare a forecast for the desired time period. Start with the time period to be forecast. The seasonal factor for that period can be identified from the adjusted seasonal indices, the trend can be determined by putting the time period in for t in the trend equation, and the cyclical factor can be estimated from the recent pattern in these factors. The forecast is then simply $F = $ seasonal $\times$ trend $\times$ cyclical.

Using these steps, you can prepare a forecast and monitor your series on a continuous basis. Again it should be mentioned that the cyclical factor is the most difficult aspect of this forecasting method. Perhaps the secret, if there is one, is for the manager to have sufficient historical data to see when the cyclical pattern begins to repeat itself. This can be used as a guide in projecting what the cycle will be for future time periods. Adjustments will undoubtedly be necessary to reflect the manager's view of the way in which the cyclical pattern might change. Alternatively, the manager might want to consider the trend and the cycle together and obtain the best possible estimates of their future values.

ADDITIONAL ASPECTS OF DECOMPOSITION METHODS

So far this chapter has focused on what the authors refer to as "classical decomposition." As the reader may guess, a number of variations of this generic approach to decomposition could be developed and applied. One of these variations, Census II, will be described below. Census II is frequently encountered in practice, and computer packages that apply it are available. (See Selected References for additional information.)

Following a brief summary of the Census II decomposition, one additional type of analysis—percentage change—is outlined and illustrated.

Census II Method

The Census II method, developed by Julius Shiskin of the U.S. Census Bureau, has been used widely over the last 40 years by the bureau, by several other government agencies, and recently by many business enterprises. Census II was introduced in the middle 1950s. In principle it is similar to the classical decomposition method, but it contains refinements and elaborations that make the results more appropriate for certain types of applications. In addition to seasonality, Census II provides a great amount of information about the trend cycle in the data. Some of the refinements incorporated in this version of decomposition follow.

1. The original data are corrected for working-day or trading-day differences. This has to be done primarily to monthly data, since the number of working or trading days varies from month to month (and year to year), thus influencing sales or any other variable to be forecast.

2. A rough calculation of the seasonal factors is obtained using the ratio of the original data to a moving average whose length is equal to that of seasonality. This step is exactly the same as that used in classical decomposition.

3. Extreme values are eliminated through the use of statistical control principles (values that are above or below a certain range, such as ± 3 standard deviations, are modified or dropped), and refined and final seasonal factors are recalculated. These seasonal factors are projected a year in advance.

4. Irregular movements are identified, smoothed, printed, and subsequently used to forecast.

5. The month-to-month cyclical movements are identified by extracting the seasonal and irregular elements.

6. Graphs and summary measures that pinpoint the importance of each of the components of any time series (seasonal, cyclical, trend, and irregular or random) are provided, and clues to forthcoming turning points in the series are identified. The months of cyclical dominance (MCD) are computed and used in preparing final estimates of the trend cycle.

From this description it can be seen that Census II is much more elaborate than the classical decomposition method, even though it uses the same concept of decomposition. The procedure in Census II is much more refined, it uses more statistics-based tests, and it does a much better job of adjusting the seasonal and irregular elements and separating them from the cyclical and trend components of a time series. Finally, it has been tested repeatedly on hundreds of thousands of series, and its validity and accuracy of results have been proven, not theoretically (as in sophisticated mathematical methods of forecasting), but empirically. For these reasons Census II is appealing to managers and is gaining acceptance as a method for decomposing the data and forecasting, even though from a statistical point of view there may be some theoretical weaknesses when the decomposition principle is employed.

Percentage Change Values

There are several percentage change values (more correctly, mean absolute percentage change values), each of which involves finding the percentage change of each value from the value of the previous month or period. Four percentage change values are commonly used—one for the original data and one for each of the major components of the time series (seasonality, trend cycle, and randomness).

The percentage change values for the original data series can be used as a comparison for evaluating the other percentage changes and as a benchmark, like the naive methods described in Chapter 4, against which the performance of other quantitative forecasting methods can be compared. These values are computed by finding the mean (average) absolute percentage change (MAPC) from one observation to the next in a data series.

For the original data series, denoted by X, this percentage change is defined as follows:

$$\text{MAPC}_x = \frac{\sum_{t=1}^{n-1} 100 \left| \frac{X_{t+1} - X_t}{X_{t+1}} \right|}{n - 1} \tag{6-9}$$

where

t = the time period
n = number of observations in the data series
X_i = the data series value at period i.

As an illustration, the data of Table 6-1 for a French paper product's sales can be used. The resulting computations give

$$\text{MAPC}_x = \left(\sum_{t=1}^{47} 100 \left| \frac{3043.539 - 3017.604}{3043.539} \right| \right.$$

$$+ \left| \frac{2094.350 - 3043.539}{2094.350} \right| + \cdots$$

$$+ \left. \left| \frac{3881.604 - 3596.765}{3881.604} \right| \right) \middle/ 47$$

$$= \frac{\sum_{t=1}^{47} 100\ (0.0085 + 0.4532 + \ldots + 0.0734)}{47} = 24.26.$$

The value of 24.26 for $MAPC_x$ means that the average fluctuation (from period to period) of the data series X is 24.26%.

It should be noted that this value is exactly the mean absolute percentage error (MAPE) that would be obtained if Naive Forecast 1 (described in Chapter 4) had been applied, that is $MAPC_x = MAPE_{NFI}$. Thus, as described in Chapter 4, this value of 24.26% serves as a benchmark or reference against which other forecasting methods can be compared. Only methods that improve over this 24.26% MAPE are worthy of further consideration.

Using a computational procedure completely equivalent to Equation (6-9), we can obtain the mean absolute percentage change of the deseasonalized data series as follows:

$$MAPC_{x'} = \frac{\sum_{t=1}^{n-1} 100 \left| \frac{X''_{t+1} - X''_{t}}{X'_{t+1}} \right|}{n-1} \qquad (6\text{-}10)$$

where $X'_{t+1} = X_t/S_j$, that is, X'_t is the deseasonalized actual data series. Continuing with the French paper product example, we note that for the data of Table 6-1, the deseasonalized data series, X'_t, consists of

$$X'_1 = \frac{X_1}{S_1} = \frac{3017.604}{1.12619} = 2679.48$$

$$X'_2 = \frac{X_2}{S_2} = \frac{3043.539}{1.0998} = 2767.36$$

$$X'_3 = \frac{X_3}{S_3} = \frac{2094.350}{0.76289} = 2745.28$$

$$\cdot$$
$$\cdot$$
$$\cdot$$

$$X'_{47} = \frac{X_{47}}{S_3} = \frac{3596.765}{0.76289} = 4714.66$$

$$X'_{48} = \frac{X_{48}}{S_4} = \frac{3881.604}{1.03941} = 3734.43.$$

Using this deseasonalized data series, we can compute $\text{MAPC}_{X'}$ using Equation (6-10)

$$\text{MAPC}_{X'} = \left(\sum_{t=1}^{47} 100 \left| \frac{2767.36 - 2679.48}{2767.36} \right| \right.$$

$$+ \left| \frac{2745.28 - 2767.36}{2745.28} \right| + \ldots$$

$$\left. + \left| \frac{3734.43 - 4714.66}{3734.43} \right| \right) \Big/ 47$$

$$= \sum_{t=1}^{47} 100 \frac{(|0.0318| + |-0.0080| + \ldots + |-0.2625|)}{47} = 6.88.$$

This means that the average fluctuation (from period to period) of the deseasonalized data series X'_t is 6.88%. This is the same value obtained for the mean absolute percentage error using Naive Forecast 2 as a reference forecast (see Chapter 4), that is, $\text{MAPC}_{X'} = \text{MAPE}_{\text{NF2}}$. Thus, as described in Chapter 4, this value of 6.88% can serve as a benchmark against which other forecasting methods can be compared.

If the difference between MAPC_X and $\text{MAPC}_{X'}$ is large, there is substantial seasonality in the original data series. Therefore, only forecasting methods that can effectively deal with seasonality need be considered. If the difference is small, then seasonality is much less important and other methods (that do not emphasize seasonality) may be suitable.

Two other MAPC values can also be computed using an equation equivalent to Equation (6-8) or Equation (6-9), but with a different data series. If the randomness or error series is used—that obtained by eliminating seasonality and the trend cycle—the result is MAPC_R. If the trend-cycle series (the last column in Table 6-11) is used, the result is MAPC_{TC}.

The mean absolute percentage change values provide extremely useful information to forecast users. This information helps the forecasters understand a data series and decide where to concentrate forecasting efforts. For instance, in a series where the percentage change in trend cycle is large, the forecaster must be concerned about cyclical fluctuations (recessions and booms). In a series in which MAPC_X and MAPC_R are about the same, not much can be done to obtain a better forecast, because most of the fluctuations in the data are random. In such a case, using Naive Forecast 1 may produce quite good results.

Returning to the French paper product data of Table 6-1, the complete set of MAPC values is

$MAPC_X$ (original data) = 24.26
$MAPC_{X'}$ (seasonally adjusted, that is, deseasonalized data) = 6.88
$MAPC_R$ (randomness or error) = 5.71
$MAPC_{TC}$ (trend cycle) = 2.30.

These percentage changes indicate that seasonality is very important, and the errors to be expected using Naive Forecast 2 would be in the neighborhood of 6.88%. With randomness in the series of 5.71%, this value serves as a limit to expected forecasting errors, unless the trend-cycle component could be predicted accurately. If that could be done, the improvement in this case would be an additional 2.3%. Thus, the minimum forecasting error could be as low as 3.41% if all trend-cycle changes could be predicted. Since this generally is not possible, the forecasting errors would most likely range between 3.41 and 5.71%.

SELECTED REFERENCES FOR FURTHER STUDY

Bails, D. G., and L. C. Peppers, 1982. *Business Fluctuations*, Prentice-Hall, Englewood Cliffs, NJ.

Berman, J. P., 1979. "Seasonal Adjustment—A Survey," *TIMS Studies in the Management Sciences*, vol. 12, North-Holland, Amsterdam, pp. 45–57.

Dagum, E. B., 1982. "Revisions of Time Varying Seasonal Filters," *Journal of Forecasting*, 1, no. 2, pp. 20–28.

Makridakis, S., and S. C. Wheelwright, (Eds.), 1987. *The Handbook of Forecasting: A Manager's Guide*, 2nd ed., Wiley, New York.

Makridakis, S., S. C. Wheelwright, and V. E. McGee, 1989. *Forecasting: Methods and Applications*, 3rd ed., Wiley, New York.

Shiskin, J., 1961. "Tests and Revisions of Bureau of the Census Methods of Seasonal Adjustments," Bureau of the Census, Technical Paper 5.

———, 1957. "Electronic Computers and Business Indicators," National Bureau of Economic Research, Occasional Paper 57.

Shiskin, J., A. H. Young, and J. C. Musgrave. 1967, "The X-11 Variant of the Census II Method Seasonal Adjustment Program," Bureau of the Census, Technical Paper 15.

CHAPTER 7

AUTOREGRESSIVE/MOVING AVERAGE (ARMA) METHODS

In Chapter 5, several time-series methods were presented. Starting with single exponential smoothing, these methods based a forecast on a weighting (smoothing) of past data in a time series.

In chapter 6, the decomposition method of time-series analysis and forecasting was introduced. This approach identified the type of data patterns present—trend, seasonal, and cycle—and prepared forecasts for each of those patterns as part of predicting future values of the time series.

In this chapter, a number of more general and theoretical time-series methods are described. These methods can deal with any data pattern. However, in most cases the manager must understand the method well enough to select the most appropriate specific model from the set available for that method. In a very real sense, using these methods instead of the exponential and decomposition methods of Chapters 5 and 6 simply trades the task of matching narrower methods to fit the data for the task of selecting directly a specific statistical model from the general class of ARMA models.

A basic tool for applying most of these advanced methods—autocorrelation—is the focus of the first part of this chapter. Following that, a variety of ARMA models are described, and the methodology proposed by Box and Jenkins for selecting among these models is summarized. Next, an application of this methodology is described. The final portion of this chapter outlines briefly several additional time-series methods—Parzen's ARARMA models, AEP filtering, Kalman filtering, Lewandowski's FORSYS, and multivariate ARMA models.

AUTOCORRELATION

The autocorrelation among successive values of a time series is a key tool in identifying the basic pattern and determining an appropriate model corresponding to a data series. As will be described in Chapters 8 and 9, the concept of correlation between two variables is straightforward. It is the association (mutual relationship) between two variables and describes what tends to happen to one of the variables if there is a change in the other.

The degree of this relation is measured by the *correlation coefficient*, which varies between $+1$ and -1. A value close to $+1$ implies a strong positive relationship between the two variables. This means that when the value of one variable increases, the value of the other tends to increase also. Similarly, a correlation coefficient close to -1 indicates the opposite—increases in one variable will be associated with decreases in the other. A coefficient of 0 indicates that the two variables are unrelated—no matter what happens to one variable, nothing can be said about the value of the other.

An *autocorrelation coefficient* is similar to a correlation coefficient except that it describes the association (mutual relationship) among values of the same variable but at different time periods. To see what is meant by this, suppose we construct a number of artificial variables from a single variable by changing the time origin of the data. For example, as shown in Figure 7-1, variable B can be constructed from variable A by simply dropping the first value of A and letting the second value of A be the starting value of B.

In Figure 7-1, variables A and B can be treated as two separate and distinct variables, even though they both come from the same data set. In a similar manner we can construct Figure 7-2, in which it can be seen that variable Y_1 is exactly the same as variable Y, except that Y_1 begins with the second value of Y, that is, -2. We can also see that Y_2 is another artificial variable that begins with the third value of Y, that is, 5. Continuing in this way, we can construct Y_3 by starting with the fourth value of Y, and so on. It is obvious that since Y has a finite number of data points and since Y_1 starts with the

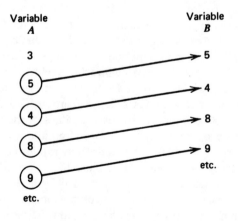

Figure 7-1   Creating Time-Lagged Variables.

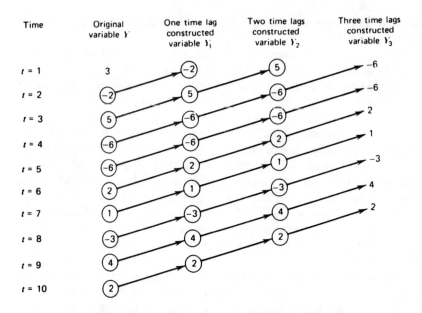

Figure 7-2 Constructing Time-Lagged Variables.

second value of Y, the last value of Y_1 will be missing, the last two values of Y_2 will be missing, the last three values of Y_3 will be missing, and so on.

We can now consider Y and Y_1 as two variables and calculate their correlation coefficient, Y and Y_2 as another two variables, Y and Y_3 as still another two, and so on. for each of these sets or pairs of variables there is a corresponding correlation coefficient, the meaning of which is of interest. A coefficient of 0.80 between Y and Y_1, for example, will imply that successive values of Y with one period (lag) between them (this is how Y_1 was constructed) are positively correlated with each other and thus tend to move in the same direction. Similarly a coefficient of -0.70 between Y and Y_2 will tell us that successive values of Y two periods (time lags) apart are negatively correlated and tend to move in opposite directions. However, since variables Y_1, Y_2, Y_3, . . . are actually all derived from the same original variable Y, we call such an association auto- (that is, self-) correlation. Thus, *autocorrelation* is a measure of association among successive values of the same variable.

Autocorrelations provide important information about the structure of a data set and of its patterns. In a set of completely random data the autocorrelation among successive values will be close to, or equal to, 0, but data values of strong seasonal or cyclical character will be highly autocorrelated. Figure 7-3, for instance, presents the autocorrelations (ρ_k) of different time lags of monthly temperatures in the Paris region. These autocorrelations

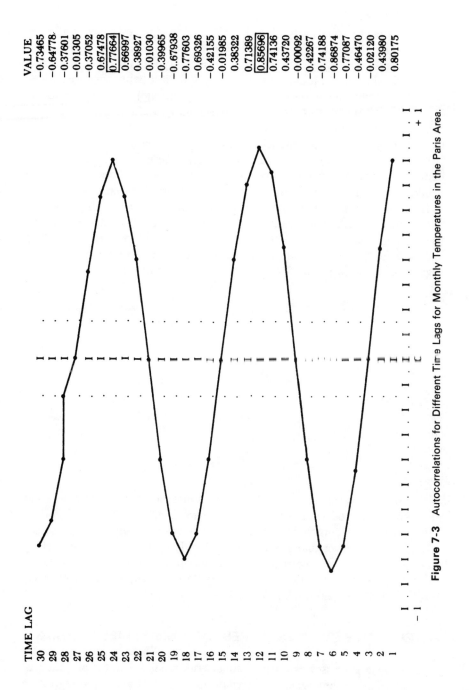

TIME LAG	VALUE
30	−0.73465
29	−0.64778
28	−0.37601
27	−0.01305
26	−0.37052
25	0.67478
24	0.77664
23	0.66997
22	0.38927
21	−0.01030
20	−0.39965
19	−0.67938
18	−0.77603
17	−0.69326
16	−0.42155
15	−0.01985
14	0.38322
13	0.71389
12	0.85696
11	0.74136
10	0.43720
9	−0.00092
8	−0.42267
7	−0.74188
6	−0.86874
5	−0.77087
4	−0.46470
3	−0.02120
2	0.43980
1	0.80175

Figure 7-3 Autocorrelations for Different Time Lags for Monthly Temperatures in the Paris Area.

129

reveal a strong seasonal pattern, since their highest values occur every 12 time periods. The ρ_{12} of 0.86, for example, implies a positive relation among the temperatures every 12 successive months. It is this type of information gained by the calculation of autocorrelations that is utilized with advanced time-series approaches to identify an optimal (appropriate) forecasting model. One thing that makes this information particularly useful is that these coefficients can be used to reveal the type of data we are dealing with and to help us identify an appropriate model to be fitted to the data.

What Figure 7-3 tells us is that the temperature of months that are 12 periods apart are highly correlated (that is, 0.86). This is, of course, what we would expect, since the temperatures of each January, February, March, and so forth, are very similar. However, if we had not known previously how this data series behaved, then the autocorrelations would be very helpful in telling us that there is a seasonal pattern of 12-month duration in the data. For instance, for the temperature series whose autocorrelations are shown in Figure 7-3, an appropriate forecasting model might be either

$$Y_t = Y_{t-12},$$

$$Y_t = \frac{Y_{t-12} + Y_{t-24}}{2},$$

$$Y_t = \frac{Y_{t-12} + Y_{t-24} + Y_{t-36}}{3},$$

or

$$Y_t = \frac{Y_{t-12} + Y_{t-24} + Y_{t-36} + Y_{t-48}}{4},$$

and so on. The various advanced time-series methods allow us to determine an appropriate model using the procedures to be decribed in this chapter.

A statistical measure that is similar to that of autocorrelation and possesses several characteristics that are helpful in identifying appropriate forecasting models is *partial autocorrelation*. The computation and use of these "partials," as they are often called, are quite technical, and the interested reader should see Makridakis, Wheelwright, and McGee (1989).

ALTERNATIVE CLASSES (TYPES) OF TIME-SERIES MODELS

Three general classes or types of time-series models can, for all practical purposes, describe any type or pattern of time-series data: (1) autoregressive

(AR), (2) moving average (MA), and (3) mixed autoregressive/moving average (ARMA).

An autoregressive model is of the form

$$Y_t = \phi_1 Y_{t-1} + \phi_2 Y_{t-2} + \phi_3 Y_{t-3} + \ldots + \phi_p Y_{t-p} + e_t \quad (7\text{-}1)$$

where Y_t is the dependent variable, say, sales, and $Y_{t-1}, Y_{t-2}, Y_{t-3}, \ldots, Y_{t-p}$ are the independent variables. In this case these independent variables are values of the *same* (thus the name *auto*) variable, that is, sales, but of previous periods ($t - 1, t - 2, t - 3, \ldots, t - p$). Finally, e_t is the error, or residual term, that represents random disturbances that cannot be explained by the model.

The model described by Equation (7-1) is called autoregressive because it is like the regression Equation ($Y = a + b_1 X_1 + b_2 X_2 + b_3 X_3 + \ldots + b_p X_p + e$) that is discussed in Chapters 8 and 9. The only difference is that $X_1 = Y_{t-1}, X_2 = Y_{t-2}, X_3 = Y_{t-3}, \ldots, X_p = Y_{t-p}$ and thus the "independent" variables are simply lagged values of the dependent variable with time lags of $1, 2, 3, \ldots, p$ periods. Thus if we could (1) show that Equation (7-1) is indeed an appropriate model, (2) determine the value of p (the number of terms to be included), and (3) estimate $\phi_1, \phi_2, \phi_3, \ldots, \phi_p$, we could come up with a forecasting model to be used for prediction purposes. If, for example, $p = 3$ and $\phi_1 = 0.8, \phi_2 = 0.5, \phi_3 = -0.4$ (that is, $p = 3$ and $\phi_4 = \phi_5 = \phi_6 = \ldots = 0$), and the past values of the time series are as shown in Table 7-1, the forecast for the next period, t, would be

$$\begin{aligned} Y_t &= \phi_1 Y_{t-1} + \phi_2 Y_{t-2} + \phi_3 Y_{t-3} + e_t \\ &= 0.80(115) + 0.5(110) - 0.4(130) + e_t \\ &= 0.95 + e_t \end{aligned}$$

where e_t is some random value.

Table 7-1   Example of Forecasting Sales with an Autoregressive Model

Time period	Actual Sales	Sales Forecast	Residual or Error
$t - 5$	100	98	2
$t - 4$	120	125	-5
$t - 3$	130	131	-1
$t - 2$	110	110	0
$t - 1$	115	112	3

Not all data series can be handled with such a model. Another possible model is the moving average (MA) type of the form

$$Y_t = e_t - \theta_1 e_{t-1} - \theta_2 e_{t-2} - \cdots - \theta_q e_{t-q} \qquad (7\text{-}2)$$

where, as before, e_t is the error or residual and $e_{t-1}, e_{t-2}, e_{t-3}, \ldots, e_{t-q}$ are previous values of the error.

Equation (7-2) is similar to Equation (7-1), except that it implies that the dependent variable Y_t depends on previous values of the *error term* $(e_t, e_{t-1}, \ldots, e_{t-q})$ rather than of the variable itself. In the same way we talked about autocorrelation among successive values of Y_t, we can talk about the autocorrelation among successive values of the residuals or errors. According to Equation (7-2), the future values of sales could be predicted by utilizing the error of each of several past periods. If $q = 2$, $\theta_1 = 0.6$, and $\theta_2 = -0.3$, and the errors of the previous two periods were -50 and 70, the forecast for Y_t would be

$$Y_t = e_t - \theta_1 e_{t-1} - \theta_2 e_{t-2}$$
$$Y_t = e_t - 0.6(-50) - [-0.3(70)]$$
$$Y_t = 9 + e_t$$

where e_t is some random value that cannot be predicted.

The third class of possible models is a mixed model. Often the pattern of the data may be described best by a mixed process of AR and MA elements. The general form of a mixed model is

$$Y_t = \phi_1 Y_{t-1} + \phi_2 Y_{t-2} + \cdots + \phi_p Y_{t-p} \qquad (7\text{-}3)$$
$$+ e_t - \theta_1 e_{t-1} - \theta_2 e_{t-2} - \cdots - \theta_q e_{t-q}.$$

It is evident that Equation (7-3) is simply Equations (7-1) and (7-2) combined. It shows that future values of sales depend on both past values of sales *and* past errors between the actual and forecast values.

If $p = 3$ (with $\phi_1 = 0.8$, $\phi_2 = 0.5$, and $\phi_3 = -0.4$) and $q = 2$ (with $\theta_1 = -0.2$ and $\theta_2 = 0.3$), the forecast for period t, using the data of Table 7-1, becomes

$$Y_t = \phi_1 Y_{t-1} + \phi_2 Y_{t-2} + \phi_3 Y_{t-3} + e_t - \theta_1 e_{t-1} - \theta_2 e_{t-2}$$
$$= 0.8(115) + 0.5(110) - 0.4(130) + e_t - [-0.2(3)] - 0.3(0)$$
$$= 95.6 + e_t.$$

These types of time-series models—AR, MA, and mixed ARMA—have been in use for some time. AR models were described by Yule (1926, 1927) more than 60 years ago. In 1937 Slutsky proposed MA models, and in 1954 Wold described mixed ARMA models. In spite of such early work on all three classes of models, their development and application were severely limited, primarily for computational reasons. With the widespread availability of computers, the utilization of ARMA models became possible. One of the commonly used procedures for applying such models is that proposed by Box and Jenkins (1976).

THE BOX–JENKINS METHODOLOGY

The Box–Jenkins methodology is based on the schematic diagram shown in Figure 7-4. First a general class of forecasting models is postulated; then three stages are proposed. In stage 1 a specific model that can be tentatively entertained as the forecasting model best suited to that situation is identified. Stage 2 consists of fitting that model to the available historical data and running a check to determine whether it is adequate. If not, the approach returns to stage 1 and an alternative method from those available in the general class is identified. When an adequate model has been accepted, stage

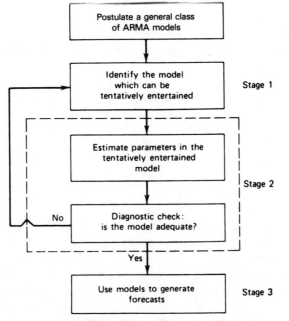

Figure 7-4 Box–Jenkins Forecasting Method.

3—the development of a forecast for some future time period—is pursued. These three stages will be described next.

STAGE 1.   Tentatively identify an appropriate model

Theoretically speaking, Equation (7-3) can fit any pattern of data. However, the values of p (0, 1, 2, . . .) and q (0, 1, 2, . . .) must be specified before the method can be applied. For instance, if $p = 1$ and $q = 0$, the ARMA model is

$$Y_t = \phi_1 Y_{t-1} + e_t. \tag{7-4}$$

Equation (7-4) is called a first-order AR (also called a Markov) model and is written as AR(1) or ARMA(1,0).

If $p = 2$ and $q = 0$, the model is an AR(2) or a ARMA(2,0) model of the form

$$Y_t = \phi_1 Y_{t-1} + \phi_2 Y_{t-2} + e_t. \tag{7-5}$$

Equation (7-5) is a second-order AR process.

When $p = 0$ and $q = 1$, the model is a first-order MA and is written as MA(1) or ARMA(0,1):

$$Y_t = e_t - \theta_1 e_{t-1}. \tag{7-6}$$

When $p = 0$ and $q = 2$, the model is an MA(2) or ARMA(0,2) model of the form

$$Y_t = e_t - \theta_1 e_{t-1} - \theta_2 e_{t-2}. \tag{7-7}$$

Finally, p and q can each be different from 0, in which case there is a mixed ARMA model. For instance, when $p = 1$ and $q = 1$, the model is ARMA(1,1) and is of the form

$$Y_t = \phi_1 Y_{t-1} + e_t - \theta_1 e_{t-1}. \tag{7-8}$$

It is interesting to realize that in Equation (7-8) e_t is influenced by Y_{t-1} and at the same time by $\theta_1 e_{t-1}$, which makes Equation (7-8) nonlinear and therefore general enough to describe a wide variety of data patterns.

Obviously p and q can take many other values, even though they rarely are larger than 2. However, the problem that remains is how to choose an appropriate order for p and q so that a model can be fitted to the data without having to try all possible combinations—a time-consuming process. This is done by examining the autocorrelation coefficients and a related measure, the partial autocorrelations.

It is not an exaggeration to say that the *most* difficult part of the Box–Jenkins methodology is identifying an appropriate model. Thus, in this section we describe the process involved without attempting to go into the theory of why it is done that way. The interested reader is encouraged to look at the many books written on the topic, several of which are cited in the Selected References at the end of this chapter.

The task of identifying a model can be subdivided into three steps: (1) achieving stationarity, (2) choosing p and q for nonseasonal data, and (3) selecting p and q and seasonal parameters for seasonal data.

Achieving Stationarity through Differencing

The basic theory behind ARMA models applies to horizontal (in statistical terminology, stationary) data only. Thus, before attempting to identify p and q in Equation (7-3), the data *must* be horizontal (without trend). If the data series contains a trend, it can be removed by taking successive differences of the data or using some other procedure to remove trends. Figure 7-5 shows how differencing is done and how data with a linear trend are detrended after differencing.

The new series in Figure 7-5 consisting of these differences is a constant because the original data were randomless. If, in addition to randomness, other patterns are present, differencing removes the trend without affecting the remaining patterns.

If the data have a seasonal pattern, in addition to the type of differencing

Data Series	First Differences	New Series
2	$4-2=2$	2
4	$6-4=2$	2
6	$8-6=2$	2
8	$10-8=2$	2
10	$12-10=2$	2
12		—

Figure 7-5   Data with Linear Trend and Their Differences.

shown in Figure 7-5 (called short or period to period), seasonal or long differencing (say, from January of one year to January of the next) might also be needed to ensure stationarity in the data.

Identifying p and q

Once the data are stationary, p and q are identified by looking at the autocorrelations and partial autocorrelations of the differentiated data. Figure 7-6 shows various shapes of autocorrelations and partial autocorrelations and the appropriate ARMA models corresponding to such autocorrelations. As a general rule, when the autocorrelations drop off exponentially to 0, the model is AR, and its order is determined by the number of partial autocorrelations that are significantly different from 0. If the partial autocorrelations drop off exponentially to 0, the model is MA, and its order is determined by the number of statistically significant autocorrelations. When

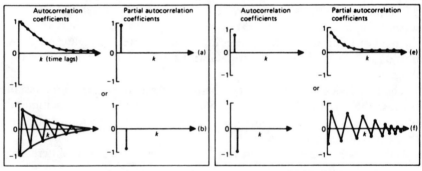

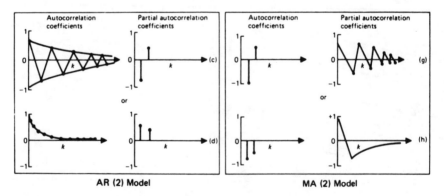

Figure 7-6 Autocorrelation and Partial Autocorrelation Functions.

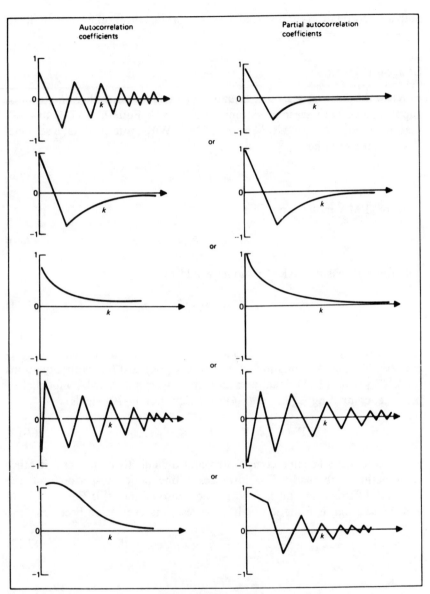

Autocorrelation coefficients

Partial autocorrelation coefficients

Mixed ARMA (1,1) Model

Figure 7-6 Autocorrelation and Partial Autocorrelation Functions.

both autocorrelations and partial autocorrelations drop off exponentially to 0, the model is mixed ARMA.

Seasonal Data

When the data are seasonal, Equation (7-3) might not suffice and must be supplemented with seasonal parameters. As with Equations (7-4) to (7-8), seasonal models can be AR, MA, or ARMA. With monthly data, a seasonal AR model would be

$$Y_t = \phi_{12} Y_{t-12} + e_t \qquad (7\text{-}9)$$

a seasonal MA model would be

$$Y_t = e_t - \theta_{12} e_{t-12} \qquad (7\text{-}10)$$

and a mixed seasonal ARMA model would be

$$Y_t = \phi_{12} Y_{t-12} + e_t - \theta_{12} e_{t-12}. \qquad (7\text{-}11)$$

Equations (7-9), (7-10) and (7-11) show seasonal AR, MA, or ARMA models only. In reality, most models include both nonseasonal and seasonal parameters. Thus a combination of Equations (7-4) to (7-8) with Equations (7-9), (7-10) or (7-11) usually makes up a seasonal ARMA model. For instance, combining Equation (7-4) with Equation (7-10) yields

$$Y_t = \phi_1 Y_{t-1} + e_t - \theta_{12} e_{t-12}. \qquad (7\text{-}12)$$

Such expressions become complicated and difficult to understand if other combinations are made. For instance, if one period-to-period and one seasonal difference are taken, and the nonseasonal model is Equation (7-6) and the seasonal is Equation (7-10), the resulting expression becomes

$$Y_t = Y_{t-1} + Y_{t-12} + Y_{t-13} + e_t - \theta_1 e_{t-1} - \theta_{12} e_{t-13} \qquad (7\text{-}13)$$
$$+ \theta_1 \theta_{12} e_{t-13}.$$

See Makridakis, Wheelwright, and McGee (1989) for a derivation of this expression.

To estimate the seasonal values of p and q (usually denoted by P and Q), the same process as used with the nonseasonal data is followed. That is, the autocorrelations and partial autocorrelations are examined, but this time the nonseasonal autocorrelations and partials are ignored and only the seasonal ones are examined. Thus with monthly data the values of 12, 24, 36, 48 and so forth are examined for patterns similar to that of Figure 7-4. Unfortunately, however, there are usually not enough autocorrelations and partials available to provide for a precise identification process such as that possible in the case of nonseasonal data. Thus, considerable judgment and trial and error are required. Fortunately, P and Q are usually 0 or 1, which makes the selection task relatively easier.

STAGE 2a: Parameter Estimation

Once a tentative model has been chosen by examining the autocorrelations and partial autocorrelations, the parameters of the model are estimated. To illustrate the process, let us assume that Equation (7-12) has been tentatively identified as the most appropriate model for our data. Thus $p = 1$, $q = 0$, $P = 0$, $Q = 1$, and there is no differencing.

Obviously, ϕ_1 and θ_{12} can take many possible values. For instance, ϕ_1 can be 0.5 and $\theta_{12} = -0.3$; or $\phi_1 = 0.2$ and $\theta_{12} = 0.4$; or $\phi_1 = -0.7$ and $\theta_{12} = -0.4$. For each set of values of ϕ_1 and θ_{12} there will be corresponding values for the errors e_t. Each of the e_t values can be squared and their sum computed, as we have done several times before. Table 7-2 illustrates the process involved. It is obvious that the mean squared error varies as ϕ_1 and θ_{12} change. The smallest is 8931, corresponding to $\phi_1 = 0.3$ and $\theta_{12} = 0.2$.

These are the values of ϕ_1 and θ_{12} that we would like because they give a minimum MSE. The process of finding the minimum mean square error and the corresponding parameters is the same as that used in exponential smoothing models.

STAGE 2b: Diagnostic Checking

Once optimal parameters (providing the minimum mean squared error) have been estimated, the errors e_t [see Equation (7-12), for example] can be examined. There are two possible findings: (1) that the errors are random,

Table 7-2   Mean Squared Errors for Values of ϕ_1 and θ_{12}

MSE	ϕ_1	θ_{12}
12,583	0.5	−0.3
20,864	0.7	−0.6
9,438	0.35	−0.1
35,863	0.9	−0.9
8,931	0.3	0.2
10,702	0.4	0.3

which means that the fitted model has eliminated pattern from the data and that what remains are random errors, or (2) that the tentatively identified model has not removed all pattern, as indicated by the fact that the e_t are not random.

Fortunately, the autocorrelations of the residuals (errors) can be computed easily. Since the autocorrelations can tell us how successive values of the residuals relate to each other, if they are random, then no autocorrelation should be significantly different from zero. This is true in Figure 7-7, which shows that the model identified is adequate. Figure 7-8, on the other hand, has several autocorrelations outside the 95% confidence interval, which implies that the fitted model has *not* eliminated all of the pattern from the data. Thus another model would be better if it removed some of the remaining pattern. Therefore the model that provided the results in Figure 7-7 is not appropriate and a new one must be identified.

STAGE 3:   Forecast Preparation

Once a model has been identified, the parameters are estimated, and the residuals are shown to be random, forecasting with that model is a straight-

```
TIME LAG                                              VALUE
24                    .    *    .                     0.00779
23                    .    I    .*                    0.23193
22                    .    *    .                     0.02446
21                    .    I  *.                      0.12614
20                    .    I* .                       0.06344
19                    .    I *  .                     0.12263
18                    .    *    .                    -0.01899
17                    .    I*   .                     0.05348
16                    . *  I    .                    -0.08049
15                    .    *    .                    -0.01780
14                    . *  I    .                    -0.08648
13                    .*   I    .                    -0.14340
12                    .    *    .                    -0.01574
11                    .    *    .                    -0.01676
10                    . *  I    .                    -0.12253
 9                    .   *I    .                    -0.04833
 8                    . *  I    .                    -0.08745
 7                    *    I    .                    -0.20262
 6                    .    *    .                     0.01471
 5                    .   *I    .                    -0.04653
 4                    .   *I    .                    -0.03957
 3                    .    *    .                     0.02190
 2                    .    I  *.                      0.13868
 1                    .   *I    .                    -0.04888
        I.I.I.I.I.I.I.I.I.I.I.I.I.I.I.I.I.I.I.I.I
        -1                  0                  +1
```

Figure 7-7   Autocorrelations of the Residuals of an Adequate Model.

```
TIME LAG                                                    VALUE
24                        .    I*  .                        0.04601
23                        .    I *  .                       0.10632
22                        .  *I    .                       -0.03505
21                        .  *I    .                       -0.06589
20                       *.    I    .                      -0.22543
19                        .*    I    .                     -0.13485
18                        .  *I    .                       -0.02727
17                        .  *I    .                       -0.03173
16                        .    *    .                       -0.00252
15                        .    *    .                       0.00569
14                        .  * I    .                      -0.08420
13                        .    I  .                         -0.36745
12                        .    I *.                         0.16444
11                        .    I    *                       0.17677
10                        .    *    .                       -0.01350
 9                        . *  I    .                       -0.12487
 8                        *    I    .                       -0.19579
 7                        .    I  *                         0.21339
 6                        .  *I    .                        -0.03896
 5                        .  I*  .                           0.03830
 4                        .  I *  .                          0.09060
 3                        .    *    .                        0.02179
 2                       *.    I    .                        -0.26520
 1                        .    I    .        *               0.44378
         I.I.I.I.I.I.I.I.I.I.I.I.I.I.I.I.I.I.I.I.I
         -1                 0                 +1
```

Figure 7-8   Autocorrelations of the Residuals of an Inadequate Model.

forward and mechanical matter. The computer program needed to carry out the calculations of identification and estimation can provide as many forecasts as the manager wishes, together with 95% or 99% confidence intervals for them.

AN APPLICATION OF THE BOX–JENKINS METHODOLOGY

To demonstrate the use of the Box–Jenkins method, we will apply it to estimating the retail sales of printing and writing papers. For more details on the model involved and the rationale for its selection, the reader can consult Makridakis, Wheelwright, and McGee (1989).

A tentative model is required to start the Box–Jenkins method. An initial form for this model can be determined by examining the autocorrelation and partial autocorrelation coefficients of the data. We can see in Figure 7-9 that the largest autocorrelation is every 12 months, which suggests a seasonal pattern of 12 months in our data. This is the type of information revealed by the autocorrelations that must be utilized to arrive at the best model. Figure 7-9 also reveals a trend in the data. This trend is indicated in Figure 7-9 by

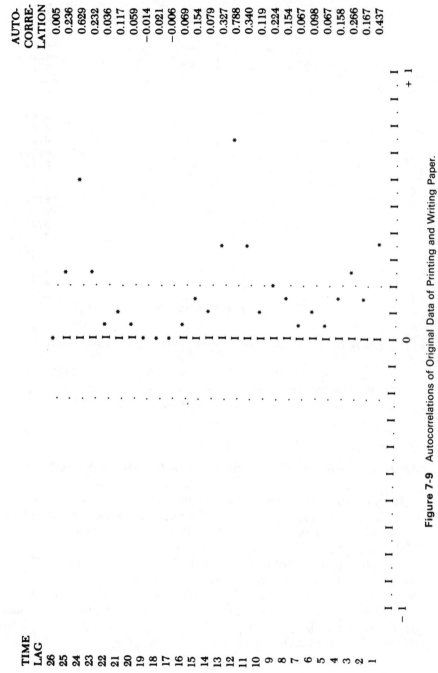

Figure 7-9 Autocorrelations of Original Data of Printing and Writing Paper.

the fact that almost all autocorrelations are greater than zero. (No trend or stationarity exists if the autocorrelations fluctuate around zero after the second or third time lag.) This means that some differencing is needed to make the data stationary. The differencing can be period to period, seasonal (that is, every 12 periods), or a combination of the two.

Figure 7-10 shows what would have happened, for example, if only one seasonal (long) difference had been taken. The resulting residuals are not stationary (they are all greater than zero), because one long difference by itself does not remove the trend. This also could have been discovered by examining the autocorrelations of the data after one short difference has been taken. In this case the autocorrelations would not fluctuate around zero.

Figure 7-11 shows the autocorrelations of the data after taking one short (that is, period-to-period) difference and one long (that, is seasonal) difference. It can be seen that the autocorrelations fluctuate around zero, which indicates that this is the appropriate level of differencing.

After the appropriate level of differencing has been determined, the autocorrelations and the partial autocorrelations are computed for that level of differencing (see Figure 7-12). Next an appropriate model is identified by examining both the autocorrelations and the partials (Figures 7-11 and 7-12) and comparing them with the theoretical ones shown in Fiture 7-6.

In examining Figures 7-11 and 7-12, the first thing to look for is which of the two patterns drops off exponentially to zero. In this instance it is Figure 7-12, the partials, that does so, indicating that a moving average model is appropriate. Once this is identified, we look at Figure 7-11 (the nonseasonal autocorrelations only) and determine that there is only *one* autocorrelation that is statistically significantly different from zero (that is, outside the parallel dotted lines—the 95% confidence interval). It should be noted that what we are doing here is completely analogous to what we will be doing in Chapters 8 and 9 when the parameters of multiple regression—$a, b_1, b_2, \ldots,$ b_k—are tested to determine whether they are significantly different from zero.

With only one significant autocorrelation, we conclude that the order of the moving average is 1, or MA(1), which is the model shown in Equation (7-6). Since the data are seasonal, a seasonal parameter must also be identified. As shown previously, not much information is available for use in doing this. Thus, the best approach is to try both MA and AR seasonal models. It is usually better to start with an MA seasonal model, because generally after taking a long difference, this model is appropriate. Therefore we assume an MA seasonal model as shown in Equation (7-10). Thus, the overall model includes one short and one long difference; it is an MA(1) in the nonseasonal portion, and an MA(1) in the seasonal. This is precisely the model shown in Equation (7-13).

The parameters ϕ_1 and θ_{12} of the model represented by equation (7-13) are

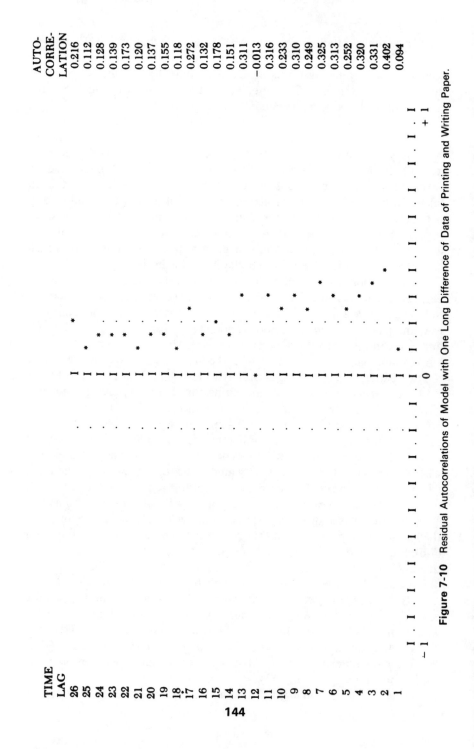

TIME LAG	AUTO-CORRE-LATION
26	0.216
25	0.112
24	0.128
23	0.139
22	0.173
21	0.120
20	0.137
19	0.155
18	0.118
17	0.272
16	0.132
15	0.178
14	0.151
13	0.311
12	-0.013
11	0.316
10	0.233
9	0.310
8	0.249
7	0.325
6	0.313
5	0.252
4	0.320
3	0.331
2	0.402
1	0.094

Figure 7-10 Residual Autocorrelations of Model with One Long Difference of Data of Printing and Writing Paper.

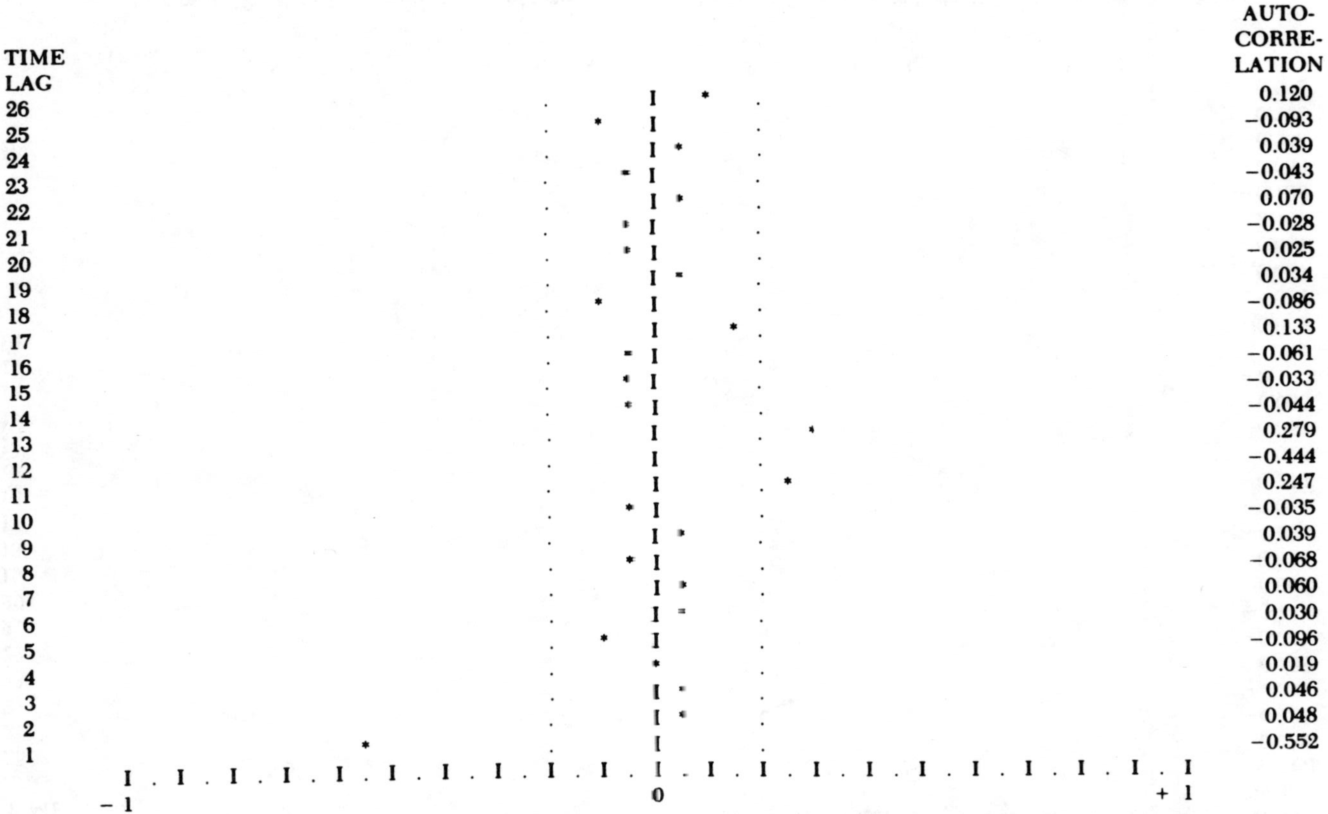

TIME LAG	AUTO-CORRE-LATION
26	0.120
25	-0.093
24	0.039
23	-0.043
22	0.070
21	-0.028
20	-0.025
19	0.034
18	-0.086
17	0.133
16	-0.061
15	-0.033
14	-0.044
13	0.279
12	-0.444
11	0.247
10	-0.035
9	0.039
8	-0.068
7	0.060
6	0.030
5	-0.096
4	0.019
3	0.046
2	0.048
1	-0.552

Figure 7-11 Autocorrelations of One Short and One Long Difference of Data of Printing and Writing Paper.

145

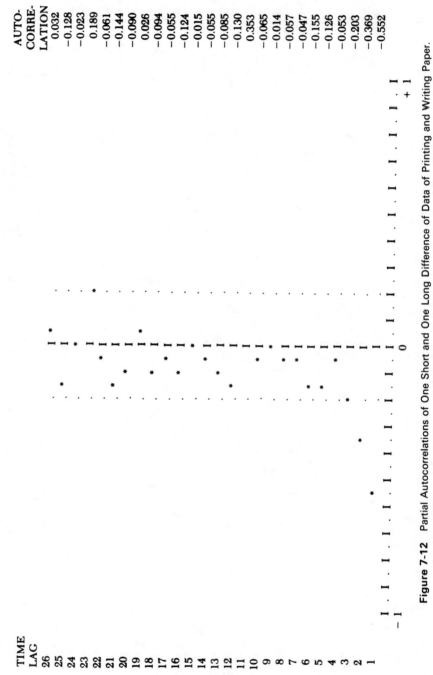

TIME LAG	AUTO-CORRE-LATION
26	0.032
25	−0.128
24	−0.023
23	0.189
22	−0.061
21	−0.144
20	−0.090
19	0.026
18	−0.094
17	−0.055
16	−0.124
15	−0.015
14	−0.055
13	−0.085
12	−0.130
11	0.353
10	−0.065
9	−0.014
8	−0.057
7	−0.047
6	−0.155
5	−0.126
4	−0.053
3	−0.203
2	−0.369
1	−0.552

Figure 7-12 Partial Autocorrelations of One Short and One Long Difference of Data of Printing and Writing Paper.

estimated using a nonlinear optimization algorithm. Computing the residual errors e_t (that is, the difference between actual and forecast values) enables us to test whether they are random, indicating an appropriate model, or nonrandom, indicating that the model is not adequate.

Figure 7-13 shows the autocorrelations of the residuals e_t for the printing and writing paper data. All of the residuals are within the dotted lines, so the hypothesis that they all came from a population whose mean is 0 and whose values are random is supported and can be accepted. Thus, the selected model is appropriate and can be used in forecasting.

The Box–Jenkins methodology for ARMA models is general. For all practical purposes, it can fit a model to all kinds of data patterns. Although it is difficult to use and requires individual involvement to determine the best ARMA model, the method is theoretically elegant and provides an excellent vehicle for illustrating the application of statistical theory to a practical forecasting situation. In the opinion of the authors, its usefulness would be

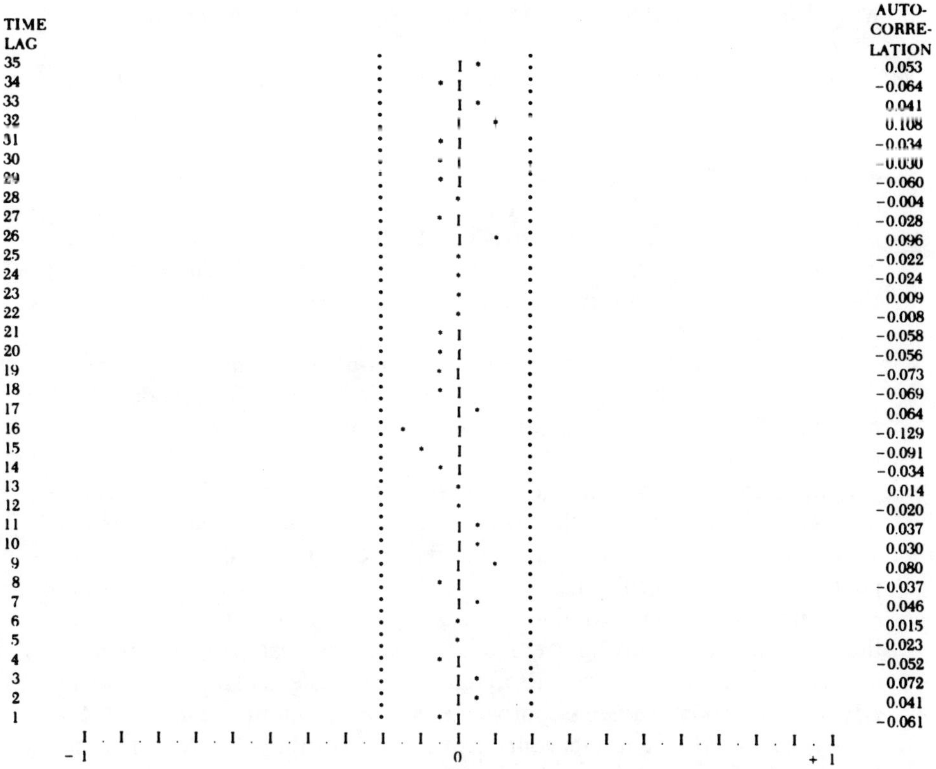

TIME LAG		AUTO-CORRE-LATION
35		0.053
34		−0.064
33		0.041
32		0.108
31		−0.034
30		−0.000
29		−0.060
28		−0.004
27		−0.028
26		0.096
25		−0.022
24		−0.024
23		0.009
22		−0.008
21		−0.058
20		−0.056
19		−0.073
18		−0.069
17		0.064
16		−0.129
15		−0.091
14		−0.034
13		0.014
12		−0.020
11		0.037
10		0.030
9		0.080
8		−0.037
7		0.046
6		0.015
5		−0.023
4		−0.052
3		0.072
2		0.041
1		−0.061

```
I . I . I . I . I . I . I . I . I . I . I . I . I . I . I . I . I . I . I
    − 1                         0                        + 1
```

Figure 7-13 Autocorrelations of Residuals of the Tentatively Identified Model.

increased if automatic, computer-based procedures were used to obtain the forecasts. Such packages are available now, and empirical research has shown that there is little difference between the forecasts prepared by analysts and those prepared automatically by computer programs.

PARZEN'S ARARMA MODELS

A major problem with the Box–Jenkins methodology is the way that stationarity is achieved through differencing. Such an approach to achieve stationarity assumes that the trend is deterministic. This means that the latest trend can influence the forecasts to a much greater extent if, for some random reason, there is a big increase or decline. Although approaches to achieve stationarity without differencing have been proposed (Meese and Geweke, 1984), it is still not clear how stationarity can be achieved in a way that provides accurate results in practice. ARARMA models present an effective way of avoiding the problem of having to deal with stationary time series only.

Parzen's approach to time-series forecasting is a very powerful one. It extends the Box–Jenkins methodology and provides a more practical alternative to time-series forecasting. Furthermore, Parzen's approach can be automated, eliminating the requirement that an analyst must select the model.

Parzen (1982) classifies time series into three categories: those having long memory, Y_t (that is, trend, seasonality, or other types of nonstationarity); those having short memory, $\tilde{Y}_t$; and those containing only "white" noise, ε_t (that is, randomness).

Instead of differencing to transform the long-memory time series Y_t into a short-memory one $\tilde{Y}_t$, Parzen recommends an AR(1) or AR(2) model whose parameters ϕ_1, or ϕ_1 and ϕ_2 can be larger than unity, in order to remove nonstationarity.

If the series is a short-memory one (that is, stationary), Parzen recommends an ARMA model so that its residual errors ε_t will be random. Parzen's approach is not as concerned about parsimony (that is, having as few parameters in the specified model as possible) as the Box–Jenkins methodology. Parzen's method is willing to sacrifice the parsimony that results from the introduction of moving average [MA(q)] terms; instead he is willing to include more autoregressive [AR(p)] terms. Thus, instead of a two-parameter ARMA(1,1) model, Parzen's approach might prefer a four-parameter AR(4) model that could give results equivalent to those of the ARMA(1,1) model. Because the long-memory series is modeled by AR terms and the short-memory series can also be modeled by AR terms (in the great majority of cases), he calls his models ARARMA. The MA terms are available but used only for special cases when an AR scheme cannot be used to produce random residuals. Figure 7-14 is a schematic of the Parzen methodology for ARARMA modeling. (The interested reader can learn more of this approach from Parzen, 1979, 1982, and from the excellent survey article by Harvey, 1984.)

Model Selection and Estimation

The first step in Parzen's approach is to decide whether the time series is long memory or short memory. If it is a long memory, there are two possibilities —either an AR(1) model is used, or an AR(2) model is used. An AR(1) model is preferred when the trend is persistent and does not include major fluctuations around the long-term pattern. An AR(2) model is preferred when the trend is moderate, that is, when it is not persistent and includes cyclical fluctuations. Parzen has developed criteria for determining (1) whether the series is long or short memory and (2) whether an AR(1) or AR(2) model should be selected.

Once an appropriate form of transformation has been chosen and the series is stationary, the next step is to select an appropriate model. This can be an AR(p), an MA(q), or an ARMA(p, q) model, although an AR(p) suffices in most cases. That is, a short memory time series can be adequately modeled by an AR(p) model (where p may be large) if parsimony is not made a paramount criterion for selection.

Determining the order (that is, the value of p) of the best AR(p) order is done using the Akaike information criterion, or another criterion, called CAT (criterion autoregressive transfer function). If the residuals of the model selected are not random, then an MA(q) or an ARMA(p, q) model must be entertained. For more details on how the ARARMA approach can be used, the reader is directed to Selected References at the end of this chapter.

A major advantage of the ARARMA approach is that it can be used automatically or semiautomatically. This eliminates the requirement for personalized analysis and the difficulties and costs that involves. A disadvantage of the approach is that computer programs for its implementation are not widely available.

AEP (ADAPTIVE ESTIMATION PROCEDURE) FILTERING

AEP filtering (Carbone and Longini, 1977) is an extension of the adaptive filtering method developed by Makridakis and Wheelwright (1977). AEP filtering does not require stationarity. Instead the user can specify a trend

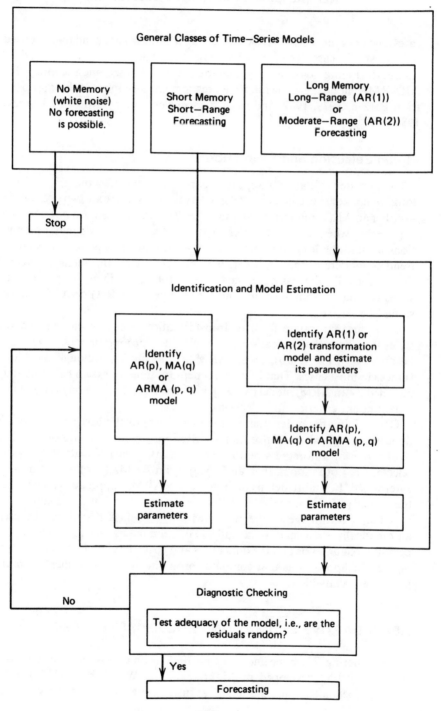

General Classes of Time–Series Models

No Memory (white noise) No forecasting is possible.

Short Memory Short–Range Forecasting

Long Memory Long–Range (AR(1)) or Moderate–Range (AR(2)) Forecasting

Stop

Identification and Model Estimation

Identify AR(p), MA(q) or ARMA (p, q) model

Identify AR(1) or AR(2) transformation model and estimate its parameters

Identify AR(p), MA(q) or ARMA (p, q) model

Estimate parameters

Estimate parameters

Diagnostic Checking

Test adequacy of the model, i.e., are the residuals random?

No

Yes

Forecasting

150

(linear, quadratic, etc.) in addition to assuming an autoregressive model. Equation (7-14) shows the general form of the AEP model, which is made up of three parts. The first part contains the terms $a_{0t} + a_1 t + \ldots + a_{qt} t^q$. These terms take care of the trend in the data. The second part includes the autoregressive terms $\phi_{1t} X_{t-1} + \phi_{2t} X_{t-2} + \ldots + \phi_{pt} X_{t-p}$. Note that the parameters have a t in addition to 1, 2, ..., p. This is to indicate that their values change (adapt) at each time period in order to follow changes in the data pattern. That is, AEP filtering (like all other forms of filters) does not require that the parameters of the model be fixed. Instead they are continuously updated as new information (data) becomes available.

The third part contains L seasonal indices (denoted by I) which take care of the seasonality in the data. Note that the first two parts of Equation (7-14) are multiplied by the seasonal indices to include seasonality, which is thus assumed to be multiplicative.

The AEP model takes the form

$$X_t = [a_{0t} + a_{1t} t + \ldots + a_{qt} t^q + \phi_{1t} X_{t-1} + \ldots + \phi_{pt} X_{t-p}]$$
$$\times [I_{1t}^{z_{1t}} \times I_{2t}^{z_{2t}} \times \ldots \times I_{Lt}^{z_{Lt}}] + e_t. \tag{7-14}$$

The model is specified by three parameters: q, which determines the power of the long-term polynomial (long-term memory) (for example, if $q = 2$, a quadratic function is assumed); p, the number of autoregressive terms to describe short-term variations (short-term memory); and L, the length of seasonality. The z_t terms in the formulation take a value of 1 if we are in season 1 at time t; otherwise they are equal to 0. As indicated, the values of a_j, ϕ_i, and the seasonal indices I_k are not constant as they are in other models. Rather, they are continuously updated as new data become available. This is done as follows:

$$a_{jt} = a_{j(t-1)} + |a_{j(t-1)}| \frac{\hat{e}_t}{\hat{X}_t} \times \frac{t^j}{\overline{t}} \times \mu_t \tag{7-15}$$

$$\phi_{it} = \phi_{i(t-1)} + |\phi_{i(t-1)}| \frac{\hat{e}_t}{\hat{X}_t} \times \frac{X_{t-i}}{\overline{X}_i} \times \mu_t$$

$$I_{lt} = I_{l(t-1)} + I_{l(t-1)} \frac{\hat{e}_t}{\hat{X}_t} \times z_{lt} \times \mu_t$$

where $\hat{e}_t$ is the one-step-ahead error, $\hat{X}_t$ is the estimated value of X_t computed from parameters obtained at time $t - 1$.

In updating, the adjustments AEP makes to the parameters are propor-

Figure 7-14 The Parzen Approach to ARARMA Modeling.

tional to the previous values of such parameters. In addition, the time adjustment of the damping factor allows the system to gear the speed of learning to prevailing conditions. The principle applied to time-adjust the damping factors is similar to that used in adaptive response rate exponential smoothing. AEP can be run in a completely automatic form.

KALMAN FILTERS

Kalman filtering is the most general adaptive estimation procedure. In AEP updating of the parameters is done automatically through the model itself. In Kalman filtering there are many possibilities available that allow us to update not only the model parameters but also the model itself. The difficulty with Kalman filtering is that the user must assign his or her own probabilities as to how the parameters or the model itself should be updated. Adaptive AEP and other filters are all special cases of Kalman filtering.

Another name for Kalman filtering is Bayesian forecasting, a term used by Harrison and Stevens (1971) to describe applications of Kalman filters to forecasting situations.

The basic Kalman filtering model proposed by Harrison and Stevens is

$$Z_t = \mu_t + S_{i,t} + e_t \tag{7-16}$$

$$\mu_t = \mu_{t-1} + \beta_t + \delta\mu_t \tag{7-17}$$

$$\beta_t = \beta_{t-1} + \delta\beta_t \tag{7-18}$$

$$S_{i,t} = S_{i,t-1} + \delta S_{i,t} \tag{7-19}$$

where e_t, $\delta\mu_t$, and $\delta\beta_t$ are normally distributed with means of 0 and variances of v_e, v_μ, and v_β, respectively, and where $Z_t = \log X_t$ and μ_t, β_t, and S_t are the logarithms of the level, trend, and seasonality of the series.

The Kalman filtering approach starts with some preliminary estimates of the level μ_t, the trend β_t, and the seasonality S_t. As new observations become available, the estimates (μ_t, β_t, and S_t) are updated using Equations (7-17), (7-18), and (7-19), respectively. Moreover, Equation (7-16) is used for forecasting purposes.

LEWANDOWSKI'S FORSYS

FORSYS (FORecasting SYStem) is a forecasting method used in Europe by several large companies. Practical in its approach, it incorporates several ideas that make its application attractive.

FORSYS is similar to Winters' exponential smoothing except that the three parameters α, β, and γ are not fixed (as in Winters' method) but are adaptive. Their updating is handled with an estimation procedure called OPS (see Lewandowski, 1979).

The main contributions of FORSYS are that it incorporates special events or actions and that it distinguishes short- and long-term trends while forecasting.

Special Actions and Other Types of Adjustments

FORSYS allows the user to adjust the data for special events such as working-day variations and temperature fluctuations. Such adjustments are made both to the historical data and for forecasting. Special events can be promotions, advertising campaigns, changes in prices, stockouts, competitors' advertising campaigns or promotions, new product introductions, and similar events that influence sales in a nonrandom fashion in the short term (usually for six or fewer periods).

If a special event is unique and very important, statistical methods such as intervention analysis can be used to assess its impact on sales, assuming that the influence of such an event can be estimated judgmentally in an accurate manner. However, for small repetitive events one does not have the time or resources to run sophisticated methods to assess the impact of every special event. This is where FORSYS provides a workable and useful alternative. Moreover, once the various special events and their influences have been recorded, FORSYS provides a historical record of these events, which can be consulted to determine the influence of similar future events on sales.

Working-day adjustments are needed because different months have a different number of working days, *varying* by as much as 20% between successive months. FORSYS, like CENSUS II, allows working-day adjustments as a standard option. This can improve forecasting accuracy considerably.

Adjustments for temperature are extremely important for some products such as beer, ice cream, and heating oil. FORSYS allows for temperature variations and provides the option of specifying a nonproportional influence of temperature changes on sales.

Finally, FORSYS facilitates the incorporation of sales objectives into quantitative forecasts. This is done by adjusting the model's forecasts in such a way that they become equal to those specified through imposed objectives. However, this is not done proportionally; instead, more of the upward changes are assigned to more distant future periods. This reflects the fact that in the short term, imposed objectives cannot alter events significantly because of inertia.

Short- to Long-Term (SL) Forecasting

The principle of SL forecasting is that short-term fluctuations (such as the effects of a recession) in the data are not necessarily permanent. They do not, therefore, have to influence long-term forecasting, which must be based on longer term trends and patterns in the data.

To obtain SL forecasting, FORSYS varies the trend parameter of the exponential smoothing model it uses. Figure 7-15 shows two forecasts, one when the value of the trend is very small (long-term forecast) and one when it is large (short-term forecast). These forecasts, together with the original data, are plotted in Figure 7-15. The SL curve forecasts are found by moving along the different forecasting curves on the right-hand side of Figure 7-15. FORSYS works with these two curves, and possibly others in between, to determine when to switch form one curve to another in selecting the SL forecast.

MULTIVARIATE TIME-SERIES METHODS

The various time-series methods described in this and the preceding two chapters are called *univariate* methods because they include only one variable. This might be adequate in many situations—in particular during the short term when a series has momentum and does not change dramatically

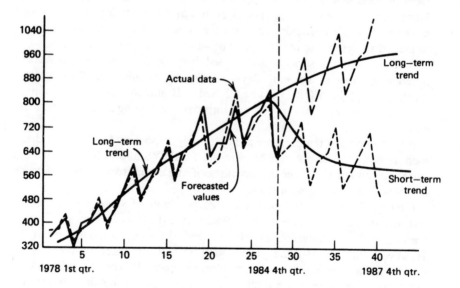

Figure 7-15   Short- and Long-Term Forecasts as Determined by FORSYS.

over the time horizon in question. However, in the medium and long term, univariate methods might not be as appropriate since external events (such as advertising campaigns or price changes) can influence future sales.

Multivariate models attempt to capture and measure the influence of external, independent factors on the dependent variable, say, sales. This is very analogous to multiple regression, which we will cover in Chapter 9. The multivariate ARMA models can be used to combine the concepts of multiple regression with those of univariate time-series models. Equation (7-20) shows this more precisely. The dependent variable is Y, and there are also several independent variables, all of which (along with the dependent variable) are expressed as univariate ARMA models:

$$
\begin{aligned}
Y_t = {} & \delta_1 Y_{t-1} - \delta_2 Y_{t-2} - \cdots - \delta_r Y_{t-r} \qquad\qquad (7\text{-}20)\\
& + \omega_0 X_{t-b} - \omega_1 X_{t-b-1} - \cdots - \omega_s X_{t-b-s}\\
& + \zeta_0 Z_{t-c} - \zeta_1 Z_{t-c-1} - \cdots - \zeta_v Z_{t-c-v}\\
& + \xi_0 W_{t-d} - \xi_1 W_{t-d-1} - \cdots - \xi_u W_{t-d-u} + e_t.
\end{aligned}
$$

To apply Equation (7-20), several steps are required. First, appropriate independent variables (such as X, Z, and W) must be identified. These variables must influence the dependent variable Y in a way that is statistically significant. Second, the number of terms of Y, X, Z and W, must be identified. Third, the values of b, c, and d must be found. These values indicate the number of periods before t that X, Z, and W, respectively, lead the independent variable Y. For instance, if $b = 2$, $c = 1$, and $d = 3$, a change in X will influence Y two periods later, a change in Z will influence Y one period later, and a change in W will influence Y three periods later. The values of b, c, and d must be greater than 0 in order to take real advantage of Equation (7-20). Finally, the parameters δ, ω, ζ, and ξ must be estimated.

There are several procedures for applying Equation (7-20) to actual data: three approaches are best known. These are (1) the transfer function models, (2) the vector autoregressive (VAR) models, and (3) the Kalman filtering approach. A short description of each is provided next.

Transfer Function Models. Box and Jenkins (1976) popularized this approach, which consists of three steps. First, the dependent variables and each of the independent variables are prewhitened. This is done by using a univariate ARMA model on each variable in such a way that the residuals of each of the variables to be included in the transfer function model are random. Second, a model relating the dependent and the independent variables is identified using the residuals (prewhitened values) of each series. The principle for doing so is that the real relationship between the dependent and the independent variables can be found only after spurious correlations caused by trend, seasonality, and other external patterns have been eliminated. Box and Jenkins provide guidelines for identifying appropriate models using the cross correlations or the impulse response function. These allow the user to determine r, s, v, and u, as well as b, c, and d, [see Equation (7-20)]. Third, once the appropriate model has been identified and its parameters are estimated, any systematic errors that are left are modeled through a univariate ARMA model.

VAR Models. Vector autoregressive (VAR) models are simpler than transfer function models, and they are geared toward economic and business data more than are transfer function models, which are most appropriate for engineering applications. The principle of VAR models is a combination of theory (to select appropriate independent variables) and appropriate estimation procedures (to come up with the appropriate values for r, s, v, and u, as well as b, c, and d).

Concerning the theory, the user must understand the factors that influence the variable to be forecast and, if possible, the lag structure (that is the number of periods) between changes in the independent variable and their influence on the dependent variable. If the lag structure is not obvious, experimentation with the data will help the forecaster discover it.

The identification and estimation procedure for VAR models can be based on one of the following:

1. Litterman's (1979) Bayesian approach to VAR models.

2. Parzen's (1982) method for identifying VAR models using appropriate loss functions.

3. Sims's (1982) random coefficient VAR models.

4. Hsiao's (1982) use of final prediction error.

For more details of these and other additional procedures, see Kling and Bessler (1985).

Kalman Filtering. Kalman filtering models are the most general of all multivariate models. At the same time, they require the fewest computations since they are recursive, that is, they update the parameters of the model in a new way similar to exponential smoothing as new data become available. The difficulty with Kalman filtering models is that they require information about the model structure and the variance and covariance of the errors that is not readily available in business applications. This is the reason why Kalman filters are not used at all, as far as we are aware, among businesses.

SELECTED REFERENCES FOR FURTHER STUDY

Abraham, B., and J. Ledolter, 1983. *Statistical Methods for Forecasting*, Wiley, New York.

Box, G. E. P., and G. M. Jenkins, 1976. *Time-series Analysis*, rev. ed., Holden-Day, San Francisco.

Brillinger, D. R., 1975. *Time-Series Data Analysis and Theory*, Holt, Rinehart and Winston, New York.

Carbone, R., 1984. "AEP Filtering," in S. Makridakis et al. (Eds.), *Forecasting Accuracy of Major Time Series*, Wiley, Chichester, England.

Carbone, R., and R. I. Longini, 1977. "A Feedback Model for Automated Real Estate Assessment," *Management Science*, 24, pp. 241–248.

Cleary, J. P., and H. Levenbach, 1982. *The Professional Forecaster*, Lifetime Learning Publications, Belmont, CA.

Cryer, J. D., 1986. *Time Series Analysis*, Duxbury Press, Boston.

Fildes, R., 1984. "Bayesian Forecasting," in S. Makridakis et al. (Eds.) *Forecasting Accuracy of Major Time Series*, Wiley, Chichester, England.

———, 1979. "Quantitative Forecasting—The State of the Art: Extrapolative Models," *Journal of Operational Research Society*, 30, no. 8, pp. 691–710.

Granger, C. W. J., and P. Newbold, 1977. *Forecasting Economic Time Series*, Academic Press, New York.

Harrison, P. J., and C. F. Stevens, 1971. "A Bayesian Approach to Short-Term Forecasting," *Operational Research Quarterly*, 22, no. 4, pp. 341–362.

Harvey, A. C., 1984. "A Unified View of Statistical Forecasting," *Journal of Forecasting*, 3, no. 3, pp. 245–275.

Hsiao, C., 1982. "Autoregressive Modeling and Causal Ordering of Economic Variables," *Journal of Economic Dynamics and Control*, 4, pp. 243–259.

Kling, J., and D. A. Bessler, 1985. "A Comparison of Multivariate Forecasting Procedures for Economic Time Series," *International Journal of Forecasting*, 1, pp. 5–24.

Lewandowski, R., 1979. *La prevision à court terme*, Dunod, Paris

———, 1982. "Sales Forecasting with FORSYS," *Journal of Forecasting*, 1, no. 2, pp. 205–214.

Litterman, R., 1979. "Techniques of Forecasting Using Vector Autoregressions," 115. Federal Reserve Bank of Minneapolis, MN, Working Paper.

Makridakis, S. and S. C. Wheelwright, 1979. "Adaptive Filtering: An Integrated Autoregressive Moving Average Filter for Time Series Forecasting", *Operational Research Quarterly*, vol. 28, pp. 877–888.

Makridakis, S., S. C. Wheelwright, and V. E. McGee, 1989. *Forecasting: Methods and Applications*, 3rd ed., Wiley, New York.

Meese, R., and J. Geweke, 1984. "A Comparison of Autoregressive Univariate Forecasting Procedures for Macroeconomic Time Series," *Journal of Business and Economic Statistics*, 2, pp. 191–200.

Nelson, C. R., 1973. *Applied Time-Series Analysis*, Holden-Day, San Francisco.

Newbold, P., 1983. "ARIMA Model Building and the Time Series Analysis Approach to Forecasting," *Journal of Forecasting* 2, no. 1, pp. 22–35.

O'Donovan, T. M., 1983. *Short Term Forecasting: An Introduction to the Box—Jenkins Approach*, Wiley, Chichester, England.

Parzen, E., 1982. "ARARMA Models for Time-Series Analysis and Forecasting," *Journal of Forecasting*, 1, no. 1, pp. 66–82.

———, 1979. "Forecasting and Whitening Filter Estimation," *Studies in Management Science* 12, pp. 149–166.

Sims, C., 1982. "Policy Analysis with Econometric Models," *Brooking Papers on Economic Activity*, no. 1, pp. 802–816.

Slutsky, E., 1937. "The Summation of Random Causes as the Source of Cyclic Processes," *Econometrica*, 5, pp. 105–146.

Thomopoulos, N. T., 1980. *Applied Forecasting Methods*, Prentice-Hall, Englewood Cliffs, NJ.

Wold, H., 1954. *A Study in the Analysis of Stationary Time Series*. 1st ed. 1938, Almqvist & Wiksell, Stockholm.

Yule, G. U., 1927. "On the Method of Investigting Periodicities in Disturbed Series, with Special Reference to Wolfer's Sunspot Numbers," *Philosophical Transactions* A, 226, pp. 267–298.

———, 1926. "Why Do We Sometimes Get Nonsense-Correlations between Time Series? A study in Sampling and the Nature of Time Series," *Journal of Royal Statistical Society*, 89, pp. 1–64.

CHAPTER 8

SIMPLE REGRESSION METHODS

In the preceding three chapters, several major classes of time-series forecasting methods were examined—exponential smoothing, decomposition, autoregressive/moving average, and filters. Various models within each class were presented, models appropriate for different patterns of data and different conditions.

In this chapter and the next two, we will examine another approach to forecasting—explanatory methods. It is one thing to fit a model (such as an exponential smoothing model) to a time series. It is quite another to come up with other variables that relate to the data series of interest and to develop a model that expresses the way the various variables are related.

Thus these chapters introduce a new concept in the attempt to forecast. A forecast will be expressed as a function of a certain number of factors or variables that influence its outcome. Such forecasts do not necessarily have to be time dependent. Developing an explanatory model facilitates a better understanding of the situation and allows experimentation with different combinations of inputs to study their effects on the forecasts. In this way, explanatory models can, by their basic formulation, be geared toward intervention—influencing the future through decisions made today.

In the application of simple regression, the focus of this chapter, we assume that a relationship exists between the variable we want to forecast (the "dependent" variable) and another variable (the "independent" variable).

Furthermore, we assume that the basic relationship is linear. Thus when we discuss simple linear regression, we mean relationships where Y, the item to be forecast, is a linear function of X, the independent variable. Obviously there are many situations in which this is not a valid assumption; for example, if we were forecasting monthly sales and it was believed that those sales varied according to the seasons of the year, such an approach would be inappropriate (unless the nonlinear seasonality were first transformed into a linear form). It may be, however, that if we were forecasting the same sales items, but on an annual basis, these sales could be modeled using a linear

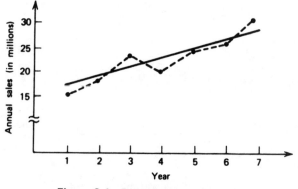

Figure 8-1   Projecting Annual Sales.

relationship. Figure 8-1 represents the pattern of data points that might exist when we look at annual sales.

It can be seen in Figure 8-1 that a straight line sloping upward (that is, a trend going upward) as we go from left to right would give a fairly good approximation of future sales. This was the kind of pattern that we saw in Chapter 5 that could be handled with Holt's linear exponential smoothing. In this chapter, however, we consider a method of handling the same type of pattern, which has different characteristics than the linear smoothing technique.

Figure 8-1 and those that we have considered in earlier chapters all involve forecasting some variable in terms of the time period. Thus, if we were to graph each of these situations, we would have the time variable on the horizontal axis and the variable that we wish to forecast on the vertical axis. Simple regression analysis is a technique that can deal with this type of relationship. We therefore assume that the independent variable X is the time (for example, X can take the values of 1, 2, 3, 4, 5, 6, 7, or 1982, 1983, 1984, 1985, 1986, 1987, 1988, in Figure 8-1).

There are a number of situations where we may want to forecast one variable on the basis of its relationship with two or more independent variables, one of which may be time. Multiple regression analysis, the topic of the next chapter, deals with this type of situation.

Simple regression also can be used when the single independent variable is not time. Consider, for example, a forecasting need faced by a large mail-order house. Each day a tremendous amount of mail is received, much of it containing orders that have to be filled. The mailing department has learned through experience that the number of orders to be filled seems to be related to the weight of the mail. They feel that it would be extremely useful to them if they could weigh the mail when it arrives in the morning and use that weight to predict the number of orders that will have to be filled that day, so they can schedule the time of the people who will fill those orders and decide whether overtime will be necessary.

As a first step in determining whether a relationship exists between mail weight and orders, they have kept a record over several days of the weight of the mail each day and the corresponding number of orders. These pairs of values can be plotted on a graph to identify the relationship between the weight of the mail and the number of orders, if such a relationship exists. It is evident from Figure 8-2 that there is a relationship between the weight of mail and the number of orders. This means that as the weight of mail increases, so does the number of orders. Furthermore, such a relationship is called linear because increases (or decreases) in the amount of mail bring proportional increases (or decreases) in the number of orders received.

The linearity of the relationship can be seen by looking at Figure 8-2 and realizing that the best way of describing the relationship between the weight of mail and the number of orders is the straight line that passes through the middle of all the points that denote weight of mail and number of orders. Figure 8-2 is called a scatter plot or diagram. It helps us visualize, graphically, relationships (or lack thereof) between pairs of variables. The straight line in Figure 8-2 is called the regression line, which can be computed statistically (see below), thus allowing us to measure the extent of the relationship between weight of mail and number of orders, that is, how much the number

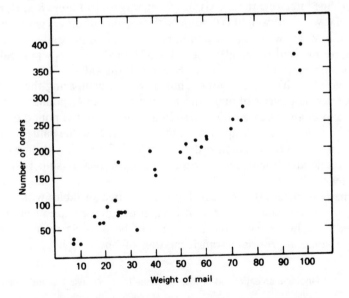

Figure 8-2 Plot of the Number of Orders and Mail Weight.

of orders will increase (or decrease) when the weight of mail increases (or decreases). If such a relationship can be measured, it is obvious that it can be used by the department to forecast the number of orders to be filled each day by the weight of mail received. Such knowledge can improve planning by assigning the right number of people to process orders each day.

This requires an explanatory model between weight and the number of orders. The method we shall examine in this chapter will allow us to obtain such a model through the statistical method of simple regression.

In the use of simple regression, the starting point is the assumption that a basic relationship exists between two variables and can be represented by some functional form. Mathematically it can be written as

$$Y = f(X).$$

This states that the value of Y is a function of (or depends on) the value of X. If it is assumed that the relationship is linear, it can be written as

$$\hat{Y} = a + bX.^* \tag{8-1}$$

Since this is the general form of any linear relationship, it is important that the reader understand just what this means. Suppose that the value of X is 0. In such a case $\hat{Y}$ would have the value a. Thus a is the point at which the straight line intersects the Y axis. If we refer again to Figure 8-2, this would mean that when the weight is 0 pounds, the number of orders would have the value of a, which we would reason to be 0, because if no mail is received, no orders are received (by mail). The value of b in Equation (8-1) is called the regression coefficient and indicates how much the value of $\hat{Y}$ changes when the value of X changes one unit. Thus, if we are comparing the number of orders from 40 pounds of mail with the number from 41 pounds of mail, we would expect an increase of b orders from that additional pound of mail. In the next section of this chapter we discuss exactly how the values of a and b can be computed for the mail-order example. Before doing so, however, it is useful to discuss briefly the concept of a linear relationship between two variables.

In many instances the relationship between two variables with which the manager is concerned is linear. In others, although the relationship does not appear to be linear when plotted, it might be possible to make it linear through some appropriate transformation of one of the variables, which

---

*We use $\hat{Y}$ to indicate an estimated or forecast value for Y. We use Y to indicate an actual or observed value.

would result in a new variable that does have a linear relationship with the other variable.

A simple example will help to illustrate this point. Suppose we have two variables Y and W, whose relationship can be written as $\hat{Y} = a + b/W$. There is not a linear relationship between Y and W. However, if we let $X = 1/W$, this equation can be rewritten as $\hat{Y} = a + bX$, which is a linear relationship.

It is also possible to transform exponential relationships into linear ones through the use of logarithms. Many other nonlinear relationships can therefore be made (transformed to become linear). Although we realize that the topic of transforming nonlinear relationships is not an easy one, we want to point out that such transformations are possible and enhance the applicability of regression analysis to many more types of relationships than just linear ones. The interested reader can find more details in Makridakis, Wheelwright, and McGee (1989).

There are many situations in which regression analysis can be applied successfully and appropriately. The two main strengths to its application in forecasting, are (1) regression analysis can be used to explain what happens to the dependent variable through changes in the independent variable(s), and (2) it uses a statistical model to discover and measure the relationship if one exists. Later on in this chapter we shall see just how this can be done.

DETERMINING THE PARAMETERS OF A STRAIGHT LINE

In the preceding section the notion of a linear relationship that could be represented mathematically as $\hat{Y} = a + bX$ was presented. However, unless the values of a and b can be estimated, the mangaer cannot use the relationship between X and Y to forecast. What is needed, therefore, is a means of estimating the values of a and b. These values are referred to as parameter estimates in the equation for a straight line. Several methods can be used to estimate these parameters. Perhaps the most straightforward technique is to plot the historical observations, as in Figure 8-2 for the mail-order example, and to draw visually a line that passes through the middle of these points. In the mail-order case the line would begin at 0.0 and pass approximately midway among the historical points. Once this is done, the values of the parameters a and b could be read off the graph. Since a is the point at which the line intersects the Y axis, its value would be 0 in this example, and the value of b would be the increase in Y (the number of orders) for a unit (one-pound) increase in X.

Although the graphical method can work fairly well in this example, we often have several hundred observations that are widely scattered. Thus it can be difficult to draw a straight line that in some sense will give the best approximation of the relationship. What is needed is a technique for determining the values of a and b that can be used consistently and gives the "best" result. Regression analysis uses such a method, referred to as the *method of least squares*. To see how it fits a straight line to historical observations, we consider a simple example that includes only four observations,* the values of which are plotted in Figure 8-3. The dependent variable (the item we want to forecast) is the cost of production per unit, and the independent variable (the item that determines the cost of production) is the number of units produced. Thus we would like to determine the relationship between the cost and the number of units in such a form that when we specify the number of units to be produced we can forecast (estimate) their cost.

The dashed line in Figure 8-3 approximates the straight line whose equation is $\hat{Y} = a + bX$ and for which we shall determine the values of a and b. We shall use the method of least squares to determine these values in such a way that the line represents the "best" linear relationship for these four points.

The rationale of the method of least squares is that the distance between the actual observations Y and the corresponding points on the line $\hat{Y}$ should be minimized. More precisely, the criterion is that the sum of the squared

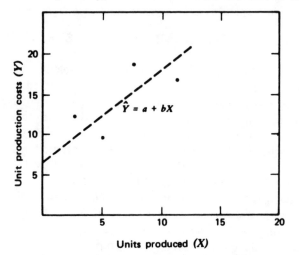

Figure 8-3 Forecasting Production Costs Based on the Number of Units Produced.

*The reader should note that for practical purposes, regression analysis can be applied successfully only when many data points are available. Here we have chosen an example with only four data points to keep the arithmetic at a minimum and to focus attention on the concepts.

errors between the actual cost Y and the estimated $\hat{Y}$ found through the regression line should be kept as small as possible by appropriately choosing a and b. To see what this involves, we consider Figure 8-4, in which the observed values (costs) are labeled Y_1, Y_2, Y_3, and Y_4, the deviations (errors) from the regression line (estimated costs) are labeled e_1, e_2, e_3, and e_4, and the points (costs) estimated by the regression line are labeled $\hat{Y}_1$, $\hat{Y}_2$, $\hat{Y}_3$, and $\hat{Y}_4$. The latter points are what we would forecast by using the regression line with values of X_1, X_2, X_3, and X_4, respectively.

In this figure each of the deviations (errors) can be computed as $e_i = Y_i - \hat{Y}_i$, and each of the values of the regression line can be computed as $\hat{Y}_i = a + bX_i$. The method of least squares determines the values of a and b in such a way that the sum of the squared deviations $\Sigma e_i^2 = \Sigma(Y_i - \hat{Y}_i)^2$ is minimized (hence the name *least squares*).

Through calculus we can determine the values for a and b in such a way as to minimize the sum of squared errors, that is, Σe_i^2. Such values for a and b are found by applying the following two formulas:

$$b = \frac{\Sigma XY/n - \overline{XY}}{\Sigma X^2/n - \overline{X}^2} \tag{8-2}$$

$$a - \overline{Y} \quad b\overline{X} \tag{8-3}$$

where

$$\overline{Y} = \frac{\Sigma Y}{n} \quad \text{and} \quad \overline{X} = \frac{\Sigma X}{n}$$

and n is the number of observations (data points) with which the regression is estimated.

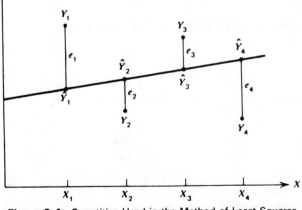

Figure 8-4 Quantities Used in the Method of Least Squares.

To see how these computations can be made in practice, we return to the example given in Figure 8-3. The data, the relevant computations, and the resulting equation for the regression line are given below. The data and computations to find the values of a and b are as follows:

Cost Y	Units X	Y^2	X^2	XY
8	3	64	9	24
11	2	121	4	22
16	5	256	25	80
15	7	225	49	105
$\Sigma Y_i = 50$	$\Sigma X_i = 17$	$\Sigma Y_i^2 = 666$	$\Sigma X_i^2 = 87$	$\Sigma X_i Y_i = 231$

$$\bar{Y} = 50/4 = 12.5$$
$$\bar{X} = 17/4 = 4.25.$$

Then

$$b = \frac{\Sigma XY/n - \bar{X}\bar{Y}}{\Sigma X^2/n - \bar{X}^2} = \frac{231/4 - 12.5(4.25)}{87/4 - (4.25)^2} = 1.254$$

$$a = Y - bX = 12.5 - 1.254(4.25) = 12.5 - 5.33 = 7.17$$

Thus

$$\hat{Y} = 7.17 + 1.254X.$$

The values found using the regression equation $\hat{Y} = 7.17 + 1.254X$ are as follows:

$\hat{Y}$	e	$\hat{Y} - \bar{Y}$	$Y - \bar{Y}$
10.93	−2.93	−1.57	−4.5
9.68	1.32	−2.82	−1.5
13.44	2.56	0.94	+3.5
15.05	−0.95	3.45	+2.5
	$\Sigma e_i = \Sigma(\hat{Y}_i - \bar{Y}) = 0$		$\Sigma(Y_i - \bar{Y}) = 0$

To illustrate further how the method of least squares can be applied, we return to the mail-order example discussed earlier in this chapter. Table 8-1 lists some of the relevant data needed in calculating a and b.

Using Equations (8-2) and (8-3), we obtain

$$b = \frac{\Sigma XY/n - \bar{X}\bar{Y}}{\Sigma X^2/n - \bar{X}^2} = \frac{337,987/30 - 47.3(177.4)}{89,592.9/30 - (47.3)^2} = 3.84$$

$$a = 177.4 - 3.84(47.3) = -4.36.$$

Thus

$$\hat{Y} = -4.4 + 3.8X.$$

Now if a manager wants to forecast what the number of orders will be for a given weight of mail, he or she can do so using this equation. For example, if the company received 45 pounds of mail, the manager would estimate that the number of orders $\hat{Y}$ would be

$$\hat{Y} = -4.4 + 3.8(45) = 166.6.$$

The reader will recall that earlier we reasoned that if no mail were received, no orders would be received (by mail). If we applied the foregoing equation to the extreme, however, it would say that if no mail were received, the company would receive -4.4 orders, which is clearly absurd. This points up the need for applying managerial judgment when using regression analysis results and for identifying a range within which the linear relationship holds but outside of which it may have little meaning. In this example the company probably receives several pounds of mail each day unrelated to actual orders, which would explain why on an average more than one pound of mail must be received before any orders are received, as stated by the regression equation.

Furthermore, it is possible to determine the regression line in such a way that the value of a is equal to 0. The reasoning for doing so can be seen in the next section when the statistical significance of the values of a and b is discussed. At this point we can say that if the manager wants a to equal 0, he or she can recalculate the regression equation (most computer programs allow the user to force the regression equation to pass through 0, that is to make a equal to 0), which becomes:

$$\hat{Y} = \frac{b}{A} X.$$

Table 8-1 Data for Applying the Method of Least Squares in the Mail-Order Example

(1) Observation	(2) Weight of Mail X (Pounds)	(3) Number of Orders Y	(4) X²	(5) Y²	(6) XY
1	70.6591	254.272	4991.30	64,654.10	17,964.10
2	48.3784	199.311	2340.47	39,725.00	9,642.35
3	19.8185	64.693	392.77	4,185.22	1,282.12
4	39.8517	162.644	1588.16	26,453.20	6,481.65
5	50.1270	195.664	2512.71	38,284.20	9,808.02
6	68.4879	238.021	4690.59	56,653.80	16,301.50
7	55.7871	219.089	3112.21	48,000.00	12,222.40
8	96.7574	392.389	9361.99	153,969.00	37,966.60
9	40.5927	151.125	1647.76	22,838.70	6,134.55
10	52.7543	210.728	2783.01	44,406.30	11,116.80
11	7.2491	33.963	52.55	1,153.49	246.20
12	73.2380	256.993	5363.80	66,045.50	18,821.70
13	96.3148	347.976	9276.54	121,087.00	33,515.20
14	18.1598	65.733	329.77	4,320.86	1,193.70
15	93.5000	377.330	8742.26	142,378.00	35,280.40
16	25.4237	83.491	646.36	6,804.89	2,097.24
17	24.0767	82.211	579.68	6,758.64	1,979.37
18	74.6311	281.124	5569.80	79,030.70	20,980.60
19	53.1468	180.763	2824.58	32,675.20	9,606.97
20	28.5609	86.153	815.72	7,422.41	2,460.62
21	10.5201	23.890	110.67	570.74	251.32
22	21.1329	98.291	446.59	9,661.13	2,077.17
23	58.9518	206.030	3475.31	42,448.50	12,145.90

24	60.6061	221.245	3673.10	48,949.40	13,408.80
25	24.4888	105.029	599.70	11,031.00	2,572.03
26	16.7616	77.943	280.95	6,075.26	1,306.47
27	7.6762	24.240	58.92	587.62	186.08
28	60.8193	224.298	3698.99	50,309.60	13,641.70
29	94.3726	369.987	8906.18	136,891.00	34,916.60
30	26.8395	88.626	720.35	7,854.70	2,378.70

$\Sigma X = 1419.6 \quad \Sigma Y = 5322\,0 \quad \Sigma X^2 = 89,592.9 \quad \Sigma Y^2 = 1,281,220 \quad \Sigma XY = 337,987$

$\bar{X} = 1419.6/30 = 47.3$

$\bar{Y} = 5322.0/30 = 177.4$

The versatility and real power of simple regression have been explained only partly so far. Although we have developed the equations necessary to specify the most appropriate linear relationship, two other questions are of concern. First, what is the reliability of the forecasts based on a given regression line? For example, if this forecasting method indicates in the mail-order example that the number of orders will be 166.6, how certain can the manager be that the actual number of orders will not fluctuate between, say, 146.6 and 186.6? Second, when is it not appropriate to say that one variable is influenced by another because no real relationship between the two can be established? (These two questions are discussed in the next section).

THE PRECISION AND SIGNIFICANCE OF A REGRESSION EQUATION

It is possible to make statistical statements about the significance of the regression equations. The use of the statistical properties will also allow us to make statements about the likelihood that future values will vary from the forecast by certain amounts, the confidence that we can place in having determined the most appropriate straight line, and the accuracy of the coefficients a and b.

Several questions concerning the significance of an application of regression analysis can be dealt with in statistical terms. We consider three of them at this point:

1. Is the regression coefficient b significantly different from 0, or did it just occur by chance? The same question can be asked about the value of a.

2. What level of confidence can be placed in the regression coefficients a and b, that is, how precise is the estimate of a or b? For what range of values around a or b can the manager be confident that the true values of a or b are within those ranges?

3. How confident can the manager be when making a forecast $\hat{Y}$ that the actual value of Y will lie within a range around that forecast value, that is, what is the precision of $\hat{Y}$?

Turning first to the question of the significance of the regression coefficient b, we would like to know whether the true value of b is really different from 0. (If b is not different from 0, the best model will be $Y = \bar{Y}$.) Since we have estimated the value of b on the basis of a limited number of observations, we might have found a value different from 0 merely by chance. Thus what we would like to do, using statistics, is to say: if we suppose that the true value of b is 0, what is the likelihood (or chance) that we could have had our specific value of b?

The statistic needed to determine the significance of a regression coefficient is the standard error of that coefficient. For b this can be computed using Equation (8-4)

$$SE_b = \frac{\sqrt{\Sigma(Y_i - \hat{Y}_i)^2/(n - 2)}}{\sqrt{\Sigma(X_i - \bar{X})^2}} \tag{8-4}$$

The numerator in this equation is called the standard deviation of regression.

This is the square root of the sum of the squared errors ($e_i = Y_i - \hat{Y}_i$) adjusted for degrees of freedom. The denominator is the square root of the sum of the squared deviations of X from the mean $\bar{X}$. Because there is a lot of arithmetic involved in computing SE_b, the standard error of b, this computation is usually done as an integral part of a computer program. To see how this standard error can be applied in practice, we can compute it for the mail-order example:

$$SE_b = \frac{\sqrt{\Sigma(Y_i - \hat{Y}_i)^2/(n - 2)}}{\sqrt{\Sigma(X_i - \bar{X})^2}}$$

$$= \frac{14.63}{149.3} = 0.098.$$

The value of the standard error tells us something about the precision of the estimated regression coefficient b (whose value was found to be 3.8). By making the assumption that the various values of b (which can be found from many different samples, of size 30, of weight of mail and number of orders) are normally distributed, we can establish the maximum possible error in the estimated value of b (it is related to the value of the standard error of 0.098). Thus, in the worst case scenario, which would include practically all cases, the real value of b cannot be outside the range of $b \pm 3SE_b$, or 3.8 ± 0.294. That is, b can vary from about 3.5 to 4.1. This means that the real value of b cannot be 0 for any practical purposes.

Alternatively, we can compute the number of standard errors our value of b is from 0. Since $b = 3.8$ we divide 3.8 by 0.098 and obtain about 38. Thus the b value we computed is approximately 38 standard errors from 0. Using a table of t values, we find that the likelihood of computing a regression coefficient in error by 40 standard errors or more is essentially 0. Therefore, we can conclude with an almost 100% certainty that the regression coefficient is significantly different from 0 in this case.

Although the statistical theory behind standard errors may seem complicated, its application is straightforward, particularly when a computer program is used. Table 8-2, for instance, shows the computer output for the mail-order example using ISP (Interactive Statistical Program). The Y (denoting Yes) next to the regression coefficient b (POUNDSM) means that the real value of b is significantly different from 0. That is, increases or decreases in the weight of mail influence the number of orders not by chance but in a consistent, statistical manner. Furthermore, under the heading P Value, the value of 0 signifies the probability that the value of the computed coefficient is equal to 0.

The same computations can be found concerning the value of a. In this case the standard error of a is equal to 5.35, which means that the computed t-test for $a = -4.4$ is -0.82. Furthermore, the P Value is equal to 0.42, which indicates that the likelihood that the real value of a will be equal to 0 is high.

Table 8-3 shows the same computer output as Table 8-2, except that the value of a has been forced to become 0. The regression equation can be seen to be

$$\hat{Y} = bX$$

$$\hat{Y} = 3.77X.$$

The final point that we deal with here is the significance of an individual forecast. We would like to know, once we have found the values of a and b

Table 8-2   Regression Results of the Mail-Order Example Using ISP

Variable	Coefficient	Standard Error	t Test	Signif	P Value
a	-4.374343	5.348527	-0.818	N	0.420
POUNDSM	3.84204	0.09787115	39.256	Y	0.000

Critical t value from table ($\alpha = 0.05$) $= 2.048$.
$R^2 = 0.982$; R^2(adjusted) $= 0.982$; $R = 0.991$;*
F^2 test $= 1541.04$; standard deviation of regression $= 14.65156$;
observations $= 30$; degrees of freedom for numerator $= 1$, for denominator $= 28$.
F value from table ($\alpha = 0.05$) $= 4.17$.

*The symbol for the square of the correlation coefficient above is R^2 while in equations (8-6) and (8-7) we use r^2. This is so because the computer does not distinguish between simple regression where r^2 is used and multiple regression (see next chapter) where R^2 is used.

Table 8-3 Regression Results of the Mail-Order Example Using ISP

Variable	Coefficient				P
a	0.0	Standard Error	t Test	Signif	Value
POUNDSM	3.772725	0.04953009	76.170	Y	0.000

Critical t value from the table (α = 0.05) = 2.048.
R^2 = 0.982; R^2(adjusted) = 0.981; R = 0.991;
F Test = 1504.44; standard deviation of regression = 14.82550;
observations = 30; degrees of freedom for numerator = 1, for
denominator = 28.
F value from table (α = 0.05) = 4.17.

in our regression equation and have substituted a value of X into that
equation, how confident we can be that the true value of Y will be around the
value computed with $\hat{Y} = a + bX$. That is, we would like to have a confidence
interval around this computed value of $\hat{Y}$.

The basis for establishing the confidence interval of a specific forecast value
is the standard error of forecast SE_f, which can be computed using

$$SE_f = \left(\sqrt{\frac{\Sigma(Y_i - \hat{Y}_i)^2}{n-2}}\right)\left(\sqrt{1 + \frac{1}{n} + \frac{(X_f - \bar{X})^2}{\Sigma(X_i - \bar{X})^2}}\right). \qquad (8-5)$$

As with the standard error of the regression coefficient SE_b, it can be seen
that the first factor in Equation (8-5) is simply the standard deviation for the
errors e_i (adjusted for degrees of freedom), or the standard deviation of
regression. The second factor in expression (8-5) is an adjustment for how far
we are from $\bar{X}$ in making our forecast (that is, the difference between X_f and
$\bar{X}$), and the number of observations n used in determining the regression
equation. Note that if the values of X_i are not close to the mean $\bar{X}$ and n is
large, the second factor in Equation (8-5) is approximately equal to 1 and the
standard error of forecast, SE_f is simply the standard deviation of the regression. If, however, n is small, or if the values of X_i are close to the mean $\bar{X}$, or
if the value being forecast X_f is far from $\bar{X}$, then the second factor in Equation
(8-5) will be greater than 1, and the standard error of forecast will be larger
than the standard deviation.

In the forecast we made earlier, the value of X was 45 pounds. Thus we can
substitute this value for X_f in Equation (8-5) and obtain

$$SE_f = 14.6\sqrt{\left[1 + 0.03 + \frac{(45 - 47.3)^2}{2446}\right]} = 14.6(1.03) = 14.9.$$

In this example there is little adjustment in the standard deviation value of 14.6 because X is close to the mean value $\bar{X}$. If we want to establish a confidence interval for our estimate of Y (where we had $\hat{Y} = -4.4 + 3.8(45) = 166.6$), this interval will be $166.6 \pm 2(14.9)$. Thus, we are 95% certain that the true value of Y (that is, orders to be filled) will be between 136.8 and 196.4 when we receive 45 pounds of mail. Note that we use a value of 2 to multiply the standard error because we assume a 95% confidence interval, in which case the t value required to multiply the standard error is close to 2 (the exact value is 2.045). If we had wanted a 99.8% confidence interval, we should have multiplied the value of the standard error by about 3. Alternatively, if we had wanted a 68% confidence interval, we should have multiplied the standard error by the approximate value of 1. (See Figure 8-5 for confidence intervals of 68%, 95%, and 99.8%.)

The fact that the confidence interval surrounding a forecast varies according to the distance we are from X is shown in Figure 8-5. As a practical matter, the usable range of X values—where the regression can be applied confidently—depends on the amount of data used, the spread of X values around their mean, and how well the regression model captures the variation in these data.

From the mail-order example the amount of information that can be obtained from making these tests of significance should be evident. In this

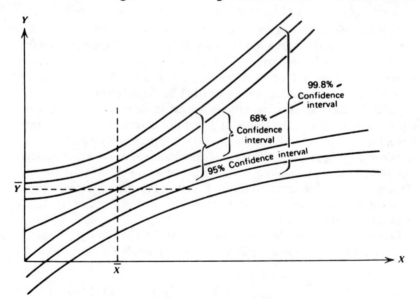

Figure 8-5   Ranges of Confidence of Individual Forecasts.

instance we found that the regression coefficient b was significantly different from 0 and that its true value would lie between 3.5 and 4.1. In addition, we found that in estimating the number of orders included in 45 pounds of mail we could be 95% sure that the orders would be between 136.8 and 196.4. Since this is a wide range, it would require management to contemplate the uncertainty surrounding the most likely forecast of 166.6 and take steps to deal with situations where the orders to be filled are around the two extreme ranges.

In concluding this section on signifiance, we want to emphasize one point: the role that the sample size plays in this area. (The sample size is simply the number of observations used in determining the regression line.) As a sample size becomes larger, the width of the confidence interval becomes smaller, as can be seen in Equation (8-5). Thus if we had 100 observations in the mail-order example, the confidence interval on a specific forecast (for example, for 45 pounds of mail) would usually be narrower than it was when we had only 30 observations. Any time the manager can obtain additional observations before computing a regression line, he or she should do so.

One of the advantages of simple regression analysis is that once the relationship $\hat{Y} = a + bX$ has been determined, it can be used to make any number of forecasts simply by inserting the value of X for which a forecast of Y is desired. One caution: the basic relationship should be assessed periodically. If the manager has some reason to believe that a change may have taken place, it will be necessary to collect a new set of data and recompute the values of a and b.

SIMPLE CORRELATION

The assumption made in the three preceding sections that dealt with simple regression is that one variable is dependent on another. Often two variables may be related, although it is not appropriate to say that the value of one of the variables depends on or is influenced by the value of the other. In such a situation, the correlation between the two variables can be found. The coefficient of correlation r is a relative measure of the degree of relationship that may exist between two variables. This coefficient can vary from 0 (which indicates no correlation) to ± 1 (which indicates perfect correlation). When the correlation coefficient is greater than 0, the two variables are said to be positively correlated; when it is less than 0, they are said to be negatively correlated. For simple regression, the sign of the correlation coefficient is always the same as the sign of the regression coefficient b.

The correlation coefficient can be found using the formula

$$r = \frac{n\Sigma X_i Y_i - \Sigma X_i \Sigma Y_i}{\sqrt{n\Sigma X_i^2 - (\Sigma X_i)^2}\ \sqrt{n\Sigma Y_i^2 - (\Sigma Y_i)^2}} \tag{8-6}$$

To compute the correlation coefficient we need to substitute the various sums in Equation (8-6) by their values as shown in Table 8-1. The value of r, therefore, is

$$r = \frac{30(337,987) - 1419.6(5322)}{\sqrt{30(89,592.9)(1419.6)^2}\ \sqrt{30(1,281,220) - (5322)^2}}$$

$$= \frac{10,139,610 - 7,555,111.2}{\sqrt{672,522.84}\ \sqrt{10,112,916}} = \frac{2,584,498.8}{2,607,904.7} = 0.991.$$

Since the value of r equals 0.991 (very close to 1), there is a very strong positive correlation (association, relationship) between the weight of mail received and the number of orders to be filled. As one goes up, so does the other.

The advantage of a correlation coefficient is that it is a relative measure and, as noted, it varies between 0 and ± 1. Thus it is easy to recognize the strength of a relationship between any two variables. A correlation coefficient close to 1 means a very strong relationship. One that is close to 0 indicates a weak relationship or none at all. On the other hand, if we want to measure how much X influences Y, then the value of the regression coefficient b is needed. In this sense the correlation coefficient r and the regression coefficient b provide us with complementary information. This is why all simple regression computer programs compute both b and r.

Another useful statistical measure in regression analysis is r^2. The formula for finding r^2 is given by

$$r^2 = \frac{\text{explained variation*}}{\text{total variation}} = \frac{\Sigma(\hat{Y}_i - \bar{Y})^2}{\Sigma(Y_i - \bar{Y})^2}. \tag{8-7}$$

r^2 varies between 0 and 1 and is a measure of the goodness of fit. It tells us [see Equation (8-6)] the percentage of the total variation explained by the regression line. In a perfect regression, where the errors between actual Y_i and

---

*It is called *explained* because it improves (that is, reduces) the variation or error over the alternative to the regression line, which is to use the mean value $\bar{Y}$, as a way of forecasting. The amount of improvement, that is, $\hat{Y}_i - \bar{Y}$, is then the *explained variation* of regression, over and above that of the mean.

estimated $\hat{Y}_i$ are 0, the value of r^2 will be equal to 1. If r^2 is close to 0, the regression equation $\hat{Y}_i = a + bX_i$ does not explain much more than if the mean ($\hat{Y} = \bar{Y}$) is used as an alternative to the regression line.

Table 8-4 shows the total variations between the production costs Y_i used previously and their mean $\bar{Y} = 12.5$. If each of these four distances $Y_i - \bar{Y}$ is squared and the values are summed, the sum will provide us with the denominator of Equation (8-7). The calculations can be seen in Table 8-4. the explained variations (deviations) can also be seen in Table 8-4 as the difference between $\hat{Y}_i$ and $\bar{Y}$. If these variations are squared and the values summed, the sum will provide us with the numerator of equation (8-7). The ratio of the two squared sums is the value of r^2. Thus,

$$r^2 = \frac{\Sigma(\hat{Y}_i - \bar{Y})^2}{\Sigma(Y_i - \bar{Y})^2} = \frac{23.204}{41} = 0.566.$$

This means that the regression line $\hat{Y} = 1.254 + 7.17X$ explains 56.6% of the total variation in costs by the variation in the amount of units produced. Obviously, with only four data points this statement may not mean much. However, if a larger amount of data ia available, r^2 will tell us what percentage of the total variation in Y is explained by variations in X.

Let us now compute r^2, or the coefficient of determination, as r^2 is also known, for the mail-order example of the preceding sections. Again we will use Equation (8-7),

$$r^2 = \frac{\Sigma(\hat{Y}_i - \bar{Y})^2}{\Sigma(Y_i - \bar{Y})^2} = \frac{808}{823} = 0.982.$$

The appropriate interpretation here is that for the 30 sample observations that were used in fitting the regression line, 98.2% of the variation from the mean $\bar{Y}$ was explained by that regression line $\hat{Y} = -4.4 + 3.8X$. Thus, almost all changes in the number of orders received every day can be explained by the weight of the mail received that day. The remaining 1.8%, which cannot be explained, is caused by random factors (for examples, some people might use heavy envelopes and paper) or by other variables in addition to weight (such as requests for information as a result of an advertising campaign).

In simple regression the square root of r^2 is equal to the simple correlation coefficient. This can be verified in the case of the mail-order example. The square root of 0.982 is equal to 0.991, the correlation coefficient computed using Equation (8-6).

Another useful statistical measure used in regression analysis is the F ratio. This is given by

Table 8-4 Total and Explained Variations for the Production Cost Example

Observation	Actual Cost Y	Mean Cost $\bar{Y}$	Value Estimated by Regression Line $\hat{Y}$	Total Variation $(Y_i - \bar{Y})^2$	Explained Variation $(\hat{Y}_i - \bar{Y})^2$
1	8	12.5	10.93	20.25	1.465
2	11	12.5	9.68	2.25	7.952
2	16	12.5	13.44	12.25	0.884
4	15	12.5	15.95	6.25	11.903
				$\Sigma(Y_i - \bar{Y})^2 = 41$	$\Sigma(\hat{Y}_i - \bar{Y})^2 = 23.204$

$$F = \frac{\Sigma(\hat{Y}_i - \bar{Y})^2/(k - 1)}{\Sigma(Y_i - \hat{Y}_i)^2/(n - k)} \qquad (8\text{-}8)$$

where n = sample size (number of observations)

k = number of variables (k = 2 for simple regression).

It should be readily apparent from Equation (8-8) that the value of the F statistic is similar to the r^2 calculation—except that it uses the "unexplained" variance in the denominator and it is dependent on the value of the sample size n. As n gets larger, the number in the denominator in the F statistic gets smaller and the F statistic increases in value.

The F test for the mail-order example is

$$F = \frac{\Sigma(\hat{Y}_i - \bar{Y})^2/(k - 1)}{\Sigma(Y_i - \hat{Y}_i)^2/(n - k)}$$

$$= \frac{808/1}{14.63/28}$$

$$= 1540.$$

This value of F must be compared with the appropriate entry in a statistical table of F-test values to determine its significance for a given confidence level. However, because most computer programs provide this value, it is not necessary to know how to use such a table. What is necessary is that the F value computed using Equation (8-8) be greater than the corresponding value from the table, which in our case (using a 95% confidence interval) is equal to 4.18. In the mail-order example, where the computed F is 1540, which is much larger than 4.18, we conclude that the relationship between the number of orders and the weight of mail is statistically significant (that is, it is not the result of chance).

Let us now determine the significance of the relationship we computed for the simple example of four data points. The reader will recall that we found that $r^2 = 0.566$, or 56.6% of the variation was explained. Using equation (8-8), we can compute the F statistic for this example as

$$F = \frac{23.2/1}{17.8/2} = 2.61.$$

To determine whether the relationship $\hat{Y} = -4.4 + 3.8X$ is significantly different from 0, we have to compare this F value of 2.61 with the corresponding value from the F table. At the 95% level and for four observations such a value is 6.61. Thus in this example, even though $r^2 = 0.566$, we *cannot* say with any confidence that the regression line is significantly different from 0. That is, the relationship between units produced and cost may well be the result of chance, because the computed F of 2.61 is smaller than the corresponding value of 6.61 from the F table.

The importance of computing the overall significance of a regression equation should be emphasized. Only when the manager can say that it is significant does it make sense to use the regression equation to forecast. That is, if the sample size is so small or the relationship so weak that it is not significant, even though the coefficient of determination may be close to 1, the manager should not base a forecast on those data and the corresponding regression line.

THE REGRESSION EQUATION AS A MODEL

The regression equation $\hat{Y} = a + bX$, like any other form of equation, can be thought of as an abstract model that represents some aspect of reality. When, for example, we say that Y represents sales and X represents time, what we are actually doing is making an abstract model. We try to simplify reality and represent it in terms of the interaction of two factors only. As managers are well aware, however, this is a gross simplification; reality is much more complex. Sales are not influenced by time alone, but by a myriad of other factors such as GNP, prices, competitors' actions, transportation costs, production costs, advertising, government policies, or even the illness of a salesperson. Then how can we ignore them?

In any modeling effort there is a choice: we can either construct a simple model that may not completely duplicate reality, or we can build a complex model that is more accurate, but also requires a large amount of effort and resources to be developed and manipulated. Even if the most sophisticated model could be developed, there would still be some part of reality that could not be explained by the model. The number of factors in real-life phenomena is infinite.

To capture the fact that a part of the real process cannot and will not be explained by a regression model, we can use the term u to denote the variations unexplained by the model. This term is often called the *disturbance term*, or *white noise*, and it plays an important role in most forecasting methods.

Thus to be precise, our simple regression equation is not $\hat{Y} = a + bX$, but $Y = a + bX + u$, even though the term u is seldom needed for calculation or any other practical purpose. Its theoretical meaning is that the forecast can vary from the estimated value $\hat{Y} = a + bX$ by an amount u, the error, which we can estimate in probabilistic terms, as we learned in the preceding sections of this chapter. It becomes obvious, however, that the magnitude of the error u will vary from model to model. Theoretically the more variables we introduce, the smaller the range of values taken on by u. There is a limit, however, to the number of variables we can employ, since they introduce more complexity and higher cost. Thus we want to introduce the smallest number of variables (the principle of parsimony) and at the same time achieve a range of values for u as small as possible.

For the regression equation $Y = a + bX + u$ to be statistically correct, u must have the following properties:

1. The mean value of u must be equal to 0, because many factors that influence Y are not included in the regression equation. However, their influence is of opposite directions, so they tend to offset one another on average.

2. The error term u must be a random variable. At any time period, some of the factors not included in the equation will influence Y more than others. This may result in a positive or negative u. However, as long as the individual values of u at each time period are random (not the result of any systematic pattern), their effect on the estimated value of Y can be determined probabilistically. Basically, we want the errors to be independent of one another.

3. The disturbance term u must be *normally distributed*. (A *normal distribution* is commonly referred to as a bell-shaped curve dispersed around the mean value of 0.) This is a consequence of the large number of factors that influence Y that are not included in the regression equation. In this case, as in many others, it is more probable that extreme variations will cancel themselves out and thus be observed only infrequently, whereas in the majority of cases the errors will be clustered around the mean value. Such a pattern results in a normal distribution.

4. The variance of u must be constant. This means that the error term must neither increase nor decrease within the entire range of observations.

Violations in these properties of u can result in serious trouble, since the complete regression model

$$Y = a + bX + u$$

will no longer be correct. As we shall see in Chapter 9, however, there are ways of minimizing the likelihood that any of these properties will be violated in a specific application.

From now on, as we have done before, we imply $Y = a + bX + u$ when we write a regression equation, even though u will not be included. Thus we use the term $\hat{Y}$. That is

$$Y = a + bX + u$$

but we will use

$$\hat{Y} = a + bX.$$

The same is true for multiple regression, where

$$Y = a + b_1 X_1 + b_2 X_2 + b_3 X_3 + \ldots + b_n X_n + u$$

but we will use

$$\hat{Y} = a + b_1 X_1 + b_2 X_2 + b_3 X_3 + \ldots + b_n X_n.$$

Finally, when we use the sample data to estimate $\hat{Y}$, the difference between the estimate $\hat{Y}$ and the actual Y is the regression, or residual error. We have denoted such a value by e. The residual error e is different from u, because it is the result of a specific and limited sample, whereas u would exist if it were possible to have an extremely large sample or even to include all the data. Like u, e must fulfill the four properties mentioned above.

In the next chapter the concept of regression will be extended to include more than one independent variable, and methods of testing the assumptions concerning the four properties required of u or e will be presented.

SELECTED REFERENCES FOR FURTHER STUDY

Chatterjee, S., and B. Price, 1977. *Regression Analysis by Example*, Wiley, New York.

Draper, N., and H. Smith, 1981. *Applied Regression Analysis*, 2nd ed., Wiley, New York.

Intrilligator, M. D., 1978. *Econometric Methods, Techniques, and Applications*, Prentice-Hall, Englewood Cliffs, NJ.

Johnson, J., 1972. *Econometric Methods*, 2nd ed., Prentice-Hall, Englewood Cliffs, NJ.

Makridakis, S., S. C. Wheelwright, and V. E. McGee, 1989. *Forecasting: Methods and Applications*, 3rd ed., Wiley, New York, chaps. 5 and 6.

Pindyck, R. S., and D. L. Rubenfeld, 1976. *Econometric Models and Economic Forecasts*, McGraw-Hill, New York.

Wetherill, G. B., 1986. *Regression Analysis with Applications*, Chapman and Hall, London.

Wonnacott, H., and R. J. Wonnacott, 1986. *Regression: A Second Course on Statistics*, Krieger, Melbourne.

CHAPTER 9

MULTIPLE REGRESSION

In Chapter 8 simple regression and correlation were introduced and discussed. In simple regression the basic proposition is that an independent variable can be used to predict the value of some dependent variable (the quantity to be forecast) on the basis of a linear relationship between the two variables. In the major example in that chapter the variable to be forecast was the number of orders received daily by a mail-order house. The independent variable on which that forecast was based was the weight of all mail for that day. In many decision-making situations more than one variable can be used to explain or forecast a certain dependent variable. For example, in the mail-order situation the day of the week, as well as the weight of mail received, might be used to predict the number of orders.

In situations where more than a single independent variable is necessary to forecast accurately, simple regression is not adequate. The idea of simple regression can be generalized, however, through the technique of multiple regression to allow the manager to include more than one independent variable. This chapter examines the extension and application of the basic principles of simple regression to situations in which several independent variables affect the outcome of some dependent variable.

The specific example we will use in this chapter to illustrate the principles and concepts of multiple regression and multiple correlation concerns the forecasting of annual sales for a company in the glass business. Table 9-1 lists some of the historical information that this company, California Plate Glass (CPG), has gathered.

This table contains data not only on the variable company sales (net sales), but also on two other variables, annual automobile production and the number of building contracts awarded annually. The management of CPG believes that its net sales are closely tied to these other two industries, since its major customers are automobile producers and building contractors. We assume that as a part of the planning process, top management has asked for a forecast of corporate sales on an annual basis for the next five years.

Table 9-1   Historical Data Relating to CPG Sales

·Year	Net Sales, CPG, (Millions of Dollars)	Automobile Production (Millions of Units)	Building Contracts Awarded (Millions of Starts)
1972	280.0	3.909	9.43
1973	281.5	5.119	10.36
1974	337.4	6.666	14.50
1975	404.2	5.338	15.75
1976	402.1	4.321	16.78
1977	452.0	6.117	17.44
1978	431.7	5.559	19.77
1979	582.3	7.920	23.76
1980	596.6	5.816	31.61
1981	620.8	6.113	32.17
1982	513.6	4.258	35.09
1983	606.9	5.591	36.42
1984	629.0	6.675	36.58
1985	602.7	5.543	37.14
1986	656.7	6.933	41.30
1987	778.5	7.638	45.62
1988	877.6	7.752	47.38
1989 (est.)		6.400	48.51
1990 (est.)		7.900	51.23
1991 (est.)		8.400	57.47
1992 (est.)		8.600	61.03
1993 (est.)		8.900	66.25

Although the results of simple regression analysis may be satisfactory for forecasting sales, management probably would prefer to use the information it has on automobile production and building contracts at the same time; that is, since management knows that both factors are important and that they move somewhat independently of each other, it would like to be able to forecast net CPG sales as a function of both automobile production and building contracts awarded. Mathematically such a relationship could be written as

net sales CPG = f(automobile production, building contracts awarded).

This equation states that net sales for the company depend on two independent variables—automobile production and building contracts awarded. Although several different forms of the equation could be written to show the relation between these variables, a straightforward one would be

$$\hat{Y} = a + b_1 X_1 + b_2 X_2 \tag{9-1}$$

where $\hat{Y}$ = estimated value of CPG annual sales
    X_1 = annual automobile production
    X_2 = annual building contracts awarded.

From this equation it can be seen that if either X_1 or X_2 were elimiated, we would have the same situation that we handled with simple linear regression. Since we have more than one independent variable (X_1 and X_2), the regression is known as *multiple*. Note that in Equation (9-1) the dependent variable (the one we wish to forecast) is expressed as a linear function of the independent variables X_1 and X_2.

Just as we used the method of least squares in Chapter 8 to find the coefficients a and b, we can use the same idea here to estimate the best values for a, b_1, and b_2. In simple linear regression that method amounted to fitting a straight line to the data points in a manner that minimized the sum of the squared errors. We represented that graphically by letting one axis represent Y and the other X. In the case of two independent variables, X_1 and X_2, we need a three-dimensional graph. The situation, however, is completely analogous to two dimensions, but we now have three axes, Y, X_1, and X_2, and we are trying to fit a plane to the data points available. We do that by minimizing the sum of the squared deviations from the plane.

In general, we could have several independent variables and we could still apply the method of least squares to solve for the values of a, b_1, b_2, . . . , b_k. Multiple regression allows us to determine the estimated values of these parameters using the principle of least squares.

When we move beyond the case of simple regression, the computations and mathematics become quite complicated, although they follow the same basic concepts of simple regression. Because of this complexity, we will not go into the details of the formulas required to estimate the values of multiple regression parameters. We will assume that the manager has at his or her disposal a computer program for multiple regression that can handle all of these calculations. The use of multiple regression is not recommended, unless some kind of computer is available.

APPLICATION OF MULTIPLE REGRESSION ANALYSIS

To achieve a better understanding of the concept of multiple regression, we can use the data given in Table 9-1 and apply the method of least squares to obtain values for a, b_1, and b_2 in Equation (9-1). In the first step we state just what the problem is and how we want to go about solving it. We assume that the task is to forecast the company's sales for the next five years (1989–1993) and that these forecasts will be based in part on the estimated values of automobile production and building contract awards for those years. Since we have a number of historical observations in Table 9-1, we would like to determine values for a, b_1, and b_2 on the basis of these historical values and then use Equation (9-1) to forecast the future values of company sales.

Using this historical information and a multiple regression computer program, we obtain the following results: $a = 19.1$, $b_1 = 35.7$, and $b_2 = 10.9$. Thus our equation for forecasting company sales can be written as

$$\hat{Y} = 19.1 + 35.7X_1 + 10.9X_2 \qquad (9\text{-}2)$$

This states that on the basis of our historical observations (years 1972–1988), the best linear equation is the one shown in Equation (9-2). Note that the historical values we used in developing the equation were in millions of dollars for net sales, in millions of units for automobile production and in millions of starts for building contracts awarded. It is important to remember that the actual values of the parameters depend on the units that we used in estimating them. Thus it would be incorrect to interpret Equation (9-2) to mean that automobile production is much more important than building contracts in determining company sales, simply because 35.7 is larger than 10.9. If we had used different units for expressing automobile production, our coefficient for X_1 could have been smaller than our coefficient for X_2.

The proper interpretation of the values in Equation (9-2) is that when both X_1 and X_2 are 0, company sales Y will have a value of $19.1 million, and that when automobile production increases by one million units, company sales will increase by $35.7 million (other things, i.e. building contracts awarded, being held constant). Thus the coefficients in our equation generally provide the manager with a rough idea of how changes in each of the independent variables influence the value of the dependent variable Y. In order to forecast sales for each of the next five years we need to substitute estimated values for X_1 and X_2 in Equation (9-2). For the year 1989, these values are, for example, 6.4 and 48.51, respectively. Thus our estimate of sales for 1989 would be

$$\hat{Y} = 19.1 + 35.7(6.4) + 10.9(48.51)$$
$$= 776.3(\$ \text{ millions}).$$

Similarly, the computations for years 1990 through 1993 can be made by using the appropriate values for automobile production and building contracts awarded.

It should be noted that this approach for forecasting requires that we have estimates of the values of the independent variables (in this case, X_1 and X_2). Thus in formulating a multiple regression equation, the manager will want to consider for which independent variables good estimates of future values will be available. The two variables used in this case would seem reasonable, since for economic reasons the country would most likely prepare long-range forecasts of those variables to help in general economic planning. The manager must keep in mind that the accuracy of the forecast for annual sales depends *in large part* on the accuracy of the forecast for building contracts awarded and automobile production. When these independent variables are in error, there is clearly going to be a compounding effect in terms of the error in the annual corporate sales forecast.

A final point about this example is that the forecasts for years 1989 through 1993 were made without first checking the significance of the parameters or the appropriateness of the equation on which those forecasts were to be based. These questions will be taken up in a later section.

MULTIPLE CORRELATION AND THE COEFFICIENT OF DETERMINATION

It will be recalled that in simple regression we computed a statistic called the coefficient of determination, which was simply the ratio of the explained variation to the total variation. The same ratio can also be computed in multiple regression, where again it is the explained variation over the total variation. This coefficient of determination, denoted by R^2, can take on values from 0 to 1, the latter representing a situation in which all the variation in Y is explained. The actual formula for calculating the coefficient of determination in this case is exactly the same as that used for simple regression:

$$R^2 = \frac{\Sigma(\hat{Y}_i - \bar{Y})^2}{\Sigma(Y_i - \bar{Y})^2}. \tag{9-3}$$

Returning to the example of annual sales of CPG, we compute the coefficient of determination, using Equation (9-3), as 0.976. This means that 97.6% of the variation in annual sales can be explained by the combined variation in automobile production and building contracts awarded.

Table 9-2   Simple Correlation Matrix

	CPG Sales	Automobile Production	Building Contracts
CPG sales	1.000	0.688	0.948
Automobile production	0.688	1.000	0.530
Building contracts	0.948	0.530	1.000

In multiple regression it is possible to compute the individual coefficient of correlation for *each of the pairs of variables*. Thus a simple correlation coefficient could be computed for company sales and annual automobile production. Another simple correlation coefficient could be computed for annual sales and building contracts awarded. Finally, a correlation coefficient could be computed for annual automobile production and annual building contracts awarded. These three different correlation coefficients are usually referred to as the simple correlations, since they involve only two variables. They are most often represented in a correlation matrix like that shown in Table 9-2.

The simple correlation matrix is of value to the manager using multiple regression, because it indicates how each pair of variables is correlated. Thus most computer programs that perform multiple regression analysis include the computation of the simple correlation matrix. (Later in this chapter some of the uses of the simple correlation matrix are described.)

TESTS OF SIGNIFICANCE

An important question that must be answered before the results of multiple regression analysis can be used in forecasting future values is that of statistical significance. The computation of the coefficients in the regression equation is based on the use of a sample of historical observations. Consequently the reliability of forecasts based on that regression equation will depend largely on this specific sample of observations that were used in its development. Thus, the question of significance is really: how reliable are forecasts that are based on a multiple regression analysis of a given sample of data?

Although there are many tests of significance, three major ones should be mentioned in connection with multiple regression. The same three tests were discussed in Chapter 8 for simple regression.

The first test of significance that the manager should be concerned with in using multiple regression is a test that indicates the overall significance in the regression equation. The test used for this is the *F* statistic. (This test was

described in Chapter 8 in connection with the significance of simple regression.)

The value of the F statistic is the ratio of the *explained variance* to the
unexplained variance. This can be written mathematically in two equivalent
forms. One form is

$$F = \frac{\Sigma(\hat{Y}_i - \bar{Y})^2/(k - 1)}{\Sigma(Y_i - \hat{Y}_i)^2/(n - k)} \tag{9-4}$$

where n = number of observations (data points).
k = number of coefficients.

Alternatively, it can be written as

$$F = \frac{R^2/(k - 1)}{(1 - R^2)/(n - k)} \tag{9-5}$$

where R^2 is the coefficient of determination.

Although both forms of this equation give the same numerical value for the
F statistic, Equation (9-5) is generally easier to use because the coefficient of
determination R^2 usually will have been calculated. In the example of the
CPG Company we have already computed the coefficient of determination as
$R^2 = 0.976$. Because we used 17 observations in determining the values of
our parameters a, b_1, and b_2 and because we have three coefficients in our
regression equation, Equation (9-5) yields

$$F = \frac{0.976/(3 - 1)}{(1 - 0.976)/(17 - 3)} = \frac{0.976}{0.024}\left(\frac{14}{2}\right) = 284.9.$$

For the F statistic the appropriate decision rule concerning significance at the
95% confidence level is that 284.9 be greater than the corresponding value
from the table of F values. Since this value is 3.74, which is much smaller than
284.9, we can conclude that the regression equation is significant.

The second test involves testing the significance of the individual coefficients in the regression equation. Essentially, the question is whether the
value of each coefficient is significantly different from 0 or whether it occurred
by chance. This test consists of calculating the standard error for each of the
coefficients and then using that error to determine whether the value of the
coefficient is significantly different from 0.

The actual computation of the amount of standard error in each coefficient
is generally included in the computer program that performs multiple regres-

Table 9-3   Tests of Significance of CPG Company Regression Equation

Coefficient	Coefficient Value	Standard Error	t test $\left(\dfrac{\text{Coefficient Value}}{\text{Standard Error}}\right)$	Value from Table ($\alpha = 0.05$)	Is Coefficient Value Significant?
a	19.1	51.9	0.37	2.145	No
b_1	35.7	10.1	3.55	2.145	Yes
b_2	10.9	0.97	11.17	2.145	Yes

sion. In most cases these results are given in the form of the t test for each of these coefficients. This t test can be used directly to determine the significance of each coefficient.

The results of the t test computations for the CPG sales example are given in Table 9-3. As we can see, the t test is simply the value of the coefficient divided by the standard deviation of that coefficient. Thus, it indicates the number of standard deviations that the computed value is different from 0. Table 9-3 shows that for a, the constant term in the regression equation, the computed value of 19.1 is only 0.37 standard deviation from 0. For b_1 and b_2 the number of standard deviations from 0 is much greater, 3.55 and 11.17, respectively.

The rule for determining whether a coefficient is significantly different from 0 at the 95% confidence level is that the absolute value of the computed t test must be greater than the corresponding value from the table.

In Table 9-3 it can be seen that the constant term a is *not* significantly different from 0, but both coefficients b_1 and b_2 are significantly different from 0. The fact that the value of a, the constant term, is not significantly different from 0 means that, on the basis of statistics, the manager has no reason to assume that the value of 19.1 is any more likely than a value of 0.

The third test of significance that the manager may wish to undertake entails calculating the standard error of a forecast. This allows confidence intervals to be developed around forecasts based on the regression line. Generally a 95% confidence interval is used. In Chapter 8 we developed the equation used for computing the standard error of forecast for simple regression. This equation represented the standard deviation of the size and the distance that the independent variables are from their mean values. The standard error of forecast for multiple regression is analogous to this, but since two or more independent variables are involved, it is difficult to visualize it graphically.

Because of the complexity of computing the standard error of forecast, this measure is generally included in the computer programs for multiple regression analysis. Once the standard error of forecast has been obtained, the manager can use it to develop a confidence interval around any forecast. For example, the manager could have a 95% confidence level (assuming that the past pattern will remain the same during the forecasting phase) that the actual value would lie within ± 2 standard errors from the forecast value.

For the CPG example, the standard error of forecast associated with the mean value of the independent variables is 40.8. Thus if we wanted to prepare a forecast using the mean values of automobile production and building contracts awarded, we could be 95% confident that the actual value would fall in an interval of roughly ± 81.6 units around the forecast value. (Note that 81.6 equals two times the standard error of forecast.) The exact value of this interval could be found using the appropriate formula. Finally, it should be noted that the value ± 81.6 is in terms of millions of dollars, since those are the units of Y.

With each basic test of significance performed, the user will gain a better understanding of the multiple regression equation and the level of reliability that can be placed on the forecasts developed from it. However, managers must also be aware that, like all statistical methods, regression is built on certain assumptions. When those assumptions are violated, the technique can become unreliable and even misleading when applied in practice.

ASSUMPTIONS INHERENT IN MULTIPLE REGRESSION ANALYSIS

Four basic assumptions are made each time multiple regression is used in practice. An understanding of these assumptions and of the conditions necessary to meet them is important if regression analysis is to be used wisely.

In this section we discuss briefly each of these assumptions, the means of recognizing possible violations, and the methods of correcting them. Much has been written about the technical aspects of these assumptions, but this is generally beyond the scope of this text. The reader desiring additional information on these four points is referred to the Selected References at the end of this chapter.

The first assumption in regression analysis is that a linear relationship exists. This assumption states that the dependent variable is linearly related to each of the independent variables. (Technically, the assumption of linearity refers to linearity in the coefficients.) As shown in Chapter 8, a number of nonlinear relationships can be transformed into linear ones. Thus this restriction is not nearly so binding in practice as it may appear on the surface.

When the assumption of linearity is not met, the usual way of achieving linearity is to transform the variables into new variables that do exhibit linear relationships with Y. As a practical step, the manager is usually well advised to graph the relationships between the dependent variable Y and each independent variable X_i to determine whether the linearity assumption has been met. An individual graph for each pair of variables can help identify any nonlinearities.

The second basic assumption in regression analysis is that of constant variance of the regression errors. This is often referred to by the technical name *homoscedasticity*. The technical term for the lack of constant variance is *heteroscedasticity*. This assumption states that the forecasting errors must be constant over the entire range of observations. In other words, the residuals e_i of the regression remain constant over the entire range from beginning to end. Figure 9-1(a) describes the kind of pattern that exists when constant variance is present. Figure 9-1(b) describes a situation in which the residuals increase as the value of the independent variable increases, and thus the assumption of constant variance is not met. This type of nonconstant variance is found often in real forecasting situations. Figure 9-1(c) presents a different kind of nonconstancy in the variance. Thus to meet the assumption of constant variance, a pattern like that shown in Figure 9-1(a) must exist.

The third basic assumption in regression is that the residuals are independent (random) of one another. This means that each residual value is independent of the values coming before and after it. In technical terms, when this assumption is not met, it is said that serial correlation (or autocorrela-

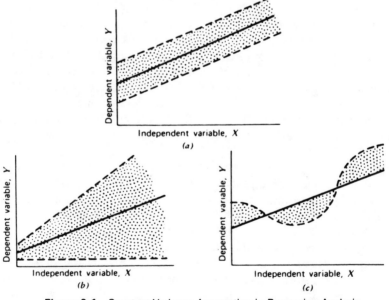

Figure 9-1   Constant Variance Assumption in Regression Analysis.

tion) exists among successive residual values. The means of identifying independence of the residuals include a graphical representation of those values, examining the sign (plus or minus) of the residuals, or computing the Durbin–Watson (D–W) statistic. Figure 9-1(c), for instance, represents not only the lack of constant variance, but also a pattern in the residuals in which their signs change from plus to minus and back to plus as the value of the independent variable increases. The (D–W) statistic, which can be used to test for the presence of autocorrelation, is beyond the scope of this book, although a value of this test between about 1.5 and 2.5 implies an absence of autocorrelation among the residuals. Again computer programs usually include the computed value of the D–W statistic and the corresponding ranges (from a table of D–W values) that indicate whether or not the residuals are independent (random).

When the residuals are not independent, an important independent variable may have been omitted or a nonlinearity may exist among the variables used in the regression equation. Thus, rather than the equation capturing the basic underlying pattern with the residuals representing random errors, those residuals still include part of the basic pattern. If that pattern can be captured by the regression equation, more accurate forecasting is possible.

Two remedies arc commonly used to eliminate autocorrelation in the residuals. First, an additional independent variable may be required to capture some of the variation in the dependent variable that could not be explained by existing independent variables and thus resulted in systematic, nonrandom errors. Second, the wrong functional form (such as, linear instead of exponential) may have been used in the regression equation. If neither a new variable nor a transformation of an existing variable can be devised that will eliminate autocorrelation, the method of first differences is often useful. Essentially, this method finds a new variable that has as its observed value the difference between each subsequent pair of observations for all variables. Thus if a series of observations with values 5, 8, 6, 4, and 7 were observed, the first differences for this set of data would be 3, -2, -2, and 3. If the first differences are computed for each of the variables in the regression equation, the regression coefficients can be recomputed using those differences as the observed values. (See Chapter 7, where the method of differencing was discussed as a way of eliminating trends from the data.)

When the independent variables exhibit strong autocorrelation, the variances are under- or overestimated, which makes the tests of significance invalid and the value of R^2 erroneous. The values of the regression coefficients $a, b_1, b_2, \ldots, b_k$ will be correct statistically and can be used, but nothing can be said about their significance as long as the residuals are autocorrelated.

The fourth basic assumption that the manager needs to consider in applying multiple regression analysis is that the residual values, if plotted, should be approximately normally distributed. This assumption is generally not restrictive, since the residuals represent the outcome of a large number of unimportant factors that influence the dependent variable, each to a relatively insignificant degree.

Thus, on the average, the influence of the factors will be cancelled out if the right model has been used. To check the assumption of normality one should plot the residuals and make sure they form a bell-shaped (normal) curve. If this assumption is not met, the tests of significance and the confidence intervals developed from them may be incorrect.

A final practical concern with multiple regression is the possibility of multicollinearity. Multicollinearity can develop when two or more of the independent variables are highly correlated. Technically the result is a near singular matrix, which has the same effect as trying to divide one number by another extremely small number. (You may recall that dividing a number by 0 gives a result of infinity.) If multicollinearity exists, the result is extremely large numbers that cannot be handled by the computer. The regression coefficient and all other output from the computer may, therefore, be erroneous. It should be stressed that multicollinearity is a computational (not a multiple regression) problem, because present-day computers are not big enough to handle the large numbers involved when two or more independent variables are highly correlated.

Multicollinearity is a real and frequent problem in economic and business data because of the high correlation between the different factors, such as population, GNP, personal disposable income, corporate sales, and corporate profits. One should be aware of its existence when selecting independent variables and when actually collecting data. The goal is to use independent variables that are not highly correlated (as a rule of thumb, the correlation between the independent variables included in the regression should not exceed $+0.7$ or be smaller than -0.7). If they are highly correlated, they provide redundent information that does not improve the explanatory power of the regression. [See Chapter 6 of Makridakis, Wheelwright and McGee (1989) for a more complete discussion of multicollinearity.]

USING MULTIPLE REGRESSION ANALYSIS IN PRACTICE

In the preceding sections of this chapter we have talked about the many considerations involved in applying multiple regression analysis and showed how the technique can be used in a straightforward example. In this section we bring together these different aspects relating to the application of regression analysis by developing a set of procedures that the manager can use and showing how these procedures can be used in a specific situation.

The fact that regression analysis is a forecasting technique based on understanding and measuring the extent of relationships means that the manager must identify those factors that appear to influence the variable to be forecast. One of the great advantages of multiple regression is that a number of different relationships can be hypothesized and tested with little effort when a computer program is available for doing so. Thus, the procedure that we outline will really go beyond the formulation of a regression equation and will describe how in a specific situation a manager might hypothesize certain relationships and then use regression analysis to determine which is the most appropriate. Nine basic steps are listed and described.

1. *Formulation of the Problem.*   First the manager must state what the problem is and what it is that will be explained or predicted. This formulation should begin with a description of the decision-making situation and an identification of the variable or variables to be forecast rather than with the forecast itself. At the end of the formulation step a number of independent variables should have been identified and the dependent variable to be forecast should have been defined. This can be done by talking to people who are actually working in the area of concern and who are forecasting the dependent variable. Their experience and the factors they use when forecasting need to be considered when the manager is formulating the problem and hypothesizing possible solutions.

2. *Choice of Economic and Other Relevant Indicators.*   Although problem formulation should identify some of the independent variables to be included, it is also necessary to identify additional possible influential factors and to determine which of them would be suitable for inclusion in the regression equation. This suitability must be based on the availability of data not only for historical periods but also for future periods for which the forecast is to be prepared. Some of the factors that are generally relevant include historical data relating to the company's operations and economic series relating to the general economy and the industry. Theoretically derived variables, as well as those identified through experience, must also be considered.

3. *Initial Test Run of Multiple Regression.*   The initial run should include all the data on the independent and dependent variables and several transformations in case some of the relationships are not linear ones. It also may include the testing of a few plausible regression equations to observe the results that can be obtained. A useful output of this test run is the simple correlation matrix used in step 4.

4. *Studying the Matrix of Simple Correlations.* Careful selection of the variables, or their possible transformations, to include in the regression equation is fundamental to developing better forecasts from this method. The key is to pick independent variables (1) whose simple correlations are not bigger than 0.7 or smaller than -0.7 and (2) that add to the explanatory ability of the regression equation. The correlation coefficients between the independent and dependent variables being selected should be sufficiently larger than 0. (It should be remembered that the rule of thumb concerning multicollinearity does not always hold; this means that a value smaller than 0.7 or larger than -0.7 may result in multicollinearity, while a value larger than 0.7 or smaller than -0.7 may not.) At the end of this step the manager should have identified five or six alternative regression equations that seem promising and can be tested further.

5. *Deciding among Individual Regressions.* After a number of regression equations have been considered in step 4, a computer program should be used to estimate the coefficients of those regression equations on the basis of the data. For each of these regression equations, the manager can consider the significance of the entire regression, of the regression coefficients, and of the standard error of forecast. Once a regression equation has been found whose independent variables significantly influence the dependent variable, the usual procedure is to attempt to increase the R^2 value by introducing additional independent variables, checking each time to be sure that the tests of significance are still met.

6. *Observing the Value of R^2.* Once all regression coefficients have been found to be statistically significant and the standard error of the forecast is considered acceptable, the value of R^2 needs to be considered. R^2 tells us the percentage of variation in the dependent variable explained through the regression equation. If this percentage is small, the regression equation does not explain enough of the variation in the dependent variable. More independence may be required to explain the variation in the dependent variable and improve the value of R^2. The R^2 value provides a subjective measure that tells us the degree of the explanatory power of our regression equation. In some cases, as in medical research, unless R^2 is practically equal to 1, the regression equation cannot be used. In other cases even a small value of R^2 can be accepted as long as all regression coefficients are statistically significant and step 7 below has been completed.

7. *Checking the Validity of the Regression Assumptions.* Once a good equation (one that passes steps 5 and 6) has been identified, the manager must consider whether such a regression equation meets the four assumptions outlined in the preceding section. If it does not, appropriate steps should be

taken to correct violations of the assumptions, or additional regression equations must be developed and tested. It must be remembered that high values of R^2 are meaningless when the D–W statistic is not in the appropriate range. If the test is not satisfied, it is advisable not to trust the regression equation no matter how large the value of R^2. Similarly, violation of the other assumptions can result in problems whose magnitude, however, is not as serious as when the D–W test indicates that the residuals are not random.

8. *Preparing a Forecast.* Once the manager has found a regression equation (1) whose regression coefficients are statistically significant, (2) that gives a sufficiently high value for R^2, and (3) that meets the assumptions inherent in regression, he or she can use the equation for forecasting purposes. In doing so, he or she should consider the confidence interval for individual forecasts and the accuracy of the values for the independent variable. As we pointed out earlier, most forecasts are based on estimated values of the independent variables rather than on actual values. Thus their validity needs to be determined, because if the forecasts of the independent variables are in error, the forecast of the dependent variable Y is also likely to be in error.

9. *Using the Regression Equation to Increase Understanding.* Quite often the biggest benefit from regression analysis is not in forecasting, but in explaining and helping us understand better some situations of interest. Consider, for instance, the regression equation we found for forecasting CPG's sales. This equation was

$$\hat{Y} = 19.1 + 35.7X_1 + 10.9X_2.$$

Suppose that the value of X_1 (automobile production) could not be forecast. Is the regression equation useless? Not at all. We know that for each additional million cars produced, the sales of CPG will increase by $35.7 million. This can be useful information by itself, because it can help us plan more effectively even though accurate forecasts of automobile production may not be available.

AN APPLICATION OF REGRESSION

As an example of how the preceding steps might be applied in developing an appropriate regression equation for forecasting, let us consider a company whose marketing manager wishes to forecast corporate sales for the coming year and to understand better the factors that influence them. The first step

Table 9-4 Forecasting Data for 1970 through 1988 (Semiannual)

(1) Personal Disposable Income (PDI) (Millions of Dollars)	(2) Dealers' Allowances (Thousands of Dollars)	(3) Price (Dollars)	(4) Product Development (Thousands of Dollars)	(5) Capital Investments (Thousands of Dollars)	(6) Advertising (Thousands of Dollars)	(7) Sales Expenses (Thousands of Dollars)	(8) Total Industry Advertising (Thousands of Dollars)	(9) Company Sales (Thousands of Dollars)
398	138	56.2058	12.1124	49.895	76.8621	228.80	98.205	5540.39
369	118	59.0443	9.3304	16.595	88.8056	177.45	224.953	5439.04
268	129	56.7236	28.7481	89.182	51.2972	166.40	263.032	4290.00
484	111	57.8627	12.8916	106.738	39.6473	258.05	320.928	5502.34
394	146	59.1178	13.3815	142.552	51.6517	209.30	406.989	4871.77
332	140	60.1113	11.0859	61.287	20.5476	180.05	246.996	4708.08
336	136	59.8398	24.9579	-30.385	40.1534	213.20	328.436	4627.81
383	104	60.0523	20.8096	-44.856	31.6456	200.85	298.456	4110.24
285	105	63.1415	8.4853	-28.373	12.4570	176.15	218.110	4122.69
277	135	62.3026	10.7301	75.723	68.3076	174.85	410.467	4842.25
456	128	64.9220	21.8473	144.030	52.4536	252.85	93.006	5740.65
355	131	64.8577	23.5062	112.904	76.6778	208.00	307.226	5094.10
364	120	63.5919	13.8940	128.347	96.0677	195.00	106.792	5383.20
320	147	65.6145	14.8659	10.097	47.9795	154.05	304.921	4888.17
311	143	67.0228	22.4940	-24.760	27.2319	180.70	59.612	4033.13
362	145	66.9049	23.3698	116.748	72.6681	219.70	238.986	4941.96
408	131	66.1843	13.0354	120.406	62.3129	234.65	141.074	5312.80
433	124	67.8651	8.0330	121.823	24.7122	258.05	290.832	5139.87
359	106	68.8892	27.0486	71.055	73.9126	196.30	413.636	4397.36
476	138	71.4177	18.2208	4.186	63.2737	278.85	206.454	5149.47

415	148	69.2775	7.7422	±6.935	28.6762	207.35	79.566	5150.83
420	136	69.7334	10.1361	7.621	91.3635	213.20	428.982	4989.02
536	111	73.1628	27.3709	127.509	74.0169	296.40	273.072	5926.86
432	152	73.3650	15.5281	−49.574	16.1628	245.05	309.422	4703.88
436	123	73.0500	32.4918	100.098	42.9984	275.60	280.139	5365.59
415	119	74.9102	19.7127	−40.185	41.1346	211.25	314.548	4630.09
462	112	73.2007	14.8358	58.153	92.5180	282.75	212.058	5711.86
429	125	74.1615	11.3694	57.963	83.2870	217.75	118.065	5095.48
517	142	74.2838	26.7510	27.088	74.8921	306.80	344.553	6124.37
328	123	77.1409	19.6038	59.343	87.5103	210.60	140.872	4787.34
418	135	78.5910	34.6881	1-1.969	74.4712	269.75	82.855	5035.62
515	120	77.0938	23.2020	125.420	21.2711	328.25	398.425	5288.01
412	149	78.2313	35.7396	29.558	26.4941	258.05	124.027	4647.01
455	126	77.9296	21.5891	13.007	94.6311	232.70	117.911	5315.63
554	138	81.0394	19.5692	42.352	92.5448	323.70	161.250	6180.06
441	120	79.8485	15.5037	−21.558	50.0480	267.15	405.088	4800.97
417	120	80.6394	34.9238	148.450	83.1803	257.40	110.740	5512.13
461	132	82.2843	26.5496	−17.584	91.2214	266.50	170.392	5272.21

is to determine just why this forecast is needed and how it will be used. We will suppose that the marketing manager wants it for at least four reasons: (1) to supply her with estimates needed as her part in the corporate planning activity, (2) to give her an idea of the kind of staffing requirements she will have in sales and sales service to handle the company's increased sales, (3) to help in planning budget allocations for advertising, dealer discounts, and so on, and (4) to help her make better policy decisions concerning price, advertising, and product development expenditures.

With this initial identification of the problem, the marketing manager might well sit down with the sales manager and others in her marketing organization to determine the factors that might affect the company's sales. Let us suppose that they come up with the following model:

sales = f(personal disposable income, dealers' allowances, prices,

product development expenditures, capital investments,

advertising, sales expenses, total industry advertising, random

effects).

Clearly, some of these factors will have a more important effect than others on the company's sales; others may turn out to be unimportant. Since any one of them, however, may have an important impact, it is useful to gather data on all of them at this early stage in the process. Thus the next step is to gather the information on these eight independent variables as well as on the dependent variable, company sales. Table 9-4 presents semiannual data covering the period from 1970 through 1988.

After these data have been collected, an initial multiple regression run can be made. As a starting point the regression equation

$$\hat{Y} = a + b_1 X_1 + b_2 X_2 + \cdots + b_8 X_8$$

can be used. This equation contains all eight independent variables. Some may not be important, but including them all initially gives a good starting basis. The results of applying a computer program by using the foregoing regression equation and the data in Table 9-4 are shown in Table 9-5. The second column in Table 9-5 lists the value of the constant term of the equation and the coefficient for each of the eight independent variables.

As can be seen in Table 9-5, not all the coefficients in this regression equation are significant. Looking at the t ratios in column 4 and comparing them to the corresponding values from the table, one can determine which coefficients are significant at the 95% level. It can be seen that independent

Table 9-5   Regression Equation for Semiannual Sales

(1) Variable	(2) Parameter Value	(3) Standard Error	(4) t Ratio	(5) Significant
Constant	2926.09	612.386	4.778	Yes
1 = PDI	3.809	1.528	2.491	Yes
2 = dealer allowances	5.064	3.138	1.613	No
3 = price	− 17.126	7.998	− 2.141	Yes
4 = product development expenditures	− 10.258	6.274	− 1.635	No
5 = capital investments	1.515	0.746	2.029	Yes
6 = advertising	8.053	1.778	4.528	Yes
7 = sales expenses	3.864	2.702	1.430	No
8 = total industry advertising	− 0.539	0.377	− 1.428	No

$R^2 = 0.912$; standard deviation of regression = 243.247;
Durbin–Watson statistic = 2.39146; F test = 1144.
t value from table ($\alpha = 0.05$) = 1.96.
F value from table ($\alpha = 0.05$) = 2.27

variables 2, 4, 7, and 8 (dealer allowances, product development expenditures, sales expenses, and total industry advertising, respectively) are not significantly different from 0 in terms of their impact on sales. This result could be due either to a lack of a significant relationship between variables 2, 4, 7, and 8 and Y or it could be due to multicollinearity between some of the variables, since both R^2 and the F test are large.

At this point the marketing manager can examine the simple correlation matrix shown in Table 9-6 to see how each independent variable is related to the company's sales. The bottom line of this table shows these correlations between the company sales (dependent variable) and each of the independent variables. We can see that variables 2, 4, and possibly 8 have a relatively small correlation with company sales. Variable 7, however, whose coefficient was not significant in Table 9-5, seems to have a fairly high correlation with company sales. The problem here is that multicollinearity does exist between variables 1 and 7. (The coefficient of correlation is 0.903.) This means that we need to drop either 1 or 7 from our regression equation. If we examine the correlation between sales and variable 1 and sales and variable 7, we see that the correlation is higher with variable 1. Thus we choose to eliminate variable 7 from our regression equation.

The marketing manager can now test an additional regression equation in which variables 2, 4, 7, and 8 have been eliminated. The new equation to be

Table 9-6 Simple Correlation Matrix for Semiannual Sales

	(1)	(2)	(3)	(4)	(5) Variable Name	(6)	(7)	(8)	(9)
Variable	PDI	Dealer Allowances	Price	Product Development	Capital Investments	Advertising	Sales Expenses	Total Industry Advertising	Company Sales
1	1.000	−0.069	0.555	0.160	0.131	0.199	0.903	−0.020	0.742
2	−0.069	1.000	0.028	0.005	0.149	−0.119	−0.051	−0.145	0.009
3	0.555	0.028	1.000	0.438	−0.063	0.252	0.630	−0.182	0.285
4	0.160	0.005	0.438	1.000	0.217	0.102	0.361	−0.128	0.031
5	0.131	−0.149	−0.063	0.217	1.000	0.277	0.228	−0.063	0.410
6	0.199	−0.119	0.252	0.102	0.277	1.000	0.132	−0.197	0.526
7	0.903	−0.051	0.630	0.361	0.228	0.132	1.000	−0.019	0.667
8	−0.020	−0.145	−0.182	−0.128	−0.063	−0.197	−0.019	1.000	−0.175
9	0.742	0.009	0.285	0.031	0.410	0.526	0.667	−0.175	1.000

tested can be written as

$$\hat{Y} = a + b_1 X_1 + b_3 X_3 + b_5 X_5 + b_6 X_6.$$

The results for this regression analysis are presented in Table 9-7. As can be seen from this new regression equation, all the t ratios are statistically significant, which indicates that the term and each of the regression coefficients (b_1, b_3, b_5 and b_6) is significantly different from 0. If the F test is greater than 2.69, the entire regression equation is significant. Finally, the value of R^2 is equal to 0.781, which indicates that 78.1% of the fluctuations in sales are explained by the regression equation shown in Table 9-7. In practical terms the accuracy of this equation can be seen from Table 9-8, which gives the residuals (the difference between actual values and those predicted by the equation) and expresses those residuals as a percentage of the actual values. Since the greatest error is 14.76%, it can be assumed that the regression equation is quite adequate in explaining past sales. Furthermore, the standard deviation of regression has a value of about 260. This means that we can be 95% confident that our actual value will lie within $\pm \$520,000$ (± 2 standard deviations, that is $\pm 260,000$ of the forecast value in the area of the mean.

Now the regression equation determined in Table 9-7 can be checked to see whether it conforms to the four basic assumptions. The equation does represent a linear relationship, the tests of significance are satisfied, the R^2 is good, and it appears that the regression equation is a good representation of this situation. The residuals are about constant. They are neither larger nor smaller in the beginning or at the end, as can be seen from Figure 9-2, which plots the residuals over time. The value of the D–W test is 2.31, which is close to the allowable range of 1.72 to 2.28. Finally, the residuals are about normally distributed, as shown in Figure 9-3, which plots the residuals in the form of a histogram.

The regression equation can now be used to prepare a forecast. This requires that values of X_1, X_3, X_5, and X_6 be estimated and then substituted in the regression equation to compute an estimate for Y. The equation also can be used to understand better the relative impact of at least a handful of factors on company sales. The precise equation taken from Table 9-7 is

$$\hat{Y} = 3276.55 + 5.70X_1 - 15.18X_3 + 1.55X_5 + 7.57X_6$$

where X_1 = personal disposable income
X_3 = price per ton (in dollars)
X_5 = capital investments (in thousands of dollars)
X_6 = advertising (in thousands of dollars)
$\hat{Y}$ = semiannual sales (in thousands of dollars).

Table 9-7 Regression Equation for Semiannual Sales

Variable	Dependent Variable is 9 = Sales			
	Parameter Value	Standard Error	t Ratio	Significant
Constant	3276.55	393.68500	8.32276	Yes
1 = PDI	5.69570	0.74394	7.65613	Yes
3 = price	−15.1783	6.96706	−2.17859	Yes
5 = capital investments	1.55114	0.70495	2.20033	Yes
6 = advertising	7.57419	1.77507	4.26698	Yes

R^2 = 0.781; R = 0.884; standard deviation of regression = 259.829; degrees of freedom = 33;
Durbin–Watson statistic = 2.31183; F test = 471.2
t value from table = 2.03.
F value from table = 2.69.

Table 9-8 Regression Results for Semiannual Sales (Predicted, Residuals and % Errors)

Actual	Predicted	Residuals	Percentage Error
5540.39	5349.89	190.501	3.43841E-02
5439.04	5180.44	258.598	4.75449E-02
4290.00	4468.90	− 178.895	− 4.17005E-02
5502.34	5620.87	− 118.530	− 2.15417E-02
4871.77	5235.68	− 363.912	− 7.46982E-02
4708.08	4505.83	202.256	4.29594E-02
4627.81	4539.03	88.783	1.91847E-02
4110.24	4717.04	− 606.794	− 0.14763
4122.69	3991.78	130.914	3.17545E-02
4842.25	4543.44	298.814	6.17097E-02
5740.65	5509.08	231.570	4.03385E-02
5094.10	5069.99	24.105	4.73197E-02
5383.20	5311.28	71.915	1.33593E-02
4888.17	4482.32	405.854	8.30277E-02
4033.13	4198.47	− 165.336	− 4.09943E-02
4941.96	5054.38	− 112.418	− 2.27476E-02
5312.80	5254.56	58.234	1.09612E-02
5139.87	5088.84	51.020	9.92636E 03
4397.36	4945.73	− 548.365	− 0.124703
5149.47	5376.45	− 226.977	− 4.40777E-02
5150.83	4733.14	417.690	8.10918E-02
4989.02	5314.13	− 325.107	− 6.51645E-02
5926.86	5977.36	− 50.498	− 8.52030E-03
4703.88	4669.05	34.821	7.40262E-03
5365.59	5132.04	233.550	4.35273E-02
4630.09	4752.48	− 122.386	− 2.64328E-02
5711.86	5603.36	108.498	1.89951E-02
5095.48	5363.63	− 266.150	− 5.22326E-02
6124.37	5702.99	421.383	6.88044E-02
4787.34	4728.74	58.606	1.22419E-02
5035.62	5248.74	− 213.121	− 4.23227E-02
5288.01	5396.88	− 108.870	− 2.05881E-02
4647.01	4682.28	− 35.263	− 7.58850E-03
5315.63	5429.94	− 114.307	− 2.15039E-02
6180.06	5968.57	211.487	3.42208E-02
4800.97	4922.02	− 121.043	− 2.52122E-02
5512.13	5287.97	244.161	4.06669E-02
5272.21	5316.98	− 44.769	− 8.49161E-03

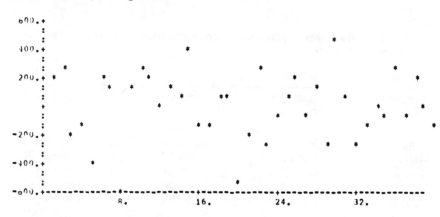

Figure 9-2 Plot of the Residuals for the Company Sales Regression Showing Their Constancy over Time.

The R^2 value of 0.781 tells us that the regression equation explains 78.1% of the total variation, that is, that variations in X_1, X_3, X_5, and X_6 explain 78.1% of the variation in the sales. The marketing manager must know the levels of precision and confidence that are associated with the values she inserts for the independent variables, to ensure that her forecast of semian-

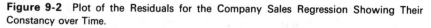

Figure 9-3 Histogram of the Residuals for the Company Sales Regression Showing that They Are Approximately Normally Distributed.

nual sales will be as accurate as this regression equation allows. Thus the same types of approaches used to increase the accuracy of the sales forecast need to be applied to increase the accuracy of the estimates of the independent variables.

In addition, the marketing manager can gather a great deal of information from the regression equation. For instance, the constant value 3276.55 means that this portion of company sales is not explained by fluctuations in the four independent variables. If this constant term is large, it suggests that there may be additional independent variables that might explain more of the dependent variable. Identifying such variables also may increase the value of R^2, which indicates that 21.9% (100 − 78.1) of the total variation in sales is still unexplained.

Furthermore, the manager knows that as personal disposable income increases by \$1 million (assuming that the remaining variables remain constant), company sales will increase by \$5700. This is important information that might be used, for instance, for long-term planning purposes. Similarly, when capital investments and advertising increase, so do sales. It is interesting to note that for every dollar spent on advertising (assuming all other factors remain constant), the return is \$1.55 in current period sales. This means that for every dollar spent on advertising, the return on sales is 55 cents more than what was spent, which is important information to consider in deciding how much to spend on advertising. Finally, it can be seen that the coefficient corresponding to price is negative. This means that when the price increases, sales will decrease. In fact, a \$1.00 price increase decreases sales by \$15.18 million. Similarly, a \$1.00 price decrease will increase sales by \$15.18 million. In spite of the caution that must be exercised in interpreting and using these results, regression analysis is an extremely powerful tool that can be used in a wide range of situations for both understanding and forecasting (see also Chapter 15).

SUMMARY

In the preceding sections we have considered some of the details of applying multiple regression in practice. There are also a number of general considerations that the manager should keep in mind in evaluating the appropriateness of this technique in comparison with other techniques. The major strength of multiple regression analysis is that it is an explanatory method that allows us to determine (estimate) virtually any kind of linear relationship that might exist between a dependent and one or more independent variables.

There are, of course, some drawbacks to the use of multiple regression.

One is that it requires estimates for the independent variables before a forecast can be made. Another is that most managers are reluctant to get into its details and to understand fully the power that it can bring to bear on a forecasting problem. (We hope this chapter will show that the method is very understandable and that by mastering some of the basic principles of its application, managers can use it wisely in a broad range of situations.)

Another potential drawback is the tendency to think that any time a high R^2 exists, the regression equation is automatically a good one. For this to be the case, the assumptions of regression must be satisfied and sufficient data must be available (at least 30 observations). A last point is that regression can be used reliably when and only when the relationship between the independent variables and the dependent variable does not change. If that relationship does change, it becomes necessary to collect a new set of data in order to redetermine the regression equation.

Given the substantial experience that has been gained by researchers and practitioners alike in the application of multiple regression, it is not surprising that a number of variations and modifications have been developed. Such things as stepwise regression (automatically selecting and then evaluating additional variables to be added to the basic regression equation), lead and lagged variables (shifting the time reference to create new variables), and dummy variables (creating variables with a value of 0 or 1, for example, to represent a seasonal factor) are just a few of these. The interested reader can pursue these in Makridakis, Wheelwright, and McGee (1989) and in Selected References.

SELECTED REFERENCES FOR FURTHER STUDY

Chatterjee, S., and B. Price, 1977. *Regression Analysis by Example*, Wiley, New York.

Clearly, P. J., and H. Levenbach, 1982. *The Professional Forecaster: The Forecasting Process through Data Analysis*, Lifetime Learning Publications, Belmont, CA.

Draper, N. R., and H. Smith, 1981. *Applied Regression Analysis*, 2nd ed., Wiley, New York.

Fildes, R., 1985. "Quantitative Forecasting—The State of the Art: Econometric Models," *Journal of Operational Research Society*, 36, no. 7, pp. 549–580.

Granger, C. W. J., 1980. *Forecasting in Business and Economics*, Academic Press, New York.

Gujarati, D., 1978. *Basic Econometrics*, McGraw-Hill, New York.

Hanke, J. E., and A. G. Reitsch, 1981. *Business Forecasting*, Allyn & Bacon, Boston.

Intrilligator, M., 1978. *Econometric Models, Techniques and Applications*, Prentice-Hall, Englewood Cliffs, NJ.

Johnston, J., 1972. *Econometric Methods*, Prentice-Hall, Englewood Cliffs, NJ.

Makridakis, S., and S.C. Wheelwright, 1978. *Interactive Forecasting*, 2nd ed., Holden-Day, San Francisco.

Makridakis, S., and S. C. Wheelwright (Eds.), 1979. *Forecasting. TIMS Studies in the Management Sciences*, vol. 12, North-Holland, Amsterdam.

Makridakis, S., S. C. Wheelwright, and V. E. McGee, 1989. *Forecasting: Methods and Applications*. 3rd ed., Wiley, New York.

Pindyck, R. S., and D. L. Rubinfeld, 1976. *Econometric Models and Economic Forecasts*, McGraw-Hill, New York.

Theil, H., 1971. *Principles of Econometrics*, Wiley, New York.

Wallace, D. T., and J. L. Silver, 1987. *Econometrics: An Introduction*, Addison-Wesley, Reading, MA.

Whetherill, G. B., 1986. *Regression Analysis with Applications*, Chapman and Hall, London.

Wonnacott, H., and R. J. Wonnacott, 1986. *Regression: A Second Course on Statistics*, Krieger, Melbourne.

CHAPTER 10

ECONOMETRIC MODELING

The previous two chapters have dealt with simple and multiple regression. Applying simple regression requires little statistical knowledge, limited data, and only moderate computational effort. (Even programmable calculators are adequate for the computations.) Multiple regression, on the other hand, requires more knowledge, more data, and a computer to do the computations. Whereas use of simple regression can be a mechanical task entrusted to a clerical level of operations, multiple regression requires a better understanding of the various steps involved to come up with an adequate regression equation.

In the same way that simple regression is a special case of multiple regression, multiple regression is a special case of econometric models. While multiple regression involves a single equation, econometric models can include any number of simultaneous multiple regression equations. The term *econometric models* is used in this book to denote systems of linear multiple regression equations, each including several *interdependent variables*. It should be noted that this is not the only usage of the term econometrics, since there are those who use it as a general term to cover simple, multiple, and systems of multiple regression equations. The more limited definition used in this chapter appears to be the most common usage at this time.

The objective of this discussion of econometrics is *not* to provide the level of detailed information needed to develop such models. Rather it is to interpret their use in a practical sense. This section will review the main ideas and concepts underlying econometric models, present the main advantages and difficulties involved, describe the statistical methods used, and, finally, discuss the role of econometric methods as a forecasting tool.

Perhaps the best starting point for understanding the basics of econometric forecasting is regression. Regression analysis assumes that all of the independent variables included in the regression equation are determined by outside factors, that is, they are *exogenous* to the system. In economic or organizational relationships, however, such an assumption is often unrealistic. To illustrate this point, one can assume that sales $= f$(GNP, price, advertising). In regression, all three independent variables are assumed to be exogenously determined; they are not influenced by the level of sales itself or by each other. This is a fair assumption as far as GNP is concerned, which, except for very large corporations, is not influenced directly by the sales of a single firm. However, for price and advertising there is unlikely to be a similar absence of influence. For example, if the per-unit cost (and thus price) decreases as sales volume increases (and vice versa), different levels of sales will result in different per-unit costs (and thus prices). Furthermore, advertising expenditures will certainly influence the per-unit price of the product offered, since production and selling costs determine the per-unit price. The price in turn influences the magnitude of sales, which consequently can influence the level of advertising. Furthermore, since advertising increases sales, it can also influence the per-unit costs and, therefore, price. These interrelationships point to the mutual interdependence among the variables of such an equation. Ordinary regression analysis is incapable of dealing with such interdependence if it is to be preserved as part of the explanatory model.

The relationship above can be more correctly expressed by a system of simultaneous equations that can deal with the interdependence among the variables. Although very simplistic, the following econometric model might represent these interdependencies:

$$
\begin{aligned}
\text{sales} &= f\,(\text{GNP, price, advertising}) \\
\text{production cost} &= f\,(\text{number of units produced, inventories,} \\
&\qquad \text{labor costs, material costs}) \\
\text{selling expenses} &= f\,(\text{advertising, other selling expenses}) \qquad\text{(10-1)} \\
\text{advertising} &= f\,(\text{sales}) \\
\text{price} &= f\,(\text{production cost, selling expenses, administration} \\
&\qquad \text{overhead, profit}).
\end{aligned}
$$

In place of one regression equation expressing sales as a function of three independent variables, the set of five simultaneous equations (10-1) expresses sales and the independent variables as a function of each other plus other exogenous factors. The relationship among these variables can be represented schematically as shown in Figure 10-1.

The basic premise of econometric modeling is that everything in the real world depends on everything else. The world is becoming more aware of this interdependence, but the concept is very difficult to deal with at an operational level. The practical question is, of course, where to stop considering these interdependencies.

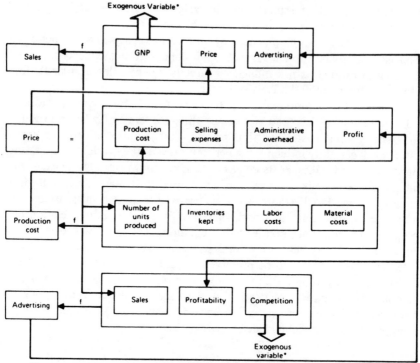

Exogenous Variable*

*Exogenous variables are not determined within the system.

Figure 10-1 A Simple Econometric Model.

One could develop an almost infinite number of interdependent relation-ships, but data collection, computational limitations, and estimation problems restrict one in practice to a limited number of relationships. In addition, the marginal understanding, or forecasting accuracy, does not increase in proportion to the effort required to include an additional variable or equation after the first few. In econometric models, a major decision is determining how much detail to include, since more detail inevitably means more complexity.

In an econometric model one is faced with many tasks similar to those in multiple regression analysis. These tasks include:

1. Determining which variables to include in each equation (specification)

2. Determining the functional form (that is, linear, exponential, logarith-mic, etc.) of each of the equations

3. Estimating in a simultaneous manner the parameters of the equations

4. Testing the statistical significance of the results

5. Checking the validity of the assumptions involved.

Steps 2, 4, and 5 do not differ in their basic approach from those of multiple regression, although they require much more sophistication to achieve. Therefore, they will not be discussed further in this chapter.

The reality of econometric models is that their development and application are far more complex than is the case for multiple regression models. These complexities and the associated costs place such applications beyond the scope of most managers and most medium-sized firms. However, several econometric forecasting services—including DRI, the Wharton School, Chase Econometric Associates, and Mapcast (GE)—provide econometric forecasts on a subscription basis, making it practical for many more firms to apply the results of this approach to their internal forecasts.

Because of the complexities of econometric methods and the fact that most managers do not develop them, but use only their results, we will focus in the next two sections of this chapter on only two aspects of these methods. First, an application of econometrics will be discussed to illustrate the nature of the problems to which they can be applied and ways in which they might be of help to a manager. Second, some of the advantages and disadvantages of the approach will be discussed, since successful use of econometric results generally hinges on management's understanding of such characteristics.

AN APPLICATION OF AN ECONOMETRIC MODEL

One difficulty in describing applications of econometric models to business forecasting is that they are generally proprietary, and detailed information about them is not readily available. However, many of these applications are described in the literature in terms of their structure and purpose. One such application is detailed in Wise (1975). This article reports on the application of econometric modeling to predicting prices and quantities (supply and demand) for iron and steel scrap. This section will describe the general structural form of this model and some of its applications in practice.

The prices of scrap iron and steel have often behaved in unexpected ways. Since these prices and their impact on supply and demand have a major effect on the profits of companies in the steel, scrap, and related industries, a substantial number of organizations are concerned with their forecasting. As the actual values shown in Figure 10-2 demonstrate, domestic scrap usage (and exports) has not always moved consistently with prices, and vice versa. At times scrap prices have risen, even though scrap consumption has de-

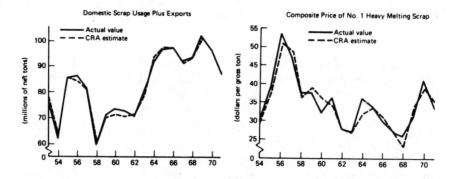

Figure 10-2   Econometric Forecast versus Actual for Quantity and Price Movements of Ferrous Scrap.

creased. At other times prices have fallen, while usage has increased. These seemingly inconsistent patterns of market behavior can be explained when the full complexity of the scrap market is understood. Many important factors interact simultaneously, however, making simple analysis impossible and defying intuition. The econometric approach to predicting scrap volumes and their prices is one way of handling these complexities. Through the concepts of econometrics that have been described previously, such a model can account simultaneously for the interaction of such factors as steel output, pig iron cost, exports of scrap, government policy, technological advances, and inventories.

The model described here was developed by Charles River Associates of Boston for its customers. Basically it provides the following for those who use its outputs:

1. A source of scrap prices for one- and two-year, and sometimes longer, profit forecasts

2. A source of market information to help top management keep tabs on its scrap purchasing operation

3. A source of short-term price forecasts that make inventory speculation possible and of information corroborating that provided by scrap purchasers to treasurers and top management who must approve funds for large-scale inventory buildup

4. Some special long-term scrap price forecasts that are suitable for use in preparing new facility plans.

In terms of the performance of this particular econometric model, Figure 10-2 summarizes actual domestic scrap usage plus exports from 1954 to 1971 and also provides actual and forecast values of the composite price of scrap for that same period. These results indicate the relative accuracy of such an approach in this particular situation.

A key determinant of the success of an econometric model for forecasting is the basic design of the model itself. Before an econometric model can be developed, a structural representation of the items that it represents and the various factors that it needs to include must be built. For the scrap situation such a structural representation is presented in Figure 10-3. This figure includes items that affect scrap demand and supply and items of general economic influence.

Once the basic structural relationship of different variables has been determined, the data can be collected. These data will be used in the same way that observations were used in estimating multiple regression coefficients in Chapter 9. In many instances these data must come from published sources or be collected for the specific model in question. As discussed previously, one of the reasons for the proprietary nature of econometric models, such as the one for forecasting ferrous scrap quantities and prices, is that the data are difficult to find and the process of developing the model is expensive.

A major advantage claimed by those who develop econometric models for forecasting purposes is that those same models can be used to perform extensive sensitivity analyses relevant to other issues of decision making. For example, in the case of the ferrous scrap model, developments on the supply or demand side or changes in government legislation may affect the quantities and price of ferrous scrap. These can be converted into assumptions suitable for incorporation in the model and tested in terms of the model's sensitivity to those changes and their influence on the factor being forecast.

In many instances, additional steps in forecasting and planning can be closely tied to the use of the econometric model, especially within a single corporation. One such application reported in *Sales and Marketing Management* (1975) is illustrated in Figure 10-4.

In this example several different forecasting and decision-making models have been linked to integrate more completely the forecasting and planning tasks. The econometric model provides annual sales forecasts that can be used as the starting point for the planning process.

Thus, the econometric model expresses the relationship between company sales and a variety of economic indicators, such as GNP, personal consumption expenditures, and capital spending plans. A second model can be used at a micro level to provide smooth estimates of monthly sales by product and seasonal factors, as well as perhaps incorporating still a third model based on a single multiple regression equation that will show the impact of past promotions on sales.

These three different forms of forecasting can then be used as the major source of input for projecting annual sales by product group. They can, in

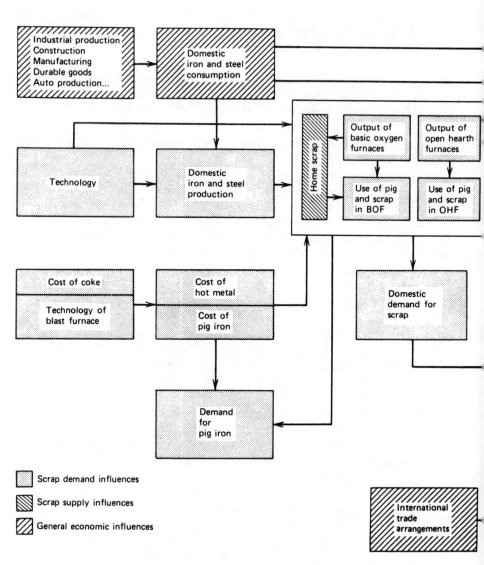

Figure 10-3 Factors Included in the Econometric Model of Ferrous Scrap.

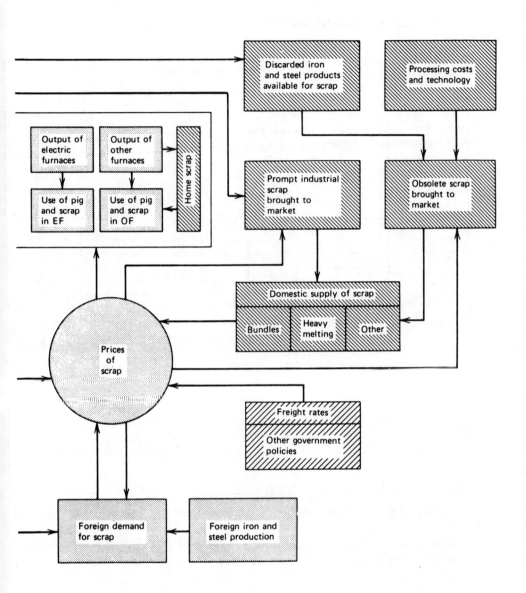

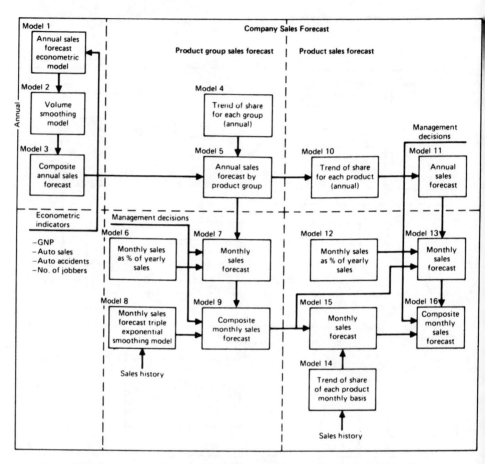

Figure 10-4   Integrating Econometric Forecasts with Other Forecasts within a Company.

turn, serve as the basis for other forecasting models, for decisions being made at more detailed levels, and for setting up performance review and evaluation procedures.

ADVANTAGES AND DRAWBACKS OF ECONOMETRIC MODELS

The main advantage of econometric models lies in their ability to deal with interdependencies. If a government, for example, would like to know the impact of a 10% tax reduction aimed at stimulating a recessionary economy, econometric models provide one alternative for estimating that. A tax cut will have direct and immediate effects on increasing personal disposable income and decreasing government revenues. It will also tend to influence inflation, unemployment, savings, capital spending, interest rates, and the like. Each of these in turn will influence personal disposable income and therefore taxes of subsequent years. Through a series of chain reactions, the 10% decrease will affect almost all economic factors. These interdependencies must be considered if the effect of the tax cut is to be predicted reasonably.

Econometric models are useful tools for increasing one's understanding of the way an economic system works, how an industry behaves, or to what extent various decisions might affect a business firm. Thus, their major purpose is to test and evaluate alternative policies and determine their influence on critical variables. These goals, however, are somewhat different from forecasting, where the main objective is predicting rather than under-standing or doing sensitivity analyses per se. Complex econometric models are not always more accurate in forecasting than simpler time-series approaches. It is important to distinguish between econometric models used for policy purposes and econometric models used for forecasting. They are two different things. In the former usage, there is little doubt as to the usefulness and uniqueness of econometric models. For forecasting usage they must be examined more carefully and in the right perspective (see Chapter 15).

Econometric models for forecasting can generally be much simpler and involve fewer equations than those designed for policy study. The main purpose of forecasting versions is to derive values for independent variables so that they do not have to be estimated externally. In the final analysis, the question is whether the extra burden required for developing and running an economic model justifies the extra costs and complexities involved.

A major weakness of econometric models is the absence of a set of rules that can be applied across different situations. This makes the development of econometric models highly dependent on the specific situation and requires the involvement of skilled experienced economericians. Finally, once a model is developed, it cannot be left to run on its own with no outside interference. Continuous monitoring of the results and updating for periodic changes are needed. This explains why much of the work in this area is done by specialized firms who can supply technical skills as well as data bases.

SELECTED REFERENCES FOR FURTHER STUDY

Butler, W. F., and R. A. Kavesh (Eds.), 1966. *How Business Economists Forecast*, Prentice-Hall, Englewood Cliffs, NJ.

Chow, G. C., 1983. *Econometrics*, McGraw-Hill, New York.

Pindyck, R., and D. Rubinfeld, 1980. *Econometric Models and Economic Forecasts*, McGraw-Hill, New York.

Plasmans, J. E. (Ed.), 1981. *Econometric Modelling in Theory and Practice*, Kluwer Academic, Amsterdam.

"Special Report: Forecasting for High Profits," 1975. *Sales and Marketing Management*.

Spivey, W., and W. J. Wrobleski, 1979. *Econometric Model Performance in Forecasting and Policy Assessment*, American Enterprise Institute, New York.

Wallace, D. T., and J. L. Silver, 1987. *Econometrics: An Introduction*, Addison-Wesley, Reading, MA.

Wise, K. T., 1975. "Scrap: Prices and Issues," *Iron and Steelmakers*, May, pp. 23–32.

MANAGEMENT JUDGMENT IN FORECASTING

CHAPTER 11

EXPLAINING THE PAST VERSUS PREDICTING THE FUTURE*

In Part B the major quantitative methods were described. A major, implicit assumption in using these methods is that the patterns or relationships are constant. This implies that a model is fitted to *all* available data. The choice of the methods to be used is a matter of personal preferences, with some guidelines drawn from empirical studies and experience (see Chapters 15, 16, and 18). Once a method has been selected, the specific model that *best fits* the available data is found and used for predicting the future. The model that best fits commonly means the one that minimizes the mean error (MSE), the mean absolute percentage error (MAPE), or some other criterion. This approach to model selection was used throughout Part B, and the MSE was usually minimized. In some methods, such as regression (Chapters 8 and 9) and ARMA (Chapter 7), the residual errors of the model (namely, $e_t = X_t - F_t$) need to be random, constant, and normally distributed. In other methods (exponential smoothing, Bayesian forecasting) there is no restriction about the residual errors, although it is desirable that they be random, constant, and normally distributed.

Two assumptions are implicit in the approach to model selection used in Part B. First, the model that "best" fits the available historical data will also be the best model to predict beyond these data (the future). Second, the model that "best" forecasts one period ahead will also be best for predicting two, three, . . . , m periods ahead. These assumptions, however, do *not* hold true for the great majority of real-world economics or business series. One way to show that the model that best fits the past data is not necessarily the best model to forecast for the future is by computing the rank correlation between the best, second best, third best, and so on, methods in the model-fitting phase and the best, second best, third best, and so on, methods when

*This chapter is based on S. Makridakis, "A New Approach to Statistical Forecasting," INSEAD Working Paper 1987/20.

Table 11-1 Among-Method Model Selection Using Different Selection Criteria

Methods	Fitting Model	Forecasting Horizons										Average of Forecasting Horizons					
		1	2	3	4	5	6	8	12	15	18	1–4	1–6	1–8	1–12	1–15	1–18
		Average MAPE: All Data (111)															
Single exponential smoothing	8.6	7.8	10.8	13.1	14.5	15.7	17.2	16.5	13.6	29.3	30.1	11.6	13.2	14.1	14.0	15.3	16.8
Dampen trend exponential smoothing	10.1	7.8	10.2	12.4	14.4	15.9	16.8	18.1	14.0	30.6	30.6	11.2	12.9	14.2	14.3	15.7	17.2
Holt's linear exponential smoothing	8.6	7.9	10.5	13.2	15.1	17.3	19.0	23.1	16.5	35.6	35.2	11.7	13.8	16.1	16.4	18.0	19.7
Long-term memory AR (p) model	6.8	9.6	8.6	10.3	12.2	13.6	14.1	14.7	14.7	18.0	24.5	10.2	11.4	12.3	12.7	13.3	14.3
Above four methods combined	8.2	7.7	9.2	10.8	12.9	14.4	15.2	14.8	13.8	26.2	26.6	10.1	11.7	12.6	13.2	13.9	14.2
Automatic AEP filter	10.8	9.8	11.3	13.7	15.1	16.9	18.8	23.3	16.2	30.2	33.9	12.5	14.3	16.3	16.2	17.4	19.0
Bayesian forecasting	13.3	10.3	12.8	13.6	14.4	16.2	17.1	19.2	16.1	27.5	30.6	12.8	14.1	15.2	15.0	16.1	17.6
Box Jenkins ARMA models	0.0	10.3	10.7	11.4	14.5	16.4	17.1	18.9	16.4	26.2	34.2	11.7	13.4	14.8	15.1	16.3	18.0
Lewandowski's FORSYS	12.3	11.6	12.8	14.5	15.3	16.6	17.6	18.9	17.0	33.0	28.6	13.5	14.7	15.5	15.6	17.2	18.6
Parzen's ARARMA models	8.9	10.6	10.7	10.7	13.5	14.3	14.7	16.0	13.7	22.5	26.5	11.4	12.4	13.3	13.4	14.3	15.4
Method with best MSE model fit	6.7	8.4	8.3	11.2	13.8	14.3	16.0	17.8	17.0	33.9	34.6	10.4	12.0	13.5	14.1	15.9	18.0
Method with best MAPE model fit	6.1	8.4	8.9	11.9	15.0	15.1	16.7	19.5	15.4	31.6	31.6	11.0	12.7	14.3	14.4	15.8	17.5
Best MAPE out-of-sample	n.a.	7.6	8.5	10.0	12.3	13.1	14.2	16.1	14.2	18.3	20.4	9.6	10.9	12.2	12.5	13.1	13.8
Best MSE out-of-sample	n.a.	7.0	8.4	9.6	12.3	13.4	14.6	16.4	14.2	18.6	20.5	9.3	10.9	12.1	12.5	13.1	13.8
Combine 2 best MAPE out-of-sample	n.a.	7.4	8.8	10.0	12.1	12.9	14.1	15.7	13.4	19.1	20.6	9.6	10.9	12.2	12.3	13.1	13.9
Combine 3 best MAPE out-of-sample	n.a.	7.3	8.6	9.8	12.6	13.5	14.9	16.7	12.7	18.2	20.5	9.6	11.1	12.6	12.7	13.4	14.1
Combine 4 best MAPE out-of-sample	n.a.	7.2	8.6	9.7	13.0	13.7	14.8	17.9	12.6	18.5	21.1	9.6	11.2	12.8	12.9	13.7	14.4
Combine 2 best MSE out-of-sample	n.a.	7.3	8.8	9.6	11.8	12.7	14.2	15.6	13.3	19.3	20.7	9.3	10.8	12.0	12.2	13.0	13.8
Combine 3 best MSE out-of-sample	n.a.	7.1	8.3	9.8	12.6	13.4	14.9	16.4	12.8	18.3	20.5	9.4	11.0	12.5	12.6	13.3	14.0
Combine 4 best MSE out-of-sample	n.a.	7.1	8.3	9.7	13.0	13.6	14.9	17.8	12.6	18.5	21.1	9.5	11.1	12.7	12.9	13.6	14.3
Combine best MSE and MAPE	n.a.	7.2	8.4	9.3	12.2	12.8	14.3	15.9	14.2	18.4	20.4	9.3	10.7	11.9	12.3	12.9	13.7
Combine best MSE, MAPE and rank	n.a.	7.7	8.7	10.0	12.7	13.0	13.8	15.3	14.4	20.3	20.7	9.8	11.0	12.2	12.5	13.2	13.7
Reference	n.a.	7.5	8.2	9.8	12.8	13.0	13.9	15.3	13.7	16.3	20.9	9.6	10.9	11.9	12.3	12.7	13.4
Best in confidence intervals	n.a.	7.5	8.4	9.8	12.3	12.5	13.6	14.4	14.0	15.8	20.5	9.5	10.7	11.6	12.0	12.5	13.2

[a] n.a. indicates not available.

forecasting for 1, 2, 3, 4, . . . , 18 forecasting horizons. When a forecasting competition (see Chapter 15) computed rank correlations between how well eight methods fitted past data and how they forecast these data (see Table 11-1), they were found to be small to start with (about 0.20) and dropped to 0 after forecasting horizons longer than four periods (Makridakis, 1986).

The implications of the fact that the model that best fits the available data might *not* be the best model for forecasting have only recently been considered. Even during the 1970s this possibility was not mentioned in the most popular forecasting or econometric textbooks (Box and Jenkins, 1970; Johnston, 1972). Thus, no serious effort was made to validate the ability of the selected model to accurately forecast for future periods. This was partly because *all* data were used to develop the "best" model, and partly because of the belief (originated in physical sciences) that a "true best" model exists, and that such a model could be correctly identified and used for forecasting. Inasmuch as most series used in the economic and business areas are short, measurement errors abound, and controlled experimentation is not possible; the basic premise that the "best" model fitted to past data exists and that it can be identified is not valid. Furthermore, the assumption that such a model is also the best one to forecast beyond the historical data is not necessarily correct.

CONSTANT VERSUS CHANGING PATTERNS OR RELATIONSHIPS

Firgure 11-1 shows monthly international airline passengers (in thousands) between 1949 and 1981. The data are divided into three segments. Segment A consists of 144 observations (1949 to 1961), which are the infamous airline data widely used in forecasting literature since the early 1960s (Box and Jenkins, 1970; Brown, 1963). Segment B includes data from 1961 to 1967, and segment C includes data after 1967. This means that the methods presented in Part B cannot be used for all of the data of Figure 11-1 (the pattern is not constant), although they can be used for segments A and B.

Although the majority of forecasting methods would provide equally good forecasts for data series when there are no changes in established patterns or relationships (see Figure 11-2 for an example), the forecasts and their accuracy will vary substantially when the changes in patterns or relationships do occur. It is necessary, therefore, to understand how various methods forecast when such changes take place, since this is the key to understanding how to improve forecasting accuracy.

Figures 11-3 to 11-5 show three kinds of pattern change during forecasting.

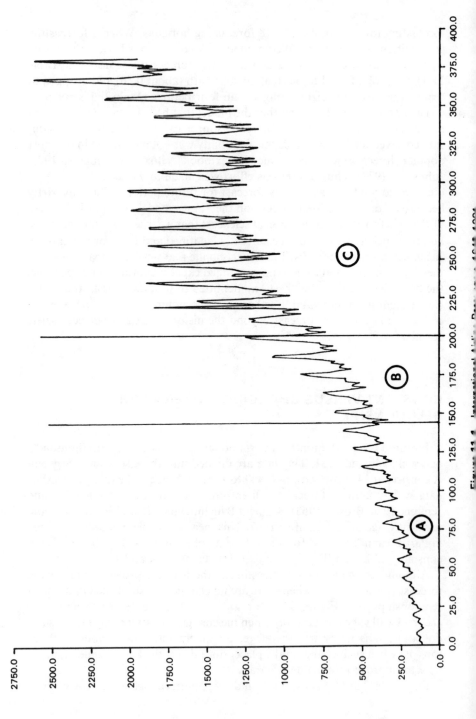

Figure 11-1. International Airline Passengers 1949–1961

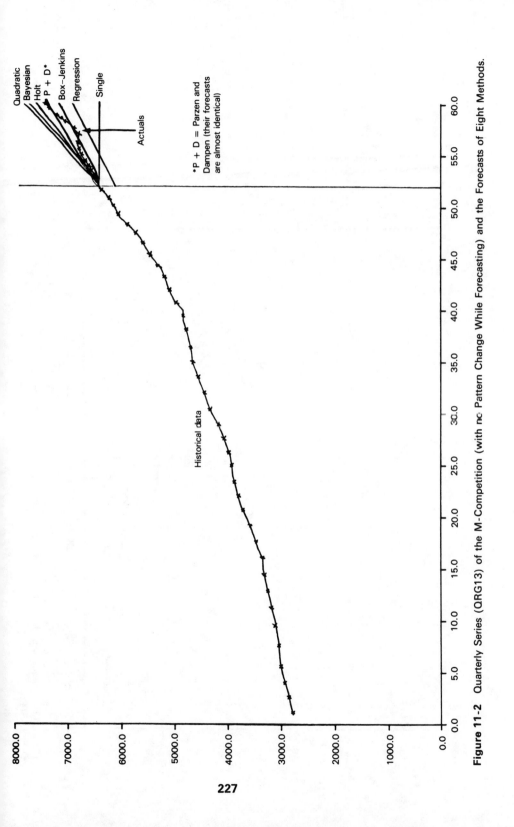

Figure 11-2 Quarterly Series (QRG13) of the M-Competition (with no Pattern Change While Forecasting) and the Forecasts of Eight Methods.

227

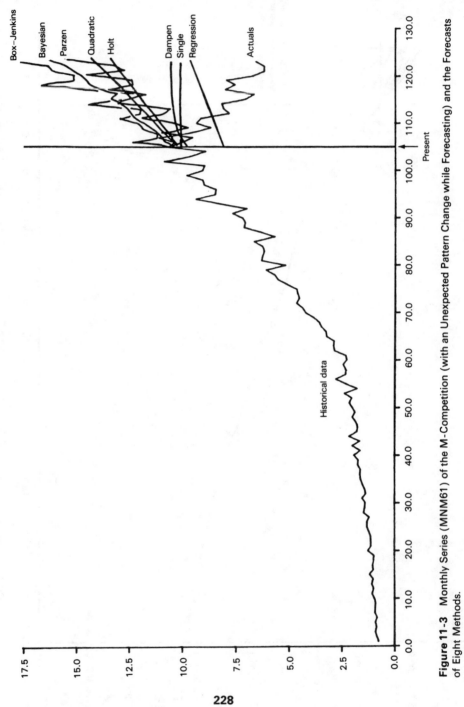

Figure 11-3 Monthly Series (MNM61) of the M-Competition (with an Unexpected Pattern Change while Forecasting) and the Forecasts of Eight Methods.

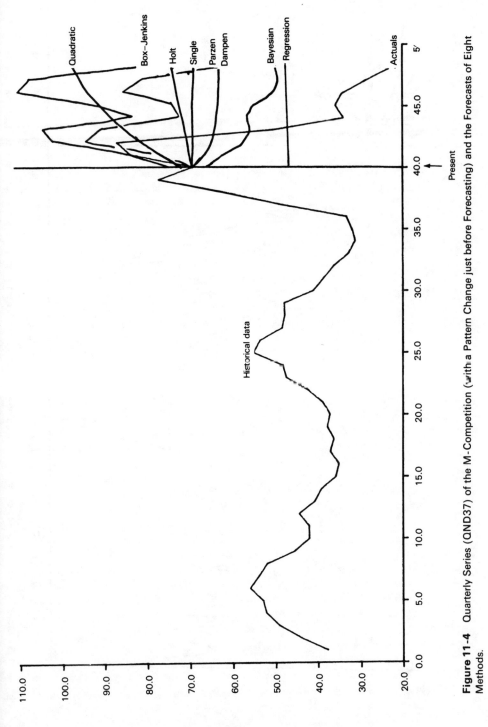

Figure 11-4 Quarterly Series (QND37) of the M-Competition (with a Pattern Change just before Forecasting) and the Forecasts of Eight Methods.

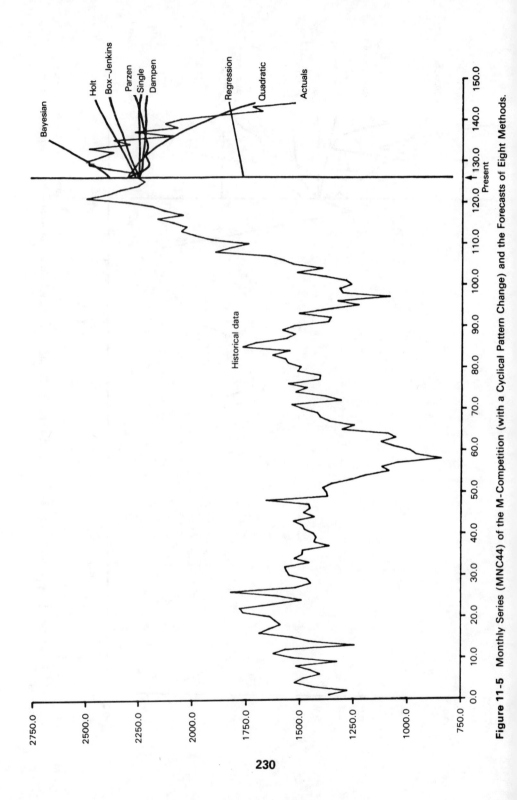

Figure 11-5 Monthly Series (MNC44) of the M-Competition (with a Cyclical Pattern Change) and the Forecasts of Eight Methods.

(The data of the three figures have been deseasonalized to better illustrate pattern changes and their consequences.) In Figure 11-3, the exponential-growth trend changed into an abrupt decline. There was nothing in the past data to indicate that such a change was forthcoming. It was impossible, therefore, to have anticipated a pattern change without inside judgmental knowledge. All methods, except for single exponential smoothing, forecast a continuation of the established trend. (Single exponential smoothing always forecasts horizontally at the most recent smoothed data level.) Contrary to the data of Figure 11-2, where the trend continued and single exponential smoothing did not forecast accurately because it assumed no trend, in Figure 11-3 exponential smoothing performs the best, since all methods (except linear trend regression) forecast by extrapolating the established exponential trend.

The data of Figure 11-4 start increasing at period 34 and do so until period 39. The figures then decrease for two consecutive periods. Two methods (Box–Jenkins and quadratic smoothing) ignore the latest two-period decline and forecast a continuation of the recent increase from periods 34 to 39. Bayesian forecasting assumes that the decline in periods 39 and 40 is not random and forecasts by extrapolating the downward trend, implicitly assuming the latest decline to be permanent. By so doing, the Bayesian procedure produces forecasts that beat all other methods. Linear trend regression ignores all fluctuations around the trend line, assuming them to be random, and extrapolates the trend to arrive at linearly growing forecasts. The forecasts of the other methods are between those of regression and Box–Jenkins. Interestingly, single exponential smoothing does pretty well, although it ignores both the initial increase (periods 34 to 39) in the actual data and the subsequent two-period decline (see Figure 11-4). The series in Figure 11-4, contrary to the series in Figure 11-3, has in its past provided indications that it *might* decline after several periods of continuous increase. Because such a decline has happened twice in the past, one could therefore have anticipated a similar decline in the future and have forecast in this light.

The data of Figure 11-5 reach a trough at period 96; then they increase (with small interruptions) until period 120, at which point they start declining until period 125. Finally, there is a single increase at period 126. Bayesian forecasting, although doing best with the data of Figure 11-4, does worst with those of Figure 11-5. It assumes a growing trend, thus providing increasing forecasts. Quadratic exponential smoothing, which did the worst with the data of Figure 11-4, now does the best by ignoring the increase in the last period and forecasting a continuing decline from periods 120 onward. The forecasts of the other methods are between those of quadratic smoothing and Bayesian forecasting. The series of Figure 11-5 is similar to that of Figure 11-4 in that several declines after persistent increases, similar to the latest one, have occurred in the past. It is not unreasonable, therefore, to anticipate (although the exact timing may not be predictable) that similar declines may occur in the future during forecasting.

Three observations should be made at this point. First, the forecasts of the various methods are all over the graph when a pattern change occurs (see Figures 11-3–11-5) during the forecast period. (This is one reason why combining various methods by simple arithmetic averaging does well—see Chapter 15.) Second, the accuracy of the methods depends on whether the latest nonrandom change in pattern is temporary or permanent (Makridakis, 1986). Some methods, such as Bayesian forecasting, are reactive in extrapolating recent changes in the data pattern by assuming them to be permanent. Other methods are slower in identifying and extrapolating the continuation of nonrandom changes in the data. Linear trend regression, for instance, ignores all changes around the long-term trend, while single exponential smoothing assumes a no-change (trend) situation. Third, single exponential smoothing seems to do well, not because it can predict pattern changes, but rather because its forecasts are robust, staying in the middle of the data and usually in the middle of the forecasts of the various methods when pattern changes occur. This seems to be a good strategy, at least for the short term, since empirically the accuracy of single exponential smoothing for one-period-ahead forecasts was found to be the best of all methods in the M-competition (see Chapter 15) which compared the forecasting accuracy of all major time series methods.

PREDICTING THE FUTURE INSTEAD OF EXPLAINING THE PAST

For any forecasting approach to be realistic and practically relevant it must avoid the two major problems facing the traditional approach to statistical forecasting: (1) selection based upon how well a model fits available data for one-period-ahead forecasts, and (2) assuming constancy of patterns or relationships.

Initially, the desired characteristics of the new approach might seem contradictory. Any time-series model, for instance, must be based on past data. At the same time, we know that the future may not be the same as the past. Furthermore, all data should be used to develop the forecasting model (otherwise some information might be lost); at the same time we advocate that out-of-sample testing be done. These seemingly contradictory requirements can be achieved simultaneously if we are willing to reconceptualize our approach to statistical modeling and forecasting.

Instead of using all data points to develop a forecasting model we can use some part of the data points initially to develop the model and make the forecasts. Since actual data exist beyond those used to develop the model, the *actual* forecasting accuracy of the model can be tested *for each of the forecasts.* Accuracy measures (such as MAPE, MSE, or median) for 1, 2, 3, . . . , m-period-ahead forecasts can, therefore, be found. Once such measures have been found, one more data point can be used, m forecasts again made, and their actual forecasting accuracy recorded. The process can be repeated, each time using one more data point, until all observations except one have been used. This type of testing (sliding simulation) can be called out-of-sample; it is shown schematically in Figure 11-6.

Once the sliding simulation has been completed, *actual* (not model fitting) one-step, two-step, . . . , m-step-ahead accuracy measures are available. The average of these measures for each of the m forecasting horizons can, therefore, be computed. Thus, model selection can be based on actual out-of-sample forecasting performance without any loss of information, since in the final analysis *all* data have been used. This type of model selection is fundamentally different from the approach used in Part B in two respects. First, model selection is based on forecasts of out-of-sample data. Second, forecasting performance is measured and model selection is done, in addition to one period ahead, for two, three, . . . , and m-step-ahead forecasts.

WITHIN-METHOD MODEL SELECTION

Given a particular method, some optimization criterion can be used to select an appropriate model. In the case of, say, single exponential smoothing this means finding seasonal indices (if there is seasonality) and optimal parameter values. This "best" model can be used to make 18 forecasts and compute various errors measured. Then the first 25 data points can be used to find the model that best fits this augmented set and make m new forecasts. This optimization process can continue, each time computing the optimal model, until all but one of the data points have been used in the model-fitting process.

Since at each step of the simulation, 18 forecasts are computed and their out-of-sample accuracy is found, it is possible to try alternative models (for example, using different values for α) and record how well these models perform for each of the 18 forecasting horizons. It is not necessarily true that the best model for 1 forecasting horizon is also the best for 2, 3, . . . , 18 horizons. The sliding simulation allows us to record the out-of-sample per-

STEPS

1. Decide on some appropriate models and/or methods.

2. Use the first s data only and make m forecasts for each model or data.

3. Compute some accuracy measures to find out how well each of the models or methods forecasts the actual data for each of m forecasting horizons.

4. Use one more data point and make m forecasts.

5. Compute accuracy measures desired.

6. Continue adding one extra data point each time (until there are no more data left).

7. Compute some accuracy measures

8. Find the average error for each forecasting horizon and accuracy measure for each model or method.

9. Select the model or method for *each* forecasting horizon which performs best for the accuracy measures you consider most appropriate.

Historical Data

| 1 | 2 | 3 | 4 | 5 | 6 | . | . | $n-2$ | $n-1$ | n |

Forecasts

| 1 | 2 | 3 | 4 | ... | $s-1$ | s | 1 | 2 | ... | m |

Accuracy Measures

| 1 | 2 | ... | m |

Forecasts

| 1 | 2 | 3 | 4 | ... | $s-1$ | s | $s+1$ | 1 | 1 | 2 | ... | m |

Accuracy Measures

| 1 | 2 | ... | m |

| 1 | 2 | 3 | 4 | ... | $s-1$ | s | $s+1$ | $s+2$ | 1 | 1 | 2 | ... | m |

Accuracy Measures

| 1 | 2 | ... | m |

Period	Accuracy Measure 1	Accuracy Measure 2
s	1 2 3 4 ... $m-1$ m	1 2 3 4 ... $m-1$ m
$s+1$	1 2 3 4 ... $m-1$ m	1 2 3 4 ... $m-1$ m
$s+2$	1 2 3 4 ... $m-1$ m	1 2 3 4 ... $m-1$ m
$n-1$	1 2	1 2
n	1	1
Average	1 2 3 4 ... $m-1$ m	1 2 3 4 ... $m-1$ m

Figure 11-6 Visualization of the Sliding Simulation and the Steps Required.

formance at each step of the simulation. Thus, when the simulation is over, the model that does the best for 2, 3, . . . , 18 periods ahead can be selected. (The best model for one-step-ahead forecasts is the same as the model that best fits the past data.) Table 11-1 shows the MAPE for the M-competition data for each of 18 forecasting horizons using the approaches described in Part B. That is, fitting the best model to the past data minimizing the MSE of one-step-ahead forecasts. In addition, it shows the results for selecting the best model for 2, 3, . . . , 18 periods ahead, and minimizing MSE at each forecasting horizon in the manner shown in Figure 11-6. The result is a substantial improvement in the forecasting accuracy. The optimal values of X are different at various forecasting horizons, which confirms the need to use different models, depending on how long into the future we wish to predict.

AMONG-METHODS MODEL SELECTION

Another way to avoid fitting a model to past data for one-period-ahead forecasts only is to select a few appropriate methods and then choose the best among them on the basis of out-of-sample comparisons. In empirical work we have found four methods that are (1) simple, (2) complementary, (3) intuitive, and (4) automatic. These methods are single, Holt's, and damped exponential smoothing, and a long-term autoregressive model similar to that of Parzen described in Chapter 7. An optimal model for each of these four methods can be found based on all data (that is, using the approach of minimizing MSE described in Part B). However, instead of obtaining forecasts based on each of these optimal models, we will use the sliding simulation described earlier. This means that the first 24 data points can be used and 18 forecasts made by each of the four methods. Then the first 25 data points are used and 18 forecasts made, and so on until all but one of the data have been used.

Once the sliding simulation (see Figure 11-6) has been completed, information about how well each method has performed during the out-of-sample testing for 1, 2, 3, . . . , m periods ahead is known. On the basis of this information, the method that does the best for one period ahead is selected to forecast one period ahead, the method that does the best for two periods ahead is selected to forecast for two periods ahead, and so on. This allows us to (1) select the best method on the basis of out of sample (that is, future) information and (2) select the best method for each of the m forecasting horizons we intend to forecast.

Table 11-2 shows the results for different methods using the approaches of Part B and the sliding simulation described in this chapter.

Table 11-2 Within-Method Model Selection Using as Criterion the Model that Minimizes MSE for Each Forecasting Horizon

Method	Model Fitting[a]	Forecasting Horizon										Average of Forecasting Horizons					
		1	2	3	4	5	6	8	12	15	18	1–4	1–6	1–8	1–12	1–15	1–18
		Average MAPE: All Data (111)															
Parzen ARARMA (M-competition)	8.9	10.6	10.7	10.7	13.5	14.3	14.7	16.0	13.7	22.5	26.5	11.4	12.4	13.3	13.4	14.3	15.4
Single (optimal model fitting)	8.6	7.6	10.8	13.1	14.5	15.7	17.2	16.5	13.6	29.3	30.1	11.6	13.2	14.1	14.0	15.3	16.8
Single (optimal out-of-sample)	n.a.	7.8	10.4	12.2	13.5	14.4	15.7	14.9	13.4	24.9	25.1	11.0	12.3	13.1	13.0	14.1	15.2
Dampen-trend (optimal model fitting)	10.1	7.8	10.2	12.4	14.4	15.9	16.8	18.1	14.0	30.6	30.6	11.2	12.9	14.2	14.3	15.7	17.2
Dampen-trend (optimal out-of-sample)	n.a.	8.2	9.6	12.1	12.7	14.8	17.2	18.6	15.5	27.3	27.3	10.6	12.4	13.9	14.2	15.2	16.6
Holt (optimal model fitting)	8.6	7.9	10.5	13.2	15.1	17.3	19.0	23.1	16.5	35.6	35.2	11.7	13.8	16.1	16.4	18.0	19.7
Holt (optimal out-of-sample)	n.a.	7.9	10.3	11.9	13.6	15.0	15.7	17.8	14.0	28.0	26.8	10.9	12.4	13.8	14.1	15.3	16.4
Quadratic (optimal model fitting)	8.7	8.8	11.8	15.0	16.9	21.9	24.1	35.7	29.7	56.1	63.6	13.1	16.4	20.3	22.2	25.9	30.2
Quadratic (optimal out-of-sample)	n.a.	8.8	11.0	14.9	14.6	16.8	18.6	22.3	26.5	36.2	47.2	12.3	14.1	15.8	16.9	19.2	22.3
		Average MAPE: Yearly Data (20)															
Parzen ARARMA (M-competition)	9.6	7.6	7.7	12.8	16.0	20.5	18.0	0.0	0.0	0.0	0.0	11.0	13.8	13.8	13.8	13.8	13.8
Single (optimal model fitting)	11.4	6.2	9.1	16.3	21.0	23.6	25.4	0.0	0.0	0.0	0.0	13.1	16.9	16.9	16.9	16.9	16.9
Single (optimal out-of-sample)	n.a.	6.1	8.0	15.7	20.9	23.4	24.5	0.0	0.0	0.0	0.0	12.7	16.4	16.4	16.4	16.4	16.4
Dampen-trend (optimal model fitting)	15.1	6.9	9.6	15.2	20.3	23.4	20.9	0.0	0.0	0.0	0.0	13.0	16.0	16.0	16.0	16.0	16.0
Dampen-trend (optimal out-of-sample)	n.a.	6.6	7.1	11.9	18.7	26.1	24.4	0.0	0.0	0.0	0.0	11.1	15.8	15.8	15.8	15.8	15.8
Holt (optimal model fitting)	12.9	5.6	7.2	11.9	16.2	19.0	16.5	0.0	0.0	0.0	0.0	10.2	12.7	12.7	12.7	12.7	12.7
Holt (optimal out-of-sample)	n.a.	5.7	6.7	10.9	14.1	17.7	15.9	0.0	0.0	0.0	0.0	9.4	11.8	11.8	11.8	11.8	11.8
Quadratic (optimal model fitting)	11.1	7.0	8.6	11.8	16.0	20.7	17.4	0.0	0.0	0.0	0.0	10.9	13.6	13.6	13.6	13.6	13.6
Quadratic (optimal out-of-sample)	n.a.	7.3	6.8	11.3	12.4	15.5	15.1	0.0	0.0	0.0	0.0	9.5	11.4	11.4	11.4	11.4	11.4
		Average MAPE: Quarterly Data (23)															
Parzen ARARMA (M-competition)	7.7	6.8	7.6	12.0	16.5	21.1	20.4	21.0	0.0	0.0	0.0	10.7	14.1	16.7	16.7	16.7	16.7
Single (optimal model fitting)	7.7	9.0	12.0	14.4	20.5	21.0	21.9	22.6	0.0	0.0	0.0	14.0	16.5	18.5	18.5	18.5	18.5
Single (optimal out-of-sample)	n.a.	9.1	10.7	11.4	15.6	17.1	17.4	18.1	0.0	0.0	0.0	11.7	13.6	15.4	15.4	15.4	15.4

Dampen-trend (optimal model fitting)	9.6	8.8	8.6	11.9	19.7	22.3	24.8	26.6	0.0	0.0	0.0	12.2	16.0	19.3	19.3	19.3	19.3	19.3
Dampen-trend (optimal out-of-sample)	n.a.	9.5	8.6	12.7	13.7	17.1	21.9	22.0	0.0	0.0	0.0	11.1	13.9	16.6	16.6	16.6	16.6	16.6
Holt (optimal model fitting)	7.2	9.2	10.4	17.1	25.1	30.3	32.2	39.2	0.0	0.0	0.0	15.4	20.7	25.9	25.9	25.9	25.9	25.9
Holt (optimal out-of-sample)	n.a.	7.4	10.6	14.4	20.3	21.1	21.5	21.2	0.0	0.0	0.0	13.2	15.9	17.9	17.9	17.9	17.9	17.9
Quadratic (optimal model fitting)	7.9	11.1	12.5	21.1	32.0	39.2	46.0	66.6	0.0	0.0	0.0	19.2	27.0	35.6	35.6	35.6	35.6	35.6
Quadratic (optimal out-of-sample)	n.a.	10.0	12.1	22.4	25.2	28.1	29.5	34.0	0.0	0.0	0.0	17.4	21.2	24.6	24.6	24.6	24.6	24.6

Average MAPE: Monthly Data (68)

Parzen ARARMA (M-competition)	9.0	12.7	12.6	9.6	11.7	0.2	11.8	14.3	13.7	22.5	26.5	11.4	12.1	12.6	12.6	12.6	13.9	15.4
Single (optimal model fitting)	8.0	7.9	10.9	11.7	10.5	11.6	13.2	14.4	13.6	29.3	30.1	11.0	12.0	12.6	12.6	14.5	16.5
Single (optimal out-of-sample)	n.a.	7.9	11.1	11.4	10.5	10.8	12.5	13.8	13.4	24.9	25.1	10.7	11.6	12.0	13.0	13.6	15.1
Dampen-trend (optimal model fitting)	8.7	7.8	11.0	11.8	10.9	11.6	12.9	15.2	14.0	30.6	30.6	11.0	12.1	13.0	13.0	15.0	17.1
Dampen-trend (optimal out-of-sample)	n.a.	8.2	10.7	12.0	10.5	10.7	13.5	17.4	15.5	27.3	27.3	10.4	10.9	12.5	13.4	14.9	16.7
Holt (optimal model fitting)	7.9	8.2	11.5	12.3	11.4	12.5	15.2	17.7	16.5	35.6	35.2	10.9	11.8	13.5	14.8	17.2	19.5
Holt (optimal out-of-sample)	n.a.	8.7	11.3	11.3	11.2	12.2	13.7	16.7	14.0	28.0	26.8	10.6	11.4	12.8	13.6	15.3	16.6
Quadratic (optimal model fitting)	8.6	12.5	13.8	12.1	15.3	18.7	25.3	29.7	56.1	63.6	11.7	13.7	16.6	20.4	25.7	11.0
Quadratic (optimal out-of-sample)	n.a.	8.8	11.8	13.5	11.5	13.4	16.0	18.4	26.5	36.2	47.2	11.4	12.5	13.9	16.0	19.2	23.0

[a] n.a. indicates not available.

237

WITHIN- AND AMONG-METHODS SELECTION

Finally, it is possible to combine the within- and among-methods selections. This requires that the best model of each of the four methods be found using the within-method model selection described. Then on the basis of the forecasts obtained from the best model for each of the four methods, another selection is done to choose the best method for each of the forecasting horizons.

The proposed approach to statistical forecasting makes theoretical sense. Equally important, when tested empirically with the M-competition data (see Makridakis, 1988), it provided superior results in terms of improved forecasting accuracy.

The sliding simulation provides additional possibilities beyond improved forecasting accuracy. First, realistic confidence intervals can be built for each of the m forecasting horizons. Such intervals need not be symmetric, since information about underestimates as well as overestimates around the most likely out-of-sample forecasts is collected. In addition, through an analysis of extreme errors, it is possible to warn forecasting users about *unusual* errors and help them think of ways to prepare to face such errors.

In this chapter we have proposed a new approach to forecasting. Such an approach aims at eliminating the problem of explaining (fitting) the past data and developing optimal one-step-ahead forecasting models. The new approach is based on the principle that model selection must be done on actual out-of-sample forecasting performance. Such selection is made on two levels. First, the best model (within-method selection) of a single method is chosen. Second, the best method among several, run in parallel, is selected. Both the within-method and the among-methods selections are done on out-of-sample comparisons. Furthermore, the within- and between-methods selections can be combined. In the new approach we do not assume that a unique method exists that can forecast best for all series and forecasting horizons. A different model or method can be selected for various series, and for each forecasting horizon, on the basis of the actual out-of-sample performance of the method or model for this specific forecasting horizon.

The empirical testing of the proposed approach shows large improvements in forecasting accuracy. Such improvements extend to both short, medium, and long forecasting horizons, different types of data (yearly, quarterly, monthly), and other classifications. Finally, the improvements come both within method, when the best model is chosen on the basis of out-of-sample information, and among methods, when the best method is chosen on the basis of out-of-sample information. Combining the within- *and* among-methods selections might further improve forecasting accuracy.

SELECTED REFERENCES FOR FURTHER STUDY

Armstrong, J. S., 1986. "Research on Forecasting: A Quarter-Century Review, 1960–1984," *Interfaces*, 16, no. 1, pp. 89–109.

Box, G. E. P., and G. M. Jenkins, 1970, *Time Series Analysis: Forecasting and Control*, Holden-Day, San Francisco.

Brown, R. G., 1963. *Smoothing, Forecasting and Prediction of Discrete Time Series*, Prentice-Hall, Englewood Cliffs, NJ.

Carbone, R., and S. Makridakis, 1986. "Forecasting when Pattern Changes Occur beyond the Historical Data," *Management Science*, 32, no. 3, pp. 257–271.

Gardner, E. S., and E. McKenzie, 1985. "Forecasting Trends in Time Series," *Management Science*, 31, no. 10, pp. 1237–1246.

Gardner, E. S., and S. Makridakis (Eds.), 1988. "The Future of Forecasting," *International Journal of Forecasting*, 4, no. 3, pp. 325–331.

Jenkins, G. M., 1982. "Some Practical Aspects of Forecasting in Organizations," *Journal of Forecasting*, 1, no. 1, pp. 3–23.

Johnston, J., 1972. *Econometric Methods*, 2nd ed., McGraw-Hill, New York.

Mahmoud, E., 1984. "Accuracy in Forecasting: A Survey," *Journal of Forecasting*, 3, pp. 139–159.

Makridakis, S., 1988. "Metaforecasting: Ways of Improving Forecasting Accuracy and Usefulness," *International Journal of Forecasting*, 4, no. 3, pp. 467–492.

———, 1986. "The Art and Science of Forecasting; An Assessment and Future Directions", *International Journal of Forecasting*, vol. 2, pp. 15–39.

———, 1981. "Forecasting Accuracy and the Assumption of Accuracy," *Omega*, 9, no. 3, pp. 307–311.

Parzen, E., 1982. "ARARMA Models for Time Series Analyses and Forecasting," *Journal of Forecasting*, 1, pp. 67–82.

Priestley, M. B., 1979. "Discussion of the Paper by Professor Makridakis and Dr. Hibon," *Journal of the Royal Statistical Society*," 142, pt. 2, pp. 127–129.

Russel, T. D., and E. E. Adams, Jr., 1987. "An Empirical Evaluation of Alternative Forecasting Combinations," *Management Science*, 33, no. 10, pp. 1267–1276.

Schnaars, S. P., 1986. "An Evaluation of Rules of Selecting an Extrapolation Model on Yearly Sales Forecasts," *Interfaces*, 16, no. 6, pp. 100–107.

Williams, W. H., and M. L. Goodman, 1971. "A Simple Method for the Construction of Empirical Confidence Limits for Economic Forecasts," *Journal of the American Statistical Association*, 66, pp. 752–754.

CHAPTER 12

JUDGMENTAL APPROACHES TO FORECASTING

The chapters in Part B dealt with quantitative forecasting methods. In this and the next chapter, a second major class of forecasting methods—judgmental—is considered. Although judgmental methods are the most widely used approach to forecasting (Dalrymple, 1987), their substantial limitations and pitfalls often go unrecognized by practitioners.

In this chapter we begin by reviewing the major types of judgmental methods—jury of executive opinion, sales force composites, anticipatory surveys, and individual subjective assessments. The second half of the chapter considers three categories of problems commonly associated with these methods—the quest for supporting evidence, overconfidence in judgments, and overconformity among group members (often referred to as "groupthink").

In Chapter 13, the major types of biases and limitations are outlined and illustrated, using evidence from a number of recent studies. Approaches for overcoming these types of bias are presented, and overall guidelines for the use of such judgments, the use of models based on the development of such judgments, and the use of quantitative models like those outlined in earlier chapters are provided.

THE JURY OF EXECUTIVE OPINION

The jury of executive opinion approach, summarized and illustrated by the Conference Board (1978), is one of the simplest and most widely used forecasting approaches available (see Dalrymple, 1987; Mentzer and Cox, 1984). In its most basic form, it consists of corporate executives sitting around a table and deciding as a group what their best estimate is for the item to be forecast. One of the main drawbacks of this approach is that because it puts the estimators in personal contact with one another, the weight assigned to each executive's assessment will depend in large part on the role and personality of that executive in the organization. Thus the greatest weight will not necessarily be given to the assessment made by the executive with the best information or the best ability to forecast the future.

When using this approach, a company generally brings together executives from sales, production, finance, purchasing, and administration so as to achieve broad coverage in experience and opinion. A number of companies provide the executives involved in this assessment process background data on the economy and various factors within the company that may be useful in assessing forecasts. This factual assistance can help to separate those areas for which judgment is most important from those for which historical information is particularly relevant. Making this separation often helps the group to move toward a more precise evaluation of the factors that affect the forecast.

In one variation of the jury of executive opinion approach, the jury is periodically requested to submit its estimates in writing. These written estimates may then be reviewed by the president or an executive vice-president who makes a final assessment on the basis of the opinions expressed, or they may be averaged to arrive at a representative forecast. Executives often perceive that this has the advantage that the president or executive vice-president may have learned from experience which executives are generally biased in which direction and can appropriately weight each individual's estimate. As will be outlined in Chapter 13, the evidence on the appropriateness of doing this is mixed.

The advantages cited for the jury of executive opinion approach to forecasting are that it provides forecasts quickly and easily; it does not require the preparation of elaborate statistics; it brings together a variety of specialized viewpoints (it pools experience and judgment); and many times it may be the only feasible means of forecasting, especially in the absence of adequate data, or when substantial changes are taking place in the environment. In addition, it is also possible to make the forecasts become a reality. As might be expected, the disadvantages also are related to the important role of intuition and unaided judgment in this approach. For example, it is often inferior to more systematic (quantitative) forecasting methods that do not rely so heavily on opinion. In addition, this method requires costly executive time, disperses responsibility for accurate forecasting, and may present difficulties in making breakdowns by products, time periods, or markets for operating purposes.

SALES FORCE COMPOSITE METHODS

The sales force composite approach to forecasting consists of obtaining the views of individual salespeople and sales management as to the future sales outlook. This method is frequently used and has been the focus of studies by the Conference Board and others. In describing the technique, the Conference Board (1978) has divided its use into three general categories: the grass roots approach, the sales management technique, and the distributor's approach.

In the grass roots approach, the process begins with the collection of each salesperson's estimate of probable future sales in his or her territory. These estimates may be made privately by the salesperson on forms provided for that purpose, or they may be made by the salesperson in consultation with a branch or regional manager. Often these assessments are associated with the annual budgeting and planning cycle of the company. Once the salespeople have made their individual assessments, the results for the district or region are cumulated and forwarded to the central office, where a composite forecast is put together. It is common practice to have the salespeople estimate demand by classes of products and often by customer so that the final composite can provide forecasts on several different dimensions—geographic area, product line, customer size, and so on. The checks and balances generally used in the application of this approach are based mainly on the judgment and assessment of district salespeople and top management as to the reasonableness of individual salespersons' estimates. It is also common practice for a corporate staff group to make an independent estimate of demand and use that as a basis for cross-checking the composite results.

The advantages cited for the sales force composite approach are that it uses the specialized knowledge of those closest to the marketplace, it places responsibility for the forecasts in the hands of those who can most affect the actual results, and it lends itself to the easy breakdown of the forecasts by territory, product, customer, or salesperson. The disadvantages are in many cases very similar to those found in consumer surveys (see the next section). Often salespeople are either overly optimistic or overly pessimistic. At other times they are unaware of broad economic patterns that may affect demand in their territory for various product lines. (Some companies have sought to overcome this weakness by giving salespeople information on general economic projections before they make their estimates.)

As an alternative to the grass roots approach, the sales management technique is often used. This approach uses the specialized knowledge of the sales executive staff rather than assessments by individual salespersons. The rationale is that the sales executives generally possess almost as much information as the individual members of the sales force and the executives can be trained to make better assessments over time. Sometimes this approach involves only high-level executives. Then it begins to resemble the jury of executive opinion, except that most executives come from sales or marketing. One advantage claimed for using only sales executives rather than individual salespersons is that it reduces the time required to obtain such forecasts. However, it also means that the individual salespersons will not be committed to the forecast nearly as much as they would have been had they prepared their portion of it.

The wholesaler, or distributor, approach to the sales force composite method is generally used by manufacturing concerns that distribute their products through independent channels of distribution rather than through direct contact with the users of their products. In such instances, this approach looks very much like the survey method described in the next section of this chapter. It involves asking each distributor of the product for information as to the size and quantity of the company's product lines that they expect to sell in the next quarter or the next year. To promote interest and improve the validity of results, some companies give their distributors comparisons of previous sales forecasts and actual performance. Alternatively, they may provide similar data designed to encourage the cooperating distributors to evaluate their sales prospects objectively. Some companies have gone one step farther: they help their distributors do their own forecasting and planning, and as a spin-off from that, the manufacturing company receives better forecasting information. The use of computers and networking among distributors and manufacturers further increases the usefulness of such an approach as a forecasting tool.

ANTICIPATORY SURVEYS AND MARKET RESEARCH-BASED ASSESSMENTS

Both the jury of executive opinion and the sales force composite approaches to forecasting rely on a type of "expert" knowledge concerning future trends and the translation of those into specific forecasts. An alternative to using a handful of experts is to sample the population whose behavior and actions will determine future trends and activity levels of the items in question. Several surveys based on a sampling of intentions are prepared on a regular basis. Two of these of particular interest to forecasters deal with business plant and equipment expenditures and purchases of consumer durables. After a review of these, the use of market research techniques to gather survey information for an organization-specific need will be discussed.

Business fixed investment consists of nonresidential structures and producer variables. Statistical series for past expenditures are usually available, but the short-term fluctuations in actual expenditures can be substantial and the pattern can change because of cyclical factors. Many planners and forecasters find it useful to consider surveys aimed at determining the intentions of business in this area, such as the U.S. Department of Commerce–Securities and Exchange Commission Survey published quarterly in the *Survey of Current Business*. This survey is one of the most widely used in the area of business plant and equipment expenditures. Although the sample is not particularly large, it does provide useful information in many situations.

The Commerce–SEC survey is published in the third month of each quarter. At each publication date, a revised estimate of expenditures for the current quarter and the survey results for the next quarter are published. In December the estimate for the second quarter of the next calendar year is also included, and the March issue contains estimates for the calendar year even though three months have passed. With these yearly estimates, the revised first-quarter estimate, and the second-quarter estimate, the forecaster can project the expenditures for the last half of the calendar year.

A second survey in the area of business plant and equipment expenditures is published by McGraw-Hill in *Business Week*. This survey, published twice a year, concentrates on large firms in order to pick up the big capital expenditure programs. Surveying large firms may contain some biases when business activity changes, but it may also provide a useful source of data to forecasters.

McGraw-Hill conducts a preliminary survey early in the fourth quarter and releases its results in November. This date is generally late enough that most large firms have pretty well fixed their expenditures for the following year, and yet early enough to provide the forecaster with information that is useful in planning for the following year. McGraw-Hill then resurveys during the spring of the year and publishes that result in April. Usually this second survey is much more accurate than the first, since most business budgets are operational by then. Both the fall and spring surveys prepared by McGraw-Hill contain forecasts for multiple years in advance.

The Commerce–SEC and the McGraw-Hill surveys also include requests for information that serves as an internal check on the firmness and validity of the responses. Essentially, these requests try to cover three questions: (1) Do expenditure plans allow for changes in the price of capital goods? (2) What is the firm's own forecast of sales or GNP? (3) What are its present and anticipated rates of capacity utilization?

A third survey of business plant and equipment expenditures is conducted by the Conference Board. This survey of capital appropriations is reported quarterly. It is based on a sample of 1000 manufacturing firms that account for a substantial portion of the total capital expenditures in the United States. The survey picks up plans that are reasonably firm since it reports capital appropriations to which boards of directors have made commitments. This survey has been particularly helpful to many forecasters in picking up turning points in the plant and equipment series.

A second type of survey often found useful by forecasters deals with consumer purchasing of durables. These surveys can be useful in many situations. Perhaps the best known of the consumer surveys are those conducted by the Survey Research Center (SRC) of the University of Michigan. SRC publishes an index that contains information about consumer sentiment (what the consumer thinks about the economy) and consumer buying plans.

Several other consumer surveys are available. These include *Consumer Reports*, published by Consumers Union, *Consumer Buying Intentions*, a survey published by the United States Bureau of the Census in its current population reports; and *Consumer Buying Prospects*, a quarterly pamphlet published by the Commercial Credit Company. Unfortunately, most of these consumer surveys do not adequately record the consumer's feelings and intentions or determine the firmness of consumer attitudes. Studies evaluating the effectiveness of such surveys have found that generally they are not very adequate in predicting turning points, but they do give some indication of the rate of change in the near term.

As an alternative to published surveys, forecasters can simply survey their customers by mail, telephone, or personal interview. The method used depends on the number of companies or individuals to be surveyed and the amount of detail sought. To increase the accuracy of customer forecasts, many of those conducting such surveys seek to obtain information from more than one source in each customer company that is surveyed. For example, the production manager as well as the purchasing agent may be questioned.

The general goal of such corporate surveys is to determine how much of a given product the consumer firm plans to use. Sometimes the inquiry is limited to the customer's expected use of the company's brand of the product, but at other times it may relate to the customer's use of several related items as well.

Closely related to surveys as a forecasting tool is the entire field of market research. Market research indicates not only why the consumer is or is not buying (or is or is not likely to buy), but also who the consumer is, how he or she is using the product, and what characteristics the consumer thinks are most important in the purchasing decision. Such information can often be helpful to the forecaster preparing estimates of market potential and market share for various products and services.

Skill is required to design market research studies that will reveal such relationships and determine their validity. Sometimes a single factor may upset an otherwise strong correlation. The trick is to recognize and correct for such factors. For example, a chemical manufacturer found that there was an apparent relation between industrial employment and the sales of one of its products. Through market research, however, some disturbing variations were identified. Through the appropriate design of this market research it was discovered that an industry using exceptionally large quantities of the chemical was concentrated in a few localities. High consumption in the one industry and its concentration in a few localities were distorting the normal relationship between industrial employment and demand for the company's products. By adjusting regional figures to correct for this distortion, sales and industrial employment were very closely correlated. This correlation allowed industrial employment figures and projections to be used as the basis for forecasting the company's product sales.

As an example of the role of market research, one can consider the situation described by Chambers, Mullick, and Smith (1974) involving the picture phone. Forecasts were prepared in the late 1960s that projected sales of the picture phone entering the rapid-growth stage by 1973. It was assumed in the projections that the product features and price would be sufficiently appealing to the customer and that the method of transmission would be both feasible and sufficiently economical to ensure this rapid growth. The picture phone was subsequently introduced for market testing in Pittsburgh and New York City. The market tests showed that the demand was extremely low because of high costs and other related problems, and that significant improvements in transmission methods were needed to achieve lower cost and to make volume feasible. It was concluded from the tests that although a large market for picture phones was still likely, it would probably not emerge for several years and then—as the test indicated—the initial market would be for communications within and between corporations.

SUBJECTIVE PROBABILITY ASSESSMENTS

Subjective probability estimates are commonly used to incorporate individual judgment into forecasting. However, this approach handles the forecasting problem somewhat differently. The previously mentioned assessment procedures generally aim at a single point estimate (the expected value of a random variable or, more commonly, the most likely value) as the forecast. In the case of subjective probability estimates, an attempt is made to identify a range of values (the probability distribution) for the uncertain event. In practice, only a finite number of outcomes of the variable are specified, and the judgmental assessment involves determining the probabilities associated with each of these outcomes. For example, the company faced with forecasting its sales for a certain product line might specify three or four different levels of sales covering the full range of possible outcomes and then subjectively assess the probability associated with achieving each level of outcome.

Considerable work has been done by those who have developed the technique of decision analysis in regard to alternative procedures for assessing probability distributions as an integral part of forecasting and decision making. Rather than cover all of these, this section will summarize some of their main conclusions. Winkler (1987) gives a good comprehensive summary of judgmental probability assessment methods, including techniques for situations with discrete outcomes.

One of the original developers of decision analysis, Schlaifer (1959) has summarized some of the important aspects involved in the direct judgemental assessment of subjective probabilities along the following lines.

1. Uncertainty concerning events that individually may have a substantial effect on the item being estimated should be separated wherever possible. The decision maker should not attempt to assess directly a probability distribution for the variable in question that combines several different elements of uncertainty. Rather, it is better to apply the individual's judgment and experience to the problem in smaller increments by estimating distributions for each of several different uncertain events and then combining them through the use of decision analysis

2. An advantage of separating those individual events that may have a substantial effect on the outcome of the uncertain quantity or the variable in question is that the decision maker is likely to feel that for each individual event the assessed probability should be unimodal and smooth.

3. If the decision maker feels that the probability distribution should be unimodal and smooth for a particular event, the distribution can be assessed by making a few separate assessments at various points on the cumulative function, plotting those points, and then fitting a smooth curve to them.

4. If only a very small probability is to be assigned to any individual value or outcome of an event, the decision maker can assess points on the cumulative function by selecting various fractiles (such as the 0.25, 0.5, and 0.75 fractiles) and specifying the outcome that corresponds to each of them.

In addition, the decision maker may be able to improve the accuracy of the subjective probability assessment by relating it to historical frequency by understanding more fully the rules of probability assessment and the implications of various shapes in those probability distributions.

Another approach to obtaining such probability assessments is that outlined by Spetzler and Stael von Holstein (1975). Although they do not disagree with the approach outlined above, these authors place more emphasis on ways to get assessors to think carefully about the forecasting problem (see Chapter 13).

Generally, studies in this field (see von Winterfeldt and Edwards, 1986) have found that even individuals who know a lot about the variable to be forecast may have trouble making subjective probability assessments unless they are given guidance as to how these assessments can be made. Thus an important step in this approach is to guide those making the assessments. They may need to practice by assessing the probability of various levels of the New York Stock Exchange Index, GNP, or some other variable rather than starting immediately with the key item in a forecast.

MAJOR PROBLEMS WITH JUDGMENTAL METHODS

The methods described thus far rely on judgment and/or subjective information/knowledge, thus they are called judgmental. More specifically they require (1) the gathering of relevant information, (2) the analysis (processing) of that information to determine its impact on the item being forecast, and (3) the integration of that impact with specific plans and decisions. Unfortunately, empirical evidence suggests that each of these three activities often leads to a major problem in the resulting forecast. These three problems—the quest for supporting evidence, overconfidence in results, and overconformity among group members—will be examined in the remainder of this chapter. It should be noted before doing so that a number of specific actions can be undertaken to overcome or limit these problems. A number of those are summarized below, and others are included in several of the references that are cited.

The Quest for Supporting Evidence

Considerable evidence has been gathered in the past 20 years regarding the means by which people gather and interpret data. Wason (1960, 1972), a psychologist, has developed an experimental approach for studying such data activities that is particularly relevant to judgmental forecasting. In one such experiment, subjects are asked to identify the rule used to generate a series of numbers. For instance, a decision rule might be even numbers in a progression of 2. The numbers 2, 4, 6, and so on could be generated by that rule, as could 20, 22, 24, and so on. However, the numbers 3, 5, and 7, or 2, 3, and 4 could not be generated by that rule.

Subjects are asked to determine the generating rule by proposing sequences of three numbers, to which the experimenter answers yes or no: yes when the three numbers could have been generated by the yet-to-be-discovered decision rule and no when they could not have been. For the rule suggested above, the answer for the sequence 2, 4, 6 would have been yes. For the sequence 20, 22, 24 it also would have been yes. However, for 3, 5, 7 it would have been no.

The purpose of this experiment is to determine how quickly subjects reach a conclusion as to the generating rule and the correctness of the rule identified. The results are that people are quick to decide that they know the rule generating the series of numbers, and usually they are wrong. This holds true even when they are told at the outset that they should be careful and not rush to reach conclusions as to the generating rule. Moreover, even if the experimenter establishes a side bet with the subjects (to provide additional incentive to exercise caution), the results are unchanged. Subjects make the same mistakes again and again, first in the way they search for information to form hypotheses as to the generating rule and then in the way they attempt to verify (confirm) these hypotheses.

The way that subjects typically formulate questions and pursue alternative explanations is directly relevant to forecasting. They first formulate a hypothesis about the type of the decision rule generating the series of numbers. Then they give a sequence of three numbers that confirms the hypothesis they have formulated. Thus, if they think that the generating rule is a sequence of increasing numbers, they ask if the numbers 4, 5, and 6 are generated by the rule. If their hypothesis is an increasing sequence by twos, they will ask if the numbers 1, 3, and 5 are generated by the rule, and so on. In other words, subjects look primarily for supporting evidence to prove the generating rule hypothesis they have already formulated. Wason found that about 90% of the questions asked by subjects in this experiment were of the type that could be called "search for supporting (confirming) evidence."

Unfortunately, this type of search for evidence is not the most appropriate one for discovering an unknown relationship or testing an hypothesis. No matter how much supporting evidence is collected, one can never be sure that the hypothesis has been tested adequately. The only way to be sure that the formulated hypothesis is correct is to look for evidence to disprove it. For instance, if a manager believes that advertising increases sales, he or she can never be certain that this is true simply by continuing to spend more money on advertising. Sales might be increasing because of any of several reasons, and advertising might have no influence at all.

The only way to prove that advertising does influence sales is to stop advertising. If that is done and sales decrease, then one would be much more certain that there is a relationship between sales and advertising than would be the case when only supporting evidence (such as increasing the advertising budget) is obtained. Obviously, stopping advertising altogether is not something that many managers would be willing to experiment with in real life.

There is too much at stake. However, there are other ways to collect disconfirming evidence without going to the extreme of stopping all advertising.

Overconfidence in Judgments

A counterintuitive result of a number of studies by psychologists is that as the amount of information increases in a judgmental setting, predictive ability does not necessarily improve. Instead, the main effect of the additional information tends to be overconfidence in judgement. This is particularly true when the additional evidence is of a supporting nature. Results comparable to those shown in Table 12-1 have been obtained from a number of other studies. These results raise a dilemma for decision makers in that they are contrary to the "conventional wisdom" that the more information available, the better will be the decisions. It appears that the optimal amount of information reaches a plateau very quickly, and additional information improves only the confidence of the decision makers that they are right, not the quality of the decision.

Alpert and Raiffa (1982) asked their subjects to predict certain values and to provide 98% and 99.8% confidence intervals for those values. To avoid problems of interpretation of the 98% and 99.8% intervals, they asked alternatively for minimum/maximum values and astonishingly low/ astonishingly high values. More than 38% of the actual values were outside the range of astonishingly low and astonishingly high values given by the respondents. In other words, the respondents considerably underestimated uncertainty, or alternatively, they were overconfident in their answers.

Overconformity among Group Members (Groupthink)

Many forecasts are made in groups. The jury of executive opinion is one of the most popular forms of forecasting (Dalrymple, 1987; Mentzer and Cox, 1984). Most managers spend a good part of their lives in groups, and the dynamics of interactions in cohesive groups—groupthink—need to be understood to avoid the disadvantages and problems of group forecasting.

Table 12-1   Performance of 32 Judges on the 25 Item Case-Study Test

Measure	M Score				P	p
	Stage 1	Stage 2	Stage 3	Stage 4		
Accuracy (%)	26.0	23.0	28.4	27.8	5.02	0.01
Confidence (%)	33.2	39.2	46.0	52.8	36.06	0.001
Number of changed answers		13.2	11.4	8.1	21.65	0.001

Some useful findings on groupthink have been reported by Janis (1972) and Janis and Mann (1982). As a basis for his analysis of groups, Janis defined ingroups and their major characteristics. He has identified six potential problems of groupthink that he has observed from his research on ingroups.

Ingroups are made up of individuals who know each other well and enjoy or feel comfortable being together and belonging to the same group. Members of ingroups tend to support each other and unite against external threats. Ingroups are widespread in business, government, and military organizations. The following four factors affect the way ingroups operate and influence the extent of groupthink, that is, the group decision-making process:

1. *High Cohesiveness.* Ingroups develop a high degree of cohesiveness among their members, which is manifested by a feeling of "belongingness" to the group and a desire to support fellow members. The results are increased conformity to group norms through group pressure, sometimes directly, but more often indirectly, the suppression of internal dissent, the emergence of group conformity, and the absence of critical thought processes during the group meetings.

2. *Strong Leadership.* In hierachical organizations strong leaders, or other influential group members, have considerable influence on ingroup feelings. The opinion of the leader, or other influential members, becomes instrumental and increases group pressure for a unanimous opinion.

3. *Lack of Objective Search and Evaluation.* Ingroups tend to develop their own internal modus operandi for making decisions. However, because of the informality and the trust among the group members, few attempts are made to find alternative courses of action. Furthermore, the fair alternatives considered often are evaluated superficially. Because ingroups operate informally, the members know and trust each other, and they attempt to minimize internal disagreement.

4. *Insulation of the Group.* As the ingroup becomes more cohesive, its members tend to insulate themselves from the rest of the world. This means that outside opinions are not sought or, when given, they are largely ignored.

The four factors outlined are not, of course, equally likely and influential in all ingroups. However, as stronger ties develop among the members of ingroups and as interaction among them increases, chances are that cohesion, strong leadership, superficial search and evaluation of alternatives, and insulation will develop and influence the quality of group decision making.

The major consequence of ingroups is consensus-seeking behavior among group members. This includes a nondeliberate suppression of opposing opinions, and an unconscious attempt to avoid critically scrutinizing the advantages and drawbacks of available alternatives. Furthermore, as ingroups become more cohesive, the symptoms of groupthink become more dominant, with the result that any thoughts that are considered to deviate from the group consensus are suppressed. The results for group forecasting are six types of problems:

1. *Illusions of Invulnerability.* Groups tend to make more risky decisions than individuals. Responsibility for decisions made in groups is "shared" so that no single member feels responsible. Furthermore, the deliberations in the group make the members feel secure in that they think all dangers have been considered, and each member trusts the combined wisdom of the others in the group. However, ingroups tend to be overly optimistic. They ignore threatening signals and therefore are willing to take (unknowingly) more risk.

2. *Collective Rationalization.* Ingroups tend to develop collective rationalization to discount warning or threatening signals. Furthermore, they find explanations (often very elaborate) as to why things did not turn out as expected. Negative feedback is ignored and outside criticism is brushed aside as irrelevant. In this respect, ingroups tend to develop elaborate defenses to avoid criticism, to protect the group against outside threats, and to reassure the group that its decisions are correct.

3. *Belief in the Inherent Morality of the Group.* Ingroups believe they are morally right in their decisions. They tend, therefore, to ignore the ethical or moral consequences of their decisions and actions. Certain things are not said in group meetings. For instance, members are not willing to question the ethical and moral standards of the group or the wisdom of its leader. All group members are presumed to have a high degree of ethics and an unquestionable sense of morality. Thus, there is no point in questioning such a fact.

4. *Pressure on Dissenters.* The consensus-seeking behavior among ingroup members is further reinforced through pressure applied on dissenting opinions. This pressure may be direct or indirect (by excluding dissenting members from the inner clique and eventually from the ingroup itself).

5. *Self-Censorship.* Dissension among ingroup members holding opposite opinions is often achieved through self-censorship. Those holding opposing opinions tend to voice them mildly, or avoid saying anything altogether, so as not to raise hostile feelings against themselves from the other group members. This self-censorship is, quite often, nondeliberate. Group members with opposing opinions are unwilling to speak up about their views,

because they believe no one else shares them, further reinforcing the self-censorship of opposing ideas.

6. *Self-Appointed Mind Guards.* Ingroup members appoint themselves as protecting guards against information they feel might be threatening to the censorship leader or other group members. This filtering of information can prevent negative evidence from reaching group deliberations, which further reinforces unanimity among the group members and the view that their opinions are correct.

Janis has identified many case studies of situations in which groupthink symptoms (and problems) have resulted in disastrous decisions by groups of extremely intelligent individuals. In particular, he has analyzed the decision that led to the fiasco of the Bay of Pigs invasion, decisions that led to the Korean War, those that escalated the Vietnam War, the Pearl Harbor disaster, and the energy crisis (Janis, 1972; Janis and Mann, 1982).

In theory, it should be possible to do a number of things to minimize the problems of groupthink. Practically speaking, however, these problems are extremely difficult to solve. Ingroups exist because they provide security and a sense of belonging for their members. Ingroups guard members against outside threats and aim at maintaining harmony among their members. To achieve such objectives, members must minimize internal conflict and support each other. However, these very characteristics of ingroups are also the biggest threats because they reduce critical evaluation, encourage unwarranted concurrence-seeking behavior, and limit the serious consideration of alternatives.

The remedy for groupthink problems is to facilitate critical evaluation of decision-making processes without destroying the ingroup. This may involve assigning group members positions on various decisions considered by the group. Alternatively, members can be assigned the role of the devil's advocate for specific decisions. Furthermore, the leader should not become an advocate of a particular point of view or solution—at least in the early stages—and force the other members toward his or her position. Rather, he or she should be nonpartisan, adopting an impartial stance until the group can develop its own opinions. In addition, ingroups could invite independent, outside evaluations when important decisions are considered. Such outside help should be concentrated on evaluating warning signals from competitors or enemies and assessing advantages or drawbacks of the alternatives being considered. Similarly, well-respected outsiders could be invited to sit in on group deliberations when important decisions are considered. These outsiders should be asked to think of alternatives not considered by the group, and to provide independent opinions considered by the group.

Conditions for Ingroups in Organizations
1. High cohesiveness
2. Strong leadership
3. Lack of objective procedures for search and appraisal
4. Insulation of the group

→

Major Characteristics of Ingroups
Concurrence-seeking behavior among group members

→

Symptoms of Groupthink
1. Illusion of invulnerability
2. Collective rationalization
3. Belief in inherent morality of the group
4. Pressure of dissenters
5. Self-censorship
6. Self-appointed mind guards

→

Consequences of Groupthink in Terms of Defective Decision Making
1. Incomplete survey of alternatives
2. Incomplete survey of objectives
3. Failure to examine risks of preferred choice
4. Poor information search
5. Selective bias in processing
6. Failure to reappraise alternatives
7. Failure to work out contingency plans

→

Remedies for Groupthink
1. Critically evaluating members
2. Assigning the role of devil's advocate to a group member
3. Nonpartisan leader
4. Outside, independent evaluations
5. Invited outside experts participating in critical group discussions
6. Not ignoring warning signals of competitors
7. Reassess important decisions by inviting open expression of residual doubts

Figure 12-1 Schematic Presentation of Groupthink and Its Consequences (Adapted from Janis, 1972).

Finally, ingroups would do well to reassess important decisions and encourage the expression of residual doubts by dissenting group members before group decisions are implemented. Although such procedures may be time consuming, they are necessary and beneficial, especially when outside evaluations have not been obtained. The issues and problems discussed in this section of groupthink are summarized in Figure 12-1. The importance and frequency of group forecasting are such that it would be difficult to overemphasize these characteristics.

SELECTED REFERENCES FOR FURTHER STUDY

Alpert, M., and H. Raiffa, 1982. "A Progress Report on the Training of Probability Assessors," in D. Kahneman, et al. (Eds.), *Judgment under Uncertainty: Heuristics and Biases*, Cambridge University Press, Cambridge, England.

Angus-Leppan, P., and V. Fatseas, 1986. "The Forecasting Accuracy of Trainee Accountants Using Judgmental and Statistical Techniques," *Accounting and Business Research*, Summer.

Anon., 1978. *Sales Forecasting*, Conference Board, New York.

Asch, S. E., 1965. "Effects of Group Pressure upon the Modification and Distortion of Judgment," in H. Proshansky and B. Seidenberg (Eds.), *Basic Studies in Social Psychology*, Holt, Rinehart and Winston, New York.

———, 1956. "Studies of Independence and Conformity: A minority of One Against an Unanimous Majority," *Psychological Monographs*, 70.

Beach, L. R., V. Barnes, and J. J. J. Christensen-Szalanski, 1986. "Beyond Heuristics and Biases: A Contingency Model of Judgmental Forecasting," *Journal of Forecasting*, 5, pp. 143–157.

Chambers, J. C., S. K. Mullick, and D. D. Smith, 1974. *An Executive's Guide to Forecasting*, Wiley, New York.

Dalrymple, D. J., 1987. "Sales Forecasting Practices: Results from a United States Survey," *International Journal of Forecasting*, 3, pp. 379–392.

Einhorn, H. J., and R. M. Hogarth, 1982. "Prediction, Diagnosis, and Causal Thinking in Forecasting," *Journal of Forecasting*, 1, no. 1, pp. 22–36.

Funder, D. C., 1987. "Errors and Mistakes: Evaluating the Accuracy of Social Judgment," *Psychological Bulletin*, 101, no. 1, pp. 75–90.

Janis, I.L., 1972. *Victims of Group Think*, Houghton Mifflin, Boston.

Janis, I. L., and I. Mann, 1982. *Decision Making: A Psychological Analysis of Conflict, Choice and Commitment*, 2nd ed. Free Press, New York.

———, 1971. "Group Think," *Psychology Today*, November, pp. 43–77.

Kahneman, D., and A. Tversky, 1979. "Intuitive Prediction: Biases and Corrective Procedures," *TIMS Studies in the Management Sciences*, vol. 12, North-Holland, Amsterdam, pp. 313–327.

Lawrence, M., and S. Makridakis, 1988. "Factors Affecting Judgmental Forecasts and Confidence Intervals," *Organizational Behavior and Human Decision Processes*, forthcoming.

Lewin, K., 1947. "Group Decision and Social Change," in T. Newcomb and E. Hartley (Eds.), *Readings in Social Psychology*, Henry Holt, New York.

Lichtenstein, S., B. Fischhoff, and L. D. Phillips, 1977. "Calibration of Probability: The State of the Art to 1980," in H. Jungermann and E. de Zeenw (Eds), *Decision Making and Change in Human Affairs*, Reidel, Dordrecht, The Netherlands.

Mentzer, J. T., and J. E. Cox, 1984. "Familiarity Application and Performance of Sales Forecasting Techniques," *Journal of Forecasting*, Vol. 3, pp. 27–36.

Oskamp, S., 1965. "Overconfidence in Case Study Judgment," *Journal of Consulting Psychology*, 29, pp. 261–265.

Schlaifer, R., 1959. *Probability and Statistics for Business Decisions*, McGraw-Hill, New York.

Simon, H. A., and A. Newell, 1970. "Human Problem Solving: The State of the Theory in 1970," *American Psychologist*, 26, no. 2, pp. 145–159.

Slovic, P., B. Fischhoff, and S. Lichtenstein, 1977. "Behavioral Decision Theory," *Annual Review of Psychology*, 28, pp. 1–39.

Spetzler, C. S., and C. A. S. Stael von Holstein, 1975. "Probability Encoding in Decision Analysis," *Management Science*, 22, pp. 340–358.

Tversky, A., and D. Kahneman, 1973. "Availability: A Heuristic for Judging Frequency and Probability," *Cognitive Psychology*, 5, no. 2, pp. 207–232.

Wason, P. C., and P. N. Johnson-Laird, 1972. *Psychology of Reasoning: Structure and Content*, Batsford, London.

———, 1960. "On the Failure to Eliminate Hypotheses in Conceptual Tasks," *Quarterly Journal of Experimental Psychology*, 12, no. 19, pp. 129–140.

Winkler, R. L., 1987. "Judgmental and Bayesian Forecasting," in S. Makridakis and S. C. Wheelwright (Eds.), *The Handbook of Forecasting: A Manager's Guide*, 2nd ed., Wiley, New York.

Winterfeldt, D. von, and W. Edwards, 1986. *Decision Analysis and Behavioral Research*, Cambridge University Press, Cambridge, England.

Wright, G., and Wyton, P. (Eds.), 1987. *Judgmental Forecasting*, Wiley, Chichester, England.

CHAPTER 13

BIASES AND LIMITATIONS IN JUDGMENTAL METHODS

Humans can master many activities involving muscular movements because feedback is frequent and precise, making continued improvement possible. For example, when playing tennis or skiing, it is easy to know how well you are doing. In tennis, if the stroke is bad, the ball will go "out." In skiing, if you make an incorrect movement, you lose your balance and fall. Learning tennis or skiing is made easier by the fact that mistakes (errors) are easy to identify and can be used to learn; the feedback is frequent and precise. At every instant, information is available that can be used to evaluate progress and facilitate learning.

Unfortunately, in many future-oriented activities in general and forecasting in particular, feedback is neither frequent nor precise. Therefore, evaluation is difficult and learning is problematic. It is the absence of exact, timely feedback that makes judgmental methods so prone to errors (in the form of biases) and so difficult to correct and improve systematically (learn).

In modern times there has been a great deal of interest in human judgments. How do people make decisions? How rational are these decisions? Do they follow certain principles? Can decision making be improved? Can mistakes of judgment be avoided? A variety of views have been expressed regarding such questions. Three very different ones are the following:

What a piece of work is a man! How noble in reason! How infinite in faculty! . . . the beauty of the world!

Shakespeare (*Hamlet*, 2.2.313)

The capacity of the human mind for formulating and solving problems is very small compared with the size of the problems whose solution is required for objectively rational behavior in the real world.

H. Simon and A. Newell (1971)

Errors of judgment are often systematic rather than random, manifesting bias rather than confusion. Thus, man suffers from mental astigmatism as well as from myopia, and any corrective prescription should fit this diagnosis.

D. Kahneman and A. Tversky (1973)

Recent work in management science and psychology has shattered Shakespeare's conception of human judgment as a noble and rational process. Simon and Newell (1971) discuss what is referred to as "bounded rationality." They point out that because people have limited information-processing capacity, they cannot deal directly with large problems. Instead they use simplifying heuristics in their problem-solving efforts. In the end, they look for satisficing rather than optimizing solutions since in the complex environment in which we live, optimizing is well beyond our present intellectual abilities.

Kahneman and Tversky (1973) have pursued a different path than that proposed by Simon and Newell. Through clever experimental work they have illustrated a wide range of judgmental biases and limitations that seriously affect the quality of human decision making. They have made judgmental or cognitive work a popular field in psychology. Among other things, this field is concerned with how people make decisions, and thus it has direct relevance and applicability to forecasting.

This chapter draws heavily on the work of Kahneman, Slovic, and Tversky (1982) and that of Hogarth and Makridakis (1981). It begins with an overview of the major biases and limitations identified in the field of cognitive or judgmental psychology. Next, those aspects particularly relevant to judgmental approaches to forecasting are discussed and their implications explored. Finally, simple decision models of judgmental approaches are described as a way of introducing consistency in decision making.

AN OVERVIEW OF JUDGMENTAL BIASES AND LIMITATIONS

There are two key findings from cognitive or judgmental psychology relating to human judgment: (1) the human ability to process information is limited, and (2) people are adaptive. To understand the process of judgment, it is necessary to specify the context in which it occurs. From the psychology literature we know that people are strongly motivated to understand, and thus control, the environment in which they live. This search for understanding and control is the raison d'être of forecasting, planning, and strategy. The actual outcomes people experience, however, depend not only on their own actions, but also on events outside their control (that is, chance). Figure 13-1 provides a conceptual model of the judgment process.

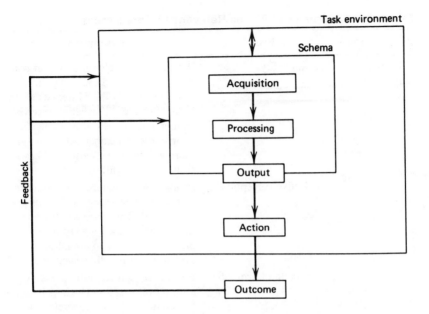

Figure 13-1 Conceptual Model of Judgment (Based on Hogarth, 1975).

The model implicit in Figure 13-1 involves three elements in mutual interaction—the person, the task environment within which the person makes judgments, and the actions resulting from that judgment that later can affect both the person and the task environment.

In Figure 13-1, the person is represented by his or her "schema," that is, the person's belief and value system relative to the judgment task. The process of judgment is decomposed into (1) the acquisition of information, (2) the processing of the information accessed, and (3) the output. The output represents action that, together with external factors, yields an outcome. The outcome then feeds back into the person's schema and can affect the task environment through self-fulfilling or self-defeating actions. At the same time several interdependencies exist: the person's schema affects the perception of the environment and its complexity, the problem identification, the tasks involved, the type of action required, the objectives, and so forth.

Considerable evidence indicates that superficial information searches and processing biases cause significant error in human decision making (Slovic et al., 1977; Lewin, 1947; Janis and Mann, 1982). To relate this evidence to future-oriented decisions, Table 13-1 summarizes the major sources of bias, organized according to the stages of information processing indicated in Figure 13-1. Table 13-1 also briefly describes each type of bias.

Of crucial concern to forecasters are the conditions under which the biases

Table 13-1   Judgmental Biases Relevant to Forecasting

Stage of Process	Bias	Description
Information acquisition	Availability	People tend to rely on data that come easily to hand and mind; e.g., forecasters may modify their forecasts on the basis of chance information received from acquaintances or news media. People also remember better and give more weight to the most vivid cases in their environment.
	Selective perception	People tend to ignore or discount information inconsistent with their prior hypotheses. Thus forecasters who are favorably disposed toward a new product are likely to attend to evidence that it will be successful.
	Concrete information	Forecasters sometimes rely less on abstract information (such as base-rate sales data) than on "concrete" information (such as the well-articulated opinion of a valued customer). This is a bias when the former is more valid.
	Illusory correlation	Two unrelated variables may seem to be related (because of chance, in small samples, or by not controlling for antecedent variables). This may cause the forecaster to base his or her forecast on the wrong premise.
	Data presentation	Data can be displayed in graphs or tables in a variety of misleading ways. Forecasters can overlook assumptions and qualifications underlying exhibits in reports and be blinded to omissions of important facts.
Information processing	Inconsistency	Forecasters may be unable to apply a consistent judgmental strategy. One who seizes new kinds of information or applies a different forecasting technique to each forecasting situation may be less accurate overall than one who applies a consistent approach.
	Conservatism	Virtually the opposite of inconsistency conservatism may cause people not to

Table 13-1 (*Continued*)

Stage of Process	Bias	Description
		weigh heavily enough information that is newly received; e.g., a forecaster may ignore early warning signs that a product is declining in fashion.
	Anchoring and adjustment	Forecasters sometimes fix on particular reference points and adjust their forecasts only with respect to them. A typical example is making next year's sales forecast a given percentage of current year's sales.
	Law of small numbers	People often assume that small samples are actually characteristic of the population from which they are drawn. An example would be basing sales forecasts on small-scale qualitative studies, such as focus groups.
	Justifiability	People may base their forecast on a processing rule that is "justified" with an apparently rational argument, even when the rule is inappropriate; e.g., a forecast could be based on a sophisticated model developed for an altogether different purpose.
Output	Wishful thinking	People tend to consider more probable those outcomes that they prefer. Some salespeople who tend toward optimism are likely to overestimate the sales they can make in a given period.
	Illusion of control	Any activity toward an uncertain outcome can lead people to feel they have some control over the outcome. Simply making a forecast may cause people to have more confidence in it than is justified.
Feedback	Outcome irrelevant learning structures	Observed outcomes of previous forecasts (e.g., accurate forecasts during stable growth period) may provide an incomplete picture of the situation, which leads to misplaced overconfidence in one's ability to forecast.

Table 13-1   (*Continued*)

Stage of Process	Bias	Description
	Misperception of chance fluctuations	When a forecaster has observed an unexpectedly high number of successful products, he or she might give higher probability than justified to the appearance of a product failure. This is known as the gambler's fallacy.
	Success or failure attribution	There is a tendency for a forecaster to attribute successful forecasts to his or her own skill and inaccurate forecasts to chance or other environmental factors.
	Hindsight	People are rarely surprised by events that have already happened. It is easy to come up with a causal explanation after the fact, but hard to find it prospectively.

Source: Hogarth and Makridakis (1981), pp. 117–120.

described in Table 13-1 occur and their consequences for decisions aimed at coping with the future. Figure 13-1 indicates that understanding of a judgmental task—as represented in the person's schema—is mediated by several stages of information processing and links with the environment. In particular, links between the person's schema, actions, outcomes, and feedback to the schema are crucial. If the action–outcome–feedback links are short and frequent, the individual is in a good position to learn about, and thus comprehend, the probable effects of actions on outcomes. Short links enhance the ability to improve decision making through taking corrective actions. The opposite is true when the links are infrequent, long (in time), and subject to distortion. This suggests that people will have difficulty providing adequate inputs in many forecasting, planning, and decision-making situations where action–outcome–feedback links are neither short nor clear.

The judgmental performances people exhibit through motor skills are considerable. For example, complex judgmental tasks are accomplished when one drives a car or walks on a crowded sidewalk. These situations are characterized by short, precise, frequent action–outcome–feedback loops. Humans have considerable facility for making the judgments needed to perform complex motor tasks, but not for making decisions that require complex conceptual judgments. Indeed, most of the biases documented in Table 13-1 have been demonstrated in situations where short, precise, and frequent loops have been lacking or, when present, have not necessarily been readily interpretable by the individual. Interestingly, experiments that have examined intuitive decision-making skills in dynamic environments involving interdependent, sequential judgmental tasks coupled with feedback or performance indicate that people can be quite efficient in such a setting (see Murphy and Winkler, 1977).

Suggestions for overcoming some important judgmental biases enumerated in Table 13-1 have been provided by Hogarth (1981), Kahneman and Tversky (1979), and Spetzler and Stael von Holstein (1975). In particular, these authors provide procedures to guard against overconfidence in judgment, and ways of making sure that available objective information is taken into account. In addition, each of the three problems addressed in the preceding chapter is relevant to a review and minimizing of the biases listed in Table 13-1. This is the case in part because of the similarities between several aspects of group and individual behavior.

JUDGMENTAL BIASES PARTICULARLY RELEVANT TO FORECASTING

Some biases and limitations are particularly common and significant in their impact on forecasting situations. Knowing the way in which those arise and how they might be overcome can substantially improve the performance of judgmental forecasting methods. Seven of these suggested by Armstrong (1984) will be addressed in this section.

Overconfidence in Judgment

Before continuing, please read the following sentence and then answer the two questions asked below:

FINISHED FILES ARE THE RESULT OF YEARS OF SCIENTIFIC STUDY COMBINED WITH THE EXPERIENCE OF YEARS.

Please do not reread the sentence above.
Please indicate the number of F's that appear in the sentence [   ].
How confident are you of your answer above? Indicate your confidence on a scale of 0 to 100 with 0 indicating no confidence and 100 indicating full confidence [   ].

Table 13-2 shows how 83 MBAs and executives have answered these two questions. If you are one of the more than 90% who did not give the correct answer (there are, in fact, six F's in the sentence), you might be surprised. However, this is not the most striking aspect of Table 13-2. What strikes one the most is that there is no relationship between how certain one is of one's answer and the correctness of that answer. (The correlation between these two, in fact, is almost 0.) In other words, the mere fact that someone believes strongly about the accuracy of his or her forecast of the number of F's is not an important factor to take into account in deciding whose predictions are to be trusted. Table 13-2 shows that people who are unsure about the accuracy of their prediction can be as correct as those who are completely certain.

Below is a variation of the question you just answered. It is different because it does not restrict the respondent to a single reading of the sentence. (On average, the sentence is read a little more than three times.)

FINISHED FILES ARE THE RESULT OF YEARS OF SCIEN-
TIFIC STUDY COMBINED WITH THE EXPERIENCE OF
YEARS.

Please indicate the number of F's that appear in the sentence above
[   ].

How confident are you of your answer above? Indicate your confidence on a scale of 0 to 100 with 0 indicating no confidence and 100
indicating full confidence [   ].

How many times did you read the sentence "FINISHED . . . OF
YEARS"? [   ].

The responses of a sample of MBAs and executives to this experiment are given in Table 13-3. What is even more striking in Table 13-3 is the dramatic increase in the confidence of the respondents: 56% of the respondents are 100% certain that they have the right answer (compared with 11% of the respondents in Table 13-2). Furthermore, another 10% are 99% certain, and an additional 14% are between 90% and 98% certain of the correctness of their answers. In other words, about 80% of the respondents feel more than 90% certain that they identified the correct answer. Of those 80%, only 23% were correct and the remaining 57% were wrong.

The reader might want to reflect on the implications of these results for the practice of forecasting and its use as an input to planning and decision making. First, it seems that people are overconfident about the accuracy of their forecasts; second, additional information drastically increases that confidence, but often has little impact on the accuracy of the predictions.

Table 13-2 Correctness of Responses Predicting the Number of F's in a Sentence and Confidence in the Accuracy of Those Responses[a]

Level of confidence	Number of F's Counted									Total
	1	2	3	4	5	6	7	8	9	
100		1	2	2						5
95			1	1	1					3
90				1						1
85			1							1
80		4	5		1	1				11
75		1	2	2		2				7
70			1	1	1	1				4
60		1	1		2		1			5
50	1	7	1		2			1	2	14
40	1	2			1				1	5
30			4		2				1	7
25				2						2
20		3	3	2	1	1			1	11
10			2		3		1		1	7
Total	2	19	23	11	14	5	2	1	6	83

[a] Sample: 83 MBA students and executives.

Table 13-3 Results of Table 13-2 Experiment when Rereading of the Sentence Is Permitted

Level of confidence	Number of F's Counted							Total
	1	2	3	4	5	6	12	
100		3	20	4	9	18	1	55
99			4		2	4		10
98			1		1	1		3
95			3		2	1		6
90			1		2	3		6
85			1					1
80			3		1	1		5
75			2					2
70								—
60								—
50						1		1
Total		3	35	4	17	29	1	89

(The mean number of F's predicted by those who had read the sentence only once was about 4; for those who read it more than once, it was 4.3.) Third, accuracy and confidence are not correlated. Those who are the most confident are not necessarily the most accurate forecasters.

Illusory Correlations

This bias can be illustrated using Figures 13-2 and 13-3. Several groups of MBAs and executives were given Figure 13-2, and asked to predict the actual sales for 1993. Other groups were given Figure 13-2, and, in addition, Figure 13-3, with the information that it was a set of forecasts made by a computer model. Both sets of groups were asked to predict the sales of Electrack (a new electronic game) for the year 1993. The predictions of the groups given Figures 13-2 and 13-3 were quite different from those of the groups given Figure 13-2 only. For the former, using Figures 13-2 and 13-3, the pessimistic estimate was 65,000 units, the most likely estimate was 90,000, and the optimistic estimate was 120,000. For the groups using Figure 13-2 only, 130,000 was the pessimistic forecast, 183,000 was the most likely, and 247,000 was the optimistic case. That is, the forecasts of one group were about double those of the other.

What accounts for the big difference in the responses of the two groups? Obviously, the second group weighted the computer predictions heavily. It did not take much persuasion for them to accept the results of the model, even though the model was based on four actual data points, an insufficient number to develop a statistical model or to use it confidently to predict future levels of sales.

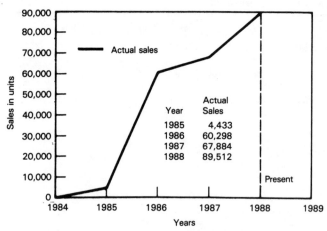

Figure 13-2   Actual Sales of Electrack Provided for Forecasting 1993 Sales.

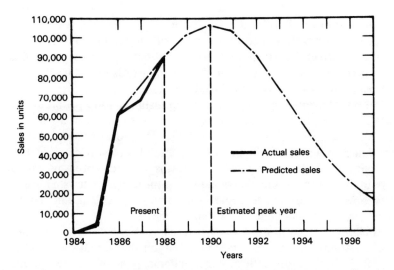

Figure 13-3 Actual and Predicted Sales of Electrack. Predictions are Based on a Computer Model.

Unfortunately, because of the strong need to master and control the environment, most of us are highly motivated to see patterns in the environment where there might be none. This need to infer patterns is referred to in psychology as *illusory correlation*. This judgmental bias is of critical importance to forecasting. At the very least, forecasters using the results of quantitative models should look at the estimated variance of the predictions to get some idea of the extent of the future uncertainty. Obviously, the variance of the four data points in this case is quite large and can help the forecast user obtain a realistic idea of the uncertainty involved.

Finally, the most interesting aspect of the data used in Figures 13-2 and 13-3 is that the four data points called "sales of Electrack" are nothing more than the first four random numbers from the table of random numbers shown in Table 13-4. The prospect that the sales may be completely random is not contemplated by any of the respondents. Rather they decide quickly that a pattern must exist in the data and then infer this pattern, which is subsequently used in forecasting. In this case, as in many others, the data are random; thus, any inferred pattern is illusory.

Availability Bias

This problem, which refers to the human tendency to recall situations and events selectively, has been illustrated by Tversky and Kahneman (1973). These authors asked their subjects whether the letter K tended to come most often in the first or third position in English words. More than two-thirds of the subjects answered that K occurred more often in the first position. This, however, is incorrect. These authors discovered that the reason for such an answer was that the subjects could think of many words that started with K but not many that had K as their third letter.

Illustrations of availability bias abound. For instance, some people are still afraid to fly on airplanes. A major reason for this is that when an airplane crashes, it gets large headlines. Such an accident, therefore, is recorded in our memory much more vividly than deaths resulting from bicycle accidents or falls in bathtubs. Bicycle and bathtub deaths are not given prominent coverage in the newspapers or shown in prime-time televison news. However, statistics show that many more people die from bicycle accidents and bathtub falls than are killed in commercial airline crashes.

A bias closely related to availability is *recency*. People tend to remember information about recent events more easily than that about older events. Such recent facts, therefore, influence their judgment and introduce a recency bias.

Table 13-4   Table of Random Numbers[a]

Random numbers	04433	80674	24520	18222	10610	05794	37515
used to denote	60298	47829	72648	37414	75755	04717	29899
the sales of Elec-	67884	59651	67533	68123	17739	95862	08034
track	89512	32155	51906	61662	64130	16688	37275
	32653	01895	12506	88535	36553	23757	34209
	95913	15405	13772	76638	48423	25018	99041
	55864	21694	13122	44115	01601	50541	00147
	35334	49810	91601	40617	72876	33967	73830
	57729	32196	76487	11622	96297	24160	09903
	86648	13697	63677	70119	94739	25875	38829
	30574	47609	07967	32422	76791	39725	53711
	81307	43694	83580	79974	45929	85113	72268
	02410	54905	79007	54939	21410	86980	91772
	18969	75274	52233	62319	08598	09066	95288
	87863	82384	66860	62297	80198	19347	73234
	52360	46658	66511	04172	73085	11795	52594
	74622	12142	68355	65635	21828	39539	18988
	04157	50079	61343	64315	70836	82857	35335
	86003	60070	66241	32836	27573	11479	94114
	41268	80168	20351	09636	84668	42486	71303

[a] Based on parts of *Table of 105,000 Random Decimal Digits*, Interstate Commerce Commission, Bureau of Transport Economics and Statistics, Washington, D.C.

Anchoring

This bias can be illustrated by the following experiment conducted by Tversky and Kahneman (1973). Subjects were asked in two groups to predict the percentage of the nations in Africa that were members of the United Nations. The two groups of subjects were given the same question, but a different starting value was given to each one of the groups. To select a starting value, a wheel that gave a random outcome was spun in the presence of the subject. The subject was then asked to revise this number upward or downward to obtain his or her response. The information given as a starting value, selected randomly, was either 10% or 65%. The predictions made by the two groups of subjects varied considerably. The group that was given 10% as a starting value gave answers on average that said 25% of the African nations were in the United Nations. In contrast, the predictions of the group given the starting value of 65% on average predicted that 45% of the African nations were in the United Nations.

Anchoring biases are very influential in forecasting. Consider a sales forecasting meeting aimed at determining the growth rate in company sales for next year. According to the anchoring bias, the outcome would be different if an initial estimate of 10% were advanced (in particular if the person proposing such an estimate is the president of the company) instead of 4%. Anchoring biases are also persistent in many aspects of our daily lives. Rooted in conservatism, they also help explain why additional weight is given to "more concrete" evidence. For instance, if you know of a friend who says to you that he has bought a car of a certain type and the car has turned out to be a lemon, you tend to give more weight to this information (availability bias), and you tend to be unwilling to change your mind (anchoring) even though you can find much more complete and representative information in reports published by consumer protection groups that have tested many cars of the type in question.

Hindsight Bias

People are rarely surprised by events that have already happened, even though those same people may have considerable difficulty predicting the same events. Once a certain event has taken place, people find it easy to explain it, or to conclude that they knew it would happen as it did. The "Monday morning quarterback" phenomenon illustrates hindsight bias well. Everyone can tell you what should have been done after the game is over.

In forecasting applications, hindsight biases can be troublesome. For instance, imagine a forecaster who has predicted a future event, and for some reason that prediction turns out to be wrong. If his immediate response is to justify his prediction, explaining that it was not his fault that it was wrong, the real explanation of the forecasting error will not be found and the same mistakes could be repeated later in a similar situation. In other words, learning is difficult or impossible if one is unwilling to accept errors. This requires guarding against hindsight bias. It seems that a major advantage of Japanese managers is their ability to accept mistakes and use the information on why such mistakes were made to avoid future ones (Morita, 1986). Since hindsight biases hinder learning, it is extremely important to be willing to accept mistakes and, thus, to avoid hindsight biases.

The effects of hindsight bias can be reduced by recording the reasons given for various forecasts, so that after the event it is possible to identify the real reasons for forecasting errors and to compare them with the earlier assumptions. This is what "tracking" is all about.

Underestimating Uncertainty

One of the major consequences of the judgmental biases mentioned is that the uncertainty associated with future events is seriously underestimated. This is due partly to the psychological need to master and control the environment (illusion control) and partly to the way information is collected (selective perception, hindsight bias, and looking for supporting evidence —see Chapter 12) and processed. The end result is significantly underestimating uncertainty and viewing the future as much more certain than it is (O'Connor, 1989). A realistic assessment of uncertainty is one of the most crucial aspects of judgmental forecasting (Makridakis and Hibon, 1987).

Inconsistency in Judgment

This bias can be better understood by considering two similar decisions taken on two different mornings. The first morning is a Monday following a relaxing weekend near the sea. The weather was beautiful and you had a marvelous time. The second morning is after a late evening and night of sickness. You did not sleep much, and you dragged yourself into the office only because you felt obliged to do so.

Unless you are superhuman, you will no doubt make two very different decisions about the same situation on these two mornings. Unfortunately, our moods and several other factors have a significant influence on our decisions and actions and introduce inconsistency into our judgment. Inconsistency in day-to-day routine decisions introduces bias and can result in either actual or opportunity losses for the organization.

HUMAN JUDGMENT VERSUS MODELS OF HUMAN JUDGMENT

In a classic study, Bowman (1963) showed that managerial decision making could be improved through the use of some simple decision rules. One of these simple rules was to base future planning decisions on the average of the three most recent decisions made by the same manager. Similarly, performance was improved by using simple quantitative forecasting models.

Bowman's findings have been replicated and expanded by several other studies (Kunreuther, 1969; Ebert, 1972; Remus, 1978). The consistency resulting from the application of the same decision rule outweighs the disadvantages from applying such a mechanical procedure to make decisions. That is, it was shown that intuitive judgment is inferior to decision rules where repetitive situations are concerned. In the field of psychology, Bowman's findings have been extended to a wide variety of decision-making situations. Psychologists have found that modeling a judge's decision-making process and using that model provide more accurate results than the judge's own decisions.

Models of judgment improve on intuitive decision making mainly by eliminating inconsistencies. One of the most interesting studies of this type is that by Dawes (1979, 1986). Some of the comparisons developed by Dawes are shown in Table 13-5. Five approaches were compared: the results of

Table 13-5   Correlations between Predictions and Actual Results

Example	Judge	Judge Model	Random Regression Model	Equal Weighting Model	Optimal Linear Model
Prediction of neurosis vs. psychosis	0.28	0.31	0.30	0.34	0.46
Illinois students' predictions of GPA[a]	0.33	0.50	0.51	0.60	0.69
Oregon students' predictions of GPA[a]	0.37	0.43	0.51	0.60	0.69
Prediction of later faculty ratings at Oregon	0.19	0.25	0.39	0.48	0.54
Yntema & Torgerson's (1961) experiment	0.84	0.89	0.84	0.97	0.97

Source: R. M. Dawes, "The Robust Beauty of Improper Linear Models in Decision Making," *American Psychologist* (1979), 34, 7, pp. 571–582.
[a] GPA = grade point average.

judgmental decisions (judge); the results from applying the decision rules underlying the judgmental decisions (judge model); the results from decisions taken by a regression model that included the correct variables but whose weights (parameters) were determined randomly except that they were constrained to have the correct plus or minus sign (random regression model); a regression model that included the correct variables but whose weights (parameters) were all given the same value $1/p$, where p was the number of variables (equal weighting model); and a statistical regression model that included the correct variables with optimal parameter values (optimal linear model). As can be seen from Table 13-5, even a largely random regression model does better than intuitive judgment in the great majority of cases.

SUMMARY

The conclusion of studies such as those cited above is not that judgmental forecasting approaches suffer from limitations and biases. These studies suggest the importance of understanding the advantages and disadvantages of such judgment and the limitations and biases of the resulting forecasts. Also, in cases where quantitative models (often very simple) have been compared to human judgment, the results have shown that the predictive accuracy of such quantitative models is as good as that of intuitive judgment where routine decisions are involved.

All of the studies that compare quantitative models with human judgment refer to repetitive situations where little or no systematic change in the environment takes place. We have seen that when systematic changes from established patterns or relationships take place, quantitative models are of little use. This is where human judgment is indispensable. We would propose, therefore, that in forecasting and planning situations, decision rules and quantitative models should be applied to situations involving little or no systematic change from established patterns or relationships. In cases where systematic changes are taking place, decision makers should rely more heavily on judgment that is concentrated on determining the extent and implications of such change (see Chapter 16 for a more detailed discussion).

An important question, of course, is knowing when a change is taking place. This aspect of forecasting and planning, known as monitoring, has been neglected in the literature among forecasting practitioners (see Chapter 14). The results of monitoring can be used as a basis for deciding what approach to forecasting is most appropriate.

One final conclusion is that since improvement and learning require feedback and evaluation, errors in one situation must be compared with errors in similar situations to determine the extent of their significance. In the final analysis, errors must be looked at not as mistakes, but as an integral part of the learning process, to be fully utilized rather than ignored.

SELECTED REFERENCES FOR FURTHER STUDY

Armstrong, J.S., 1984. "Relative Accuracy of Judgment and Extrapolative Methods in Forecasting Annual Earnings," *Journal of Forecasting*, 2, no. 4.

Bowman, E.H., 1963. "Consistency and Optimality in Managerial Decision Making," *Management Science*, 10, no. 1, pp. 310–321.

Dawes, R.M., 1986. "Forecasting One's Own Preferences," *International Journal of Forecasting*, 2, pp. 5–14.

———, 1979. "The Robust Beauty of Improper Linear Models in Decision Making," *American Psychologist*, 34, no. 7, pp. 571–582.

Ebert, R.J., 1972. "Environmental Structure and Programmed Decision Effectiveness," *Management Science*, 19, no. 4, pp. 435–445.

Funder, D.C., 1987. "Errors and Mistakes: Evaluations of the Accuracy of Social Judgment," *Psychological Bulletin*, 101, pp. 75–90.

Hogarth, R., 1981. "Beyond Discrete Biases: Functional and Dysfunctional Aspects of Judgmental Heuristics," *Psychological Bulletin*, 90, pp. 197–217.

Hogarth, R., 1975. "Cognitive Processes and the Assessment of Subjective Probability Distributions," *Journal of the American Statistical Association*, 70, no. 350, pp. 271–289.

Hogarth, R., and S. Makridakis, 1981. "Forecasting and Planning. An Evaluation," *Management Science*, 27, no. 2, pp. 115–137.

Janis, I.L., and I. Mann, 1982. *Decision Making: A Psychological Analysis of Conflict, Choice and Commitment*, 2nd Ed. Free Press, New York.

Kahneman, D., P. Slovic, and A. Tversky, 1982. *Judgment under Uncertainty: Heuristics and Biases*, Cambridge University Press, Cambridge, England.

Kahneman, D., and A. Tversky, 1979. "Intuitive Prediction Biases and Corrective Procedures," *TIMS Studies in the Management Sciences*, vol. 12, North-Holland, Amsterdam, pp. 313–327.

———, 1973. "On the Psychology of Prediction," *Psychological Review*, 80, no. 4, pp. 237–251.

Kunreuther, H., 1969. "Extensions of Bowman's Theory of Managerial Decision Making," *Management Science*, 15, no. 8, pp. B-415–439.

Lawrence, M., and S. Makridakis, 1988. "Factors Affecting Judgmental Forecasts and Confidence Intervals," *Organizational Behavior and Human Decision Processes*, forthcoming.

Lewin, K., 1947. "Group Decision and Social Change," in T. Newcomb and E. Hartley (Eds.), *Readings in Social Psychology*, Henry Holt, New York.

Makridakis, S., and M. Hibon, 1987. "Confidence Intervals: An Empirical Investigation of the Series in the M-Competition," *International Journal of Forecasting*, 3, pp. 489–508.

Morita, A., 1986. *Made in Japan: Akio Morita and Sony*, Dutton, New York.

Murphy, A.H., and R.L. Winkler, 1977. "Can Weather Forecasters Formulate Reliable Probability Forecasts of Precipitation and Temperature?" *National Weather Digest*, 2, pp. 2–9.

Neuringer, A., 1986. "Can People Behave Randomly? The Role of Feedback," *Journal of Experimental Psychology*, 115, pp. 62–75.

Northcraft, G.B., and M.A. Neale, 1987. "Experts, Amateurs and Real Estate: An Anchoring-and-Adjustment Perspective on Property Pricing Decisions," *Organizational Behavior and Human Decision Processes*, 39, pp. 84–97.

O'Connor, M.J., 1989. "An Examination of Judgmental Confidence Intervals," *International Journal of Forecasting*, forthcoming.

Remus, W.E., 1978. "Testing Bowman's Managerial Coefficient Theory Using a Competitive Gaming Environment," *Management Science*, 24, no. 8, pp. 827–835.

Schwenk, C.R., 1986. "Information, Cognitive Biases, and Commitment to a Course of Action," *Academy of Management Review*, 11, pp. 298–310.

Simon, H., and A. Newell, 1971. "Human Problem Solving: The State of the Theory in 1970," *American Psychologist*, 26, pp. 145–159.

Slovic, P., B. Fischhoff, and S. Lichtenstein, 1977. "Behavioral Decision Theory," *Annual Review of Psychology*, 28, pp. 1–39.

Spetzler, C.S., and C.A.S. Stael von Holstein, 1975. "Probability Encoding in Decision Analysis," *Management Science*, 22, pp. 340–358.

Tversky, A., and D. Kahneman, 1973. "Availability: A Heuristic for Judging Frequency and Probability," *Cognitive Psychology*, 5, no. 2, pp. 207–232.

Zieve, L., 1966. "Misinterpretation and Abuse of Laboratory Tests by Clinicians," *Annals of the New York Academy of Science*, 134, pp. 563–572.

CHAPTER 14

MONITORING APPROACHES

Monitoring is an essential aspect of any forecasting situation. As outlined in the initial chapters of this book, managers must deal with two types of situations in connection with forecasting: (1) the continuation of established patterns or relationships, and (2) nonrandom (systematic) changes from established patterns or relationships. The role of monitoring, either implicitly or explicitly, is to identify the occurrence of nonrandom changes from existing patterns or relationships.

The idea of monitoring is applicable to a wide range of situations. It applies not only to forecasting situations but also to all cases where a manager would like to know when nonrandom changes from targets, patterns, or established situations are occurring. The critical element in monitoring is the selection of the type of factor to be monitored and the quantification of such a factor if it is a qualitative one.

Figure 14-1 presents data on two common types of pattern shifts—a step change and a ramp change. Figure 14-1 also indicates how some simple forecasting approaches would respond. Three aspects of these responses are central to the discussion of monitoring in this chapter. First, if such a change can be identified (monitored) early, the forecasting method can be adapted or replaced to obtain much better results both during the transition stage and later when the new pattern or relationship stabilizes. Second, when a pattern shift does occur, it is usually most visible in the forecasting errors, that is, those errors change in a systematic manner. Third, with the presence of random fluctuations, as would normally be the case, the quick separation of random effects and nonrandom pattern change becomes nontrivial.

In this chapter, two categories of approaches for monitoring will be described:

1. Automatic, quantitative procedures for determining when a pattern or relationship has changed. Such methods use a tracking signal to identify when changes in the forecasting errors indicate that such a nonrandom

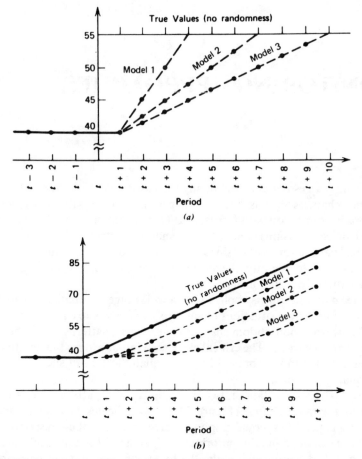

Figure 14-1 Accuracy of Three Forecasting Models. (*a*) With a Step Change, (*b*) With a Ramp Change.

shift has occurred, that is, when such errors are increasingly less likely to be simply random fluctuations.

2. Judgmental procedures, such as use of the trend-cycle component from decomposition methods, for distinguishing random fluctuations, temporary systematic changes (for example, recessions), and long-term trend changes.

AUTOMATIC MONITORING OF FORECASTING ERRORS: TRACKING SIGNALS

As a backdrop for understanding the use of tracking signals to monitor quantitative forecasting methods, it is instructive to review the concept of quality control charts. The principle of quality control is to discover as soon as possible when a process or product has deviated in a nonrandom manner from its normal value. The approach used to achieve this objective is to sample continuously the process or product and to compare the mean (average) value of that sample with the desired value.

For example, a bottler of cognac might desire to fill each bottle with 750 centiliters of product, but because of random variations the firm knows that the actual contents will sometimes be a little more and sometimes a little less than this amount. As long as the contents are within some specified range of the 750-cl target, there is no problem, that is, as long as the equipment is operating according to its expected pattern, the slight variation in content is not a concern. However, if the equipment does not work properly (that is, it begins operating according to a different pattern), the firm wants to know that quickly so the machine can be stopped, corrected (adjusted or modified), and then restarted so that a minimum of output needs to be rechecked and possibly rebottled.

A quality control chart is one technique for determining whether a process is operating as expected. Such a chart is shown in Figure 14-2. The desired mean or average is plotted as a horizontal line, and above and below it two parallel lines are drawn. The upper line is called the upper control limit (UCL) and the lower line the lower control limit (LCL). The distance between these two limits depends on the characteristics of the item being measured. In the case of the cognac bottler, the equipment specifications and its tolerances determine this distance. The actual distance used would be based on past experience when the equipment was known to be operating correctly.

The cognac bottler would periodically sample the output of the equipment, compute its mean (that is, average content per bottle), and plot that on the control chart. As long as that sample mean is within the control limits, the equipment is known to be operating correctly and the quality (volume) standards are being met. If a sample mean lies outside the control limits, the equipment is stopped and appropriate action is taken to return it to correct operation.

Automatic monitoring of a quantitative forecasting method follows the concept and principles of a quality control chart. Every time a forecast is made, its error (actual minus predicted value) is checked against the UCL and the LCL. If it is within the acceptable range, the conclusion is that the forecasting method used is operating correctly (under control), that is, the

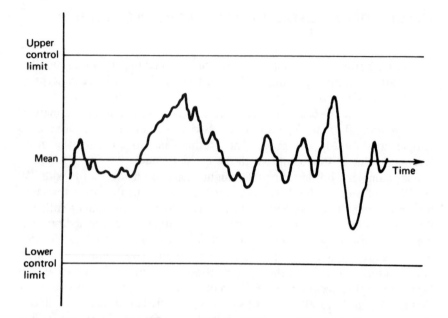

Figure 14-2 Quality Control Chart. *Note:* As long as the output of a process stays within the upper and lower control limits, it is assumed that the process is under control (that is, the fluctuations of the output values around the mean are random). When the output crosses the upper or lower control limit, the chart signals a systematic error, indicating that the process must be stopped and the cause(s) of the change (error) identified and corrected.

extrapolated pattern or relationship has not changed. If the forecasting error is outside the control limits, it indicates a systematic error and implies that something has changed, that is, there has probably been some systematic (nonrandom) change in the established pattern or relationship used for forecasting.

The objective of automatic monitoring procedures is to set the UCL and the LCL in such a way that nonrandom forecasting errors are caught as early as possible, but random errors are not mistaken for such pattern changes. The mean of the control chart is set at 0 since such a forecasting error implies a perfect forecast. The more the forecasting errors vary from 0 in some systematic way, the greater the chances that the established pattern or relationship being monitored has changed.

In an excellent review paper, Gardner (1983) has surveyed all of the major automatic monitoring procedures and classified them into four categories: (1) simple CUSUM (CUmulative SUM) tracking signals, (2) backward CUSUM control systems, (3) smoothed-error tracking signals, and (4) auto-correlation tracking signals. As summarized in Table 14-1, approaches in

Table 14-1   Advantages and Disadvantages of Automatic Monitoring Approaches

Approaches	Advantages	Disadvantages
CUSUM	Performance is independent of the model parameters and variance of the time series. More sensitive to small changes in the time series than other approaches.	Large errors are not "forgotten" once they occur. If forecasting errors are clo⌐ to or exactly equal to zero, system becomes unstable. Does not work well with independent forecasting errors.
Backward CUSUM	Performance is independent of the model parameters and variance of the time series. Most comprehensive approach—each period, all previous errors are implicitly reviewed.	The lower and upper control limits cannot be easily found. Its performance has not been tested p: actically. It requires more data to use than the other monitoring approaches. The variance of the time series must be constant.
Smoothed-error tracking signals	Easy to operate and update. Only two parameters to store. The average error is a useful, intuitive measure of how well the forecasting system is doing.	The upper and lower control limits depend on the value of the smoothing constant. It does not work well with independent forecasting errors.
Autocorrelation tracking signals	Performance is independent of the model parameters and variance of the time series. More general than the alternative monitoring approaches. Works best when forecasting errors are independent.	More complex to apply. Not recommended for exponential smoothing methods where the forecasting errors are *not* independent.

Source: Adapted from Gardner (1983).

each of the four categories have certain advantages and drawbacks and thus vary in their appropriateness for specific situations. For practical purposes, category (3) is probably the most widely used, followed by category (4), which requires a more sophisticated user. After describing each of the categories briefly, the next section will examine a smoothed-error tracking signal representative of category (3) and briefly examine an autocorrelation tracking signal representative of category (4).

Simple CUSUM Tracking Signals

First recommended by Brown (1959), this approach compares the cumulative sum (CUSUM) of the errors at the end of each time period with a smoothed value of the mean absolute deviation (MAD). If the ratio CUSUM/MAD exceeds a prespecified multiple (the control limits), the forecasting approach is reexamined to see whether the pattern has changed and thus whether some change in the forecasting approach is required. The control limit (that is, the prespecified multiple of the smoothed MAD that is allowed) can be set either to yield some desired probability of getting a "false trip" (a signal to reexamine when no pattern change has occurred, often called a Type I error) or to require a certain number of time periods to detect a change of a given size.

Backward CUSUM Control Systems

Approaches in this category, such as that suggested by Harrison and Davies (1963), are based on the notion that if we could guess when a past change in the time series occurred, then the sum of all errors since the change would be the best tracking signal available today, that is, if a change in the series occurred in period 40 and it is now period 46, then the sum of the errors from periods 40 to 46 would be more sensitive to the change than the sum from periods 1 to 46. Since there is no way of knowing the number of past periods to sum in advance, it appears necessary to maintain a battery of all possible CUSUMs. The first one is just the last error, the second is the sum of the last two errors, and so on. The number of such CUSUMs could quickly get out of hand. However, Harrison and Davies have worked out an ingenious scheme whereby all previous CUSUMs can be implicitly tested while storing only four quantities.

Smoothed-Error Tracking Signals

The earliest approach of this type, developed by Trigg (1964), was developed to overcome the disadvantages of the long memory of the simple CUSUM. Rather than taking the ratio of the actual CUSUM to the smoothed MAD, this approach uses an exponentially smoothed value of the forecast error divided by a smoothed value of the MAD. If this ratio exceeds some prespecified multiple, it signals to the forecaster that a change in pattern or relationship probably has occurred.

Autocorrelation Tracking Signals

It will be recalled from Chapter 7 that autocorrelation coefficients can be used to determine the existence of a pattern in a time series. Since error terms should be random when a forecasting approach is working correctly, the autocorrelation of adjacent errors (referred to as a first-order regression on successive errors) can be used to develop a tracking signal. Since the standard computation of the first-order autocorrelation weights all errors equally, it is necessary to discount the sums in this calculation (weighting recent errors most heavily) to convert it into a tracking signal. Control limits can then be established on the basis of the expected value of the mean squared error, the denominator in this discounted autocorrelation tracking signal.

COMPUTING THE SMOOTHED-ERROR TRACKING SIGNAL

The smoothed-error tracking signal, widely used in practice, consists of two smoothing equations and the tracking signal T. It requires the continued updating and storage of two values, E_t and M_t, as well as a value for the smoothing constant α. The updating and tracking signal equations are as follows:

$$E_t = \alpha e_t + (1 - \alpha)E_{t-1} \tag{14-1}$$

$$M_t = \alpha|e_t| + (1 - \alpha)M_{t-1} \tag{14-2}$$

$$T_t = \left|\frac{E_t}{M_t}\right| \tag{14-3}$$

where $e_t = X_t - F_t$, | | means absolute value, and α is a smoothing constant whose value is between 0 and 1, similar to that used in exponential smoothing (see Chapter 5).

Once a forecasting system is in operation, e_t is known, and Equations (14-1) and (14-2) can be computed. Then the tracking signal ratio T_t can be found using Equation (14-3). If T_t is close to 0, indicating that M_t is much bigger than E_t, it implies that the errors are random. This is so because the numerator is smoothing the actual errors (with their positive and negative values) while the denominator is smoothing the absolute values (all errors are treated as positive). When some systematic change has occurred, the forecast-

Table 14-2   Smoothed-Error Tracking Signals of Various Probabilities

Cumulative Probability that Errors Are Not Random	Independent Errors $\alpha = 0.1$	T_t Exponential Smoothing Constant (Dependent Errors)		
		$\alpha = 0.1$	$\alpha = 0.2$	$\alpha = 0.3$
0.80	0.37	0.28	0.40	0.51
0.90	0.47	0.36	0.49	0.61
0.95	**0.54**	**0.42**	**0.57**	**0.69**
0.96	0.56	0.44	0.59	0.71
0.97	0.59	0.46	0.61	0.73
0.98	0.62	0.50	0.65	0.77
0.99	0.67	0.55	0.69	0.81

ing errors will be consistently positive or negative, increasing the value of E_t in Equation (14-1). This will cause the ratio T_t of Equation (14-3) to increase (positive or negative). Once a certain limit is reached (the UCL or LCL), it implies that the errors have ceased to be random. The value of these limits depends on (1) whether or not the errors are independent and (2) the specific value of the smoothing constant α.

Table 14-2 shows, for various probabilities, the limits that would be used to determine that the forecasting errors are not random. For practical applications we would recommend that one use a 95% probability level and that the errors not be assumed to be independent. (These tracking signal limits are printed in bold type in Table 14-2.) Quite often a value of $\alpha = 0.1$ is used in Equations (14-1) and (14-2), thus making the value of 0.42 the upper and lower control limits.

The questions of whether the forecasting errors are independent requires some explanation here. Some time-series methods, such as the Box–Jenkins approach, are designed to remove any consistent pattern from the errors. In other methods, particularly exponential smoothing, one would expect the errors to be autocorrelated. The presence of autocorrelation in the errors makes a great deal of difference in the tracking signal limits that should be selected. In Table 14-2 the limits take into account the autocorrelations resulting from simple exponential smoothing of a horizontal data pattern with random noise.

As initial values for Equations (14-1) and (14-2), we can let $E_1 = 0$ and M_1 equal an estimate of the mean absolute deviation (MAD). (The MAD can be based on the errors from the model-fitting process.) We would also recommend using an α value no larger than 0.2 and assuming that the forecasting errors are not independent. Finally, it should be remembered that if the tracking signal indicates an out-of-control message, the value of E_t must be reset to 0 before continuing. (Otherwise the tracking signal would continue to be outside of the control limits.)

The Autocorrelation Tracking Signal

For models other than exponential smoothing, usually the first-order autocorrelation of the residuals is tracked to determine whether the errors are nonrandom. The tracking signal is found as follows:

$$\text{Cov}_t = e_t e_{t-1} + (1 - \alpha)\text{Cov}_{t-1} \tag{14-4}$$

$$\text{MSE}_t = e_{t-1}^2 + (1 - \alpha)\text{MSE}_{t-1} \tag{14-5}$$

$$T_t = \frac{\text{Cov}_t}{\text{MSE}_t} \tag{14-6}$$

where
α = smoothing constant for the error
Cov_t = covariance at time t
MSE_t = mean squared error at time t
T_t = tracking signal at time t.

Although Equations (14-4) to (14-6) seem difficult to understand, they are similar in principle to Equations (14-1) to (14-3). In addition, they can be applied easily. For more details, see Gardner (1983).

The forecasting errors are assumed not to be random if values of T_1 in Equation (14-6) go outside the limits ($+$ or $-$) shown in Table 14-3.

The autocorrelation tracking signal is a discounted least squares model with discount factor equal to $(1 - \alpha)$. For most applications of this signal, values of $\alpha = 0.1$ and $(1 - \alpha) = 0.9$ are recommended. Increasing the value of α makes the signal more responsive to true changes in the time series but also leads to more false alarms. The net result is that generally there is no advantage to a larger α value.

The form of Equations (14-4) and (14-5) may be confusing. It may seem that $e_t e_{t-1}$ should be multiplied by α. Also, it may seem that e_{t-1}^2 should be multiplied by α. However, there is no need to do this. Since T_t is a ratio, its value is not affected by the use of α in the first term of Equations (14-4) and (14-5).

A similar comment applies to Equations (14-1) and (14-2) for the smoothed-error tracking signal. Since T_t is again a ratio, α could be omitted in the first term of these equations. We chose to leave α in these terms because this form of these equations has become commonly used in practice.

Table 14-3 Autocorrelation Tracking
Signal for Independent Errors and
$\alpha = 0.1$, $(1 - \alpha) = 0.9$

Cumulative Probability that Errors Are Not Random	T_t
0.80	0.17
0.90	0.27
0.95	0.35
0.96	0.37
0.97	0.39
0.98	0.43
0.99	0.48

Source: Gardner (1983).

As initial values for applying this monitoring system, we can let Cov_1 equal 0 and let MSE equal the average of the first several error terms, squared, obtained during the model-fitting process. The value of α can be set to 0.9. Finally, as with the smoothed-error tracking signal, if T_t goes outside the allowable limits, Cov_t must be reset to 0 before continuing.

Illustrating the Application of Tracking Signals

Applying Equations (14-1) to (14-3) or Equations (14-4) to (14-6) is a straightforward matter if a computer or programmable calculator is available. The computations involved will be illustrated in this section and the behavior of tracking signals when a step or a ramp change occurs will be examined, both for a smoothed-error tracking signal and for an autocorrelation tracking signal.

Using Tables 14-4 to 14-6, we want to examine the application of a smoothed-error tracking signal when the errors are random, when a step change occurs, and when a ramp change occurs, respectively. (The reader might want to return to Figure 14-1 to see what such changes look like graphically.) It can be seen from Table 14-4, where the errors are random, that at no point does the tracking signal exceed 0.54 (the trigger value from Table 14-2 for a 95% confidence level). Thus the tracking signal indicates that indeed these forecasting errors are random.

As an illustration of the computations involved in developing Table 14-4, we can apply Equations (14-1) to (14-3) with $\alpha = 0.1$ for periods 14 and 15

$$E_{14} = \alpha e_{14} + (1 - \alpha)E_{13}$$
$$= 0.1(-1.721) + 0.9(0.235) = 0.039$$
$$M_{14} = a|e_t| + (1 - \alpha)M_{13}$$
$$= 0.1(1.721) + 0.9(0.699) = 0.801$$
$$T_{14} = \frac{E_{14}}{M_{14}} = \frac{0.039}{0.801} = 0.049.$$

Table 14-4 Smoothed-Error Tracking Signal T_t and Required Input Values When Residuals Are Random

Period t	Residuals e_t	Smoothed Errors E_t	Smoothed Absolute Errors M_t	Tracking Signal T_t
1	−0.992	−0.099	0.992	0.100
2	−0.319	−0.121	0.925	0.131
3	0.278	−0.081	0.860	0.094
4	0.507	−0.022	0.825	0.027
5	0.159	−0.004	0.758	0.006
6	0.611	0.057	0.743	0.077
7	1.973	0.249	0.866	0.287
8	−0.460	0.178	0.826	0.215
9	0.727	0.233	0.816	0.285
10	−0.035	0.206	0.738	0.279
11	−0.470	0.138	0.711	0.195
12	0.394	0.164	0.679	0.241
13	0.874	0.235	0.699	0.336
14	−1.721	0.039	0.801	0.049
15	−0.514	−0.016	0.772	0.021
16	−0.394	−0.054	0.734	0.073
17	1.466	0.098	0.808	0.122
18	−0.095	0.079	0.736	0.107
19	−0.164	0.055	0.679	0.080
20	0.290	0.078	0.640	0.122
21	0.754	0.146	0.652	0.224
22	−0.047	0.126	0.591	0.214
23	1.108	0.225	0.643	0.349
24	0.236	0.226	0.602	0.375
25	−0.060	0.197	0.548	0.360
26	0.001	0.178	0.493	0.360
27	0.249	0.185	0.469	0.394
28	−0.526	0.114	0.475	0.239
29	0.205	0.123	0.448	0.274
30	0.905	0.201	0.493	0.407

Table 14-5 Smoothed-Error Signal T_t and Required Input Values When a Step Change of Two Units Is Introduced at Period 20[a]

t	e_t	E_t	M_t	T_t
1	−0.992	−0.099	0.992	0.100
2	−0.319	−0.121	0.925	0.131
3	0.278	−0.081	0.860	0.094
4	0.507	−0.022	0.825	0.027
5	0.159	−0.004	0.758	0.006
6	0.611	0.057	0.743	0.077
7	1.973	0.249	0.866	0.287
8	−0.460	0.178	0.826	0.215
9	0.727	0.233	0.816	0.285
10	−0.035	0.206	0.738	0.279
11	−0.470	0.138	0.711	0.195
12	0.394	0.164	0.679	0.241
13	0.874	0.235	0.699	0.336
14	−1.721	0.039	0.801	0.049
15	−0.514	−0.016	0.772	0.021
16	−0.394	−0.054	0.734	0.073
17	1.466	0.098	0.808	0.122
18	−0.095	0.079	0.736	0.107
19	−0.164[b]	0.055	0.679	0.080
20	2.290	0.278	0.840	0.331
21	2.754	0.526	1.032	0.510
22	−1.953	0.668	1.124	0.595
23	3.108	0.311	2.069	0.150
24	2.236	0.503	2.085	0.241
25	1.940	0.647	2.071	0.312
26	2.001	0.782	2.064	0.379
27	2.249	0.929	2.082	0.446
28	1.474	0.984	2.021	0.487
29	2.205	1.106	2.040	0.542
30	2.905	0.291	2.275	0.128

[a] See Table 14-4.
[b] Step change.

Similarly,

$$E_{15} = 0.1(−0.514) + 0.9(0.039) = −0.016$$
$$M_{15} = 0.1(0.514) + 0.9(0.801) = 0.772$$
$$T_{15} = \left|\frac{−0.016}{0.772}\right| = 0.021.$$

Table 14-6 Smoothed-Error Tracking Signal T_t and Required Input
Values When a Ramp Is Introduced at Period 20[a]

t	e_t	E_t	M_t	T_t
1	−0.992	−0.099	0.992	0.100
2	−0.319	−0.121	0.925	0.131
3	0.278	−0.081	0.860	0.094
4	0.507	−0.022	0.825	0.027
5	0.159	−0.004	0.758	0.006
6	0.611	0.057	0.743	0.077
7	1.973	0.249	0.866	0.287
8	−0.460	0.178	0.826	0.215
9	0.727	0.233	0.816	0.285
10	−0.035	0.206	0.738	0.279
11	−0.470	0.138	0.711	0.195
12	0.394	0.164	0.679	0.241
13	0.874	0.235	0.699	0.336
14	−1.721	0.039	0.801	0.049
15	−0.514	−0.016	0.772	0.021
16	−0.394	−0.054	0.734	0.073
17	1.466	0.098	0.808	0.122
18	−0.095	0.079	0.736	0.107
19	−0.164[b]	0.055	0.679	0.080
20	0.790	0.128	0.690	0.186
21	1.754	0.291	0.797	0.365
22	1.453	0.407	0.862	0.472
23	3.108	0.677	1.087	0.623
24	2.736	0.274	3.071	0.089
25	2.940	0.540	3.058	0.177
26	3.501	0.836	3.102	0.270
27	4.249	1.178	3.217	0.366
28	3.974	1.457	3.292	0.443
29	5.205	1.832	3.484	0.526
30	6.405	2.289	3.776	0.606

[a] See Table 14-4.
[b] Ramp change.

In Table 14-5 a step change of two has been added at period 20 and
continues until period 30. It is interesting how fast the tracking signal detects
such a nonrandom change.

The calculations involved for period 20 are

$$E_{20} = 0.1(2.29) + 0.9(0.055) = 0.278$$
$$M_{20} = 0.1(2.29) + 0.9(0.679) = 0.840$$
$$T_{20} = \frac{0.278}{0.840} = 0.331.$$

For period 21 the calculations are

$$E_{21} = 0.1(2.754) + 0.9(0.278) = 0.526$$
$$M_{21} = 0.1(2.754) + 0.9(0.84) = 1.032$$
$$T_{21} = \frac{0.526}{1.032} = 0.51.$$

Although the tracking signal of 0.51 is close to the control limit of 0.54, it does not exceed it until period 22:

$$E_{22} = 0.1(1.953) + 0.9(0.526) = 0.668$$
$$M_{22} = 0.1(1.953) + 0.9(1.032) = 1.124$$
$$T_{22} = \frac{0.668}{1.124} = 0.595.$$

Thus in this instance it takes three periods to detect a nonrandom change. This is not long, considering that the step change introduced was rather small.

Table 14-6 is similar to Table 14-4, except that at period 20 a ramp change is introduced. This is done by adding 0.5 to the period 20 value, 1.0 to the period 21 value, 1.5 to the period 22 value, and so on. The tracking signal values (see right-hand column of Table 14-6) detect the change at period 23 where the value of the tracking signal (0.623) exceeds the control limit value of 0.54 for a 95% confidence level. Thus in this case the nonrandom pattern change is identified within four time periods.

As an illustration of how an autocorrelation tracking signal can be developed and applied, Tables 14-7 to 14-9 utilize the same basic data (error terms) as Tables 14-4 to 14-6. Starting with Table 14-7, a situation with random error terms—that is, no change in the basic pattern—is examined. The calculation of the autocorrelation tracking signal T for period 14 using

Table 14-7 Autocorrelation Tracking Signal T_t and Required Input Values When Residuals Are Random

t	e_t	Cov_t	MSE_t	T_t
2	-0.391	0.316	4.527	0.070
3	0.278	0.196	4.176	0.047
4	0.507	0.317	3.853	0.083
5	0.159	0.366	3.709	0.099
6	0.611	0.427	3.363	0.127
7	1.973	1.590	3.400	0.467
8	-0.460	-0.908	5.237	-0.173
9	0.727	-1.151	4.925	-0.234
10	-0.035	-1.062	4.961	-0.214
11	-0.470	-0.939	4.466	-0.210
12	0.394	-1.030	4.240	-0.243
13	0.874	-0.583	3.971	-0.147
14	-1.721	-2.029	4.338	-0.468
15	-0.514	0.885	5.712	0.155
16	-0.394	0.999	5.405	0.185
17	1.466	0.321	5.020	0.064
18	-0.095	0.150	6.667	0.022
19	-0.164	0.150	6.009	0.025
20	0.290	0.088	5.435	0.016
21	0.754	0.298	4.976	0.060
22	-0.047	0.232	5.047	0.046
23	1.108	0.157	4.544	0.035
24	0.236	0.403	5.317	0.076
25	-0.060	0.348	4.841	0.072
26	0.001	0.314	4.361	0.072
27	0.249	0.282	3.925	0.072
28	-0.526	0.123	3.594	0.034
29	0.205	0.003	3.512	0.001
30	0.905	0.188	3.202	0.059

Equations (14-4) to (14-6) is as follows:

$$Cov_{14} = e_{14}e_{13} + (1 - \alpha)Cov_{13}$$
$$= -1.721(0.874) + 0.9(-0.583) = -2.029$$
$$MSE_{14} = e_{13}^2 + (1 - \alpha)MSE_{13}$$
$$= (0.874)^2 + 0.9(3.971) = 4.338$$

$$T_{14} = \frac{\text{Cov}_{14}}{\text{MSE}_{14}} = \frac{-2.029}{4.338} = -0.468.$$

In this case, the value of the autocorrelation tracking signal exceeds the control limit of 0.35, yet we know the series of errors is random (that is why we selected this example). Thus this is a false alarm. Since the control limit is set for a 95% confidence level, this is simply an instance where by chance

Table 14-8 Autocorrelation Tracking Signal T_t and Required Input Values When a Step Change of Two Is Introduced at Period 20[a]

t	e_t	Cov_t	MSE_t	T_t
2	−0.319	0.316	4.527	0.070
3	0.278	0.196	4.176	0.047
4	0.507	0.317	3.835	0.083
5	0.159	0.366	3.709	0.099
6	0.611	0.427	3.363	0.127
7	1.973	1.590	3.400	0.467
8	−0.460	−0.908	5.237	−0.173
9	0.727	−1.151	4.925	−0.234
10	−0.035	−1.062	4.961	−0.214
11	−0.470	−0.939	4.466	−0.210
12	0.394	−1.030	4.240	−0.243
13	0.874	−0.583	3.971	−0.147
14	−1.721	−2.029	4.338	−0.468
15	−0.514	0.885	5.712	0.155
16	−0.394	0.999	5.405	0.185
17	1.466	0.321	5.020	0.064
18	−0.095	0.150	6.667	0.022
19	−0.164[b]	0.150	6.009	0.025
20	2.290	−0.240	5.435	−0.044
21	2.754	6.090	10.136	0.601
22	1.953	5.379	26.463	0.203
23	3.108	10.911	27.631	0.395
24	2.236	6.949	23.391	0.297
25	1.940	10.592	26.051	0.407
26	2.001	3.882	21.763	0.178
27	2.249	7.994	23.590	0.339
28	1.474	10.510	26.289	0.400
29	2.205	3.250	20.381	0.159
30	2.905	9.331	23.205	0.402

[a] See Table 14-7.
[b] Step change.

that limit was exceeded. We would expect this to happen 5% of the time. Once this happens (whether a real or a false alarm), the values of Cov and MSE must be reinitialized. Otherwise the tracking signal will continue to indicate nonrandom changes. This reinitialization can be done by setting the covariance for period 14 to 0 and recomputing MSE for period 14 as

$$\text{MSE}_{14} = e_{13}^2(4) = (0.874)^2(4) = 3.056.$$

The approach used for this reinitialization of MSE_{14} is open to interpretation and judgment. However, whatever approach is used, the reinitialized value must be large enough in relation to the covariance to provide some stability for the tracking signal (see Table 14-8).

For period 20,

$$\text{Cov}_{20} = 2.29(-0.164) + 0.9(0.15) = -0.240$$
$$\text{MSE}_{20} = -(0.164)^2 + 0.9(6.009) = 5.435$$
$$T_{20} = \frac{-0.24}{5.435} = -0.044.$$

For period 21,

$$\text{Cov}_{21} = 2.754(2.290) + 0.9(-0.24) = 6.909$$
$$\text{MSE}_{21} = (2.29)^2 + 0.9(5.435) = 10.136$$
$$T_{21} = \frac{6.09}{10.136} = 0.601.$$

Finally, in Table 14-9 the ramp change is detected at period 22. This is one period sooner than the detection by the smoothed-error signal (see Table 14-6). This is a further indication that the autocorrelation tracking signal is more sensitive but can also lead to more false alarms than the smoothed-error tracking signal.

JUDGMENTAL MONITORING OF THE TREND CYCLE

Automatic monitoring through tracking signals is particularly appropriate when large numbers of forecasts are involved (such as in inventory forecasting systems) and the objective is to distinguish random from nonrandom errors. Where one or only a few important series are involved, a judgmental monitoring of the trend cycle can be used in addition to automatic tracking signals.

Table 14-9 Autocorrelation Tracking Signal T_t and Required Input Values When a Ramp Change Is Introduced at Period 20[a]

t	e_t	Cov$_t$	MSE$_t$	T_t
2	-0.319	0.316	4.527	0.070
3	0.278	0.196	4.176	0.047
4	0.607	0.317	3.835	0.083
5	0.159	0.366	3.709	0.099
6	0.611	0.427	3.363	0.127
7	1.173	1.590	3.400	0.467
8	-0.460	0.908	5.237	-0.173
9	0.727	-1.151	4.925	-0.234
10	-0.035	-1.062	4.961	-0.214
11	-0.470	-0.939	4.466	-0.210
12	0.394	-1.030	4.240	-0.243
13	0.874	-0.583	3.971	-0.147
14	-1.721	-2.029	4.338	-0.468
15	-0.514	0.885	5.712	0.155
16	-0.394	0.999	5.405	0.185
17	1.966	0.321	5.020	0.064
18	-0.095	0.150	6.667	0.022
19	-0.164[b]	0.150	6.009	0.025
20	0.790	0.006	5.435	0.001
21	1.751	1.391	5.516	0.252
22	1.453	3.800	8.041	0.473
23	3.108	4.516	13.187	0.342
24	2.736	12.568	21.528	0.584
25	2.940	8.044	42.260	0.190
26	3.501	17.532	46.678	0.376
27	1.249	14.876	43.374	0.343
28	3.974	30.274	57.091	0.530
29	5.205	20.685	80.787	0.256
30	6.405	51.954	99.800	0.521

[a] See also Table 14-7.
[b] Ramp change.

The logic behind monitoring the trend cycle is that randomness is of no concern in the longer term and that seasonality also can be excluded in order to isolate the trend-cycle pattern. (See Chapter 6 for details.) This trend-cycle pattern can provide extremely important information about the current pattern in the variable being monitored with regard to two basic questions: (1) is a cyclical change taking place? and (2) is a change occurring in the trend?

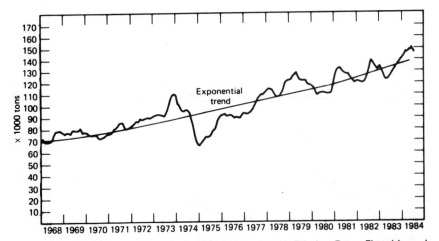

Figure 14-3 Trend and Trend-Cycle Values for a French Printing Paper Firm (through November 1984).

Unfortunately, cyclical and trend changes are interrelated and extremely difficult to separate, and they pose a fundamental problem for the forecaster. By definition, cyclical nonrandom (systematic) changes are temporary, while systematic changes in trend are permanent.

To answer the first question, the long-term trend in the data must be identified. This can be done by first specifying starting and ending periods that are considered to be "normal" in terms of the level of economic activity. That is, these starting and ending periods should not represent periods of recession or boom. The second step is to identify the trend that best fits the data between these two points. Figure 14-3 illustrates the application of this approach for the French printing paper industry. The trend was calculated using the middle of 1968 to the beginning of 1980 as the time horizon. The trend-cycle curve is found using any decomposition method (see Chapter 6). Both the trend and the trend-cycle curves are shown in Figure 14-3.

By computing the new value of the trend cycle each time a new data point becomes available, the forecasting user can obtain substantial information that can be used in monitoring for changes in patterns or relationships. In Figure 14-3, the data show that the orders for printing paper recently have risen above the long-term trend and, most recently, have started declining. The obvious concern is whether this signals the start of a recession.

Looking at Figure 14-3, we see that the latest trend-cycle values are monitored continuously. Since they do not include randomness or seasonality, any change in their value must be explained in terms of trend and cycle changes. For example, a decrease in the trend cycle might be caused by a price increase by one's own firm, a price discount by one of the competitors, and

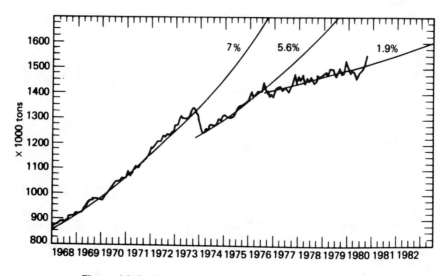

Figure 14-4   Distinguishing Changes in Trend and Cycle.

similar reasons. If no explanation can be found, one might conclude that the decrease is tied to a forthcoming recession.

Monitoring the trend cycle is a waiting game where every month the most recent data value is compared to the past values to determine whether changes in the trend cycle are occurring. The authors have found this approach to be a very useful addition to forecasting. Such knowledge often becomes the basis for future adjustments in forecasting.

It is interesting to note the cyclical ups and downs shown in Figure 14-3. Where the series is going beyond the final data point (November 1984) is not clear. Much will depend on the value for December 1984 and January 1985. If the downward pressure persists, the recent decline may become the start of a major recession. If the decline does not continue, the upturn that started in mid-1983 will continue. Thus, although precise forecasting is not possible, the likelihood of various alternatives can be weighed and their possible impact on the organization evaluated.

In order to isolate changes in trend, it is necessary first to consider whether the changes are of a cyclical nature. If changes in the trend-cycle values persist beyond the lowest (or highest) values of previous cycles, then the hypothesis that the downtrend may not be of a cyclical nature but actually a change in the long-term trend must be entertained. The validity of such a hypothesis is illustrated with the data of Figure 14-4. These data indicate several changes in trends. Figure 14-4 makes it much easier to identify such changes because the cycle in this case can be seen to be rather insignificant. Had a more substantial cycle been present, distinguishing (isolating) permanent changes in trend would have been much more difficult. Thus while an approach such as monitoring of the trend cycle can be very useful, it does require the use of management judgment.

SELECTED REFERENCES FOR FURTHER STUDY

Batty, M., 1969. "Monitoring an Exponential Forecasting System," *Operational Research Quarterly*, 20, pp. 319–325.

Brown, R. G., 1982. *Advanced Service Parts Inventory Control*, Materials Management Systems, Norwich, VT.

———, 1971. "Detection of Turning Points in a Time Series," *Decision Sciences*, 2, pp. 383–403.

———, 1967. *Decision Rules for Inventory Management*, Holt, Rinehart and Winston, New York.

———, 1963. *Smoothing, Forecasting and Prediction of Discrete Time Series*, Prentice-Hall, Englewood Cliffs, NJ.

———, 1959. *Statistical Forecasting for Inventory Control*, McGraw-Hill, New York.

Ewan, W. D., and K. W. Kemp, 1960. "Sampling Inspection of Continuous Processes with No Autocorrelation Between Successive Results," *Biometrika*, 47, pp. 363–380.

Gardner, E. S., 1985. "CUSUM vs. Smoothed-Error Forecast Monitoring Schemes: Some Simulation Comparisons," *Journal of the Operational Research Society*, 36.

———, 1983. "Automatic Monitoring of Forecast Errors," *Journal of Forecasting*, 2, no. 1, pp. 1–22.

Golder, E. R., and J. G. Settle, 1976. "Monitoring Schemes in Short-Term Forecasting," *Operational Research Quarterly*, 27, pp. 489–501.

Harrison, P. J., and O. L. Davies, 1963. "The Use of Cumulative Sum (CUSUM) Techniques for the Control of Routine Forecasts of Product Demand," *Operations Research*, 12, pp. 325–333.

McClain, J. O., 1981. "Restarting a Forecasting System when Demand Suddenly Changes," *Journal of Operations Management*, 2, pp. 53–61.

Trigg, D. W., 1964. "Monitoring a Forecasting System," *Operational Research Quarterly*, 15, pp. 271–274.

Van Dobben De Bruyn, C. S., 1968. *Cumulative Sum Tests: Theory and Practice*, Griffin, London.

CHAPTER 15

SELECTING APPROPRIATE QUANTITATIVE METHODS

The seven chapters of Part B described a variety of quantitative forecasting methods, ranging from the very simple—Naive Forecast 1 and Naive Forecast 2—to the very sophisticated—multivariate ARMA and econometric methods. The purpose of this chapter is to discuss and compare the strengths and weaknesses of the various quantitative forecasting methods. Understanding such differences is important from a practical point of view if the manager is to select appropriate forecasting methods for his or her specific situation. In addition to accuracy, the questions of cost and ease of utilization of alternative methods are considered.

FORECASTING ACCURACY: EXPLANATORY VERSUS TIME-SERIES METHODS

The empirical evidence that has been reported in recent years comparing explanatory methods (regression and econometrics) with time-series methods (exponential smoothing, decomposition, and ARMA) has not been wholly consistent. Armstrong (1978) identified 12 published studies that reported 16 different comparisons between explanatory and time-series methods. Furthermore, in a more recent reevaluation of 57 companies, he found 26 that supported the superiority of explanatory methods, while the rest favored time-series approaches (Armstrong, 1985). His conclusions, after analyzing each and attempting to evaluate their differences, is that the preference of most experts and many users for explanatory methods is not supported by empirical evidence. Spivey and Wrobleski (1980) also summarized the findings of past studies of econometric models developed in the United States and presented some newer studies. Their conclusions were that noneconometrically based forecasts appeared generally to be at least as accurate as those based on the econometric models. Furthermore, they found that the accuracy of econometric forecasts for time horizons of three or more quarters deteriorated considerably, making their utility for forecasting horizons longer than one year questionable. The same finding has recently been reported by Ashley (1988).

Thus the evidence suggests that explanatory models do not provide significantly more accurate forecasts than time-series methods, even though the former are much more complex and expensive than the latter. McNees (1982) has advanced the argument that time-series methods might do better than econometric ones, but only for the shorter term (less than one year). In the longer term, McNees states, econometric methods perform better. (This conclusion is also supported by Armstrong, 1985.) This is an interesting hypothesis, and although contrary to that of Spivey and Wrobleski (1980) and Ashley (1988), it deserves further attention through additional empirical studies. These studies should be broad based to provide a comparison of econometric methods with a full range of time-series methods.

The comparisons of explanatory methods and time-series methods should not be made on the basis of predictive accuracy alone. Explanatory models provide an extra advantage not available from time-series methods. They contribute information on how important factors affect the variable to be forecast and thus how changes in those factors will influence the forecasts. For instance, if a price increase is contemplated, there is no way to forecast accurately the effects of the price increase on sales using traditional time-series methods. Regression or econometric methods, on the other hand, can indicate the effects of such an increase. For this reason, regression and econometric methods can play an extremely important role in the overall forecasting effort, while, perhaps, short-term extrapolations should be left to time-series methods.

THE FORECASTING ACCURACY OF EXPLANATORY METHODS

One of Armstrong's (1978, 1985) conclusions after examining published evidence on econometric models is that large models are not more accurate than smaller ones. McNees (1982) has reached a similar conclusion. In addition, he found that no single forecaster or forecasting model outperformed all others consistently. Although his sample contained judgmental as well as econometric-based models of various sizes and complexity, McNees concluded that no forecasts or forecasters were consistently superior to any others. Similar conclusions were reached by Zarnowitz (1984).

The conclusion regarding large versus small econometric models goes in the same direction as that of econometric versus time-series models. It seems that forecasting accuracy does not necessarily improve with increases in complexity and statistical sophistication. However, the larger econometric models often provide additional understanding of the factors influencing the variable to be forecast. Managers should recognize this important difference between greater predictive accuracy and additional explanatory power. If a user wants maximum accuracy, he or she is better off with time-series methods, at least for forecasting horizons of less than one year. Similarly, if predictive accuracy is the primary criterion, smaller econometric models seem to perform as well as larger ones. The additional advantage of time-series methods and simpler econometric models is, of course, their lower cost.

THE FORECASTING ACCURACY OF TIME-SERIES MODELS

During the late 1970s several empirical studies compared the performance of a variety of time-series models. [See Makridakis and Hibon (1979) and Mahmoud (1984) for a review of these studies.] In addition, there has been a major competition (see Makridakis et al., 1982, 1984) in which various experts on each of the major time-series methods prepared forecasts for up to 1001 actual time series. Using a subsample of 111 of these series, Makridakis and his associates compared the accuracy performance of each of these 24 methods (representing the best they could do when applied by an expert) in terms of mean absolute percentage error (MAPE) and several other criteria. Table 15-1 presents their MAPE performance during the model-fitting time periods and for 10 different time horizons for forecasting. An average of each method's performance for all time horizons of 1 to 18 months is also shown. (Note that as a reference point, Naive Forecast 1 and Naive Forecast 2 were also evaluated.)

As a further comparison of performance, for each of the 111 data series, the 24 methods were ranked from smallest MAPE (ranked number 1) to largest MAPE (ranked number 24). The average ranking for each method across all 111 time series was then computed. The resulting data are shown in Table 15-2.

As a final means of comparison, Naive Forecast 2 (using the seasonally adjusted most recent actual value as a forecast) was applied to the 111 data series. The results were compared against each of the 24 methods, and the percentage of time that Naive Forecast 2 performed better (smaller MAPE) was computed. These data are shown in Table 15-3.

An examination of Tables 15-1 to 15-3 indicates that the conclusions regarding large versus small econometric models also hold for time-series methods: increasing complexity and statistical sophistication do not automatically mean an improvement in forecasting accuracy. This is an important finding, one that increases rather than diminishes the potential usefulness of forecasting since it indicates that model simplicity is a positive characteristic. This broadens the number of situations in which time-series forecasting (using simple methods) can be usefully (and inexpensively) applied.

Looking at these comparative results at a more detailed level, it can be seen that some sophisticated methods do better than simple methods under certain circumstances. Lewandowski's FORSYS and Parzen's ARARMA models (see Chapter 7), for example, performed well. Differences in forecasting accuracy, however small, sometimes can mean substantial savings from more effective planning and decision making. Finally, combining the forecasts of various methods seems to work extremely well, as can be seen in Tables 15-1 to 15-3. (See methods labeled Combining A and Combining B. More details on combining are presented below.)

An important issue raised by the results in Tables 15-1 to 15-3 is that of selecting an appropriate forecasting method. If the user wants to increase forecasting accuracy, a time-series method should be used. If the objective is to understand better the factors that influence the forecasting situation, then an explanatory model should be selected. In either case, the simplicity of alternative forecasting methods should not be considered automatically a negative characteristic. Some simple methods can perform extremely well under certain conditions. Before a more complex or sophisticated method is selected, it is worthwhile to evaluate the extra benefits expected in terms of increased accuracy, or better explanatory power in light of the extra complexity and costs involved.

Other important criteria, in addition to accuracy, are the cost and the complexity of the method (see Carbone and Armstrong, 1982). Simple methods are cheaper to use and easier to understand, but they are not always the most accurate. Thus higher cost and complexity need to be balanced against higher accuracy, as well as the value of even small increases in forecasting accuracy, since in specific situations they might be worth a great deal.

There appear to be three conditions that affect forecasting accuracy. These are the time horizon of forecasting, the type of data involved, and the accuracy measure applied. Makridakis and his associates (1983) report that various methods do consistently better or worse depending on these three conditions. Using the 111 data series and the 24 different methods, he concluded, for instance, that Parzen's method was always best for quarterly data, for each of the forecasting horizons when MAPE was the accuracy measure. However, it did not do as well using a mean squared error (MSE) measure, when Lewandowski's method was best on three occasions and Holt's was best on the fourth. Single exponential smoothing was the best

Table 15-1 Average MAPE of 24 Time-Series Methods Applied to 111 Data Series

Methods[a]	Model Fitting	Forecasting Horizon (Months)										Average of All Forecasts
		1	2	3	4	5	6	8	12	15	18	
Naive Forecast 1	14.4	13.2	17.3	20.1	18.6	22.4	23.5	27.0	14.5	31.9	34.9	22.3
Moving average	12.8	14.1	16.9	19.1	18.9	21.8	23.6	23.9	16.3	28.7	31.9	20.8
Single smoothing	13.2	12.2	14.8	17.4	17.6	20.3	22.5	22.7	16.1	28.8	32.5	20.1
Adaptive response smoothing	15.1	13.0	17.1	18.4	18.3	20.7	22.8	22.4	16.1	29.6	32.2	20.5
Holt's smoothing	13.6	12.2	13.9	17.6	19.2	23.1	24.9	31.2	22.6	40.4	40.3	25.1
Brown's smoothing	13.6	13.0	15.1	18.6	19.5	25.2	27.1	35.0	28.0	54.0	59.6	30.3
Quadratic smoothing	13.9	13.2	16.1	21.9	23.2	30.3	34.1	51.5	49.0	103.11	106.0	47.7
Regression	16.6	17.9	19.9	21.1	21.2	23.2	25.0	26.2	26.1	49.5	60.2	29.5
Naive Forecast 2	9.1	8.5	11.4	13.9	15.4	16.6	17.4	17.8	14.5	31.2	30.8	17.8
D moving average	8.1	10.7	13.6	17.8	19.4	22.0	23.1	22.7	15.7	28.3	34.0	20.6
D single smoothing	8.6	7.8	10.8	13.1	14.5	15.7	17.2	16.5	13.6	29.3	30.1	16.8

D adaptive response smoothing	9.8	8.8	12.4	14.0	16.4	16.7	18.1	16.5	13.7	28.6	29.3	17.1
D Holt's smoothing	8.6	7.9	10.5	13.2	15.1	17.3	19.0	23.1	16.5	35.6	35.2	19.7
D Brown's smoothing	8.3	8.5	10.8	13.3	14.5	17.3	19.3	23.8	19.0	43.1	45.4	22.3
D quadratic smoothing	8.4	8.8	11.8	15.0	16.2	21.9	24.1	35.7	29.7	56.1	63.6	30.2
D regression	12.0	12.5	14.9	17.2	18.2	19.7	21.0	21.0	23.4	46.5	57.3	25.6
Winters' smoothing	9.3	9.2	10.5	13.4	15.5	17.5	18.7	23.3	15.9	33.4	34.5	19.5
Automatic AEP	10.8	9.8	11.3	13.7	15.1	16.9	18.8	23.3	16.2	30.2	33.9	19.0
Bayesian	13.3	10.3	12.8	13.6	14.4	16.2	17.1	19.2	16.1	27.5	30.6	17.6
Combining A	8.1	7.9	9.8	11.9	13.5	15.4	16.8	19.5	14.2	32.4	33.3	17.7
Combining B	8.2	8.2	10.1	11.8	14.4	15.4	16.4	20.1	15.5	31.3	31.4	17.7
Box–Jenkins	0.0	10.3	10.7	11.4	14.5	16.4	17.1	18.9	16.4	26.2	34.2	18.0
Lewandowski	12.3	11.6	12.8	14.5	15.3	16.6	17.6	18.9	17.0	33.0	28.6	18.6
Parzen	8.9	10.6	10.7	10.7	13.5	14.3	14.7	16.0	13.7	22.5	26.5	15.4
Average	10.7	10.8	13.2	15.5	16.8	19.3	20.8	24.0	19.2	37.5	40.7	22.1

Source: Makridakis, et al. (1982, 1984).

[a]D = deseasonalized.

Table 15-2 Average Rankings of 24 Time-Series Methods Applied to 111 Data Series

Methods[a]	Model Fitting	Forecasting Horizon (Months)										Average of All Forecasts
		1	2	3	4	5	6	8	12	15	18	
Naive Forecast 1	17.4	13.5	14.5	15.2	13.8	14.9	14.0	14.1	11.1	14.0	13.2	13.83
Moving average	15.5	13.4	14.0	14.2	13.5	14.5	13.8	12.8	13.3	12.7	12.1	13.09
Single smoothing	14.8	13.4	13.7	14.1	14.4	14.2	14.1	12.7	12.7	13.1	12.8	13.20
Adaptive response smoothing	20.3	14.1	15.2	15.1	14.9	14.6	15.1	13.5	13.7	13.4	13.4	13.95
Holt's smoothing	11.9	12.0	12.8	13.0	12.7	13.6	12.6	13.4	13.9	14.3	12.6	13.25
Brown's smoothing	13.8	13.1	13.2	12.9	12.5	13.9	12.7	13.5	13.4	14.8	13.2	13.30
Quadratic smoothing	15.1	13.7	14.0	14.5	13.4	14.9	13.8	16.3	16.0	17.1	16.4	15.27
Regression	16.9	16.7	15.4	15.5	15.2	14.6	15.1	14.3	14.6	14.0	12.7	14.61
Naive Forecast 2	11.8	11.5	12.1	12.7	13.1	12.3	12.6	12.1	11.2	12.9	12.6	12.32
D moving average	9.3	12.8	13.6	14.7	14.9	14.6	14.5	13.9	12.9	12.2	14.2	13.86
D single smoothing	8.4	10.9	12.2	11.7	12.5	12.2	12.7	10.9	11.2	11.0	11.9	11.57

D adaptive response smoothing	14.5	12.7	13.8	13.4	14.2	13.3	13.9	11.7	11.9	12.6	12.9	12.72
D Holt's smoothing	4.7	10.0	10.0	10.3	10.6	10.6	10.9	11.6	12.0	12.1	11.8	11.15
D Brown's smoothing	6.3	10.8	10.4	10.3	10.0	10.2	11.1	11.8	12.2	12.2	12.8	11.47
D quadratic smoothing	8.0	11.4	11.4	11.1	10.7	11.8	11.7	14.2	15.1	15.2	14.9	13.23
D regression	12.5	14.7	13.4	14.4	14.1	12.7	13.8	12.6	12.7	12.5	11.9	12.94
Winters' smoothing		11.9	10.5	10.5	11.1	10.6	10.3	11.6	12.0	10.5	10.8	11.26
Automatic AEP	10.3	11.5	11.5	12.2	11.3	11.5	10.9	11.4	12.2	11.0	12.7	11.77
Bayesian	17.1	12.7	12.2	11.5	11.1	10.8	11.9	13.4	12.3	11.7	11.8	11.90
Combining A	7.3	10.1	10.3	9.9	10.6	10.5	10.5	10.8	10.1	10.8	11.0	10.40
Combining B	7.5	10.8	11.6	10.3	11.8	11.3	11.6	11.1	11.6	10.8	11.6	11.30
Box–Jenkins	0.0	12.4	11.3	10.5	11.2	10.5	10.8	10.8	12.4	10.7	12.1	11.53
Lewandowski	15.6	13.5	12.4	11.4	11.6	10.5	10.7	10.9	10.9	10.3	8.8	10.87
Parzen	9.4	12.5	10.7	10.9	10.6	11.2	10.8	10.8	11.0	10.1	12.1	11.22
Average	11.5	12.5	12.5	12.5	12.5	12.5	12.5	12.5	12.5	12.5	12.5	12.50

Source: Makridakis et al. (1982, 1984).

[a]D = deseasonalized.

303

Table 15-3 Percentage of Forecasts for which Naive Method 2 Performed Better than Each of 24 Time-Series Methods on 111 Data Series

Methods[a]	Model Fitting[b]	Forecasting Horizon (Months)										Average of All Forecasts
		1	2	3	4	5	6	8	12	15	18	
Naive Forecast 1	75.2	59.5	58.6	60.8	53.2	61.3	57.2	54.9	48.5	58.1	52.2	56.64
Moving average	72.1	64.0	58.1	56.8	53.2	65.3	58.6	54.4	61.0	52.9	49.3	55.96
Single smoothing	64.0	62.2	59.9	57.2	58.1	63.1	55.4	51.1	47.8	47.8	45.6	53.66
Adaptive response smoothing	93.7	68.5	68.5	66.2	63.1	64.0	60.4	58.2	64.7	57.4	57.4	60.96
Holt's smoothing	55.9	55.0	49.5	51.4	51.4	56.8	51.4	56.0	66.2	58.8	51.5	55.69
Brown's smoothing	60.4	55.9	54.1	54.1	45.9	56.8	48.6	54.9	64.7	58.8	52.9	54.19
Quadratic smoothing	64.9	59.5	55.0	58.6	53.2	62.2	54.1	69.2	67.6	69.1	64.7	62.11
Regression	76.6	73.0	64.0	63.1	59.5	60.4	59.5	59.3	72.1	58.8	54.4	61.91
Naive Forecast 2	—	—	—	—	—	—	—	—	—	—	—	—
D moving average	32.4	53.6	59.9	59.0	59.5	64.0	62.2	59.3	61.8	45.6	56.6	58.08
D single smoothing	23.4	50.9	53.6	47.3	49.1	52.7	54.1	42.9	47.1	32.4	43.4	46.04

	67.6	57.7	62.2	56.3	58.6	55.0	56.8	47.3	54.4	45.6	51.5	52.26
D adaptive response smoothing	11.7	40.5	42.3	39.6	37.8	42.3	39.6	47.3	52.9	45.6	47.1	44.11
D Holt's smoothing	16.2	43.2	45.9	41.4	37.8	39.6	42.3	46.2	50.0	47.1	52.9	45.03
D Brown's smoothing	27.9	47.7	48.6	41.4	37.8	45.0	45.0	53.8	63.2	64.7	64.7	53.21
D quadratic smoothing	53.2	64.9	55.9	57.7	52.3	48.6	48.6	54.1	54.9	44.1	50.0	51.77
D regression	28.8	45.9	39.6	36.9	41.4	40.5	38.7	48.4	55.9	42.6	41.2	45.03
Winters' smoothing	46.8	45.9	45.0	45.9	41.4	43.2	45.0	50.5	54.4	45.6	47.1	47.71
Automatic AEP	85.6	54.1	48.6	41.4	40.5	41.4	43.2	54.9	51.5	44.1	45.6	46.40
Bayesian	22.5	37.8	39.6	32.4	31.5	36.0	37.8	40.7	41.2	36.8	36.8	37.57
Combining A	24.3	51.4	48.6	39.6	41.4	43.2	44.6	46.7	51.5	37.5	42.6	44.54
Combining B	NA	53.2	43.2	38.7	40.5	38.7	45.0	46.2	57.4	39.7	51.5	46.66
Box–Jenkins	73.0	58.6	50.5	44.1	42.3	39.6	37.8	48.4	45.6	38.2	32.4	42.80
Lewandowski	47.7	52.3	43.2	42.3	38.7	45.9	44.1	42.9	48.5	39.7	50.0	45.35
Parzen												
Average	53.2	54.5	51.9	49.2	47.3	50.7	49.4	51.7	55.8	48.4	49.6	50.77

Source: Makridakis et al. (1982, 1984).
[a]D = deseasonalized.
[b]NA = not available.

method for one-period-ahead forecasts, but did not do well for longer forecasting horizons.

Figure 15-1 presents one way in which several of these results can be combined and presented. This figure compares the perceived complexity of the various methods. The complexity-cost index was supplied judgmentally by the authors of the cited study. The complexity indices used are the following:

1. Deseasonalized single exponential smoothing   2

2. Deseasonalized Holt's exponential smoothing   2.5

3. Holt–Winters exponential smoothing   3

4. Automatic AEP   6

5. Box–Jenkins   9

6. Parzen   9.5

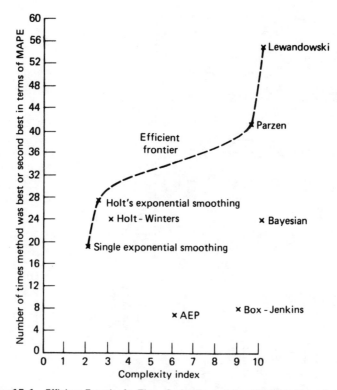

Figure 15-1   Efficient Frontier for Time-Series Forecasting Methods (Based on Makridakis et al., 1984).

7. Lewandowski   10

8. Bayesian forecasting   10

Figure 15-1 indicates a kind of "efficient frontier" for these forecasting methods. Along this frontier, a forecasting user will have to make a trade-off between higher accuracy and greater complexity. The choice will depend, ultimately, on the specific situation being considered. In the final analysis, this will be influenced by the savings that could result from increased forecasting accuracy versus the additional cost of a more complex method.

At present the question of choosing an appropriate time-series method depends on the specific situation being considered, the length of the forecasting horizon, and the organization involved. Although more details about the specific situation and the forecasting horizon will be discussed in Chapters 17, 18, and 19, the following rules can be applied.

For organizations that do not want to be in the forefront of new and sophisticated forecasting development, we recommend exponential smoothing and decomposition methods. We believe that these methods are adequate to cover all forecasting needs of small, medium, and even large organizations. In our experience these methods cover the entire spectrum of needs for a reasonable cost and effort.

For yearly data (and therefore yearly forecasts) we recommend Holt's linear exponential smoothing. For quarterly data we suggest damped trend exponential smoothing, and for monthly data single exponential smoothing. For organizations wishing to experiment with more sophisticated methods we recommend a version of Parzen's ARARMA models (or Parzen's method itself if a computer program can be found) we call the long-term AR method (see Chapter 11). If the user does not have computer programs for Holt, damped, single and the long-term AR method, we suggest SIBYL (see Chapter 22), which includes all of these methods as well as the idea of metaforecasting discussed in Chapter 11.

We urge both newcomers and seasoned forecasting users to choose methods not by how well they fit past data, but how accurately they predict the future. This is true in particular for forecasting horizons of more than one period ahead, which are usually ignored by traditional approaches to forecasting (see Chapter 11). To do so one needs to use simulation and assume that the future is not known. This is the only way to test the accuracy of different methods and then decide which method does best for each forecasting horizon and forecasting situation. As was discussed in Chapter 11, doing so substantially improves forecasting accuracy.

If a forecasting user wants the simplest of approaches, no decision rules, and no worrying about the best methods, we recommend combining. Considerable empirical evidence (see Mahmoud, 1984; Makridakis and Winkler,

1983; Russell and Adams, 1987) has shown that combining is a reliable forecasting method that does as well or better than the individual methods being combined. Furthermore, combining reduces the fluctuations in forecasting errors, which can be of considerable importance when a conservative attitude toward forecasting errors exists. Finally, as Russell and Adams (1984) have shown, by combining appropriate methods, a user can further improve forecasting accuracy. In our experience, combining single, damped, and Holt's exponential smoothing provides excellent results as these three methods are complementary.

Capturing the seasonality in the data is a must for accurate forecasting for the short term and a prerequisite for using the various methods recommended in this chapter. Although sophisticated decomposition methods are available, we believe that the classical decomposition method suffices to capture the seasonality in the data. A computer program of the classical decomposition method is, therefore, necessary. In addition to seasonality, decomposition methods isolate the trend cycle in the data; this is also necessary for medium-term forecasting. It allows management to monitor the cycle in the data (see Chapter 14) and better understand the present state of the economic, company, or specific series.

Sophisticated forecasting users can experiment with advanced methods as well as with new methodologies. In our opinion it is imperative to judge the accuracy of new methods against a yardstick. This yardstick can be, for instance, single exponential smoothing. Using a yardstick will enable the user to determine whether the extra improvements in accuracy, if any, are worth the added cost and effort required to develop and use the new method.

Finally, we would like to conclude this chapter by stressing that the forecasting method used should be intuitively appealing to management. Management does not like black boxes (no matter how accurate they may be). Thus, unless they can understand the method being used, they are not likely to use its forecasts. Intuitive appeal, as well as accuracy and cost, must be considered when a forecasting method is selected.

The forecasting accuracy of time-series methods has been examined in detail for two reasons. First, these methods provide better results in terms of accuracy than any alternative methods. Second, time series is the only forecasting field where differences in forecasting accuracy have been found to be consistent and where those differences seem to depend on various factors (for example, time horizon).

This makes it possible for a user to select the method that is best for the specific forecasting situation being considered. For instance, for forecasting involving large numbers of inventory items there is little choice but to use an automatic method that can provide mechanical, timely forecasts for each of the thousands of items for which predictions are required. Thus, simple time-series methods become much more desirable because they require limited historical data and little computer time per item (see Chapter 17). Explanatory models can be used to supplement time-series forecasting and provide information on the relationship between two or more variables. Such methods can supplement those of time-series forecasting.

CONCLUSIONS

Published empirical evidence suggests that if the criterion of accuracy is to be optimized, time-series methods are preferable to explanatory approaches, at least for shorter term horizons. It is less clear, as yet, which approach performs better for longer term forecasting. In addition, empirical studies have shown that simplicity in forecasting methods is not necessarily a negative characteristic or detriment with regard to forecasting accuracy. Therefore, the authors would advise against dismissing simple methods and moving too quickly to replace them with more complex ones. Careful study is needed to determine whether the extra complexity and accompanying costs are justified by an increase in the accuracy they provide.

SELECTED REFERENCES FOR FURTHER STUDY

Armstrong, J. S., 1985. *Long Range Forecasting: From Crystal Ball to Computer*, 2nd ed., Wiley, New York.

———, 1978. "Forecasting with Econometric Methods: Folklore versus Fact," *Journal of Business*, S1, pp. 549–600.

Ashley, R., 1988. "On the Relative Worth of Recent Macroeconomic Forecasts," *International Journal of Forecasting*, 4, no. 3.

Bell, D., and I. Kristal, 1981. *The Crisis in Economic Theory*, Basic Books, New York.

Carbone, R., and J. S. Armstrong, 1982. "Evaluation of Extrapolative Forecasting Methods," *Journal of Forecasting*, 1, no. 2, pp. 215–218.

Lewandowski, R., *La Prevision à Court Terme*, Dunod, Paris.

Mahmoud, E., 1984. "Accuracy in Forecasting: A Survey," *Journal of Forecasting*, 3, pp. 139–159.

Makridakis, S., 1982. "Forecasting Accuracy and the Assumption of Constancy," *Omega*, 9, no. 3, pp. 307–311.

Makridakis, S., and M. Hibon, 1979. "Accuracy of Forecasting: An Empirical Investigation (with Discussion)," *Journal of the Royal Statistical Society A*, 142, pt. 2, pp. 97–145.

Makridakis, S., and Winkler, 1983. "Averages of Forecasts: Some Empirical Results," *Management Science*, 29, pp. 987–996.

Makridakis, S., et al., 1984. *The Accuracy of Major Extrapolation (Time Series) Methods*, Wiley, Chichester, England.

————, 1983. "Commentary on the Makridakis Time Series Competition," *Journal of Forecasting*, 2, no. 3, pp. 259–312.

————, 1982. "The Accuracy of Extrapolation (Time Series) Methods. Results of a Forecasting Competition," *Journal of Forecasting*, 1, no. 2, pp. 111–154.

McNees, S. K., 1982. "The Role of Macroeconomic Models in Forecasting and Policy Analysis in the United States," *Journal of Forecasting*, 1, no. 1, pp. 37–48.

Newbold, P., and C. W. J. Granger, 1974. "Experience with Forecasting Univariate Time Series and the Combination of Forecasting (with Discussion)," *Journal of the Royal Statistical Society A*, 137, pp. 131–165.

Russell, T. D., and E. E. Adams, 1987. "An Empirical Evaluation of Alternative Forecasting Combinations," *Management Science*, 33, pp. 1267–1276.

Spivey, W. A., and W. J. Wrobleski, 1980. "Surveying Recent Forecasting Performance," American Enterprise Institute, Reprint 106, February.

Zarnowitz, V., 1984. "The Accuracy of Individual and Group Forecasts from Business Outlook Surveys," *Journal of Forecasting*, 3, no. 1, pp. 11–26.

CHAPTER 16

INTEGRATING JUDGMENTAL AND QUANTITATIVE METHODS

The major quantitative methods discussed in Part B are based on the assumption of constancy of patterns or relationships. When this assumption holds, established patterns and relationships can be identified and then extrapolated (or interpolated) to predict the future. In Chapter 11, the assumption of constancy was further discussed, and the difference between explaining the past and predicting the future was explored. If established patterns or relationships are not constant, the task of quantitative forecasting must be supplemented with judgment. However, as we saw in Chapters 12 and 13, judgment is not without its own problems. Quantitative methods and judgment are complementary and must be integrated to produce accurate and usable forecasts. This chapter provides a set of guidelines for integrating quantitative methods and judgment to produce final forecasts.

ADVANTAGES AND DRAWBACKS OF QUANTITATIVE AND JUDGMENTAL METHODS

Table 16-1 lists the advantages and disadvantages of quantitative and judgmental methods. The challenge for those involved with forecasting is to harness the advantages of both quantitative models and judgment while avoiding their drawbacks. Doing so involves the following eight considerations.

Choice of Method or Model

People must decide what method or model to use. Although guidelines for method or model selection are available (see Chapter 15) and some methods or models are more appropriate than others for specific situations, the final

Table 16-1   Advantages and Drawbacks of Quantitative versus Judgmental Methods for Forecasting

Consideration	Quantitative Methods	Judgmental Methods
Choice of method or model to use.	Method or model used cannot be selected on mere statistical grounds.	Choice of method or model has a major impact on forecasts but requires human judgment to be selected.
Ability to predict changes in established patterns or relationships.	Future changes cannot be predicted.	Future changes can be predicted, but they can also be ignored, or people can overreact to them.
Utilizing available information or data.	Not all information in the data is being used.	People can use inside information or knowledge, but they are also selective, biased, and inconsistent in using such information.
Adapting or adjusting the forecasts once changes have been identified.	Modifying the forecasts as a result of changes depends on the specific method being used.	Once changes have been confirmed *and* accepted, people can evaluate their effects and modify the forecasts.
Introducing objectivity in the forecasts.	Objectivity is achieved on the basis of some selection criterion (e.g., minimizing the MSE), which must be decided judgmentally.	Forecasts are greatly influenced by personal and political considerations and undue optimism or pessimism.
Determining future uncertainty.	Future uncertainty is usually underestimated by most methods.	Future uncertainty is usually underestimated by a large amount, mostly on the optimistic side.
Requiring repetitive forecasts.	The forecasts are consistent whether a method is used once or 100,000 times.	People easily get bored in repetitive forecasting situations, which introduces inconsistency in the forecasts.
Cost of method employed.	Methods are cheap to use today when computing is not costly.	People and meetings are expensive, and so are judgmental forecasts.

selection of a method or model is not value-free. Single exponential smoothing, for instance, provides conservative forecasts because it assumes a horizontal extrapolation of the most recent values. Holt's linear smoothing, on the other hand, is reactive in that it extrapolates the latest trend in the data. Quadratic smoothing is more reactive than Holt's, since it extrapolates the latest trend in a quadratic fashion. Trend regression is less reactive than single, Holt's, or quadratic smoothing (it extrapolates a linear trend but on the basis of all the data, not just what has happened lately). Similarly, the forecasts are influenced, to a great extent, by the use of a logarithmic transformation, whether or not (1) the data are differenced to eliminate the trend, and (2) an autoregressive or moving average ARMA model is used. Such decisions, although technical in nature, can have a significant influence on the forecasts and cannot be left to staff people alone. Although logarithmic transformation, for example, can help better fit a curve to past data, it would mean an exponential extrapolation of the trend, which would produce much larger forecasts than if no transformation was made. An advantage of using the sliding simulation suggested in Chapter 11 is that the final choice of a method or model and the specific options selected can be evaluated. However, managers should realize that the final selection of a method and its specific utilization are not free of value judgments since the method used affects the forecasts. This fact must be understood before decisions about the methods or models that will be selected and used to forecasts are made.

Ability to Predict Continuations or Changes in Established Patterns or Relationships

Since quantitative methods cannot predict changes in patterns or relationships, nor distinguish them as either temporary or permanent, it becomes necessary to do so judgmentally. However, people must avoid the judgmental biases discussed in Chapter 13, some of which are particularly relevant when changes in established patterns or relationships are occurring. Our approach to reduce such biases is based on minimizing inconsistency and optimism or pessimism. This can be done by starting with quantitative forecasts that assume no changes, and then modifying these forecasts judgmentally, upward or downward, to take into account forthcoming changes.

Biases can be further reduced by asking those making the judgmental forecasts to state their reasons for modifying the quantitative ones. Using the quantitative forecasts as the base and asking for reasons to change them introduces an anchoring effect, which we have found an excellent way of avoiding unnecessary changes on the part of judgmental forecasters. In a variation of this procedure forecasters can be asked to write down the changes in the quantitative forecasts they consider necessary and the reasons involved. Doing so introduces objectivity, in addition to anchoring, and makes it easier to reach a consensus since no one feels obliged to stick to his or her publicly stated forecasts.

Utilizing Available Information

Quantitative methods do not use all information contained in the past data. Adaptive models, for instance, base their forecasts on very recent information about the data but ignore information in the more distant past. In concrete terms, this downgrades, for instance, the influence of a recession that occurred a few years ago and overemphasizes an increase caused by a recent promotional campaign. On the other hand, regression methods ignore, for all practical purposes, recent changes because they give equal weight to all data. Exponential smoothing methods are between adaptive and regression ones (Makridakis, 1986). It is important to understand how different methods use the information contained in the data, because adjustments may be required, particularly when changes from established patterns or relationships are about to occur.

Judgmental forecasters can use all information available. However, such information must be presented to them in a way that minimizes biases. This would require providing all important aspects (including nonsupporting evidence) of the situation being forecast and information about similar past cases and the types of mistakes that were made. In addition, feedback should be provided to the judgmental forecasters to reflect their ability to accurately predict changes and to disclose possible reasons when their judgmental forecasts did not improve the quantitative forecasts. The purpose of such feedback is not to assign blame in case of errors, but rather to help reduce judgmental biases in forecasting and facilitate learning.

Adjusting the Forecasts Once Changes Have Been Identified

Certain quantitative methods (such as regression) are extremely slow to react to change. It becomes imperative, therefore, that the forecasts be adjusted judgmentally, or that a method capable of adapting quickly to the changed patterns or relationships be used (for example, an adaptive method).

As judgmental forecasters, people are capable of assessing the effects of changes, but they can be slow to identify changes or accept them. Thus some form of a monitoring mechanism is required (see Chapter 14) to help them identify possible changes. The procedures must be established to determine the seriousness and duration of such changes and their implications for the future. These are critical tasks that must be integrated into forecasting in a systematic procedure.

Introducing Objectivity into the Forecasts

The major advantage of quantitative methods is the objectivity of their forecasts. Once a method has been selected and a criterion (such as minimizing the MSE) for optimizing the chosen model (both judgmental tasks) has been decided, the forecasts will be the same (or very similar) regardless of the person or program that computes such forecasts. This is rarely the case, however, with judgmental forecasters, who, given the same information, can come up with very different forecasts. People are usually optimistic. Furthermore, personal or political considerations influence their forecasts. Thus, the only way to introduce objectivity is to use quantitative methods. When quantitative methods cannot be used, either a third party can be asked to make the forecasts or more than one person should predict independently the event of interest. On the other hand, we already saw that the quantitative methods cannot predict changes in established patterns or relationships. This is why it becomes critical to help judgmental forecasters achieve as high a degree of objectivity as possible by adapting the procedure described in the preceding sections.

Determining Future Uncertainty

Both people and statistical models underestimate uncertainty, sometimes considerably. Uncertainty, although difficult to accept psychologically, cannot be ignored. Pretending that it does not exist is not realistic, and it inevitably results in unpleasant surprises. We have found it useful to warn forecasting users that the uncertainty is usually greater than that estimated by quantitative models and their own judgmental estimates. To deal with uncertainty realistically would require effective ways of measuring it quantitatively (see Makridakis et al., 1987), or a willingness to accept that forecasting errors can come from several sources, all of which must be considered. As we have discussed in Chapters 12 and 13, uncertainty is not phychologically comfortable. However, psychological comfort should not prevent forecasters from being willing to understand and deal with the entire range of future uncertainty.

Requiring Repetitive Forecasts

Quantitative methods can be used when many forecasts at frequent intervals are required. Thus producing monthly judgmental forecasts for 10,000 items cannot be done practically, but it can be done by using an objective approach that can be automated and whose base is some simple quantitative method. People who are asked to forecast repetitive events at frequent intervals quickly lose interest, and they often produce forecasts that are worse than those produced by quantitative methods. On the other hand, it has been mentioned repeatedly that quantitative methods cannot predict changes in established patterns or relationships or their effects on the future. People are, therefore, the only alternative to deal with pattern changes and must concentrate their efforts on predicting such changes and their implications for the forecasts.

Costs of the Method Employed

A big advantage of quantitative forecasting methods is their inexpensiveness, particularly when simple methods can be employed at minimal cost. People and committees, on the other hand, are expensive, and they substantially increase the costs of forecasting. Thus, unless the benefits from improved forecasting accuracy are clear, it makes little sense to use people to make forecasts, particularly when the forecasts involve the continuation of established patterns or relationships that can be computed just as accurately through quantitative methods.

The forecasting process can be rationalized if people concentrate on predicting the influence on forecasting of changes in established patterns or relationships, while quantitative methods are used to predict continuations of such patterns or relationships. This would, most likely, improve forecasting accuracy and at the same time, reduce the cost of forecasting substantially.

Integrating quantitative and judgmental methods is of critical importance. Both judgment and quantitative methods exhibit advantages that must be exploited. At the same time, they have drawbacks that must be understood and avoided. In Chapters 19 to 23, several of the ideas described in this chapter will be reexamined, and practical ways of addressing them will be suggested. We would like to mention, however, that forecasting accuracy will not be achieved by abandoning quantitative methods, or by switching to more complex and sophisticated techniques. Instead, managers must recognize the advantages and drawbacks of both quantitative and judgmental methods and be capable of integrating the best of the two in a procedure that will enable them to forecast in a consistent and efficient manner. If this is done, gains in forecasting accuracy will be inevitable.

SELECTED REFERENCES FOR FURTHER STUDY

Dawes, R. M., 1986. "Forecasting One's Own Preferences," *International Journal of Forecasting*, 2, pp. 5–14.

——, 1979. "The Robust Beauty of Improper Linear Models in Decision Making," *American Psychologist*, 34, no. 7, pp. 571–582.

Fischhoff, B., 1988. "Judgmental Aspects of Forecasting: Needs and Possible Trends," *International Journal of Forecasting*, 4, no. 3.

Hogarth, R., and S. Makridakis, 1981. "Forecasting and Planning: An Evaluation," *Management Science*, 27, no. 2, pp. 115–138.

Makridakis, S., 1988. "Metaforecasting: Ways of Improving Forecasting Accuracy and Effectiveness," *International Journal of Forecasting*, 4, no. 3, pp. 467–492.

——, 1986. "The Art and Science of Forecasting: An Assessment and Future Directions," *International Journal of Forecasting*, 2, pp. 15–39.

Makridakis, S., Hibon, M., Lusk, E. and M. Belhadjali, 1987, "Confidence Intervals: An Empirical Investigation of the Series in the M-Competition, *International Journal of Forecasting*, 3, pp. 489–508.

CHAPTER 17

TECHNOLOGICAL AND ENVIRONMENTAL FORECASTING

The various methods we have discussed so far are mostly geared toward economic, marketing, financial, and other forms of business forecasting. Furthermore, such methods focus primarily on the short and medium terms. Under technological and environmental forecasting we will group a diverse range of approaches to forecasting that are focused on the long term and deal, as their name implies, with technology and the general environment. These methods cover population or demographic forecasting, raw material (including energy) availability and cost, political risk assessment, governmental and legislative forecasting, competitive forecasting, and, of course, technological forecasting. In this chapter some major approaches to deal with the forecasting of the above-mentioned areas are presented. In Chapter 21 their application to long-term forecasting is covered.

Technological and environmental forecasting do not always provide a step-by-step procedure, nor do they give their forecasts in terms of a single numerical answer. Use of these methods requires an understanding of the factors involved in each situation and a need to adapt the method to that situation. With such methods it is the expert who becomes the processor of facts, knowledge, and information, rather than some set of mathematical rules or mathematical model, as would be the case with quantitative methods. Furthermore, various experts can come up with completely different forecasts, and these forecasts cannot often be specific. In his book *Profiles of the Future*, Clarke (1973) describes the environment within which the forecaster must operate (p. xi):

He does not try to describe the future, but to define the boundaries within which possible futures must lie. If we regard the ages which stretch ahead of us as an unmapped and unexplored country, what he's attempting to do is to survey its frontiers and to gain some idea of its extent. The detailed geography of the interior must remain unknown until he reaches it.

The forecasting methods described in this chapter are used in three types of situations. First is forecasting when a given new process or product will become widely adopted. For example, a government organization may be aware of a number of scientific discoveries that have not yet been applied, and it may wish to predict the point in time at which their application will become widespread. Similarly, a company may be concerned about the time horizon for the adoption of a new development or process. As an example, we can consider the development of robotics and the problem of forecasting the point at which that technology will gain widespread industrial application. This information would be of interest to companies that manufacture or sell robots and to those who can exploit the opportunities available through the usage of robotics to improve their production and reduce their costs.

Second is predicting what new developments and discoveries will be made in a specific area. For example, certain governmental agencies might be concerned with what new medical discoveries and breakthroughs will occur. Corporations might wish to forecast new processes and technologies that will be developed in their industry over the next 15 or 20 years to help in planning plant expansion programs, long-range market development, and long-range R&D investments. Similarly, it is important to be able to predict the cost of energy and other raw materials, because increases in such costs might have critical consequences for some countries or companies.

Third is forecasting the types of changes and eventual patterns or relationships that might emerge from an area or environment that is undergoing or is about to undergo a major change (such as the international competitive environment). A major objective is to break traditional mind-sets and to identify the full range of future possibilities. Isolating emerging patterns and relationships in such a situation is also highly desirable since technological and other changes will inevitably affect societal attitudes, which in turn will affect demand for products and services and technological innovations.

Technological and societal approaches consist of four subsegments. The first, exploratory methods, start with today's knowledge, orientation, objectives, and trends and then seeks to predict what will happen and when. The second subsegment consists of normative methods that seek at the outset to assess future goals and objectives and then work backward to identify the new technologies and developments that will be most likely to lead to the achievement of these goals. The third subsegment consists of a different type of exploratory method that deals with forthcoming changes in patterns and relationships of a broad, overall nature. A fourth subsegment of methods deals with analogies.

LONG-TERM TRENDS

In several chapters in Part B we described a number of methods that help us identify the trend in our data. Such a trend will depend on two factors: (1) the start and end of the data, and (2) the type of trend (linear, exponential, S curve) we assume best fits the data. Figure 17-1 shows copper prices adjusted for inflation since 1800. The reader can easily see that if data before 1934 were not available, the trend of copper prices would appear to be increasing rapidly. Furthermore, such an increase can be assumed to be linear, exponential, or S-curve type. Obviously, one who wants to prove his or her point of view can compute the trend using selected starting and ending dates and a trend pattern that fits his or her hypothesis. From a forecasting point of view, however, such an approach can provide misleading and even dangerous results, and it is not recommended. As we discussed in Chapter 6, data are made up of trend, cycle, and seasonality. Trend and cycles, however, are intermixed, and unless dealt with properly, the trend can easily be confused with the cycle in the data. This can be easily verified in Figure 17-1, where increases and decreases in the trend pattern (consider, for example data between 1855 and 1896) depend entirely on the segment of data being used.

In our experience the only way to discover long-term trends is to use

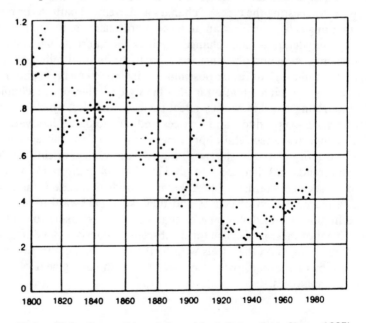

Figure 17-1   Copper Prices Adjusted for Inflation (from Simon, 1985).

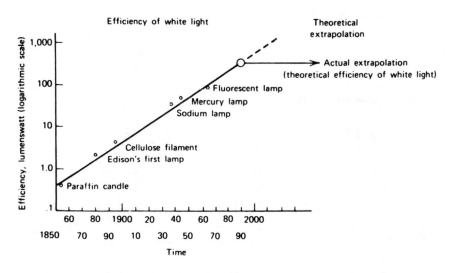

Figure 17-2 Curve-Fitting Approach to Forecasting Artificial Illumination.

long-term data. Such data must span a period of more than 100 years (that is, include at least two long wave cycles whose length is between 50 and 60 years). If such long series are not available, it is not easy to talk about long-term trends, because it is difficult to know whether the data include a cyclical component that biases the estimation of the trend.

The fact that a long-term trend has been identified does not mean it cannot change. This creates another difficulty for the long-term forecasters who must determine judgmentally when and how such a trend might change. The literature of technological forecasting provides guidelines for adjusting long-term trends using expert judgment.

Suppose that we are interested in predicting the efficiency of artificial illumination (Cetron, 1969, p. 58). We cannot extrapolate the curve indefinitely because it is not possible to exceed the theoretical efficiency of light. This means that the trend line will have to bend (see Figure 17-2) at the level of theoretical efficiency of white light, a fact that indicates the bend of the linear extrapolation toward a horizontal line.

Another method that can deal with changes in trends is trend impact analysis (Gordon and Stover, 1976). This method allows the forecaster to specify several factors that might alter the established trend and to assess probabilities for each of them. Trend impact analysis consists of a program that determines the impact of each factor on the trend on the basis of its probability of occurrence. The output of the program is the original trend with several other positive and negative trends scattered around it. This

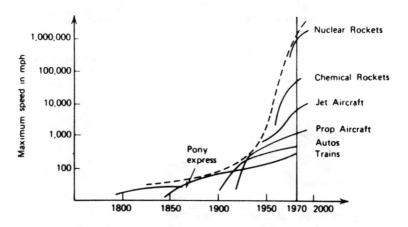

Figure 17-3   Trend Fitting Transportation Speed with an S-Curve.

display allows the forecaster to visualize possible departures from the original trend to consider the probability that each might occur.

One of the most applicable and frequently used ways of determining changes in trends is assuming that long-term trends are of the S type. An S curve (see Figure 17-3) implies a slow start, a steep growth, and then a plateau. This curve is a characteristic form of many technological developments and the sales of several products. Chambers, Mullick, and Smith (1971) reported that the sales of black-and-white and color television sets have followed an S pattern. Ayres (1969, pp. 94–142) and Jantsch (1967, pp. 143–174) also reported a number of different technologies that have followed S-type curves.

The use of an S curve in representing growth can be applied not only to a given product but also to a given technology or, even more broadly, to a given growth situation. For example, the method has been applied to forecast the maximum speed of transportation. Figure 17-3 shows transportation speeds from the pony express to the nuclear rocket (Ayres, 1969).

If the tangents of each of the individual growth curves are connected (Figure 17-3), an envelope S curve can be developed. In this case the upper limit of the curve can be recognized as the absolute or natural limits on transportation speed, such as the velocity of light. In most instances, however, predicting the point and time when a plateau will be reached, or when we will go from one S curve to another, on such an envelope S curve may be extremely difficult.

TIME-INDEPENDENT ANALOGIES

When data for identifying long-term trends are not available, it may be possible to predict the developments in one situation by analogy to a similar situation. In many cases, the forecaster can identify a trend in one part of the area that he or she thinks will lead to a similar development in another. Thus he or she can forecast the second area and its development by following the trend in the first. The difficulty arises, however, in trying to determine how the two situations or events are related. The time-independent comparison approach (Gerstenfeld, 1971) assigns the responsibility of representing this interrelationship between the two trends to the forecaster.

As a specific example of the use of the time-independent comparison method of forecasting, we can consider the plausible relationship between the maximum speed of military aircraft (the original trend) and the maximum speed of commercial aircraft (item to be forecast). Since it is reasonable to assume that the speed of military aircraft leads developments in the speed of commercial aircraft, a diagram like Figure 17-4 can be developed to relate these two trends. From this diagram the forecaster can determine that the rate of increase in speed of military aircraft is such that it will double every 10 years, whereas for commercial aircraft it will double every 12 years. Thus, by projecting increases in the speed of military aircraft, the forecaster can predict what the increases in the speed of commercial aircraft will be as well. Similarly, the development of color television may be related to that of black-and-white television, and the penetration of home computers can be

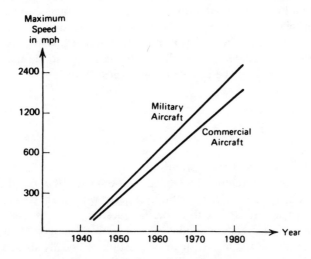

Figure 17-4   Time-Independent Technological Comparison for Aircraft Speeds.

forecast on the basis of an analogy with home telephones or stereo systems. Moreover, new products that replace old ones often can be assumed to follow a pattern similar to that of the product they replace.

At present there is great interest about the effects of the Information Revolution on many aspects of our lives, as well as the future of most firms. Although we do not have enough data to determine long-term trends resulting from the Information Revolution (which started in 1946), we have plenty of data concerning the Industrial Revolution, which started more than 200 years ago. By making the analogy that the Information Revolution will produce results similar to those of the Industrial Revolution, we can achieve a clearer view of the effects of the Information Revolution, which will enable us to forecast the long term more accurately (see Chapter 21). Table 21-5 shows important events in the Industrial and Information Revolutions. One thing is clear from such a comparison. The rate of change caused by the Information Revolution is much faster than that caused by the Industrial Revolution. Using this analogy, we can assume that it will take about 12.5 years for the Information Revolution to accomplish what took the Industrial Revolution 50 years to effect. (See Figure 21-2.) To forecast the changes between now and the beginning of the 21st century, the forecaster will first have to consider the type of changes caused by the Industrial Revolution in the past 50 years and then realize that similar changes will occur in the next 12.5 years (for more details see Makridakis, 1988, and Chapter 21).

Diffusion models (Mahajan and Wind, 1986) and substitution models (Fisher and Pry, 1972) can also be used to make time-independent forecasts. The Fisher–Pry substitution model is based on an S-curve type extrapolation. However, it simplifies the presentation of the S curve in such a way that the model becomes easier to understand and the interpretation of the results becomes more intuitive. The diffusion models described by Mahajan and Wind are more sophisticated approaches to forecasting and, as their name implies, they are based on the rate of technological diffusion.

THE DELPHI METHOD

This approach to forecasting, perhaps the most common of the nonquantitative methods, was developed by Helmer (1966b) and others at the Rand Corporation. Using the Delphi method, experts who wish to prepare a forecast form a panel to deal with a specific question, such as when a new process will gain widespread acceptance or what new developments will take place in a given field of study. Instead of meeting physically to debate the question, these experts are kept apart so that their judgments will not be influenced by social pressure or by other aspects of group behavior. An example of the use of this approach is presented below.

Phase 1.   The experts on the panel (numbering five) were asked in a letter to name inventions and scientific breakthroughs that they thought (1) were urgently needed and (2) could be achieved in the next 50 years. Each expert was asked to send his or her list back to the coordinator of the panel. From these lists a general list of 50 items was compiled.

Phase 2.   The experts were sent the list of 50 items and asked to place each of them in one of the five-year time periods into which the next 50 years had been divided, on the basis of a 50–50 probability that it would take a longer or shorter period of time for the breakthrough to occur. Again experts were asked to send their responses to the panel coordinator. (Throughout this procedure the experts were kept apart and asked not to approach any other members of the panel.)

Phase 3.   Letters were sent to the experts listing items on which there was a general consensus and asking those who did not agree with the majority to state their reasons. On items on which there was no general agreement the experts were asked to state the reasons for their widely divergent estimates. As a result, several of the experts reevaluated their time estimates, and a narrower range for each breakthrough was determined.

Phase 4.   To narrow the range of time estimates still further, the phase 3 procedure was repeated. At the end of this phase, 31 of the original 49 items of the list could be grouped together as breakthroughs for which a relatively narrow time estimate of their occurrence has been obtained. Thus the government agency that had initiated this forecasting exercise was able to obtain considerable information about the major breakthroughs and, for at least 31 of them, when they were most likely to occur.

The Delphi method, unlike many forecasting methods, does not have to produce a single answer as its output. Instead of reaching a consensus, the Delphi approach can leave a spread of opinions since there is no particular attempt to get unanimity. The objective is to narrow down the quartile range as much as possible without pressuring the respondent. Thus, justified deviant opinion is permitted by this approach. Helmer describes this characteristic of the Delphi techique as follows (1966*b*):

The effect of placing the onus of justifying relatively extreme responses on the respondents had the effect of causing those without strong conviction to move their estimate closer to the median, while those who felt they had a good argument for a deviationist opinion tended to retain their original estimate and defend it.

The Delphi method is not without disadvantages. The general complaints against it have been insufficient reliability, oversensitivity of results to ambiguity of questions, different results when different experts are used, difficulty in assessing the degree of expertise, and the impossibility of predicting the unexpected. These complaints are only relative, and the Delphi method should be judged in terms of the available alternatives. The same objections apply even more critically to the less systematic methods of forecasting.

A number of evaluative studies have been made to summarize experiences with the Delphi technique and some of its advantages and disadvantages. One of the most thorough of these is that prepared by Sackman (1975). He attempts to evaluate the Delphi approach and describes some of its variations and some alternative procedures that have been found to overcome shortcomings in the method as it was originally developed. Linstone and Turoff (1975) have added to the descriptive literature on the Delphi approach, as well as expanding discussion of its practical applications.

PATTERN: A RELEVANCE TREE METHOD

The relevance tree is a particularly interesting forecasting concept. Its origin is decision theory and the construction of decision trees to help decision makers select the best course of action from a number of alternatives. The relevance tree method uses the ideas of decision theory to assess the desirability of future goals and to select those areas of technology whose development is necessary for the achievement of those goals. The technologies can then be singled out for further development by the appropriate allocation of resources.

The initial and best known form for applying relevance trees is PATTERN (Planning Assistance Through Technical Evaluation of Relevance Numbers), an approach that has been developed and used by Honeywell Corporation for military, space, medical, and other purposes (Sigford and Parvin, 1965). The aim of the PATTERN approach (as with all variations of the relevance tree method) is to help planners identify the long-run developments that will be most important to the accomplishment of specific objectives.

As an example of the PATTERN approach and how it can be implemented, consider the situation faced by a country that has set preeminence in the areas of science and the military as its long-range goals. As a starting point in helping planners to identify the developments necessary to achieve this objective, a scenario can be prepared. This scenario will be a brief description of the future and what the situation may be like surrounding military and scientific developments. Such a scenario could be developed by some expert or long-range planner in the government. It serves mainly as a starting point for a panel of experts and need not be extremely accurate in all its details but should suggest the types of problems that must be considered when the objective is military and scientific preeminence.

On the basis of this scenario, a panel of experts can develop a relevance tree (see Figure 17-5) to show the relation between the objective and the subobjectives and to refine further those subobjectives until a level is reached at which specific technological deficiencies, or what might be thought of as areas requiring major breakthroughs, are identified. In the relevance tree shown in Figure 17-5 eight levels have been developed. The elements of the final level represent some of the nation's critical areas in which breakthroughs are required to achieve the long-run objective given on the first level.

By developing the relevance tree, the experts who have met to develop it become familiar with the various aspects of achieving that objective. In the next phase relevance numbers are assigned to each element of the tree by having the experts vote (individually on a secret ballot) on the relevance and importance of each element of the tree. Once the voting has been completed, the results can be tallied and an average of some kind can be determined for each of the elements. At this point the experts are allowed to discuss among themselves how they think the relevance numbers should be determined.

Following this phase, a set of computations must be made that will give the total relevance for each element in the tree. To compute the total relevance number, the individual relevance number for that element is multiplied by the relevance number of each element in the line above. Thus a high relevance for

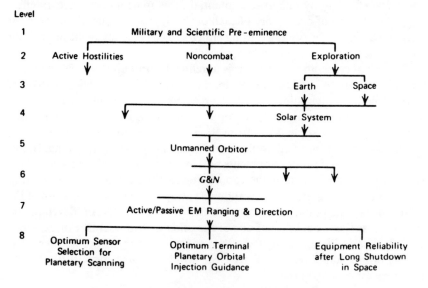

Figure 17-5   Sample Relevance Tree (PATTERN).

something like "active hostilities" would be reflected in the total relevance of all elements below it in the tree.

The final result is that the experts have developed a tree that not only indicates the breakthroughs needed to achieve a long-run objective but also tells those who will use the forecast in planning just what the relative impor- tance is of each of these breakthroughs.

The PATTERN method of qualitative forecasting is actually interactive with the planning it will affect. As critical areas are identified, the planner can make modifications in his or her long-range decisions and have the experts determine the additional breakthroughs that may be needed for the plan to be completed successfully. Thus this procedure helps the planner to carry out his or her entire function of planning by providing the advice of experts in a form that relates directly to planning concerns.

CROSS-IMPACT MATRICES

A recently developed technological method of forecasting closely related to the Delphi method is that of cross-impact matrices. A number of papers have appeared reporting applications of this methodology. A cross-impact matrix describes two types of data for a set of possible future developments. The first type estimates the probability that each development will occur within some specified time period in the future. The second estimates the probability that the occurrence of any one of the potential developments will have an effect on the likelihood of occurrence of each of the others. In general, the data for such a matrix can be obtained using either subjective assessment procedures or a method such as the Delphi approach.

The aim of cross-impact analysis is to refine the probabilities relating to the occurrence of individual future developments and their interaction with other developments to the point that these probabilities can be used either as the basis for planning or as the basis for developing scenarios that can be used in planning. An example taken from Rochberg, Goldon, and Helmer (1970) will help illustrate this methodology and its application in forecasting. In this example there are four developments that might occur in the next year. These developments are shown at the top of Figure 17-6. At the bottom of that figure, the cross-impact matrix is shown. The upward arrows in certain of the boxes in the matrix indicate where the occurrence of a certain development will increase the probability of one of the other developments. For example, if D-2, "feasibility of limited weather control," were to occur, then D-1, "one-month reliable weather forecasts," would become more probable, as noted by the upward arrow.

The interaction between the various potential developments shown in

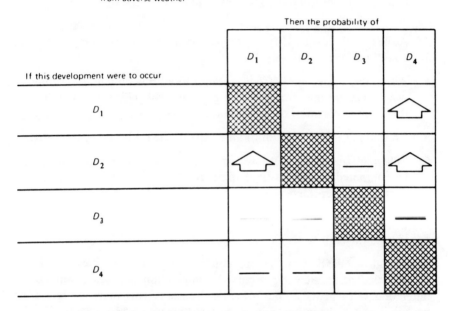

Development D_i		Probability P_i
1	One month reliable weather forecasts	.4
2	Feasibility of limited weather control	2
3	General biochemical immunization	5
4	Elimination of crop damage from adverse weather	5

Figure 17-6   Example of a Cross-Impact Matrix.

Figure 17-6 is, of course, very complex. The arrows simply indicate the nature of the relationship. Some form of expert opinion and subjective assessment would be needed to quantify that relationship. In addition, the technique of simulation is often used to refine further these probability estimates and their overall impact on the probability that each individual development will occur in the specified time period.

Through appropriate analysis of the problem and use of the guidelines suggested by those who have developed this approach to forecasting, numerical estimates of the probabilities can be filled in for each box in a cross-impact matrix. In addition, formulas can be developed for calculating changes in probabilities that will occur as different developments become a reality. Once this has been done, the matrix can be analyzed using a computer and the technique of simulation. Rochberg, Goldon, and Helmer (1970) describe the following steps for this analysis:

1. Assessing the potential interactions (the cross impact) among individual events in a set of forecasts in terms of:
    a. direction or mode of the interaction
    b. strength of the interaction
    c. time delay of the effect of one event on another.

2. Selecting an event at random and "deciding" its occurrence or nonoccurrence on the basis of its assigned probability (this is simply an application of simulation).

3. Adjusting the probability of the remaining events according to the interactions assessed in step 1.

4. Selecting another event from among those remaining and deciding its occurrence or nonoccurrence (using its new probability) as before (again, this is an application of simulation).

5. Continuing this process until all events in the set have been decided.

6. "Playing" the matrix in this way many times so that the probabilities can be computed on the basis of the percentage of times an event occurs during these repeated plays.

7. Changing the initial probability of one or more events and repeating steps 2 through 6.

Through application of this procedure, a set of probabilities can be developed that adequately represents the interaction between a number of different developments, each of which is uncertain. This analysis allows such probabilities to take into account the cross impacts of other events. Clearly, that is of help to the forecaster and planner who must consider a number of different uncertain developments.

While the basic concept of cross-impact matrices is straightforward, the detailed steps involved in its application are generally quite complex. In fact, Amara (1972) points out one of the major shortcomings of the methodology, namely that frequently the impact of various developments on each other is sequence dependent, that is, the probabilities for the impact of one development on another depend on sequences of activity rather than on individual activities. That, of course, greatly increases the magnitude of the problem and the difficulties associated with the application of this methodology. However, in spite of these shortcomings, it has found a number of useful applications in both government and business (see Linstone and Turoff, 1975; Helmer, 1977).

Table 17-1   Active Role-Playing Procedures for Forecasting Situations

Casting
Find subjects "somewhat similar" to actual participants.

Describing the situation
Furnish brief, but accurate descriptions. Specify possible outcomes.

Describing the roles
Improvise (for realism).
Stay in role at all times.
Act as the participants themselves would act, or act as the person being played would act.

Administering the session
Hold short sessions (less than one hour).
Allow for a brief preparation (10 minutes).
Prepare a realistic setting (dress, location, etc.).

Coding
Use actual outcome from the role-playing as prediction.
Ask participants to state what the outcome would have been if outcome is not reached.

Source: Armstrong (1987).

ROLE PLAYING

In the natural and physical sciences, the forecast being made can seldom change the outcome being predicted (for example, the weather forecast cannot by itself influence tomorrow's weather since people are not capable of changing the climate). In the social sciences, however, forecasts can influence the event being forecast and thus become self-fulfilling or self-defeating prophecies. In such cases, particularly when conflict is involved (such as in situations involving negotiations or competition), the role-playing approach can improve forecasting accuracy.

Role playing, as the name implies, requires individuals or groups to play a certain role and then interact with other individuals or groups playing a different role. Armstrong (1987) summarizes role playing in Table 17-1. His advice is that the potential gains in forecasting accuracy more than compensate for the extra costs of preparing and running a role-playing simulation.

FUTURIBLES AND LA PROSPECTIVE

The method of long-term forecasting known as *futuribles, futuristics*, or *La Prospective* has been developed primarily in France. Its major proponents, (de Jouvenel, 1964; Berger, 1964; Lessourne, 1979; and Godet, 1982), see it as a radically different approach from that followed by traditional forecasting methods (quantitative and technological).

The "prospective" approach advocates active participation in the creation of the future. Its proponents argue that large forecasting errors, overdependence on quantitative techniques, and, in fact, the crisis in world economic forecasting as a whole in the late 1970s and early 1980s could have been avoided by using the prospective approach. Table 17-2 contrasts seven characteristics of the prospective approach with the characteristics of traditional forecasting. Its advocates maintain that the basic philosophy of the prospective approach makes its application to long-term prediction more realistic than the traditional methods of technological and qualitative forecasting.

Futuribles criticizes the Anglo-Saxon tradition of long-term forecasting. Even the meaning of the world forecasting implies an ability to predict the future. Futuribles, on the other hand, claims that the future cannot be predicted simply because it is not as yet determined. It presumes that the

Table 17-2 Characteristics of Classical Forecasting Compared with Those of the Prospective Approach

Characteristic	Classical Forecasting	Prospective Approach
Viewpoint	Piecemeal, "Everything else being equal"	Overall approach, "Nothing else being equal"
Variables	Quantitative, objective, and known	Qualitative, not necessarily quantitative, subjective, known, or hidden
Relationships	Static, fixed structures	Dynamic, evolving structures
Explanation	The past explains the future	The future is the "raison d'être" of the present
Future	Single and certain	Multiple and uncertain
Method	Deterministic and quantitative models (econometric, mathematical)	Qualitative (structural analysis) and stochastic (cross-impact) models
Attitude toward the future	Passive or adaptive (future *comes* about)	Active and creative (future *brought* about)

Source: Godet (1979), p. 298.

future contains multiple alternatives and uncertainty. It is not yet written, but remains to be formulated through the actions of various actors involved, each with unequal powers to influence the determination of the future. The dream of August Comte that the science of social physics could be used to predict the future exactly by observing the past is considered by futuribles a mere dream, never to be realized.

Godet (1979) has provided an excellent description of the French school of thought regarding futuribles. According to La Prospective, as the French school is known, the future should be looked at as a way of understanding the past. This, of course, is not completely new. The rational expectations theory in economics is simply a way of looking at future expectations to understand present actions. For example, entrepreneurs do not start new businesses by examining past demand and prices; rather, they assess future ones. If they expect high demand and good prices in the future, they will start a new business or venture. The image of the future is, therefore, imprinted on their present outlook and determines their present actions. Expectations (that is, forecasts) influence present actions that subsequently influence future events. This cycle is never ending.

If there were a single actor capable of influencing the future through present actions, predicting the future would be much simpler. However, there are many actors and many possible futures. The future that materializes eventually is the consequence of confrontations among the various actors, the continuation of established trends, regulating factors, and constraints on actions of the various actors. Furthermore, it is clear that the various actors involved possess unequal power to determine the future.

An example of how these factors combine to determine the future will be helpful at this point. World oil prices were raised more than 18 times between 1973 and 1979. This one possible future of the early 1970s became reality because of the power of OPEC countries, which enabled them to raise prices unilaterally. But Western countries did not stand still during this process. Through a series of actions they reduced their dependence on OPEC oil, increasing their relative bargaining power and diminishing that of the OPEC countries. Concurrently, regulating factors (for example, the law of supply and demand) started to work. Higher oil prices encouraged substitution (the use of alternative energy sources) and conservation, and the higher potential oil profits resulting from higher prices brought new supply (through new explorations). The net result of the former was a decrease in demand for oil; the net result of the latter was an increase in supply. As the balance of supply and demand shifted, OPEC found itself in a difficult position. In order to maintain price control, it had to decrease production. However, this became difficult because several countries had increasing need of the oil revenues to finance their economies and achieve internal development goals (constraints).

The interplay of the various factors changed established oil consumption trends so drastically that growth rates became negative in 1982 and 1983. Moreover, the share of world oil supplied by OPEC fell to less than 25% in late 1988, down from 60% in the middle 1970s. Thus, in a period of only 10 years, significant changes occurred in the relative bargaining power of the dominant actors and their ability to mold the future for their own objectives.

According to the approach of futuribles, all future events are determined in a manner similar to that described above for oil prices. The only difference is that usually transitions are smoother, causing fewer crises and fewer discontinuities than those produced by the oil embargo. Consequently, most managers are less aware of the developments and transitions constantly taking place in the environment as the result of changes in the actions of the actors, regulating forces, constraints, and balances.

According to La Prospective, to speculate about probable outcomes, it is necessary to understand the bargaining power of the dominant actors, the elasticity of relationships, or the resistance of established trends, to change the importance of regulating factors, and the magnitude of the constraints involved. To decrease speculation and to increase the confidence in the forecasts, normative criteria must be considered. What the influential actors want and the constraints they face become critical. Such analyses can help expand the possible outcomes that will be considered in examining the future.

Since the future is uncertain, the prospective approach advocates a careful consideration of present decisions and actions. It is extremely important that these decisions and actions not deprive one of further freedom of choice. This becomes a critical aspect of coping with the future since locking oneself into an irreversible course of action leaves no freedom of movement and often results in an unsatisfactory outcome. It can be likened to locking the steering wheel of a car, throwing the keys out of the window, and then trying to steer the car down a winding road. Once the keys are gone, nothing can avert a crash as the car picks up speed. Thus, to the extent possible, one should neither overmortgage the future nor wait too long to commit and "miss the boat."

Accepting normative goals as instrumental factors in determining the future gives a better understanding as to why political, economic, and social structures break down when constraints increase beyond a certain level. Crises arise when, because of imposed constraints, the gap between reality and aspirations becomes too wide. Crises imply changes in the rules of the game and a new order of things. These changes are welcomed by some actors and rejected by others. Crises last as long as the pressure is sufficiently strong to disturb the old rules of the game but not powerful enough to impose a new order or new rules. In other words, crises continue as long as the old system is dying and the new one is not yet born. The system is in a state of transition

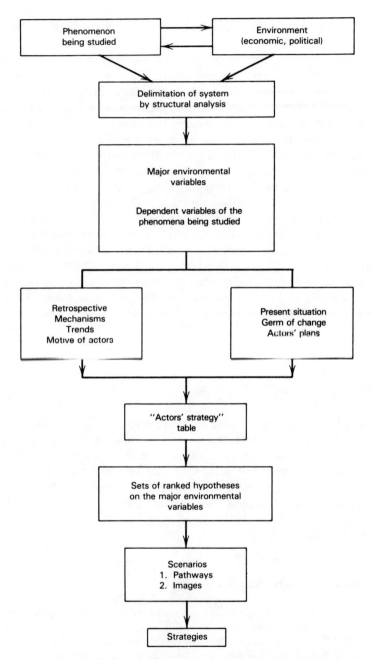

Figure 17-7 Use of Scenarios by the Prospective Approach.

of crisis proportions. While such transitions encompass dangers, they also encompass opportunities.

The foregoing views are illustrated by the world monetary and economic crises of the late 1970s and the early 1980s. The monetary crisis reflects the relative political and economic decline of the United States as the dominant world power. Other countries have not yet been willing to accept such a dominant role (changes in the relative bargaining power of the various actors). In the new relationships, the dollar is not sufficiently powerful to play its former role as the regulator of the world economic system, but it is still too powerful to be ignored. The crisis will last until another set of rules is found and accepted by the dominant participants of the monetary game. Until this happens, the transition, or crisis, will continue.

A final important tool used in the approach of La Prospective is that of scenarios. This tool is used to derive multiple futures and to explore the paths leading to them. Although they may be a stimulating exercise intellectually, scenarios traditionally have suffered from a lack of credibility. It is generally impossible to verify and validate their assumptions, to assess the plausibility of each scenario, or to assign probabilities for various outcomes. The prospective approach uses scenarios as shown in Figure 17-7. This approach, when properly used, increases the usefulness and credibility of scenarios for long-term forecasting and overcomes many of the traditional problems.

SUMMARY

Technological and qualitative forecasting approaches represent a wide range of techniques applicable to a variety of settings. Although most of these methods have been developed and applied to defense, aerospace, technology, and political or economic topics, they hold substantial potential for corporate managers and planners. This chapter, combined with the chapters of the next section, which compare and evaluate the full range of methods and their advantages and drawbacks, should provide a useful starting point for corporate applications.

SELECTED REFERENCES FOR FURTHER STUDY

Amara, R. C., 1972. "A Note on Cross-Impact Analysis: A Calculus for Sequence-Dependent Events," *Futures*, September.

Armstrong, J. S., 1987. "Forecasting Methods for Conflict Situations," in G. Wright and P. Ayton (Eds.), *Judgmental Forecasting*, Wiley, New York.

Ascher, W., 1978. *Forecasting: An Appraisal for Policy Makers and Planners*, Johns Hopkins University Press, Baltimore, MD.

Ayres, R.U., 1969. *Technological Forecasting and Long Range Planning*, McGraw-Hill, New York.

Berger, G., 1964. *Phenomenologie du Temps et Prospective*, Presses Universitaires de France, Paris.

Cetron, M. J., 1969. *Technological Forecasting*, Gordon and Breach, New York.

Cetron, M. J., and H. F. Davidson, 1977. *Industrial Technology Transfer*, Noordhoff-Leyden, The Netherlands.

Cetron, M. J., and C. A. Ralph, 1971. *Industrial Application of Technological Forecasting*, Wiley, New York.

Chambers, J. C., S. K. Mullick, and D. D. Smith, 1971. "How to Choose the Right Forecasting Technique," *Harvard Business Review*, 65, July–August.

Clarke, A. C., 1973. *Profiles of the Future*, 2nd ed., Harper & Row, New York.

Cournand, A., and M. Levy, 1973. *Shaping the Future: Gaston Berger and the Concept of Prospective*, Gordon and Breach, New York.

Fisher, J. C., and R. H. Pry, 1972. "A Simple Substitution Model of Technological Change," *Technological Forecasting & Social Change*, 3, pp. 75–88.

Gerstenfeld, A., 1971. "Technological Forecasting," *Journal of Business*, 44, no. 1, pp. 10–18.

Godet, M., 1982. "From Forecasting to 'La Prospective': A New Way of Looking at Futures," *Journal of Forecasting*, 1, no. 3, pp. 293–301.

———, 1980. *Demain les Crises: De la Résignation à l'Antifatalité*, Hachette, Paris.

———, 1979. *The Crisis in Forecasting and the Emergence of the Prospective Approach*, Pergamon, New York.

Gordon, J., and J. Stover, 1976. "Using Perceptions and Data about the Future to Improve the Simulation of Complex Systems," *Technological Forecasting & Social Change*, 9, pp. 191–211.

Helmer, O., 1979. "The Utility of Long Term Forecasting," *TIMS Studies in the Management Sciences*, vol. 12, North-Holland, Amsterdam, pp. 141–147.

———, 1977. "Problems in Futures Research—Delphi and Causal Cross-Impact Analysis," *Futures*, 9.

———, 1966a. *Social Technology*, Basic Books, New York.

———, 1966b. *The Use of the Delphi Technique—Problems of Educational Innovations*, Rand Corporation, Santa Monica, pp. 2–3.

Jantsch, E., 1973. "Forecasting and Systems Approach: A Frame of Reference," *Management Science*, 19, 12 (August).

———, 1967. *Technological Forecasting in Perspective*, OECD, Paris.

Jouvenel, B. de, 1964. *L'Art de la Conjecture*, Du Rocher, Monaco.

Kahneman, D., and A. Tversky, 1979. "Prospect Theory," *Econometrica*, 47, no. 2.

Lesourne, J., 1982. *Les Mille Sentiers de L'Avenir*, Seghers, Paris.

———, 1979. *Interfutures: Facing the Future, Mastering the Probable and Managing the Unpredictable*, OECD, Paris.

Linstone, H. A., and S. Devendra (Eds.), 1967. *Technological Substitution Forecasting Techniques and Applications*, American Elsevier, New York.

Linstone, H. A., and M. Turoff (Eds.), 1975. *The Delphi Method: Techniques and Applications*, Addison-Wesley, Reading, MA.

Mahajan, V., and Y. Wind, 1988. "New Product Forecasting Models: Directions for Research and Implementation," *International Journal of Forecasting*, pp. 341–358.

————, 1986. *Innovation and Diffusion Models of New Products Acceptance*, Ballinger, Cambridge, MA.

Makridakis, S., 1988. "Business Firms and Managers in the 21st Century, INSEAD Working Papers 3/88.

Rochberg, R., T. J. Gordon, and O. Helmer, 1970. "The Use of Cross-Impact Matrices for Forecasting and Planning," Report R-10, April, Institute for the Future, Middletown, CT.

Sackman, H., 1975. *Delphi Critique*, Lexington Books, Lexington, MA.

Sigford, J. V., and R. H. Parvin, 1965. "Project PATTERN: A Methodology for Determining Relevance in Compex Decision-Making," *IEEE Transactions on Engineering Management*, 12, no. 1, pp. 9–13.

Simon, J. L., 1985. "Controversy: Forecasting the Long-Term Trend of Raw Material Availability," *International Journal of Forecasting*, 1, pp. 85–94.

PART D

FORECASTING APPLICATIONS

CHAPTER 18

THE USE OF FORECASTING IN BUSINESS ORGANIZATIONS

The preceding chapters have described the full range of forecasting methods currently available. These methods vary from the subjective and judgmental to the quantitative and technological and from the simple to the complex. Questions that might logically be raised at this point include:

1. Which methods are used in practice? Why?

2. How consistent are the practical utilization of methods and experience gained through applications with empirical findings and theoretical expectations?

3. Do those providing staff support for forecasting (preparers) agree with managers applying forecasting (users) as to its status and contribution?

4. Where are the major opportunities for better management use of forecasting?

5. What is required to realize forecasting's full potential?

The first three of these questions will be addressed in this chapter. In the remaining chapters the last two will be discussed. This places the description of current forecasting practice in this chapter and recommendations as to what might be done to improve it in the remaining chapters of this book.

Several surveys of forecasting application and practice that have appeared in recent years are cited in Selected References at the end of this chapter. These studies provide valuable insights on the practice of forecasting and, more important, on the reasons for that practice and its development over time. Although they do not all focus on the same aspects of forecasting, these studies, taken together, present a fairly comprehensive picture, one that is surprisingly consistent in its implications and conclusions. We will draw heavily on three of these studies in this chapter (Dalrymple, 1987; Mentzer and Cox, 1984; and Wheelwright and Clarke, 1976) because of their comprehensiveness and representativeness.

In the first half of this chapter we focus on several important dimensions of forecasting practice: management familiarity with the methods, the extent of usage of each method, satisfaction with the results of that usage, the organizational levels and application areas for such use, and the perceived accuracy (and other benefits) of that use. In the second half of the chapter we focus on major differences between users and preparers as to the company's status with regard to forecasting, the skills of their counterpart in contributing to forecasting usage, and their relative roles in moving ahead with forecasting. Understanding these differences can be very helpful in explaining why forecasting's potential is seldom tapped fully, and what is required to realize that potential. The discussion of these topics sets the stage for the recommendations presented in the next chapter.

FAMILIARITY AND SATISFACTION WITH MAJOR FORECASTING METHODS

Table 18-1, which is based on the Mentzer and Cox (1984) study, indicates the level of familiarity of more than 150 U.S. managers with a number of subjective and quantitative (objective) methods of forecasting. On the basis of this table and the results of similar questions from earlier studies (see Wheelwright and Clarke, 1976; Dalrymple, 1975; and Conference Board, 1978), a number of observations can be made.

1. Forecasting users are very familiar with the subjective (judgmental) methods: jury of executive opinion, sales force composite, and customer expectations.

2. Users are much more familiar with the simpler quantitative methods than with the sophisticated ones.

3. Moving average is the most familiar of the objective methods, although, from the authors' own studies, it is not as accurate as the most familiar method, exponential smoothing.

4. The Box–Jenkins methodology is the least familiar of the methods included in Table 18-1.

5. Classical decomposition is the second least familiar method. Only about half of the respondents indicated any familiarity with this method, although it is one of the most useful, since it can distinguish the various

Table 18-1   Familiarity with Forecasting Methods (as a Percentage of Those Responding)

Method	Very Familiar	Vaguely Familiar	Completely Unfamiliar
Subjective			
Jury of executive opinion	81	6	13
Sales force composite	79	5	16
Customer expectations	73	7	20
Objective (quantitative)			
Moving average	85	7	8
Straight-line projection	82	11	7
Exponential smoothing	73	12	15
Regression	72	8	20
Trend-line analysis	67	16	17
Simulation	55	22	23
Life cycle analysis	48	11	41
Classical decomposition	42	9	49
Box–Jenkins	26	9	65

Source: Mentzer and Cox (1984).

subpatterns (seasonality, trend cycle, and randomness) of a data series and can be used to deseasonalize a data series.

The overall satisfaction of the respondents with various methods is shown in Table 18-2. It is interesting that forecasting users are less satisfied with subjective methods than with objective methods, and they are not simply neutral with regard to subjective methods. Dissatisfaction with subjective methods is higher than it is with objective methods. This finding is consistent with the empirical findings discussed in Chapter 12 and 13. A number of additional observations also can be made on the basis of Table 18-2.

1. Regression is the method with which users have the highest level of satisfaction, despite empirical findings that time-series methods are more accurate than explanatory (regression and econometric) methods. However, since regression can be used for purposes other than simply obtaining forecasts, this finding may not be surprising.

2. The method with which users were next most satisfied is exponential smoothing. This finding is consistent with the empirical studies that report that exponential smoothing is capable of considerable accuracy and is easy to understand and use.

Table 18-2   Satisfaction with Forecasting Methods (as a Percentage of Those Responding)

Method	Satisfied	Neutral	Dissatisfied
Subjective			
Jury of executive opinion	54	24	22
Customer expectations	45	23	32
Sales force composite	43	25	32
Objective (quantitative)			
Regression	67	19	14
Exponential smoothing	60	19	21
Moving average	58	21	21
Trend-line analysis	58	28	15
Classical decomposition	55	14	31
Simulation	54	18	28
Life cycle analysis	40	20	40
Straight-line projection	32	31	37
Box–Jenkins	30	13	57

Source: Mentzer and Cox (1984).

3. The methods of moving average and trend-line analysis also produced a high level of satisfaction. Furthermore, trend-line analysis had one of the smallest percentages of dissatisfied users. This finding is somewhat surprising in light of empirical evidence that suggests that neither method does very well on the criterion of accuracy, and that exponential smoothing tends to outperform both of these methods on many commonly used accuracy criteria.

4. The Box–Jenkins method was the one with which users were least satisfied *and* the most dissatisfied. (Given the amount of coverage of this method in the literature, this might be taken as a warning regarding its practical usefulness.) However, this result is consistent with the empirical findings that indicate that the method is difficult to understand and apply and frequently performs badly.

5. It is somewhat surprising that classical decomposition does not fare better in Table 18-2. One reason for this might be that it is as much a tool for analysis as a forecasting method. However, its perceived value is certainly below what the empirical evidence on performance would suggest.

THE USE OF DIFFERENT FORECASTING METHODS

Dalrymple (1987) and Mentzer and Cox (1984), like others before them, surveyed the use of different forecasting methods for different forecasting horizons. Their results, summarized in Table 18-3, suggest several points.

1. The jury of executive opinion is the most widely used forecasting method; furthermore, its usage is uniform across all forecasting time horizons. Although this method has some advantages, it also has some serious disadvantages, as discussed in Chapter 12.

2. Sales force composites and customer expectations are used less for the long term and more for the medium and short terms. Overreliance on these two methods, and on the jury of executive opinion, introduces considerable bias into forecasting. Empirical findings have shown that salespeople are overly influenced by recent events.

3. Exponential smoothing and moving average methods are used more for short-term, less for medium-term, and even less for long-term horizons, which is consistent with the empirical evidence, which indicates that these methods perform best for shorter time horizons.

4. It is surprising that the straight-line projection method is used for short-term horizons. Because of seasonality and cyclical factors, there are ups and downs in the short term that make straight-line extrapolations highly inaccurate. Even for the medium term, trend-line extrapolation is not very accurate, according to empirical studies.

5. The Box–Jenkins method is not used very much for any forecasting horizons, which is consistent with other empirical findings.

6. Finally, regression is used most often for medium-term, followed by long-term forecasting horizons. This is consistent with theoretical reasoning that postulates that in the medium and long terms, more emphasis should be placed on understanding the variables to be forecast and the factors that influence them. Thus, understanding can be aided substantially with regression analysis.

The level at which different forecasting methods are used is shown in Table 18-4. The jury of executive opinion method is used more than any other method for all forecasting levels except product forecasting, where customer expectations and sales force composite methods are used at least as much. As the level of disaggregation increases, moving average and exponential smoothing methods are used more frequently and regression is used less. (This is consistent with both theoretical reasoning and empirical findings.)

Table 18-3 Percentage of Respondents Using Techniques for Different Forecast Horizons

	Forecast Period					
Methods	Dalrymple, Short, 1–3 Months	Mentzer & Cox,[a] up to 3 Months	Dalrymple, Medium, 4 months–1 Year	Mentzer & Cox,[a] 3 Months–2 Years	Dalrymple,[b] over 1 Year	Mentzer & Cox,[a] over 2 Years
Subjective						
Sales force composite	23.1	37	34.3	36	5.2	8
Jury of executive opinion	18.7	37	29.1	42	6.7	38
Intention to buy survey	10.4 }	25	11.2 }	24	4.5 }	12
Industry survey	8.2 }		15.7 }		11.4 }	
Extrapolation						
Naive Forecast	34.3	—	17.9	—	0.7	—
Moving average	17.9	24	12.7	22	2.2	5
Percentage rate of change	10.4 }	21	13.4 }	28	8.2 }	21
Unit rate of change	9.7 }		9.7 }		4.5 }	
Exponential smoothing	9.7	24	9.0	17	6.7	6
Line extension	6.0	13	8.2	16	3.7	10
Leading indicators	3.7	—	20.1	—	7.6	—
Quantitative						
Box–Jenkins	6.0	5	3.7	6	2.2	2
Multiple regression analysis	5.2 }		11.9 }	36	4.5 }	28
Simple regression analysis	5.3 }		7.5 }		3.0 }	
Econometric models	2.2	4	10.4	9	7.5	10

[a] Adapted from Mentzer and Cox (1984).
[b] From Dalrymple (1987).

Table 18-4   Percentage of Respondents Using Different Techniques for Different Organizational Level Forecasts

Method	Industry Forecast	Corporate Forecast	Product Group Forecast	Product Line Forecast	Product Forecast
Subjective					
Jury of executive opinion	26	41	32	32	22
Customer expectations	8	12	18	18	23
Sales force composite	5	20	25	27	24
Objective (quantitative)					
Regression	18	22	21	29	12
Trend-line analysis	13	20	20	21	22
Simulation	7	9	7	4	4
Straight-line projection	6	10	11	10	11
Life cycle analysis	4	4	4	4	6
Moving average	4	9	18	19	20
Exponential smoothing	4	6	14	14	23
Box–Jenkins	2	3	3	2	6
Classical decomposition	2	4	8	7	9

Source: Mentzer and Cox (1984).

Finally, straight-line projection is used about the same amount across all levels.

The application areas where the various methods are being used are shown in Table 18-5. Production planning is the heaviest use of forecasting, followed by budgeting and strategic planning. Surprisingly, material requirements planning was one of the areas making the least use of forecasting, although it is one that could greatly benefit from accurate forecasts. Perhaps respondents did not distinguish between production planning and material requirements planning, even though forecasting often precedes material requirements planning.

Table 18-6 shows the percentage of regular use of forecasting methods by industrial and consumer firms. Overall it seems that industrial firms are

Table 18-5 Percentage of Respondents for Different Application Areas where Forecasts Are Used

	Total	Primary Decision	Secondary Decision	Tertiary Decision
Production planning	73	36	20	18
Budgeting	54	11	25	22
Strategic planning	45	6	18	26
Sales analysis	29	14	5	12
Inventory control	26	13	9	5
Marketing planning	22	8	13	0
Logistics planning	17	8	3	7
Purchasing	10	3	7	0
Material requirements planning	5	1	0	5
Product planning	4	0	0	5
		100	100	100

Source: Mentzer and Cox (1984).

348

Table 18-6 Regular Usage of Sales Forecasting Techniques by Industrial and Consumer Firms

Methods	Percent of Industrial Firms	Percent of Consumer Firms
Subjective		
Sales force composite	33.9	13.0
Jury of executive opinion	25.4	19.6
Industry survey	6.8	8.7
Intentions to buy	6.8	4.3
Extrapolation		
Naive Forecast	18.6	17.4
Leading indicators	16.9	2.2
Moving average	8.5	10.9
Unit rate of change	6.8	6.5
Percentage rate of change	5.1	15.2
Exponential smoothing	3.4	10.9
Line extension	1.7	6.5
Quantitative		
Econometric models	10.2	4.3
Multiple regression	10.2	4.3
Simple regression	5.1	2.2
Box–Jenkins		
Number of firms	59	46

Source: Dalrymple (1987).

heavier users than consumer firms. This is surprising since forecasting is usually more accurate for consumer products, because the number of customers is much larger and because cycles influence consumer goods less than industrial products.

PERCEPTIONS OF FORECASTING ACCURACY

The forecasting accuracy reported by respondents in the Mentzer and Cox 1984) study is shown in Table 18-7. As a rule, forecasting accuracy decreases as the forecasting horizon becomes longer and as the level of aggregation decreases. This has been verified with both theoretical research and empirical studies. In fact, the MAPEs shown in Table 18-7 are very similar to those found by Makridakis et al. (1982) and summarized in Table 18-8. Similar accuracies are reported by Dalrymple (1987, p. 387). A comparison of Tables

Table 18-7 Mean Absolute Percentage Error (MAPE) Reported by Forecasting Horizon and Organizational Level

	Forecasting Horizon		
Organizational Level	Short Term (3 Months)	Medium Term (3 Months–2 Years)	Long Term (Over 2 Years)
Industry forecast	8	11	15
Corporate forecast	7	11	18
Product group forecast	10	15	20
Product line forecast	11	16	20
Product forecast	16	21	26

Source: Adapted from Mentzer and Cox (1984).

Table 18-8 Typical Size (in Percent) of Forecasting Errors (MAPE) by Forecasting Horizon

	Forecasting Horizon (Time Periods)							
	1	2	3	4	6	8	12	18
Yearly	7	10	16	18	25			
Quarterly	8	12	16	25	30	37		
Monthly	9	11	12	13	18	21	24	30

Source: Makridakis et al. (1982).

Table 18-9 Criteria Applied, in Addition to Accuracy, to Evaluate Forecasting Techniques

Criteria	Responses (Percent)
Ease of use	38
Credibility	31
Cost	20
Data characteristics	4
Managerial reasons	4
Flexibility	2
	100

Source: Mentzer and Cox (1984).

18-7 and 18-8 suggests that forecasting users have an excellent idea of the magnitude of forecasting errors and how they vary according to forecasting horizon and level of aggregation.

Finally, forecasting users are most concerned about forecasting accuracy in selecting a method for a specific situation. However, as shown in Table 18-9, ease of use and credibility are important secondary concerns.

CONTRASTING USERS AND PREPARERS OF FORECASTING

In the study performed by Wheelwright and Clarke (1976), one of the major objectives was to discover how the perceptions of those whose primary role in forecasting was that of a preparer differed from the perceptions of those whose primary role in forecasting was that of a user. (Most often the former was a staff specialist and the latter was a manager.) Survey data were collected from 127 major U.S. industrial firms. All respondents indicated whether they were primarily users or preparers, and for 67 companies both a user and a preparer completed separate copies of the survey.

Companies in the Wheelwright and Clarke (1976) study were first asked to rate themselves in comparison with others in their industry on three factors relating to forecasting status:

1. Forecasting methodologies applied

2. Management use of forecasts

3. Accuracy of forecasts

Although both preparers and users gave similar responses on the status of management use of forecasts, significantly more preparers than users viewed their companies as substantially ahead of others in the industry on the other two factors. (See Table 18-10.) Over 50% of the preparers felt that they were ahead of the industry in forecasting methodologies applied, whereas just over 40% of the users felt this was the case.

The difference in the perception of preparers and users concerning the accuracy of forecasts was even more significant. Almost 50% of the preparers felt that they were ahead of their industry in terms of accuracy, but only one-third of the users felt that this was the case. This difference is important because both users and preparers are faced with the same facts about forecast accuracy. The difference, then is due to the perceived adequacy of forecast accuracy as it applies to the usefulness of the forecasts.

To understand better the difference in user and preparer perceptions of forecasting performance, Wheelwright and Clarke (1976) questioned both

Table 18-10 Company's Current Status in Forecasting (in Percent)

	Behind Industry	Average	Ahead of Industry	Total
Forecasting methodologies applied	19.1	34.2	46.7	100
Preparers only	17.1[a]	32.5	50.4	100
Users only	22.4	36.8	40.8	100
Management use of forecasts	18.2	39.4	42.4	100
Preparers only	18.1	38.5	43.4	100
Users only	18.4	40.8	40.8	100
Accuracy of forecasts	15.8	41.3	42.9	100
Preparers only	11.6	39.7	48.8	100
Users only	22.7	44.0	33.3	100

[a] 17.1% of the preparers rated their companies behind the industry in forecasting methodologies applied.

users and preparers about characteristics basic to understanding forecasting performance. On the basis of the responses given for 19 characteristics (9 for preparers and 10 for users), it was possible to identify four major groupings of these characteristics: (1) preparer's ability, (2) user's technical ability, (3) user–preparer interaction, and (4) user's management skill.

Preparer's Ability

The first of these four groups of characteristics related to the preparer's ability in forecasting and included such things as his or her understanding of the methodologies and ability to provide forecasts that met the user's needs and requirements (see Table 18-11). In these characteristics, 25 percent more preparers rated themselves good or excellent than did users. For example, preparers rated themselves much better at identifying the best technique for a given situation and providing forecasts in new situations than did users who rated them. A much larger fraction of the preparers felt that they could provide forecasting results in the management time frame required than was felt to be the case by the users. Preparers more frequently rated their forecasts cost effective than did the users. Users and preparers did agree on the ability of the preparer to understand sophisticated mathematical forecasting techniques. These differences are particularly interesting because, although technical competence (or even excellence) is attributed to the preparers by the users, the confidence of the users in the ability of the preparers to choose the best techniques or provide cost-effective forecasts is low.

Table 18-11   Differences in Perceptions of Users and Preparers of Forecasts

	Rating (Percent)
Preparer's Ability	
Understand sophisticated mathematical forecasting techniques	1
Understand management problems	−25[a]
Provide forecasts in new situations	−42
Provide forecasts in ongoing situations	−13
Identify important issues in a forecasting situation	−30
Identify the best technique for a given situation	−56
Provide cost-effective forecasts	−33
Provide results in the time frame required	−38
User's Technical Ability	
Understand the essentials of forecasting techniques	+27
Understand sophisticated mathematical forecasting techniques	+12
Identify new applications for forecasting	+5
Effectively use formal forecasts	−6
Evaluate the appropriateness of a forecasting technique	+24
User–Preparer Interaction Skills	
Understand management problems (preparers)	−25
Work within the organization (preparers)	−10
Understand management problems (users)	−5
Communicate with preparers of forecasts (users)	−1
Work within the organization in getting forecasts (users)	+2
User's Management Abilities	
Make the decisions required in their jobs	−3
Effectively use formal forecasts	−6
Describe important issues in forecasting situations	−8
Work within the organization in getting forecasts	+2

Source: Wheelwright and Clark (1976). Reprinted by permission.
[a]25% more preparers rated themselves good or excellent than did users. Rating = 100 × (percentage of users rating good or excellent − percentage of preparers rating good or excellent)/percentage of preparers rating good or excellent.

User's Technical Ability

This group of characteristics included such things as the user's understanding of forecasting methodologies, the ability to evaluate those methodologies, and the skill in using forecasts (see Table 18-11). Although most users tended to think they were better able to understand forecasting methodologies than preparers thought they were (even though the users rated themselves appallingly low), both groups seemed to agree on how well (be it very low) users could identify new applications for forecasting and how well they could effectively use formal forecasts. Thus the range of difference in perceptions concerning the user's ability is much smaller than it is for the preparer's ability.

User–Preparer Interaction Skills

Although preparers rated themselves more highly than did users on such dimensions as understanding management problems and working within the organization, both groups agreed on the user's ability to understand management problems, to communicate with the preparers of forecasts, and to work within the organization in obtaining forecasts.

User's Management Abilities

The final group of characteristics covered items ranging from the user's ability to make the decisions required by his or her job to describing issues in new forecasting situations and actually using forecasts (see Table 18-11). As was the case in evaluating the company's current status in its management use of forecasts, both users and preparers were in agreement as to management's abilities to do such things as make required decisions, effectively use formal forecasts, describe the important issues in forecasting situations, and work within the organization in getting forecasts.

Major Differences in User–Preparer Perceptions

Several important implications arise from the analysis of the mutual characterization of users and preparers. It is not surprising that the technical ability of the forecast preparer is seen as a key element of forecasting choice. Nor should it be surprising that preparers of forecasts are more favorably impressed with their efforts and abilities than are the users of their services (for whom the forecast is but a single, if important, input to their jobs).

What is perhaps most important in this analysis is the strength of the impression of the existence of a major gap between users and preparers of forecasts. This gap is reflected in the technical emphasis of the preparers and the managerial emphasis of the users. If the managers do not understand enough of the details of the forecasting methodologies to visualize new applications of them or to make reasonable demands for modifications that will lead to greater usefulness and if the preparers do not understand the application well enough to require situational integrity of their forecast methodology, what hope is there for progress in the effective use of forecasts?

The need, expressed by both users and preparers, for improved communication in the definition of forecasting problems is symptomatic of the problem. The real difficulty is probably insufficient knowledge of both preparers and users of the problems and abilities of others. There is a serious question as to whether excellent communication between the only tangentially knowledgeable user and preparer can possibly be sufficient. It may well be that an intersection of the respective spheres of knowledge may be necessary.

There was evidence in the Wheelwright and Clarke survey that the communications problems, although real, were merely symptoms of a deeper problem for many companies. The problem inherent in many companies is that in the definition of their own responsibilities and skills, both users and preparers have abdicated some tasks and skills to their counterparts. The result is that some basic skills and responsibilities are not covered (see Figure 18-1). No amount of effort to improve communication can compensate for the missing elements.

The impression gained from the Wheelwright and Clark survey is that both users and preparers would view communication improvement as bringing their own roles together at a point of tangency as in Figure 18-2. In fact, for many companies, this improved communication will leave key tasks uncovered. In particular, Table 18-12 lists four major functions and the percentage of companies in which neither user nor preparer was listed better than

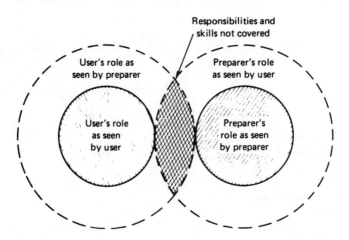

Figure 18-1   Role Perceptions of Preparers and Users of Forecasts.

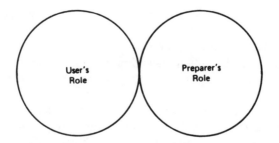

Figure 18-2   The Problem as Viewed by Users and Preparers.

adequate. Clearly, for a sizeable number of companies better communication between two people lacking in these skills is going to fall short of improving the forecasting function.

The authors believe that communication between a complex application and a sophisticated methodology is not possible with only the tangential contact between users and preparers, as shown in Figure 18-2. It is apparent from the survey that preparers must become much more of an integral part of the management process than their methodologies are called upon to serve. It should also be recognized that communication between two people when only one understands the vocabulary is tedious at best and impossible at worst. Users need to learn the basic vocabulary and concepts of forecasters and vice versa.

Table 18-12   Percentage of Companies in Which Neither User Nor Preparer Is Better than Adequate

Function	Percentage of Companies in which Neither User Nor Preparer Is Better Than Adequate
Ability to understanding the management problem	15
Identify the important issues in a forecasting situation	29.2
Identify the best forecasting technique	55.4
Identify new forecasting situations	52.3

SUMMARY

From the results of the Dalrymple, Mentzer and Cox, and the Wheelwright and Clarke surveys examined in this chapter, it appears that there are relatively few differences between theoretical and empirical results with regard to alternative forecasting methods and the results of their use in practice. However, there are significant differences between users' and preparers' perceptions. Users are more concerned about forecasting accuracy. They prefer simple rather than sophisticated methods, but they do rely much more on subjective than objective methods, particularly for aggregate forecasting tasks. Forecast preparers, on the other hand, prefer more sophisticated techniques and believe that forecasting accuracy can be improved through more complex methods. In addition, forecast preparers rate the understanding of such methods on the part of users very low.

Several lessons can be drawn from these surveys. Most important is that universities and other centers of training for forecasting must recognize that forecast users prefer simple, intuitive, easy-to-use, easy-to-comprehend methods. Thus, the majority of the treatment of forecasting must be on such methods with an overriding emphasis on how those methods can be used effectively to improve planning and other forms of decision making.

Forecasting users, that is, managers, must learn to rely much less on subjective methods. The evidence is overwhelming that human judgment does not necessarily improve accuracy over objective methods, and it usually degrades that accuracy when routine, repetitive tasks are involved. Managers also would be well advised to use moving averages and straight-line projection methods much less. They provide no real advantages over exponential smoothing methods and tend to do poorly with regard to accuracy. Empirical studies have found that methods such as Holt's linear exponential smoothing out-perform straight-line extrapolation even in the long term. Finally, forecasting users would benefit from training in the use of classical decomposition (see Chapter 6). This method provides several advantages both in forecasting and in analysis and understanding of time series.

SELECTED REFERENCES FOR FURTHER STUDY

Dalrymple, D. J., 1987. "Sales Forecasting Practices: Results from a United States Survey," *International Journal of Forecasting*, 3, pp. 379–392.

———, 1975. "Sales Forecasting Methods and Accuracy," *Business Horizons*, December.

Forecasting Sales, 1978, Conference Board, New York.

Kress, G., 1985. *Practical Techniques of Business Forecasting: Fundamentals and Applications for Marketing, Production, and Financial Managers*, Quorum Books, Westport, CT.

Makridakis, S., 1986. "The Art and Science of Forecasting: An Assessment and Future Directions," *International Journal of Forecasting*, 2, pp. 15–39.

Makridakis, S. et al., 1982. "The Accuracy of Extrapolation (Time Series) Methods," *Journal of Forecasting*, 1, no., 2, pp. 111–154.

Mentzer, J. T., and J. E. Cox, 1984. "Familiarity, Application and Performance of Sales Forecasting Techniques," *Journal of Forecasting*, 3, no. 1, pp. 27–36.

———, 1981. "Executive Familiarity and Usage of State-of-the-Art Sales Forecasting Techniques," *AMA Educator*.

Pan, J., D. R. Nichols, and O. M. Joy, 1977. "Sales Forecasting Practices in Large U.S. Industrial Firms," *Financial Management*, 7, no. 3, pp. 72–77.

Sales Forecasting, 1964, Conference Board, New York.

Wheelwright, S. C., and D. G. Clarke, 1976. "Corporate Forecasting: Promise and Reality," *Harvard Business Review*, November–December.

CHAPTER 19

FORECASTING THE SHORT TERM

In Chapter 2 the role of forecasting in planning and decision making was discussed. The various types of forecasts required to achieve different types of planning tasks for the immediate, short, medium, and long terms were described. Furthermore, the need to match the forecasting situation with the forecasting method was stressed. In this chapter (and the next two) a more pragmatic and specific approach is followed. On the basis of our experience with forecasting in business, we look at the major applications requiring forecasting and the best way of providing such forecasts. For the short term, forecasts are required for production, equipment, and personnel planning and scheduling. In addition, the size of forecasting errors needs to be estimated so that inventory levels or slack in personnel and equipment can be factored into the scheduling.

Of the three time-series patterns, the most important to forecast in the short term is seasonality. The trend is less important, because over a period of less than three months any regular increases or decreases tend to be small and dominated by seasonality. Furthermore, it is difficult to distinguish random fluctuations from changes due to the trend in a period of a few months. In the short term many forecasts (sometimes many thousands) are needed. Thus it becomes preferable to use a method that can be employed in an automatic mode and that provides conservative forecasts. In such cases single or damped-trend exponential smoothing is preferred to Holt's or quadratic smoothing. In addition, the cycle is usually not a major concern for short-term forecasting, except during periods of recessions or booms (see next chapter), which do not occur very often.

Finally it is not likely that established patterns or relationships will change permanently in the short term. Other types of changes, however, can occur which can greatly influence the sales, prices, cost, and other variables being predicted. These changes can be caused by competitors, actions, weather conditions, cartels, government legislation, and the like, giving rise to what we can call special events or actions (SEA), which will be described next.

SPECIAL EVENTS OR ACTIONS

Special events are beyond the control of an organization. A special event can be a heavy snowstorm, a promotional campaign or a price decrease by a competitor, a raw material price increase, and so on. Although most special events have temporary effects, others may have a more lasting influence, particularly if the organization does nothing to neutralize competitive actions (for example, a promotional campaign or a price decrease that succeeds in winning market share).

Special actions are deeds an organization can take to influence the future. The effect of special actions, like that of special events, is usually temporary, although gains from special actions can result in permanent benefits if the organization is successful in maintaining the benefits gained through them (such as the increases in market share obtained through an advertising campaign).

Often there is a strong interaction between special events and special actions, and vice versa. A promotional campaign by one of our competitors can increase his or her market share; however, its effect can be neutralized if we meet it with a campaign of our own. Similarly, if we decide to reduce prices, we may win temporary gains until our competitors decide to follow suit, as is usually the case. Such actions and counteractions make forecasting difficult and challenging.

A multiple regression model could estimate the combined effects of a price decrease of, say, $2.00 and an increase in the advertising budget of $300 000. However, it does so by assuming that the competitors will do nothing, which is unlikely if our price decrease and advertising reduce their market share. If they match our price decrease (or reduce the price by even more than $2.00) and increase their advertising, our benefits may disappear or even become losses. This is why it is difficult to quantify special events or actions and estimate their precise influence on the future. The circumstances that surround them are rarely the same. There are always some unique factors involved which make the quantification of special events or actions extremely difficult or impossible. In reality we are concerned with a chain of actions and reactions whose end result is hard to estimate. Managers must accept the fact that the effect of their special actions can be neutralized by competitive reactions. As they will not remain idle when they are losing market share, they cannot expect their competitors to do nothing when they attempt to grab market share from them.

Our approach to deal with special events or actions is based on recognizing their uniqueness and the impossibility of quantifying them in terms of a statistical model. Instead, the following procedure is suggested.

1. Keep track of special events or actions. This would require (a) classifying them by category (see Table 19-1), (b) recording the conditions that gave rise to them, such as a 10% price reduction, and (c) isolating and estimating their effects (see below for more details).

2. Adjust the historical data to eliminate the estimated effect of special events or actions. Otherwise the seasonality cannot be properly estimated. For example, we know of a company that used to announce their price increases in early January every year. The usual effect of an announcement of a price hike is an increase in orders before the new, higher price takes effect, followed by a reduction during and after the month the higher price is imposed. The orders this company received followed this pattern, rising above normal in December and then dropping below normal in January and February. Customers persuaded the company to announce new prices at the beginning of October, so that their budgets could reflect actual rather than estimated prices. Once this was done, September became higher than average, and October and November lower than average. The result was a very different monthly seasonal pattern that affected September, October, November, December, January, and February, which made it imperative to estimate and eliminate the effect of the price increase from the data to predict seasonality accurately.

3. Estimate the influence of forthcoming special actions on forecasting. Since the effect of special actions cannot be estimated automatically by

Table 19-1 Categories for Classifying Special Events/Actions

1. Price increases (or announcement of increases)
2. Price decreases (or announcement of decreases)
3. Price increases by competitor(s) (or announcement of price increases)
4. Price decreases by competitor(s) (or announcement of price decreases)
5. Strike
6. Strike in competitor(s)
7. Advertising
8. Competitive advertising
9. Promotion
10. Competitive promotion
11. Insufficient inventories
12. Insufficient inventories of competitor(s)
13. Introduction of new product
14. Introduction of new product(s) by competitors
15. Unusual weather conditions
16. Others

.statistical models, it must be introduced judgmentally by adjusting the quantitative forecasts. Such an adjustment can be made after consulting similar special actions taken in the past (see point 1 above). As more information about special actions is accumulated by building a base in a form similar to that shown in Table 19-1, the task of estimating the effect of future actions becomes more reliable. At some point it might even become possible to formalize the process of adjusting the forecasts for forthcoming special actions.

4.   Be ready to react to special events as soon and as effectively as possible. Because a wide range of special events cannot be predicted beforehand (such as weather or competitive actions), one must be prepared to react fast and effectively when such events occur. To react to competitive actions, an effective monitoring system might be required to find out, as soon as possible, when competitive actions commence.

An Example of Special Events or Actions

Table 19-2 shows the unit shipments (in thousands) of a pharmaceutical product sold over the counter. Figure 19-1 is a graph of such shipments. Neither Table 19-2 nor Figure 19-1 reveals the presence of special actions in the data. To isolate their influence, it is necessary to eliminate seasonality and use the deseasonalized data (see Chapter 6). The deseasonalized data (see column 3 of Table 19-2) are smoother and reveal certain periods when shipments are considerably above or below historical levels. Although randomness might be responsible for some of the extreme fluctuations, the remaining might be caused by special events or actions. In order to find out, knowledgeable people (for example, product managers) can be asked why such extreme fluctuations exist. Alternatively, written records can be consulted if such records exist. Figure 19-2 shows a plot of the deseasonalized values (column 3 of Table 19-2). Figure 19-2 and Table 19-2 show a large decline for three months in periods 16, 17, and 18, followed by a big increase in period 19. There is also a big decrease in periods 60 and 61, followed by a decline in periods 62 and 63, and a big decrease in periods 70 and 71, followed by a big increase in period 72 and a lesser decrease in period 73.

In addition to the above unusually large increases or decreases there are several others which, however, the product manager could not explain. For such increases or decreases we can do nothing and must assume that they represent randomness. For the three mentioned, however, we can attempt to estimate their impact and subsequently adjust the data.

The product manager knew that shipments were low in periods 16, 17, and 18 because there was a strike by the truck drivers which lasted for three months. As the strike was progressing, some new drivers were hired and some

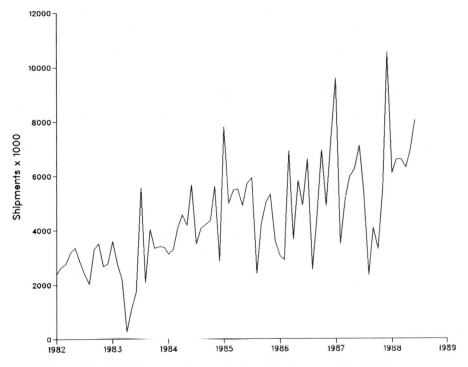

Figure 19-1   Shipments (in Thousands of Units) of Pharmaceutical Products.

of the transport was subcontracted to outsiders, but still shipments stayed well below normal. Once the strike was settled at period 19, shipments jumped considerably.

One of the problems in dealing with special events or actions is estimating their impact. This must be done by guessing what the shipments ought to have been and then computing adjustment coefficients to bring the shipments to such a level. In the case of the data of Table 19-2 the product manager estimated that shipments in period 16 were 10% of what they ought to have been, in period 17, 30%, in period 18, 50%, while in period 19 they were 150%. These coefficients can be seen in the fourth column of Table 19-2.

In a similar manner, the adjustment coefficients for periods 60 to 63 and 70 to 73 can be estimated. In period 60 the company had initiated a promotional campaign (by giving a 33.3% quantity discount below normal prices) whose effect was to increase their shipments to the discount drug stores to whom they sold their product. The discount stores, having large supplies, also reduced prices and exhibited the product in prominent displays. Thus, shipments increased during periods 60 and 61. However, once people bought the product, they were not likely to buy it again soon, since the quantity in

Table 19-2   Unit Shipments of Pharmaceutical Product (In Thousands), Deseasonalized Values and Adjustment Coefficients

Period	Shipments	Deseasonalized Shipments	Coefficients of Special Events/Actions	
1	2401.950	1894.7190	1.00	
2	2638.125	3192.0040	1.00	
3	2776.313	2753.5760	1.00	
4	3198.413	3251.4070	1.00	
5	3371.775	3226.1490	1.00	
6	2836.613	2498.7830	1.00	1982
7	2422.050	2279.9580	1.00	
8	2032.613	3362.6860	1.00	
9	3316.500	3557.0460	1.00	
10	3522.525	3267.8610	1.00	
11	2685.863	2610.5890	1.00	
12	2778.825	2704.2010	1.00	
13	3610.463	2848.0240	1.00	
14	2761.238	3340.9650	1.00	
15	2208.488	2190.4020	1.00	
16	276.375	280.9542	0.00	
17	1080.375	1033.7140	0.30	
18	1748.700	1540.4360	0.50	1983
19	5572.725	5245.7950	1.40	
20	2095.425	3466.6000	1.00	
21	4040.100	4333.1280	1.00	
22	3356.700	3114.0250	1.00	
23	3414.488	3318.7930	1.00	
24	3394.387	3303.2320	1.00	
25	3143.137	2479.3850	1.00	
26	3308.963	4003.6860	1.00	
27	4092.863	4059.3440	1.00	
28	4587.825	4663.8390	1.00	
29	4188.337	4007.4440	1.00	
30	5688.300	5010.8440	1.00	1984
31	3514.988	3308.7780	1.00	
32	4077.788	6746.1540	1.00	
33	4221.000	4527.1490	1.00	
34	4371.750	4055.6910	1.00	
35	5640.563	5482.4800	1.00	
36	2874.300	2797.1120	1.00	
37	7828.950	6175.6730	1.00	
38	4997.363	6046.5680	1.00	

Table 19-2 (*Continued*)

Period	Shipments	Deseasonalized Shipments	Coefficients of Special Events/Actions	
39	5487.300	5442.3610	1.00	
40	5535.038	5626.7470	1.00	
41	4924.500	4711.8130	1.00	
42	5736.038	5052.8970	1.00	1985
43	5944.575	5595.8310	1.00	
44	2422.050	4006.9580	1.00	
45	4213.462	4519.0640	1.00	
46	5040.075	4675.6990	1.00	
47	5344.087	5194.3030	1.00	
48	3605.438	3508.6160	1.00	
49	3075.300	2425.8740	1.00	
50	2909.475	3520.3250	1.00	
51	6939.525	6882.6930	1.00	
52	3678.300	3739.2450	1.00	
53	5834.025	5582.0560	1.00	
54	4942.087	4353.5020	1.00	1986
55	6648.075	6258.0590	1.00	
56	2560.238	4235.5710	1.00	
57	4427.025	4748.1170	1.00	
58	6972.188	6468.1280	1.00	
59	4906.913	4769.3920	1.00	
60	7386.750	7188.3830	1.20	
61	9625.388	7592.7480	1.40	
62	3509.963	4246.8860	0.75	
63	5133.038	5091.0010	0.80	
64	5994.825	6094.1520	1.00	
65	6268.688	5997.9460	1.00	
66	7138.013	6287.9020	1.00	1987
67	5364.188	5049.4920	1.00	
68	2366.775	3915.5120	1.00	
69	4102.913	4400.4980	1.00	
70	3306.450	3067.4080	0.50	
71	5555.138	5399.4490	0.90	
72	10580.140	10296.0200	1.60	
73	6117.938	4825.9830	0.80	
74	6630.488	8022.5710	1.00	
75	6633.000	6578.6790	1.00	1988
76	6323.962	6428.7420	1.00	
77	6962.138	6661.4460	1.00	
78	8077.688	7115.6650	1.00	

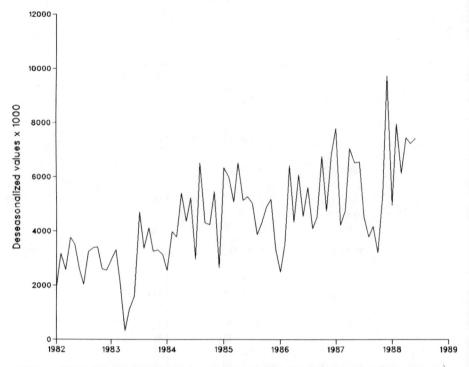

Figure 19-2 Deseasonalized Values of Pharmaceutical Shipments (in Thousands of Units).

the package could last from three to four months. Thus, shipments and sales declined for the two months following periods 60 and 61.

In period 70 one of the competitors initiated a large advertising campaign coupled with a price reduction of close to 40%. This resulted in a reduction in shipments of close to 50% in period 70 and 10% in period 71. Then as the price reduction was matched, shipments increased 40% in period 72 (see Table 19-2, column 4).

If strikes, price decreases or increases, and promotional or advertising campaigns were conducted in the same month every year, there would be no problems as far as seasonality is concerned. However, this is not the usual case. Thus, the increases and decreases associated with the promotional campaigns interfere with the seasonality in the data. The data, therefore, have to be adjusted before the true seasonality can be found.

Estimating the effects of special events or actions without a historical record of similar events or actions takes a fair amount of trial and error as well as talking to the product manager or other knowledgeable people. However, once experience has been accumulated, the adjustment process becomes easier. Table 19-2 shows the adjustments for the three special events or actions we discussed. A value of more than 1 means that the corresponding month was affected by the special event or action in a positive way. For example, the value 1.20 means 20% more than the normal. A value less than 1 indicates a negative influence, causing shipments to drop below their normal level for the corresponding month. A value of 1 means a normal month not affected by special events or actions.

Once the coefficients for the special actions have been estimated, their values can be divided into those of the shipments (see column 5 of Table 19-2). The resulting figures present adjusted shipments without the effect of special actions. These data can now be used to estimate the seasonal indices.

Table 19-3 shows the seasonality of both the original and the adjusted data. The differences are large, which further illustrates the need for adjustments. The forecasts based on the adjusted coefficients can improve forecasting accuracy considerably because seasonality is more realistic and because new promotional campaigns can be anticipated and their influence introduced into the quantitative forecasts. Obviously, strikes and competitive actions cannot usually be predicted in advance. However, once it is known that they have started, their influence can be estimated more accurately and steps taken to neutralize their influence.

In our experience, as adjustments for special events or actions are made on a continuous basis—as they occur—the deseasonalized data look smoother since seasonality can be estimated more accurately. This reduces randomness

Table 19-3 Seasonality of Original Data and Adjusted for Special Events/Actions Data

Season	Original Data Seasonal Index	Adjusted Data Seasonal Index
1	126.77	108.56
2	82.65	86.83
3	100.83	109.90
4	98.37	102.27
5	104.51	109.73
6	113.52	116.30
7	106.23	106.05
8	60.45	58.98
9	93.24	94.61
10	107.79	110.41
11	102.88	102.05
12	102.76	94.29
	1200.000	1200.000

and makes it easier to spot the cyclical changes and to monitor competitive actions and industry or economic fluctuations more effectively.

We believe that special events or actions play a critical role in short-term forecasting, and companies should consider dealing with them in the fashion suggested in this chapter. The steps required to do so are summarized below.

1. Deseasonalize the data.

2. Identify systematic variations above or below the normal level of orders, shipments, or sales that are not caused by cyclical factors.

3. Ask the product manager, or other knowledgeable people in the department, whether they can explain why such unusual fluctuations exist. It might also be possible to search for written records, if they exist, to discover promotional campaigns, price increases, or competitive actions.

4. If special events or actions can be verified, estimate their effect on orders, shipments, sales, or whatever variable is being forecast. Even if the estimation is crude, it is better than none.

5. Adjust the data and recalculate seasonality and the trend cycles.

6. If special actions are being planned, estimate their effect and adjust the forecasts accordingly.

7. Monitor competitive actions and be ready to react when a special event occurs.

8. Keep track of special events or actions by grouping them into similar categories, as suggested in Table 19-1. As the data base of such events or actions increases, so will your ability to estimate their influence in a more accurate and effective way.

9. Once you have started, make adjustments for special events or actions as they occur and keep the coefficients together with the original data so that you can make the necessary adjustments each time you use the data in order to forecast.

OTHER ADJUSTMENTS

Two other adjustments are often necessary for short-term forecasting applications. These involve working or trading day adjustments as well as an adjustment caused by fluctuations in continuous variables (such as temperature or rainfall) that can influence sales.

Working or trading day adjustments aim at removing the effect of unequal numbers of working or trading days of the same month (such as April) in different years. Since the number of working or trading days can have a profound effect on sales, its influence needs to be removed, particularly for months such as April, which sometimes includes Easter and sometimes does not. Similarly, in some businesses (such as department stores) the number of weekends in a month influences sales. However, the same month can contain four weekends one year and five weekends another year. Since sales will fluctuate on the basis of the number of weekends, this fluctuation must be removed by adjusting for the number of weekends (and possibly other nonworking days) each month.

The adjustments for working or trading days, weekends, or holidays each month are also treated in Chapter 23. The basic idea of such adjustments is that if a month has more working days (weekends or holidays) than the average, the sales will be adjusted proportionally upward or downward. For example, if the average number of working days for May is 21, but May 1988 has 22 days, the sales of May 1988 are divided (adjusted) by 1.0476 (that is, 22/21). Thus, sales are effectively reduced by 4.76%. Furthermore, if a forecast for May 1989 is required, this forecast must be multiplied by 1.0952 (May has 23 working days, that is, 23/21), effectively increasing the forecast by 9.52%.

Adjustments for continuous factors can be made in a similar spirit. If the factor (such as temperature) is above average, the historical data (such as sales) are adjusted downward in proportion to the amount the factor is above the average. Alternatively, if the factor that influences sales is below average, the sales are adjusted upward.

Table 19-4 (column 2) shows the monthly shipments of a beer brand and the corresponding temperatures. Table 19-5 gives the results of a regression run that enables us to estimate the influence of temperature on beer shipments. The last column in Table 19-4 lists the adjustment coefficients to be applied to the beer data. These are computed from the regression equation, estimated by using the shipment and temperature data. Such a regression equation is of the form

$$\text{shipments} = a + b(\text{temperature}).$$

The parameters a and b of this equation are:

$$a = 538.81$$
$$b = 81.67.$$

This means that the beer shipments have a minimum of 538,810 cases (when the temperature is zero) and increase by about 82,000 cases every time the temperature increases by 1°C.

Table 19-4   Monthly Shipments of Beer, Temperatures, and Related Information

Temperature	Shipments	Regression	Adjustment	Adjusted Shipments	
5	1028.198	485.7745	982.3045	1.0467200	
5	1074.704	473.1994	969.7294	1.1082510	
6	957.020	516.3141	1012.8440	0.9448847	
9	1280.530	783.9841	1280.5140	1.0000180	
16	1656.610	1337.2890	1833.8190	0.9033687	
23	2572.460	1917.5400	2414.0700	1.0656120	1982
29	3111.620	2440.3050	2936.8350	1.0595150	
30	3047.070	2454.6760	2951.2060	1.0324840	
25	2673.020	2100.7770	2597.3070	1.0291540	
20	2138.160	1673.2230	2169.7530	0.9854409	
13	1664.840	1098.3620	1594.8920	1.0438600	
8	1245.200	674.4011	1170.9310	1.0634270	
5	976.375	471.4030	967.9330	1.0087230	
5	994.405	471.4030	967.9330	1.0273490	
6	973.196	516.3141	1012.8440	0.9608548	
8	1193.560	674.4011	1170.9310	1.0193270	
15	1768.700	1285.1920	1781.7220	0.9926961	
22	2412.940	1854.6640	2351.1940	1.0262640	1983
27	2677.610	2213.9530	2710.4830	0.9878744	
29	2925.420	2449.2870	2945.8170	0.9930760	
27	2791.500	2204.9700	2701.5000	1.0333150	
20	2024.320	1669.6300	2166.1600	0.9345220	
12	1503.320	1028.3000	1524.8300	0.9858939	
8	1345.740	686.9761	1183.5060	1.1370790	
7	1012.610	575.5967	1072.1270	0.9444903	
6	831.199	500.1461	996.6761	0.8339715	
6	1097.840	550.4465	1046.9760	1.0485810	
11	1355.340	958.2390	1454.7690	0.9316584	
18	2042.890	1542.0830	2038.6130	1.0021010	
23	2417.560	1915.7430	2412.2730	1.0021920	1984
26	2657.780	2197.7850	2694.3150	0.9864423	
27	2716.980	2239.1030	2735.6330	0.9931846	
20	2212.530	1701.9670	2198.4970	1.0063840	
15	1825.650	1247.4660	1743.9960	1.0468210	
12	1395.700	1013.9290	1510.4590	0.9240281	
7	1283.840	629.4900	1126.0200	1.1401580	
5	943.293	469.6065	966.1356	0.9763567	
5	944.309	469.6065	966.1365	0.9774076	
6	984.787	498.3496	994.8796	0.9898555	
8	1167.270	692.3655	1188.8960	0.9818135	
14	1699.590	1189.9800	1686.5100	1.0077580	
22	2373.040	1858.2570	2354.7870	1.0077520	1985

Table 19-4 (*Continued*)

Temperature	Shipments	Regression	Adjustment	Adjusted Shipments	
27	2601.570	2206.7670	2703.2970	0.9623718	
26	2830.410	2187.0060	2683.5360	1.0547320	
22	2321.660	1872.6290	2369.1590	0.9799523	
16	1677.930	1326.5100	1823.0400	0.9204056	
11	1195.460	922.3102	1418.8400	0.8425651	
7	1356.540	652.8438	1149.3740	1.1802480	
6	907.371	492.9603	989.4904	0.9170091	
5	1007.780	469.6065	966.1365	1.0431130	
7	1008.330	580.9860	1077.5160	0.9357992	
11	1316.960	916.9208	1413.4510	0.9317340	
16	1827.750	1348.0670	1844.5970	0.9908695	
22	2480.580	1869.0360	2365.5660	1.0486220	1986
24	2481.170	2219.3420	2715.8720	0.9135818	
26	2551.610	2151.0770	2647.6070	0.9637452	
24	2251.750	2016.3440	2512.8740	0.8960890	
20	2218.740	1714.5420	2211.0720	1.0034700	
12	1521.080	1017.5220	1514.0520	1.0046440	
6	1024.970	546.8536	1043.3840	0.9823576	
5	988.489	480.3852	976.9152	1.0118480	
5	946.846	469.6065	966.1365	0.9986650	
6	1065.960	563.0216	1059.5520	1.0060540	
10	1435.430	852.2489	1348.7790	1.0642490	
14	1614.800	1220.5200	1717.0500	0.9404554	
22	2223.010	1806.1600	2302.6900	0.9653977	1987
30	2955.400	2472.6410	2969.1710	0.9953641	
28	2810.290	2309.1640	2805.6940	1.0016410	
20	2034.600	1687.5950	2184.1250	0.9315406	
16	1810.970	1371.4210	1867.9510	0.9695002	
13	1492.380	1066.0260	1562.5560	0.9550903	
8	1345.390	674.4011	1170.9310	1.1489980	
5	1176.430	469.6065	966.1365	1.2176690	
6	698.972	494.7567	991.2867	0.7051162	
7	1002.650	607.9327	1104.4630	0.9078227	
13	1608.640	1075.0080	1571.5380	1.0236140	
22	2366.600	1807.9570	2304.4870	1.0269530	
29	3010.900	2438.5080	2935.0380	1.0258470	1988
37	3635.750	3090.6170	3587.1470	1.0135490	
35	3609.290	2937.9190	3434.4490	1.0509090	
24	2385.440	1994.7870	2491.3170	0.9575054	
16	1871.860	1319.3240	1815.8540	1.0308470	
10	1498.470	848.6560	1345.1860	1.1139550	
7	1427.390	604.3398	1100.8700	1.2966050	

Table 19-5 Regression Run of Beer Shipments versus Temperatures

Dependent variable: 2 BEER

Variable	Coefficient	Standard Error	t-Test	Significant	p-Value
a	538.8074	26.41418	20.398	Y	0.000
TEMPERATURE	81.67017	1.49194	54.741	Y	0.000

The critical t-value from the table ($\alpha = 0.05$) = 1.989

R-Squared = 0.973   R-Squared adjusted = 0.973   R = 0.987
Standard deviation of regression = 120.4623
F-test = 2996.57   p-value = 0.0000
F value from table ($\alpha = 0.05$) = 3.96
Observations = 84.   Degrees of freedom for numerator = 1, for denominator = 82

Table 19-6   Seasonal Indices of the Original
Shipments and Adjusted (for Temperature)
Shipments

Season	(a) Original Data Seasonal Index		(b) Adjusted Data Seasonal Index
1	55.25	1	98.85
2	52.68	2	96.14
3	57.97	3	97.92
4	75.48	4	99.40
5	104.99	5	100.68
6	138.90	6	101.40
7	155.12	7	98.54
8	160.39	8	100.19
9	134.30	9	98.90
10	108.94	10	98.01
11	83.85	11	97.70
12	72.15	12	112.26
	1200.000		1200.000

Table 19-4 (column 3) shows the variable amount of shipments corresponding to various temperatures. Thus the first value of 485.77 is found by multiplying the temperature for January (5°C) by the regression coefficient $b = 81.67$. To this amount the constant $a = 538.81$ is added. The result is 982.30 (see column 4 of Table 19-4). This value represents the estimated shipments if we assume that no other factors affect sales except temperature. Finally, adjustment coefficients can be found if estimated shipments (column 5) are divided into actual shipments of beer (column 2). These coefficients can be seen in the last column of Table 19-4.

Table 19-6(a) shows the seasonal indices of the original beer shipments (column 2 of Table 19-4). They show a strong seasonality with shipments well below average in the winter months and much above average during the summer months. However, most seasonality shown in Table 19-6 column (a) is caused by fluctuations in temperature, which can be eliminated in a manner similar to that described above and shown in Table 19-4. If temperature fluctuations are eliminated and the seasonal indices are computed anew, their pattern is very different from before [see Table 19-6 column (b)]. The highest seasonality is now in December (because of Christmas) rather than August. The seasonality in the shipments for the other months, once temperatures have been taken into account, is very similar. This suggests the importance of temperature fluctuations on consumption and can be used to improve forecasting accuracy and consequently production scheduling, transportation, and other planning activities associated with beer production and distribution.

SELECTED REFERENCE FOR FURTHER STUDY

Lewandowski, R., 1979. *La Prévision à Court Terme*, Dunod, Paris.

CHAPTER 20

FORECASTING THE MEDIUM TERM

In the previous chapter the major adjustments in forecasting for short-term planning and scheduling were discussed. Seasonality was mentioned as the major component determining forecasting accuracy of short-term predictions when established patterns do not change. Furthermore, dealing with and predicting the influence of special events or actions on the future were described as the major challenge facing short-term forecasters since such events or actions inevitably change established patterns or relationships. In the medium term the major application requiring forecasting is budgeting. The tasks involve predicting growth rates, costs, and revenues. The challenge facing forecasters is to predict changes in growth, costs, revenues, and the other variables that influence budgets. In the medium term, unlike the short term, such changes can be large and persistent because they can be caused by cyclical factors whose duration and strength vary widely. In this chapter the forecasting needs for budgeting are described and the task of predicting cyclical turns is discussed.

Budgeting

Budgets are prepared once a year, usually between October and December, and they are updated in May or June for the remainder of the year. Budgets may cover individual products, departments, divisions, companies, or entire multicompany corporations. Moreover, they may involve geographic regions or different countries. Budgets require estimates (forecasts) of sales, prices of raw and other materials, levels of wages and salaries, selling and other expenditures, the prices of finished products, and similar variables that determine costs and revenues. On the basis of such estimates of sales, costs, and revenues, budget allocations are made covering products, projects, departments, divisions, companies, geographic regions, and countries.

The process of forecasting for budget purposes covers a time span of 13 to

15 months during which, unlike the short term, more changes in established patterns or relationships may occur, thus introducing considerable uncertainty into budgeting. Prominent among such changes are cyclical fluctuations caused by economic conditions and changes caused by fashions and other fads. Uncertainty in budgeting is proportional to the fluctuations in sales, costs, and revenues caused by cyclical factors. It becomes critical, therefore, to be aware of the amount of cyclical fluctuations in the past so that appropriate steps can be taken to deal with those that are forthcoming.

BUSINESS CYCLES

There are numerous theories as to what causes cycles in the level of economic activity. These theories cite causes ranging from random events to readjustments necessary to maintain an efficient economic system (that is, during periods of recession, cost cutting reduces inefficiencies and marginal firms disappear). Although business cycles have been studied extensively, there is little agreement as to their real causes and the means of preventing them. Despite government policies aimed at stabilizing the economy by smoothing out booms (increasing inflation) and recessions, (reducing disposal income), the act of balancing economic growth is a delicate one that does not always succeed (for example, when there is a recession during an election year despite government efforts to prevent it). Part of the reason for business cycles is consumers' and businesses' expectations that a recession or boom will arrive. Such expectations can start or intensify the recession or boom as consumers increase or cut their spending in anticipation of increases or decreases in their future income. Similarly, businesses can hire or fire personnel and can expand or reduce their capital spending, thus starting or intensifying a boom or recession.

Another real problem that is a consequence of business cycles is inventories. It has been estimated that it takes about five months for firms to realize changes in demand caused by business cycles. This means that production ignores cyclical fluctuations for many months. Excess production in this case increases inventories while insufficient production decreases inventories or even causes stockouts. Figure 20-1 shows inventories and how they fluctuate over the time span of business cycles. Such fluctuations intensify the influence of a recession on specific firms. Thus, a drop of 3 to 5% in real GNP might mean a drop of 40% in the production of a specific firm precisely because inventories have accumulated and drastic cuts in production are needed to reduce them. Cyclical fluctuations in the economy, therefore, provide the equivalent of a multiplier effect, which amplifies the effect of such fluctuations on specific industries or individual firms.

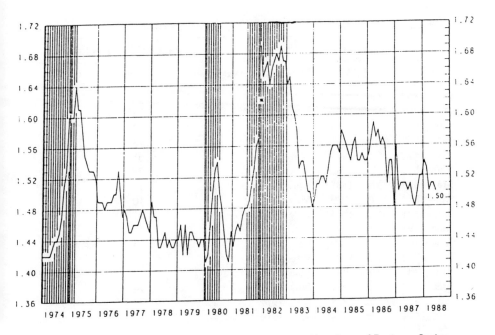

Figure 20-1 Inventories and How They Fluctuate over the Time Span of Business Cycles. Shaded Areas Represent Periods of Business Recessions. Source: U.S. Department of Commerce. Prepared by the Federal Reserve Bank of St. Louis.

Table 20-1 lists the business cycles in the United States economy since 1850, the first year that historical records were kept. An examination of this table reveals the following.

Beliefs that cycles repeat themselves at regular intervals and can be forecast are not reflected in Table 20-1. Moreover, if a similar table is constructed for specific industries or individual firms, the duration of cycles and of booms or recessions varies even more than those in the general economy. Furthermore, cycles in the general economy and those in specific industries or individual firms do not usually occur at the same time. Thus, attempts to predict business cycles mechanically have not been successful in our experience; alternative approaches must be adopted. Central to these approaches is the notion of monitoring the stage of the cycle *and* looking for warning signals of forthcoming cyclical changes.

Leading Indicators

Leading indicators which can be found both internally (such as orders received) and externally (such as unemployment claims or stock market

Table 20-1   U.S. Business Cycles 1850 through 1982

Business Cycle			Duration (Months) of:		
Trough	Peak	Trough	Expansion	Contraction	Full Cycle
Dec. 1854	June 1857	Dec. 1858	30	18	48
Dec. 1858	Oct. 1860	June 1861	22	8	30
June 1861	Apr. 1865	Dec. 1867	46	32	78
Dec. 1867	June 1869	Dec. 1870	18	18	36
Dec. 1870	Oct. 1873	Mar. 1879	34	65	99
Mar. 1879	Mar. 1882	May 1885	36	38	74
May 1885	Mar. 1887	Apr. 1888	22	13	35
Apr. 1888	July 1890	May 1891	27	10	37
May 1891	Jan. 1893	June 1894	20	17	37
June 1894	Dec. 1895	June 1897	18	18	36
June 1897	June 1899	Dec. 1900	24	18	42
Dec. 1900	Sept. 1902	Aug. 1904	21	23	44
Aug. 1904	May 1907	June 1908	33	13	46
June 1908	Jan. 1910	Jan. 1912	19	24	43
Jan. 1912	Jan. 1913	Dec. 1914	12	23	35
Dec. 1914	Aug. 1918	Mar. 1919	44	7	51
Mar. 1919	Jan. 1920	July 1921	10	18	28
July 1921	May 1923	July 1924	22	14	36
July 1924	Oct. 1926	Nov. 1927	27	13	40
Nov. 1927	Aug. 1929	Mar. 1933	21	43	64
Mar. 1933	May 1937	June 1938	50	13	63
June 1938	Feb. 1945	Oct. 1945	80	8	88
Postwar cycles					
Oct. 1945	Nov. 1948	Oct. 1949	37	11	48
Oct. 1949	July 1953	Aug. 1954	45	13	58
Aug. 1954	July 1957	Apr. 1958	35	9	44
Apr. 1958	May 1960	Feb. 1961	25	9	34
Feb. 1961	Nov. 1969	Nov. 1970	105	12	117
Nov. 1970	Nov. 1973	Feb. 1975	33	15	48
Feb. 1975	Jan. 1980	Aug. 1980	58	6	64
Aug. 1980	July 1981	Dec. 1982	11	16	27

Source: National Bureau of Economic Research.

prices) can help management foresee a forthcoming recession or boom. Leading indicators alone, however, are not a solution. First, the time between a leading indicator and an actual turn varies widely. McLaughlin (1988) has examined the number of months by which several leading indicators have led recessions in the U.S. economy in the past. The actual lead time, as shown

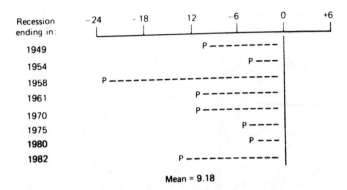

Figure 20-2   Lead Time of Leading Indicators.

in Figure 20-2, has ranged from 22 months in the 1958 recession to 3 months in the 1954 and 1980 recessions; the average lead time was 9.18 months.

Second, leading indicators can provide false signals, that is, they may go up or down *without* a cyclical turn taking place. At the time this chapter is being written (February 1988), the rate of increase in the leading indicators has been going down since July 1987. There has been a negative increase for the last three months that data have been available, and the stock market crashed in October 1987. Yet, economists and business forecasters are split on the question of whether or not a recession will hit the economy in 1988 or 1989. On the other hand, leading indicators do tell management that conditions are uncertain (as at present) and that they should look for additional signals (see the sections on anticipatory surveys and inventory changes later in this chapter).

Another practical approach proposed by McLaughlin is what he calls the five-phase economic forecasting system, which monitors the percentage changes of five indicators: (1) monetary-fiscal policy (MFP), (2) a composite of leading indicators, (3) real GNP, (4) a composite of lagging indicators, and (5) the price index.

The basic reasoning of this system is that monetary-fiscal policies will eventually affect the economy (real GNP), and the leading indicators will see such effects first. Thus changes in MFP will be followed first by changes in the leading indicators and then by changes in real GNP. Economic performance in turn will be reflected by changes in the composite index of lagging indicators. Finally, price changes will result from movements in the GNP.

Figure 20-3 indicates the substantial correspondence among the five components of the system and how peaks and valleys shift from left to right as one moves down the graph. Although the lead times are not constant from peak to peak, the set of indicators does give a general sense of the way movements in these factors are related to longer term trends and cycles.

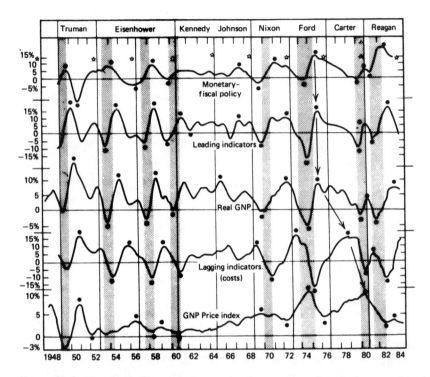

Figure 20-3 Five-Phase Economic Forecasting System. *Note*: Stars indicate presidential elections; heavy dots indicate peaks and troughs; shaded areas are recessions. All five lines are annual percentage rates. (Source: McLaughlin, 1988.)

Forecasting Business Activity Cycles Using Pressures

For many industries and individual companies, cycles are a fact of life. During the 1970s, a number of firms adopted an approach to forecasting cycles based on work done by the Institute for Trend Research, Contoocook, New Hampshire. Referred to as cycle forecasting, or pressures analysis, the approach builds on an attempt to forecast cycles for an industry, a firm, or a product. This section summarizes the steps involved in applying the pressures approach, indicates its value in some multinational manufacturing firms, and links the technique with action planning for businesses that confront business cycles as an ongoing part of their environment.

The cycle forecasting approach is relatively straightforward. Perhaps one of the best summary explanations of it is that given by Sommer (1977) in regard to its application at Parker Hannifin Corporation. The starting point is monthly data on a simple time series. For example, Table 20-2 presents

Table 20-2   Calculating Pressures for Business Cycle Forecasting

Month	Actual Orders	12-Month Moving Total (MMT)	Ratio of 12-Month Moving Totals[a] (12/12)
1972			
January	226		
February	284		
March	331		
April	292		
May	301		
June	336		
July	315		
August	277		
September	332		
October	314		
November	335		
December	362	3705	
1973			
January	370	3849	
February	407	3972	
March	498	4139	
April	411	4258	
May	406	4363	
June	421	4448	
July	387	4520	
August	382	4625	
September	393	4686	
October	487	4859	
November	423	4947	
December	500	5085	137.3
1974			
January	375	5090	132.2
February	517	5200	130.9
March	628	5330	128.8
April	581	5500	129.2
May	573	5667	129.9
June	589	5835	131.2
July	524	5972	132.1
August	519	6109	132.1
September	690	6406	136.7

[a] The ratio is multiplied by 100.

actual monthly orders (in millions of dollars) for the U.S. metalworking industry. The first step in preparing the cycle analysis, or pressures analysis, for this data series is to compute the 12-month moving total. As indicated in Table 20-2, this is simply the sum for a 12-month span. This total is placed opposite the twelfth or final month it includes. In Table 20-2, each subsequent 12-month moving total (MMT) is formed by dropping the earliest month and adding the most recent month. Thus, the second MMT value goes from February 1972 through January 1973, the third MMT value goes from March 1972 through February 1973, and so on. Using 12 months in computing the MMT eliminates any seasonality in the data.

The second step is to calculate the ratio of one 12-month moving total to the 12-month moving total one year earlier (12/12). These ratios (multiplied by 100) are indicated in the final column of Table 20-2, where each 12/12 pressure is listed opposite the MMT used as the numerator in the ratio. Thus, the 12/12 for December 1973 (a value of 137.3 in Table 20-2) is obtained by taking the 12-month moving total for December 1973, dividing it by the 12-month moving total for December 1972, and multiplying by 100. The resulting 12/12 value indicates that the 12-month moving total has increased by 37.3% over its year earlier value.

An examination of the 12/12 pressure of monthly orders shown in Table 20-2 shows that a minimum value for that ratio was reached in March 1974, which suggests that date as being the bottom of the cycle, even though this did not become obvious until several months later. These 12/12 pressure values for monthly orders also can be plotted graphically to see more clearly the amplitude and length of individual cycles for a specific time series.

This same approach to calculating pressures can be used with any of a variety of time series.

In addition, different ratios can be taken in order to see peaks and valleys in individual cycles more clearly. For example, it would be easy to calculate the ratio of 3-month moving totals for the data shown in Table 20-2 by taking the ratio for one year to those of the next. This would be referred to as a 3/12 pressure of monthly orders. (The first value in identifying a particular pressure is the number of periods included in the numerator—such as 3 months—and the second value is the number of periods between the moving totals being compared—such as 12 months. The values most commonly used in computing pressures are 1/12, 3/12, and 12/12.)

In much the same fashion that comparison of leading indicators was described earlier in this chapter, pressure values for different time series can be compared to identify cycles affecting a specific company or business unit. These pressures may simply be different pressure series for the same basic time series, or they may be pressures derived from different times series. Some

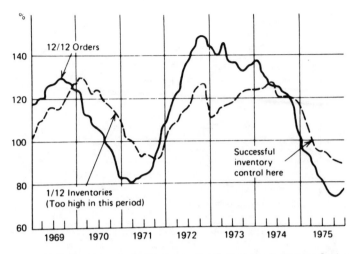

Figure 20-4   Using Order Cycles to Guide Business Inventory Cycles.

examples will help illustrate how these might be calculated and used in practice.

At Parker Hannifin Corporation, one of the relationships that was observed early in the use of the pressures technique was that certain order receipt pressure series tended to lead or lag other pressures. An illustration of this is given in Figure 20-4, where the 1/12 pressures for inventories are plotted on the same graph as the 12/12 pressures for orders. (Note that the 1/12 pressure is simply the ratio of a single month's value compared with the same month a year ago. The 12/12 pressure is the ratio of the 12-month moving total up through the current month compared with the 12-month moving total a year ago.) Comparing these two pressures on the same graph suggests that inventories continued to build in late 1969 and early 1970, even though orders had peaked and were on the decline. That six-month to one-year lag indicated that the company had been building inventories at the wrong time, in the downswing, and had failed to build them during the upswing.

Owing in part to using the 1/12 pressures of inventories and comparing them with the 12/12 pressures for orders, the company was able to control inventory buildup and production levels much more successfully during the 1973–1974 downturn than in 1969–1970. This, in turn, helped the company reduce its working capital requirements during 1975 and repay funds it had borrowed to finance much of the peak of two years earlier.

Another application of multiple pressures to guide management action is suggested in Figure 20-5. Management at Parker Hannifin had noted that its

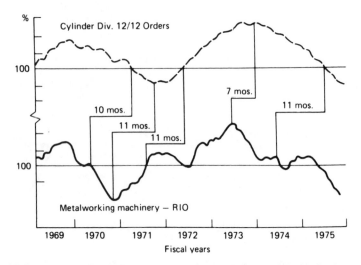

Figure 20-5   Using the Ratio of Inventories to Orders (RIO) as a Leading Indicator of the Order Cycle.

orders tended to drop drastically with even a minor cutback in customers' inventories. In fact, customer inventory swings were found to be the most significant factor affecting swings in Parker Hannifin's own business activity level. As an aid to anticipating the impact of such customer inventory adjustments on an individual division's order receipts, two pressure series were compared, as in Figure 20-5. One of those was simply the 12-month moving totals for orders (the 12/12 pressure based on data readily available within the division). The other series was made up of data representing the ratio of inventories to orders for the major customer industry. In this instance, Commerce Department data gathered through trade associations were used to develop a series representing the ratio of inventory to orders for the U.S. metalworking machinery industry. Then 12/12 pressures were computed for this series, and these were plotted on the same graph as the cylinder division's 12/12 orders.

It was found that the ratio of inventory to orders (RIO) for this major customer segment provided a leading indicator of the customer's business activity and thus a fairly accurate indicator of what was in store for one of Parker Hannifin's major divisions. While the lead time varied from seven to eleven months, it was consistently a leading indicator and thus provided additional guidance for management.

As a result of this RIO analysis, Parker Hannifin began to cut back steel and casting orders and long-term contracts, even in the face of growing orders for its own products. This was in anticipation of the downturn that this analysis predicted for early 1974.

One other example that illustrates the use of multiple pressures to predict individual cycles comes from the motor division of Reliance Electric Company. That division found that when it plotted the 1/12 pressure for order receipts on the same graph as the 12/12 pressure for order receipts, the former was a good leading indicator of the latter. This has been particularly helpful to the division in its budgeting. It enables it to anticipate the general business cycle for the coming year at the time the annual budget is being prepared, helping to avoid predictions of significant growth in a year where the cycle is on the downturn, and it allows the division to budget for even greater growth during a year where the cycle is clearly on the upturn. It has helped the motor division prepare budgets that are much more credible and has encouraged actions that are consistent both with the long-term goals of the business and the short-term realities of the cycle and the environment.

Cycle Analysis through Regression

Simons (1988) has proposed an interesting approach to analyzing business cycles and tracking their behavior. His approach is based on the assumption that the various components of a time series (trend, cycle, seasonality, and randomness) depend on each other and must therefore be determined *simultaneously*. Thus, according to Simons the traditional approach to decomposition cannot work adequately since it attempts to isolate each component of the time series separately in order to determine its importance.

Simons uses a nonlinear estimating procedure for his simultaneous decomposition. Such procedures find the optimal harmonics for the seasonal and cyclical components of the time series, which are then compared to determine those that can be grouped together. In doing so the length of seasonality and of various cycles is found. In addition, it is possible to determine how seasonality and cycles might be changing from one year to another. Figure 20-6, for instance, shows the seasonality over six years and how it has been slowly changing from one year to the next. Figure 20-7 shows the trend cycle together with the original data, and allows managers to determine the present level of the most recent cycle in comparison to the long-term trend.

BUDGETING BASED ON BUSINESS-CYCLE FORECASTS

In businesses that are traditionally cyclical in nature, a major concern of management is adjusting decisions to fit the stage of the business cycle in which it finds itself. In order to do this, many companies have found it useful to separate the problem of forecasting the business cycle from the problem of selecting those actions most appropriate for a given phase of the business

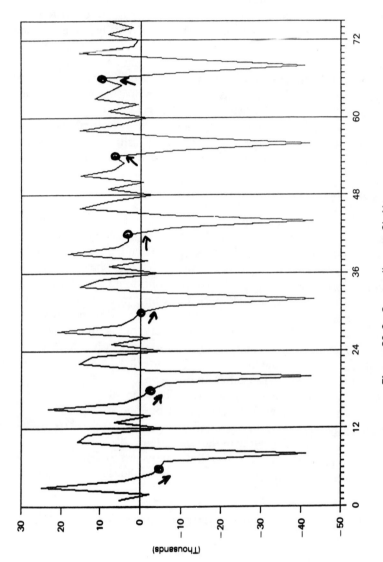

Figure 20-6 Seasonality over Six Years.

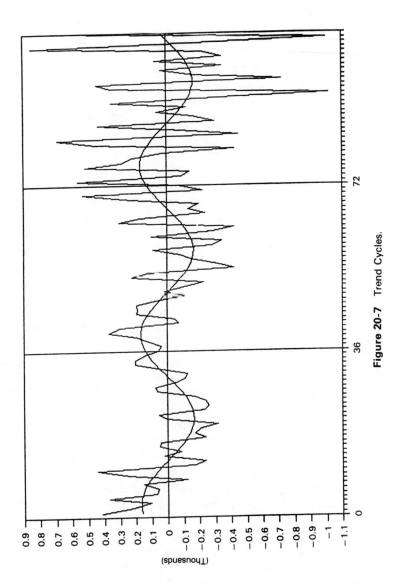

Figure 20-7 Trend Cycles.

387

Activity level

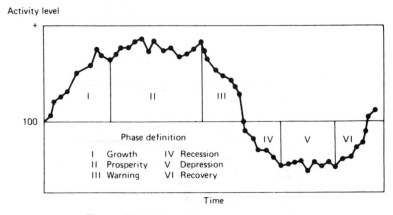

Figure 20-8 Six Phases of a Business Cycle.

cycle. Several companies associated with the Institute for Trend Research have identified a useful approach for guiding actions in various phases of the business cycle. This approach is summarized in Figure 20-8 and Table 20-3. As suggested by Figure 20-8, a business cycle can be divided into six major phases. These can be referred to in sequence as growth, prosperity, warning, recession, depression, and recovery. While many economic forecasters think of business cycles as having only two phases (or possibly four), for most management teams the use of six phases offers a distinct advantage. The problem with using only two or four phases is that a phase will then end at a major turning point (a peak or trough). If such an ending point is used for a phase, substantial debate arises as to exactly when a turning point has been reached, and when the next phase has been entered. When using six phases, where phases 2 and 5 span the upside turning point and the downside turning point, respectively, much of this debate on turning points can be eliminated.

Once a management group has agreed that its business generally goes through cycles that can be represented adequately with these six phases, there are two separable tasks to be addressed—forecasting movement through those phases and determining appropriate actions for any given phase. Again, it is extremely useful to separate those two tasks and to use pressures, leading indicators, and other cyclical forecasting techniques to handle the forecasting part of the problem. The conclusion of the forecasting activity is the identification of the phase in which the business now finds itself.

The second task of identifying the actions and responses appropriate for each phase of the business cycle can be clearly discussed and planned well in advance of actual entry into a given phase. Table 20-3 suggests one way that this might be done and indicates the responses and actions that might be appropriate for each of the six phases. People are frequently influenced a great deal by current events. They tend to believe that a boom or decline will

Table 20-3   Planning for the Six Phases of a Business Cycle

Phase	Recognition	Suggested Responses or Actions
I. Growth	Optimistic conditions	Expand work force Accelerate training Undertake plant expansions Examine outside manufacturing sources Try to build inventories
II. Prosperity	Gains in cycle chart narrow for 2 to 3 months	Stay in stock Review sales forecasts Freeze plant expansions Spin off undesired divisions Unload surplus equipment Missionary work in new fields (but don't add to costs)
III. Warning	3 months of cycle decline	Reduce inventories Make inventory curve (1/12) Start cuts in training and advertising Weed out bad products Cut hiring Reduce long-term purchasing commitments
IV. Recession	Orders fall below year-ago level	Further inventory reductions Layoffs Review purchase decisions
V. Depression	Declines in cycle chart narrow for 2 to 3 months	Freeze work force Keep skilled employees Reduce work hours if needed Order major capital equipment for next upswing Enter into long-term leases and labor contracts Prepare training programs
VI. Recovery	Gains in cycle chart, but still below 100	Rehire Build inventories Get distributors and suppliers to build inventories

go on forever. It is important, therefore, that managers agree in principle about what is appropriate for each phase. Then it becomes a matter of operationalizing and applying those general guidelines, rather than starting from scratch every time the firm finds itself in either an overcapacity or an out-of-supply situation.

Anticipatory surveys are aimed at collecting information concerning the intentions of consumers or businesses. There are three major types of anticipatory surveys:

1. Consumer attitudes and buying plans

2. Investment anticipations

3. Inventory and sales anticipations

The outcome of these surveys can be used as input to the prediction of the cycle, even though the forecasting accuracy of such surveys is not always better than naive approaches. The forecaster must bear in mind the characteristics and accuracy record of these surveys, each of which is described below.

1. *Consumer Attitudes and Buying Plans.*   The survey on consumer attitudes and buying plans (CABP) is conducted by the Survey Research Center at the University of Michigan. The survey gathers information on consumer opinions about general economic conditions and consumer buying plans. Although the forecasting record of CABP has been poor in several instances, their record is better than simply using last year's attitudes or sales data as a prediction for next year. When considered as one of many inputs, the survey can reveal a great deal about anticipated consumer actions.

2. *Investment Anticipations.*   There are two widely used investment anticipation surveys. One is prepared by the McGraw-Hill Company and is published the first week of November in *Business Week*. The other is conducted by the Office of Business Economics and the Securities and Exchange Commission (OBE–SEC) of the U.S. government. Of the two, the OBE–SEC has historically been the more accurate. Its only disadvantage is that it does not appear until March of the year to which it applies. Thus, it is of little value in preparing budgets that must be completed before the end of the previous year. The McGraw-Hill survey is much more timely for such use, although not as accurate. However, it can become a useful tool since its predictive power often has been satisfactory in the past.

3. *Inventory and Sales Anticipations.*   Besides the investment anticipation survey, the OBE–SEC also conducts inventory and sales anticipation surveys. There is general agreement that the results of the sales anticipation survey provide little help, since those surveyed are not necessarily good forecasters. (It has been shown that sales anticipations are no better than naive models.) Anticipatory data on inventories have been more accurate and more useful than naive models. They can be used together with the investment and consumers' plans to obtain information about possibly cyclical changes.

MONITORING CHANGES IN INTERNAL INVENTORIES

No matter what approach is being used to predict or monitor changes caused by business cycles, it will be necessary to decide *when* a cycle has started to affect a specific firm, and *how much* it will affect final demand. In our experience the questions of when and how much of a recession will take place cannot be answered satisfactorily unless an estimate of the changes in inventories can be made. This is particularly true for firms that keep several levels of inventories between production and selling to the final consumer. Failure to estimate changes in inventories will usually delay the realization that a cyclical turning point has occurred and will increase the negative consequences of failing to take corrective actions to reduce the effects of a recession or boom.

We believe that business organizations are not doing enough to monitor changes in their own inventories and their own warehouses or those of their distributors. Some simple procedures can be instituted to help estimate internal inventory changes. In our experience, such procedures *cannot* be based on telephoning or calling warehouse personnel or distributors; they must be supported by actual sampling surveys that measure inventory levels. The idea of sampling surveys can be carried one step further to measure inventory changes with major customers whose inventory levels can have a major impact on a company's future demand.

Although sampling surveys may involve some cost, the value of the information gathered will more than compensate for such costs. Furthermore, it is not necessary to conduct sampling surveys continuously. Rather, such surveys become necessary when the direction of the economy or industry is uncertain and concrete information is needed. Sample surveys become useful during unsettled times (as at present, February 1988), because what people think or what they plan is often different from what the actual situation is found to be after measuring some variable of interest (inventory changes in our case) quantitatively in an objective way.

OTHER CYCLES

Business cycles are not the only cycles that affect industries and firms. Several other types of medium-term cycles exist. These can be caused by fashions or fads, replacement cycles, new product announcements, governmental policies (for example, a Republican administration followed by a Democratic one, or vice versa), people's moods, raw material and energy prices, or purely random factors (such as terrorism or political upheavals in certain countries or regions). Although the causes and effects of cycles other than business cycles have not been studied as much as those of business cycles, their influence can have profound effects on many industries and companies. Moreover, predicting them can be just as difficult or more difficult than forecasting business cycles.

Managers can apply the approaches suggested in this chapter to deal with cycles other than those caused by economic factors. However, they need to realize that the difficulties and uncertainty involved in these cycles is even greater than that attending business cycles. Fads can create a billion dollar industry in a few years, one that can disappear in a few months (such as the home video game market). Similarly a fashionable product from a certain company can be a huge success one year and another product from the same company a failure the next year. The saying in the fashion industry that fortunes can be made and lost overnight is not an exaggeration. From a forecasting point of view, we can warn users of the dangers and the uncertainty involved because of the inaccurate forecasting of cycles in many fashion industries. Monitoring, in such cases, becomes critical and organizations must be flexible so they can react as quickly as possible to signals of forthcoming changes.

In this chapter we have seen the importance of cycles on budgeting and other business plans. Given that cycles have such a significant impact on almost every type of business, we have described a variety of approaches for dealing with what is one of the toughest of forecasting tasks. Each approach has its strengths and weaknesses, and none dominates the others on a consistent basis. Thus, the manager is well advised to use multiple approaches and accept the fact that cycle forecasting is an inexact endeavor, but one that must be undertaken because doing nothing usually produces even worse results. Monitoring, flexibility, and financial strength are all needed to cope with cycles whose arrival and strength cannot usually be predicted in advance.

SELECTED REFERENCES FOR FURTHER STUDY

Bails, D. G., and L. C. Peppers, 1982. *Business Fluctuations: Forecasting Techniques and Applications*, Prentice-Hall, Englewood Cliffs, NJ.

Dauten, C. A., and L. M. Valentine, 1974. *Business Cycles and Forecasting*, Southwestern Publishing, Cincinnati, OH.

Fair, R. C., 1974 and 1976. *A Model of Macroeconomic Activity*, 2 vols., Lippincott, Ballinger, Cambridge, MA.

Johnston, J., 1972. *Econometric Methods*, 2nd ed., McGraw-Hill, New York.

Makridakis, S., and S. C. Wheelwright (Eds.), 1987. *The Handbook of Forecasting: A Manager's Guide*, 2nd ed., Wiley, New York.

Makridakis, S., and S. C. Wheelwright, 1979. *Forecasting, TIMS Studies in the Management Sciences*, vol. 12, North-Holland, Amsterdam.

Makridakis, S., 1982. "Chronology of the Last Six Recessions," *Omega*, 10, no. 1, pp. 43–50.

Mass, N. J., 1976. *Economic Cycles: An Analysis of Underlying Causes*, Wiley, New York.

McLaughlin, R. L., 1988. *Turning Points* (monthly newsletter), Micrometrics, Waterburg, CA.

McNees, S. K., and N. S. Perna, 1987. "Forecasting Macroeconomic Variables," in 2nd Ed. S. Makridakis and S. C. Wheelwright (Eds.), *The Handbook of Forecasting: A Manager's Guide*, Wiley, New York.

Moore, G. H., and J. Shiskin, 1967. *Indicators of Business Expansions and Contractions*, Columbia University Press, New York.

Pindyck, R. S., and D. L. Rubenfeld, 1976. *Econometric Models and Economic Forecasts*, McGraw-Hill, New York.

Simons, L. F., 1988. "Cycle Regression Analogy: Simultaneous Decomposition," paper presented at the 8th International Symposium on Forecasting, Amsterdam.

Sommer, D. W., 1977. "Cycle Forecasting Spot Trends, " *Industry Week*, April 25, p. 71.

Stoken, D. A., 1978. *Cycles*, McGraw-Hill, New York.

U.S. Government, *Business Conditions Digest*, (monthly publication), Washington, DC.

Wise K. T., 1975. "Scrap: Prices and Issues," *Iron and Steelmaker*, May, pp. 23–32.

CHAPTER 21

FORECASTING THE LONG TERM*

In the two preceding chapters the major uses of forecasting in planning, scheduling, and budgeting were pointed out. In addition, the major tasks of forecasting were identified as predicting seasonality for the short term and predicting growth rates as well as cost and revenues for the medium term. The challenges facing forecasters were described as predicting the influence of special events or actions in the short term and cycles in the medium term. The principal use of forecasting in the long term is resource planning—capital, people, and technology—and new products and services. The major task of forecasting is to predict long-term trends and the need for new products or services in case established patterns or relationships do not change. The greatest challenge is to figure out the impact of changes in technology, competition, raw material and energy prices, population and demographics, customer attitudes and needs, and societal, legislative, and political changes in case of multinational corporations. Such changes can have a lasting impact on established trends or relationships and need to be taken into account in long-range planning.

New technologies, changing customer needs, competitive pressures, and changing demographic conditions necessitate the introduction of new products or services. New products or services, however, cannot be introduced overnight. Most of them require R&D work, some assurance that consumers will accept them, and some prediction about their future sales on which to base capital and production planning. Thus, new product forecasting becomes a major element of long-range planning and one of the most difficult and challenging managerial tasks.

---

*This chapter is based partly on S. Makridakis, 1989 "Business Firms and Managers in the 21st Century," *Long-Range Planning Journal,* forthcoming.

ASSESSING LONG-TERM FORECASTING

Long-term forecasting requires two kinds of tasks: (1) discovering established patterns or relationships, and (2) determining how such patterns or relationships may change in the future. Both of these tasks are mostly judgmental, although technological (Chapter 17) and quantitative methods (Part B) can also be useful. Before looking at patterns and relationships and how they might change, it is necessary to analyze long-term predictions made in the past to recognize the types of mistakes that were made so that they will not be repeated. These mistakes can be classified into five categories.

1. *Hidden or Complicated Assumptions.* The accuracy of long-term forecasts depends, to a great extent, on the assumptions on which these forecasts are based. Such assumptions are numerous and rarely made explicit, which leads Ascher (1978) to conclude that formulating these assumptions is as time-consuming a task as making one's own forecasts from scratch. Furthermore, forecasting users may disagree with some of the assumptions (assuming they can be figured out) but accept the rest. At present it is not possible to discover the specific influence of each assumption on the final forecasts. It is necessary, therefore, to restrict and make explicit the number of assumptions utilized. Furthermore, the influence of each assumption on forecasting must be made as clear as possible.

2. *Unfounded Predictions.* Predictions are often made without an explicit rationale. The user cannot, therefore, judge their validity and must either accept them on good faith or ignore them. Most often, managers choose to ignore them, which forces them to construct and use their own intuitive forecasts. This is particularly true with long-term forecasts whose impact on the long-term survival of the firm is critical. It becomes therefore necessary to make whatever assumptions are used explicit and the process of arriving at the forecasts clear, to increase the chances that such forecasts will be used.

3. *Long-Term Trends versus Cyclical Swings.* In addition to business and other medium-term cycles (see Chapter 20), long-term cyclical waves of up to 60 years' duration (Kondratieff, 1935; Burns and Mitchell, 1946) seem to exist. It is possible to confuse cyclical changes with changes in trends, for example, when increases in raw material prices between 1940 and 1979 were thought to be a prelude to raw material scarcities, which would impose limits on growth (Meadows et al., 1972). Similarly, the increase in oil prices that followed the 1973 oil embargo was thought to signify a permanent increase in oil prices. Cyclical changes, however, should be eliminated before a change in trend can be identified. For long-term forecasting, this is possible only

Table 21-1   Events that Happened but Were Not Predicted

The computer and the Information Revolution before 1950. (Today the computer industry is approaching $100 billions a year.)

The maximum demand for computers in the United States is 100 (forecast made in the early 1950s). In 1977 no one thought there was a market for personal computers. (Ten years later this market passed $20 billions in sales a year.)

Commercial television

The airplane

Airplane travel

Wireless communications

The atomic bomb

X-rays

Roads for cars

The maximum market for cars in Europe is 1000. (There is, after all, it was reasoned, a limit to the number of persons who will learn to drive the cars.)

"Who the hell wants to hear actors talk?" (Henry Warner, 1921)

The Walkman

The Post-it pad

Jogging shoes

Overnight mail delivery

High-temperature superconductors

when long series spanning many decades are available. Otherwise, what can be thought of as increases or decreases in a trend can be part of a long-term cycle and therefore not part of the trend.

4. *Forecasting Specific Events.*   Table 21-1 shows some important events (products or innovations) of far-reaching consequence that were not predicted in advance, and, in some cases were not forseen even a few years before they occurred. Table 21-2, on the other hand, lists events that were forecast as imminent, but did not occur until much later, or have not materialized as yet. Tables 21-1 and 21-2 show that two types of forecasting errors are possible in the long term: (1) specific events that have not been predicted can occur, and (2) events that have been predicted as forthcoming may not occur, or may occur much later than expected.

Table 21-2 Examples of Predictions That Did Not Materialize

"I am convinced that within a few years every household will have one or several flying machines." (H. Ganswindt, helicopter pioneer, 1891)

The widespread use of nuclear power

The economics of synthetic and shale oil

The feasibility of computer translation

A computer chess program becoming World Champion by 1970

Plastic paper

Plastic teeth

Instant yogurt

The extended use of robotics (predicted to be much higher than it is today)

Widespread commercial supersonic flights

Widespread utilization of magnetic-levitation trains

5. *Inability to Imagine the Extent of Technological Changes.* Most people (except science fiction writers) have been completely unable to conceive of the consequences of new technologies for their personal and professional lives. Consider, for instance, a watchmaker living 200 years ago. Could he have imagined, in his wildest dreams, that a watch that took him and his apprentices many months to construct would be produced today by a machine in less than one minute? Similarly, can we today conceive that a jumbo jet could be made in less than one hour by the middle of the next century? (See Table 21-3 to further develop this example.)

Long-term forecasting must avoid these five types of mistakes. In addition, managers need to realize its advantages and limitations. As Mendell (1985) writes, long-term forecasting does not necessarily mean predicting the future accurately. It is equally important to learn as much as possible about the future to develop the inner resources to cope with the change it will inevitably bring. In this respect long-term forecasting becomes a vehicle by which we may better understand forthcoming change and take steps to anticipate it.

LONG-TERM PATTERN RELATIONSHIP IN HUMAN HISTORY

Table 21-4 lists major innovations and breakthroughs since the dawn of human civilization that help us identify long-term trends, which should not

Table 21-3 Making Watches 200 Years Ago and Airplanes 50 Years from Now

	Fabricating a Watch 200 Years Ago	Making a Mass-Produced Watch Today	Implications
Method	The 250 or so parts needed to make a watch were made separately using the crude hand tools that existed at that time.	Digital watches are made automatically using specially designed microchips. Analogue watches are assembled semiautomatically using ready-made parts produced automatically elsewhere.	Imagine a watchmaker (or any other person) 200 years ago. Could he, in his wildest dreams, have conceived that a watch could be produced in ten minutes, or that digital watches showing time in hundreds of seconds, the day of the week the year, including multiple alarms, calculators, and a place for storing telephone numbers and appointments could exist? Could the watchmaker have imagined his skills becoming obsolete?
Time to complete task	About one month.	Less than one minute for digital. About ten minutes for analogue.	The month has become minutes, a time reduction of between 1200 and 12,000.
Cost in 1988, dollars	At the equivalent of today's wages (of workers with a similar level of skill) for a master watchmaker, an assistant, and three apprentices, plus equipment overheads, estimated cost is about $10,000.	Less than $1 for digital. About $5 for analogue.	A cost reduction by between 2000 and 10,000 times.

	Constructing a Jumbo Jet Today	Making a Mass-Produced Airplane 50 Years from Now	Implications
Method	The various premade parts are assembled by skilled workers as the body is built using an assembly-line approach.	Giant machines, guided by computers and robots, construct a conventional airplane. A new type of airplane (using a brand-new technology) is made by a single machine.	Imagine a technology that could produce a small passenger airplane in less than one hour, at a cost of about $10,000 (based on conservative estimates). Consider the implications: will there be airtraffic jams similar to those on today's highways? Will people live in the Caribbean and work in Atlanta? Will people spend their week-ends skiing in the Alps (in the winter) or the Andes (in the summer)? Will houses have two airplane garages?
Time to complete task	About two months	Less than two minutes for airplanes using the new technology.	What about vehicles (combining helicopter design with that of an airplane) that can take off and land on roofs or in back yards?
Cost in 1988, dollars	About $75,000,000.	Less than $7000 for airplanes using the new technology About $37,500 for airplanes using the old technology.	Even if the estimates are off by a factor of 10, the basic analogy and trends hold. Alternatively, consider the predictions which will be made not 50, but 100 or 150 years from now.

Table 21-4 Major Innovations or Breakthroughs that Changed Established Trends in Human History or Prevailing Attitudes

Epoch[a]	Approximate Time (Years from 1988)	Innovation or Breakthrough	Consequence or Reason
I. Technology			
A	1,750,000	Primitive tools	Extending human capabilities
B	100,000	Making and using gear for hunting	
	40,000	Making and using weapons	
D	5,500	The wheel	Reducing or making manual work easier
	4,000	Bronze and other metals	
	3,500	Boats and sailboats	
E	800	The clock, compass, and other measurement instruments	Facilitating or making mental work easier
	600	Gun powder	
	500	The printed book	
	350	Mechanical calculators	
F	210	Engines	Improving comfort or speed of transporation
	180	Railroads	
	150	Electricity	
	130	Image and sound reproduction	
G	90	Telecommunications	Increasing speed and availability of telecommunications
	85	Airplanes	
	70	Automobiles and roads	
	60	Mass-produced chemical products	

	Item
45	Nuclear weapons
40	Computers
35	Mass-produced home appliances
35	The transistor
30	Extensive use of fertilizers
30	Artificial satellites
25	Lasers
20	Micro technology (microchips, biochemistry, and genetic engineering)
20	The moon landing

H

Improving quality of arts and entertainment

Improving material quality of life

Decreasing dependence on the environment

Exploiting nature's capabilities

Using nature's resources

Adapting to changes in the environment

II. Exploiting Nature's Resources and Capabilities

		Item
A	400,000	Hunting
	300,000	Harnessing of fire
	150,000	Shelter
	20,000	Permanent settlements
	20,000	Domestication of animals
C	15,000	Agriculture
	10,000	Using animals for transportation and labor
D	3,500	Irrigation systems
	3,000	Harnessing wind power
	2,000	Using horses for transportation and labor
E	800	Using the energy of falling water
F	180	Using coal and oil for energy
H	45	Nuclear energy

Table 21-4 *(Continued)*

Epoch[a]	Approximate Time (Years from 1988)	Innovation or Breakthrough	Consequence or Reason
III. Social and Intellectual Human Achievements			
A	1,500,000	Social organization to care for children	Better mastery of the environment
	500,000	Language	
	400,000	Immigration	
C	20,000	Religion	Need for socialization
	7,000	First cities	
	5,500	Alphabet	
	5,000	Abacus	Need for knowledge
D	3,500	Money for transactions	
	3,000	Number system	
	2,500	Arts, philosophy, sciences	
	2,500	Democracy	Drive toward equality
	500	Scientific experimentation	Desire for achievement
E	500	The discovery of the New Worlds	
	475	*The Prince* by Machiavelli is written	
	400	Large-scale commerce	
	300	Scientific astronomy	
	300	Mathematical reasoning	
	210	Discovery of oxygen (beginning of chemistry)	
	200	French and American revolutions	
	150	Babbage's failed computer	
F	150	Political ideologies (communism, capitalism)	
	120	Foundations of genetics	Appreciation of arts

402

G	100	Financial, banking, and insurance institutions	
	80	The theory of relativity	Desire to reduce future uncertainty
	50	The concept of the computer is demonstrated mathematically	

IV. Medicine

D	2,500	The doctor as a healer	Curing disease
E	500	Therapy based on sound medical reasoning	Prolonging life expectancy
	300	Drugs with real medical value	
	90	X-ray	Providing better diagnostics
	55	Antibiotics	
H	30	Oral contraceptives	Preventing unwanted pregnancies
	20	Tissues and organ transplants	
	10	The CT (CAT or body) scan	

[a] A — the emergence of human domination; B — the first hard-made tools to extend human capabilities; C — the beginning of human civilization; D — the foundation of modern civilization; E — the foundations of modern science and society; F — the start of the Industrial Revolution; G — the Industrial Revolution; H — spin-offs of Industrial Revolution, the start of the Information Revolution.

Source Makridakis, S. G., Facing the future, The Free Press N.Y. Forthcoming.

be confused with long cyclical waves. A study of such innovations or break-throughs reveals the following conclusions, which are relevant for long-term forecasting:

1. The manual work performed by human beings has been supplemented (using tools to better perform certain tasks), substituted (using horses or tractors to cultivate the land), or amplified (employing levers or cranes to lift heavy weights) by a variety of means.

2. Mental work has also been supplemented, substituted, or amplified by a variety of means, although this came about much later than the changes in manual tasks.

3. There are clusters of innovations or breakthroughs that occur together within a relatively short time span.

4. The rate of innovations or breakthroughs has increased considerably in the last 200 years as a result of the discovery of machines, using mechanical energy to supplement, substitute, or amplify manual work. This discovery launched what has been called the Industrial Revolution.

5. In the late 1940s another revolution, the Information or Computer Revolution, began. This has also supplemented, substituted, or amplified work, but this time mental, and not manual. The Information Revolution has produced results similar to those of the Industrial Revolution, and it has further accelerated the rate of technological change.

6. Spin-offs from the Industrial and Information Revolutions affect all areas of our personal and family lives, entertainment, transportation, and medicine.

7. The importance of technology has increased over time. Consider, for example, the role, of technology in (a) Columbus's discovery of America and (b) Neil Armstrong's landing on the moon. Even in areas such as medicine, or in the harnessing of nature's resources or capabilities, innovations or breakthroughs depend now to a greater extent on technology than ever before.

THE INDUSTRIAL AND INFORMATION REVOLUTIONS

The Industrial Revolution brought about huge changes in employment patterns. The manual skills of farmers, craftspeople, and artisans were replicated in a machine design that could perform the same task faster, cheaper, and with less effort. A skilled shoemaker who could make less than one pair of shoes per day was replaced by a machine producing thousands of shoes in a single day. Similarly, a farmer cultivating less than one acre of land with the aid of a horse could cultivate hundreds with the use of the appropriate tractor. For the first time in the history of human civilization, hand skills acquired through many years of apprenticeship and long periods of practical experience became obsolete. The widespread introduction of machines brought unemployment to farmers, craftspeople, and artisans, and created a new form of employment—that of the factory worker. The Industrial Revolution changed long-established trends and relationships that had prevailed for thousands of years.

THE INFORMATION (COMPUTER) REVOLUTION

The Industrial Revolution substituted, supplemented, and amplified manual work by machines. The Information Revolution is substituting, supplementing, and amplifying mental work through the use of computer programs (software). The consequences of the Information Revolution are similar to those of the Industrial Revolution. Higher efficiency and better productivity are achieved by replacing people doing mental work with computer programs. Initially such replacement has taken place for repetitive, high-volume tasks (such as payrolls, billings, or processing of checks), but recently the replacement has been extended to a multitude of other tasks. The substitution of mental work by computer programs will continue into the future. Furthermore, the Information Revolution like the Industrial Revolution will continue to change established patterns of relationships.

PARALLELS OF THE INDUSTRIAL AND INFORMATION REVOLUTIONS

The parallels between the Industrial and Information Revolutions are strong—they both aim at substituting, supplementing, or amplifying human work—and of great interest for long-term forecasting purposes. At the same time there are some substantial differences between them (see Table 21-5). Such differences are likely to increase the pace of the Information Revolution in comparison to that of the Industrial Revolution (see below). Extending human manual abilities, for instance, started as early as 1,750,000 years ago (see Figure 21-1), whereas the extension of mental abilities did not take place until 40,000 years ago. Humans were mostly preoccupied with improving their chances of survival, and it was not until much later that they started to be concerned with mental activities. The prehistory, therefore, of the Indus-

Table 21-5 Similarities and Differences between the Industrial Revolution and the Information Revolution

Industrial Revolution	Information Revolution
Substitutes, supplements, or amplifies manual work through the use of tools and machines powered by mechanical energy.	Substitutes, supplements, or amplifies mental work through the use of computer programs (software).

Replace work done by people.
Make work easier or less boring by eliminating hard repetitive tasks.
Allow for more and cheaper material goods.
Improve quality and length of life.

Industrial Revolution	Information Revolution
Requires energy to produce goods. Possible side effects in terms of pollution and waste disposal.	The energy required is zero for practical purposes. There are no side effects.

The cost of developing new products and applications is considerable.
The success of the new products and applications is uncertain

Industrial Revolution	Information Revolution
Once developed and successful, a product must be produced and shipped to consumers. The cost of manufacturing and transportation is, usually, substantial.	Once developed a product or application can be reproduced and shipped at virtually no cost.

The sales and marketing costs can be substantial.

Industrial Revolution	Information Revolution
The product is destroyed when used (either at once or slowly, as with durables).	The product or application can be used an infinite number of times. The usefulness of the product or application might even improve through repetitive use.

The larger the production, the bigger the economies of scale being achieved.

Industrial Revolution	Information Revolution
Machines cannot operate on their own. They require supervision and guidance.	Computers can operate (through appropriate programs) on their own. Moreover, they can supervise and guide machines.

The techniques of the Industrial (hardware) and Information (software) Revolutions can be combined to produce superautomation.

Table 21-5   (*Continued*)

Industrial Revolution	Information Revolution
Production facilities can break down because they are made from mechanical components. Similarly, durable products (such as cars) do break down.	Information facilities, products, and applications break down much more rarely because they are not made of mechanical parts.

trial and Information Revolutions (Figure 21-1) is uneven in terms of the length of time it took each to start. The same pattern can be seen in Figure 21-2, which shows the history of the Industrial and Information Revolutions and some important corresponding events between the two. Some experts suggest that in 1988 the Information Revolution was at about the same stage as the Industrial Revolution in the 1930s. (Interestingly, the penetration of cars into the United States economy in 1935 was 17.7%; the coresponding penetration of computers today is 17%.) This suggests that it took the Industrial Revolution about 175 years to achieve what the Information Revolution has achieved in 42 years, implying that the pace of the Information Revolution is about four times faster than that of the Industrial Revolution (see Figure 21-2). Thus, the equivalent of the change brought about by the Industrial Revolution between the 1930s and today (a little more than 50 years) is likely to be achieved by the Information Revolution in about a fourth of this time, that is, 12.5 years, which will bring us to the beginning of the 21st century. At that time, society and business firms will be as far advanced in terms of the Information Revolution as today's firms are in terms of the Industrial Revolution. This will represent a considerable change.

The strong parallels between the Industrial Revolution and the Information Revolution (see Figures 21-1 and 21-2) can be utilized to predict the type of changes that will take place between now and the 21st century. The manufacturing firm in the remainder of the 20th century will be in a position similar to that of the agricultural firm since the middle of this century. This suggests that the percentage of people employed in manufacturing might drop substantially, to less than 5% of the population. (The percentage of people employed in agriculture was more than 60% of the population before the Industrial Revolution, but today it is less than 2% in the United States.) One scenario for the future suggests that manufactured products will be in plentiful supply, and competition among the firms producing them will be as fierce as it is among agricultural firms today. Competitive advantages among the various manufacturers will be few, because the same high level of technology will be available to all. Differences in the quality of products will be small

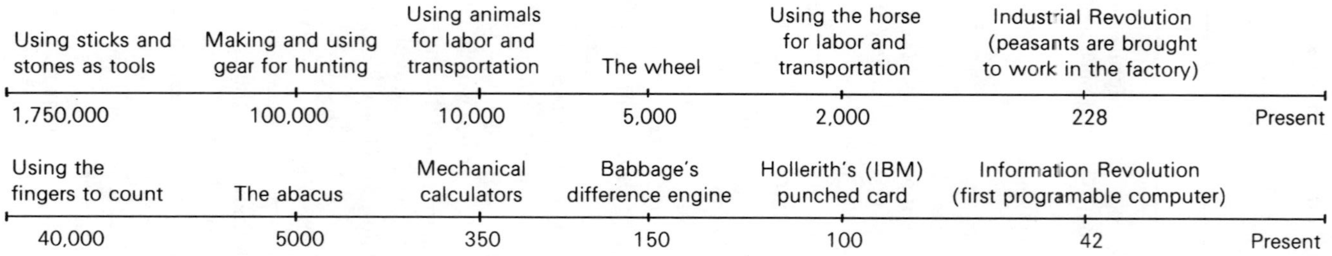

Using sticks and stones as tools	Making and using gear for hunting	Using animals for labor and transportation	The wheel	Using the horse for labor and transportation	Industrial Revolution (peasants are brought to work in the factory)	
1.750.000	100,000	10,000	5,000	2,000	228	Present

Using the fingers to count	The abacus	Mechanical calculators	Babbage's difference engine	Hollerith's (IBM) punched card	Information Revolution (first programable computer)	
40,000	5000	350	150	100	42	Present

Figure 21-1 Important Events in Human History leading up to the Industrial and Information (Computer) Revolutions (Years from Present —1988).

408

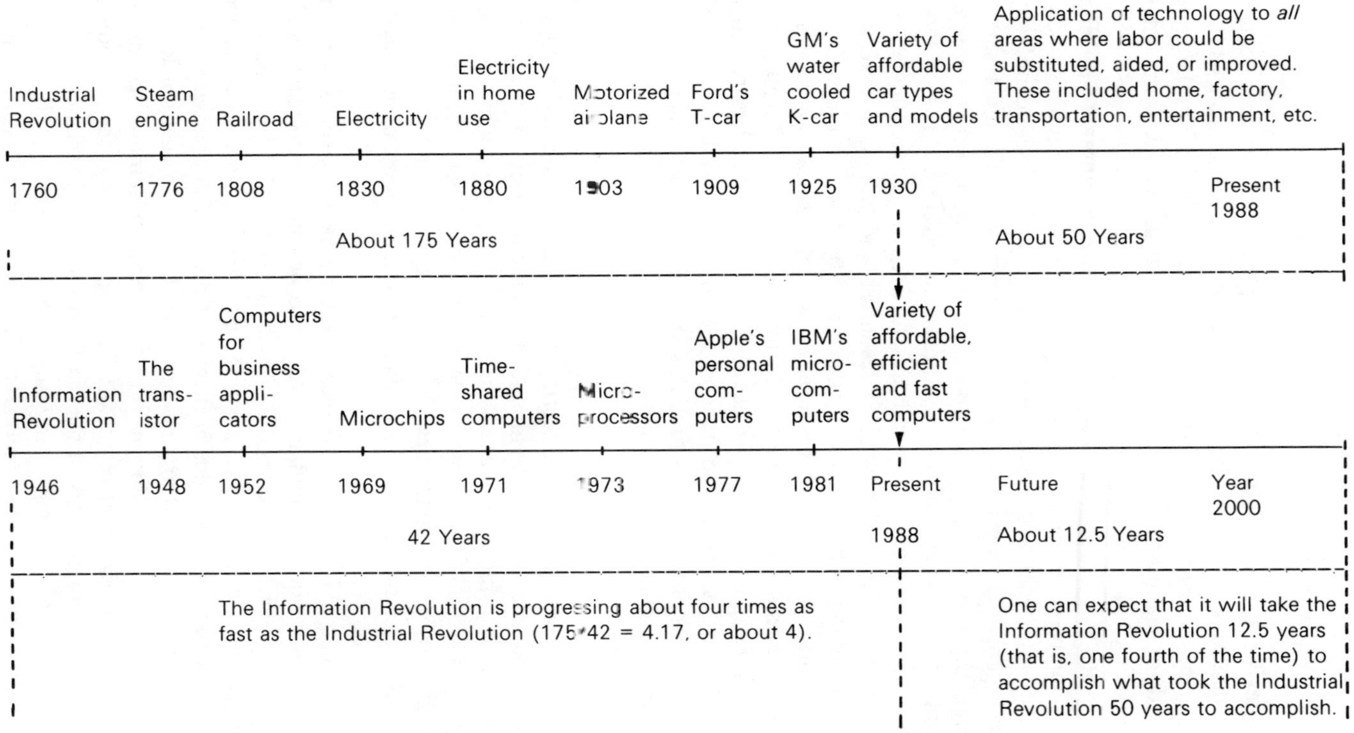

Industrial Revolution

Industrial Revolution	Steam engine	Railroad	Electricity	Electricity in home use	Motorized airplane	Ford's T-car	GM's water cooled K-car	Variety of affordable car types and models	Application of technology to *all* areas where labor could be substituted, aided, or improved. These included home, factory, transportation, entertainment, etc.
1760	1776	1808	1830	1880	1903	1909	1925	1930	Present 1988

About 175 Years

About 50 Years

Information Revolution

Information Revolution	The transistor	Computers for business applicators	Microchips	Time-shared computers	Micro-processors	Apple's personal computers	IBM's micro-computers	Variety of affordable, efficient and fast computers	Future
1946	1948	1952	1969	1971	1973	1977	1981	Present 1988	Year 2000

42 Years

About 12.5 Years

The Information Revolution is progressing about four times as fast as the Industrial Revolution ($175 \div 42 = 4.17$, or about 4).

One can expect that it will take the Information Revolution 12.5 years (that is, one fourth of the time) to accomplish what took the Industrial Revolution 50 years to accomplish.

Figure 21-2 Important Events of the Industrial and Information Revolutions.

or nonexistent, because many firms will be producing the same goods using the same technologies. Furthermore, since material needs (such as food) are finite, they will eventually be satisfied. This would slow down the growth in demand for manufactured products, and result in overacapacity similar to that existing today in agricultural production.

Together with economies of scale, competitive advantages will be gained by developing or introducing new products (mostly by combining hardware and software technologies) or creating new needs. Thus identifying new markets, creating new wants, and introducing new fads and fashions will become imperative to avoid product saturation and to achieve competitive advantages. These activities will require huge R&D budgets or enormous advertising and marketing expenditures, fueling the need for super giant firms capable of mastering the required resources and willing to take the risks necessary to develop and commercialize new products or ideas.

Biochemistry and genetic engineering will play roles as crucial as those played by chemistry and genetics during the Industrial Revolution. Their growth and importance will increase as the biochemical and genetic engineering technologies are linked to computers, lasers, and computer-driven production. Improved or new products for both consumer *and* industrial uses will appear, and new, improved industrial processes will emerge. R&D costs for biochemistry and genetic engineering will be huge, necessitating large firms capable of harnessing economies of scale. As the synergy among biochemical and genetic engineering firms, information technology companies, and the traditional manufacturing corporations becomes more critical, joint firms covering all three areas will eventually emerge. The integrating factor of such firms will be research and development and marketing and distribution capabilities, as well as the capital and human resources required to conceive, develop, manufacture, and distribute or market the new product or processes.

The Industrial Revolution has increased the personal disposable income of a large segment of the population. At the same time it has created a class of rich and superrich whose expectations and needs differ from those of the "average" consumer. Product positioning to reach the high-income segment has been a successful practice of firms that distinguish themselves and their products from those that are mass-produced. The Information Revolution will further increase spending income and create even more rich and superrich. Marketing skills in segmenting and positioning one's product will become critical ingredients in the battle to satisfy the needs of the affluent. The firms in this category can range from the very small, geared to a particular segment, to the supergiants that will apply a mixture of high-tech and individualized production to create or satisfy the needs of specific segments. Thus a form of mass-produced, customized products aimed at spending segments will become possible. (This is possible using computer-driven manufacturing systems.)

The service sector will grow substantially more than manufacturing, particularly after the Information Revolution has reached a plateau similar to that reached by the Industrial Revolution today. The growth in services will increase employment and will compensate for the decreases of workers in manufacturing. However, as service companies also automate their operations, overall employment will eventually stagnate or decrease, necessitating fewer hours of daily work, fewer days per week, or considerably longer yearly vacations. Moreover, services requiring dealing with people (such as caring for the old or sick, serving in high-quality restaurants) and those involving problems solving or creative talents will grow as it will be difficult to substitute such services by a computer program.

Changes in the service sector will be substantial, and they will be more difficult to predict. New forms of services and new types of service firms will probably emerge. Furthermore, service and marketing practices will most likely change in the 21st century. Service industries, as well as the types of service they offer, will be greatly affected by the Information Revolution, because service differentiation and customer loyalty are usually weak in the service sector. Small changes in the conception of the service being offered, its perceived utility, or the by-products of such a service can affect sales and market share drastically. Service firms will have to rethink constantly their markets or businesses and innovate or keep up with their competitors. The marketing of services will become the crucial factor determining successful service firms. Furthermore, since barriers to entry will be weak, competition will be keen, so service firms will have to be flexible and constantly monitor the environment for changes that might affect them.

In this chapter we have attempted to avoid the mistakes made by forecasters in the past when making long-term predictions about the future. By analyzing established patterns in human history (Table 21-4), a trend showing that technology has been playing an increasingly important role became obvious. This trend does not seem likely to change. Instead, it will probably accelerate through the influence of the Information Revolution. The critical assumption of the predictions made has been that an analogy exists between the Industrial Revolution and the Information Revolution. If the manager does not accept this assumption, he or she should not accept our predictions either.

Long-term forecasting presents a paradox. To be accurate, forecasts must be general in terms of the events being predicted and vague in terms of the time when these events could occur. However, to be useful, the same forecasts have to be specific and precise. This paradox can only be resolved on a case-to-case basis through individual, company-wise thinking. A list of

Table 21-6 Possible Future Innovations/Breakthroughs That Would Probably Change Established Trends and/or Prevailing Attitudes

Forecast (in Years from Now) of Widespread Application

Low	Likely	High	Innovation/Breakthrough	Consequence/Reason
Hardware-based Technology				
5	10	20	Mass global telecommunications (message/data, sound, image)	Continued substitution of unskilled and semi-skilled labor by machines
5	15	35	Super-automation (in office and factory)	Fewer hours of work
5	20	40	High temperature superconductivity	Cheaper and more plentiful products
10	20	40	Mass use of lasers	Faster transportation and speedier and less costly telecommunications
15	25	35	Mass use of lightweight super-strength materials (ceramic, plastic, synthetic metals)	
20	40	150	Super-miniaturization	
30	50	150	Super-efficient engines	
30	60	200	Hypersonic transport (air, train, other)	
Software-based Technology				
5	15	35	Super-automation (in office and factory)	Heavy substitution of office and/or service personnel by "computer-based technology
5	15	50	Widely used expert systems	Large shifts in employment patterns
20	50	100	General-purpose robots	"Automation" of homes and offices
25	50	150	Intelligent products (cars, home applicances, etc.)	Large changes in the way professional work is done
25	100	400	Real artificial intelligence	
50	200	600	Intelligent computers	
75	400	800	Intelligent robots	
100	600	1000	Super-smart specific-purpose robots	
500	5000	20000	Computers and robots that can imitate or surpass human intelligence and/or creativity	

Biochemical and Related Technologies

5	15	30	Improved agricultural production
10	20	50	Eradicating pollution
10	25	60	Improved production from animals
10	30	70	Mass-produced biochemical compounds
25	40	80	Widely used biochemical processes
15	30	100	New bio- and/or genetically engineered products
30	50	200	Altering gene structure
50	300	800	New, powerful energy sources
200	1000	5000	New forms of life

New and improved products
Cheaper and more plentiful products
Clean air and water
New and vast sources of energy

Expanding Human Presence

15	40	80	Full-scale space stations
20	50	150	Marine life
30	200	400	Colonizing the moon
100	400	1000	Colonizing planets of our solar system
10	500	Never	Communicating with extraterrestrials
1000	5000	100000	Colonizing planets beyond our solar system

Opening new frontiers to expand human presence

Medicine

10	30	50	Preventive medicine
15	40	60	General-purpose drugs
15	40	60	General-purpose vaccines
15	25	50	Expert systems for medical diagnosis
30	50	100	Mass-produced artificial organs
40	60	120	Preventive organ transplants
60	100	400	Cures and preventions before birth
150	300	2000	Growing limbs naturally

Progress towards eradicating disease
Substantially prolonging life expectancy
Improving diagnostics
Replacing the doctor with expert systems

Table 21-6 *(Continued)*

Forecast (in Years from Now) of Widespread Application

Home Life, Leisure Time, Education

Low	Likely	High	Innovation/Breakthrough	Consequence/Reason
3	6	10	Super powerful, affordable home computers	Reducing and facilitating work at home
3	6	10	Electronic post, on-line messages, ordering of goods, reservations, transfer of money and similar transactions through home computers	Improving quality and expanding entertainment coverage at home
4	8	15	Super-high fidelity sound and image systems	Performing a host of tasks by home computer
5	10	20	The Fully Integrated Home Communication Center (sound, image, telephone and computers)	Super-automated homes
5	10	20	Tele copying (buying or renting) and storing music, videos, films, books, newspapers, magazines in home computers	New forms of education and research
5	10	25	Vacation supermarkets	
5	15	25	Superautomation at home	
10	20	30	The home entertainment center (receiving programmed and live events from around the world in large, color, stereophonic TV-type sets)	
10	20	30	Home appliances programmed by computers	
15	25	35	Lifelike computer games and realistic simulations	
15	25	40	Specialized research universities	
15	30	50	Specially tailored computer education	
15	30	60	Flexible workplace in widespread use	
30	50	100	Robots as home servants	

general and vague (in terms of time) predictions is presented in Table 21-6. Individuals and companies need to evaluate them to determine which will affect them and how, and what actions and strategies they will need to succeed.

Managers often underestimate the rate and degree of technological change. Table 21-3 develops further the analogy of making a watch and an airplane. Although the implications might sound part of a science fiction story, they might turn out not to be far from reality. Business executives should, therefore, consider the consequences involved and the type of planning decisions and actions they might need to take at present, in the face of what Toffler calls future shock.

Finally, the question is often asked: "What will happen after the Information Revolution?" The answer is, "not much." Table 21-4 clearly shows that people perform manual or mental tasks. Once such tasks have been replaced to the maximum by machines or computers, there will be nothing left. The next stage will come when computers can imitate or surpass the highest of the human intellectual abilities, that is, problem solving, learning, and creativity. However, such computers are not likely to appear soon. When and if they do, it will be interesting to see if the prediction will come true that humans will be, at that time, to computers what pets are today to humans. In the meantime, humans will continue to hold a huge competitive advantage over computers because they are superb problem solvers. They can learn if given adequate feedback, and they can be creative. These talents, which must be cultivated as far as possible, will become the critical skills of the 21st century.

NEW PRODUCT FORECASTING*

Forecasting the future and profitability of new products or services is one of the most difficult and challenging management functions. The actual performance of new products or services depends on a large number of factors, which include not only consumer acceptance of the new product or service, but also economic and technological conditions, competitive forces, easiness by which the product can be imitated by competitors, cost considerations, and so on. Assessing the importance of these factors and using them to forecast the product or service revenues and profits is not an easy task. At the same time it cannot be avoided because it is difficult.

*This section draws heavily on V. Mahajan and Y. Wind, 1988. "New Product Forecasting Models: Directions for Research and Implementation," *International Journal of Forecasting*, 4, no. 3, pp. 341–358.

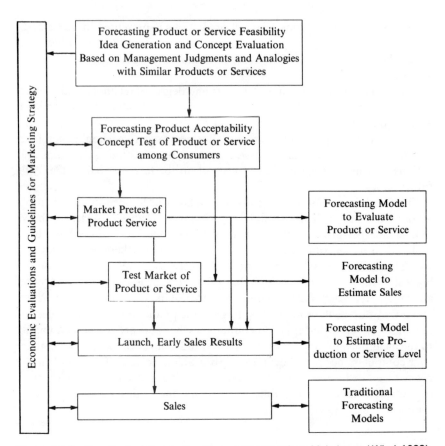

Figure 21-3 New Product Forecasting Process (Adapted from Mahajan and Wind, 1988).

Figure 21-3 provides a summary of the various aspects of the forecasting process for new products, which consists of the following five steps.

1. Forecasting the feasibility of a product or service. For example, is the product or service technologically possible? Will it be profitable? Can it be financed?

2. Forecasting the acceptability to consumers of the product or service. For example, will consumers buy or use it? How much will they spend on it? How often will it be bought or used?

3. Forecasting usage of the product or service based on pre-test-market data. How do consumers like the product or service? How can it be improved?

4. Forecasting revenues based on test-market information. What percentage of consumers will buy the product or use the service?

5. Forecasting sales from early data once the product or service has been introduced, such as, production and personnel, raw materials, advertising, and similar requirements for the short, medium, and long term.

New product or service forecasting requires information that might be found from one of the following sources:

1. *Management and Expert Judgments.*   Management's or experts' subjective estimates are used to forecast a new product's likely performance.

2. *Analogous Products.*   A product with characteristics similar to those of the new product under consideration is used to forecast its likely performance.

3. *Consumers.*   Based on consumer responses, the likely performance of a new product is derived by estimating people's awareness of the product as well as information about trial sales and subsequent repeat purchasing.

These three types of information sources are used at the different stages of the new product development process (see Figure 21-3) for which they are most appropriate. Management's subjective estimates and analogy-type information are usually used at the idea or concept screening stage, prior to the undertaking of a consumer-based evaluation study. If the initial forecast of management gives the "go ahead" signal, a study among consumers is conducted. The next stage involves forecasts based on data generated by consumers. These forecasts are evaluated by management in order to decide whether or not to continue with pretesting the new product or service. If a "go" decision is reached again, a test market is undertaken, and the data from the test market are used in a test-market-based forecasting model. Finally, if the product is introduced (regionally or nationally), the early sales results are monitored carefully and used in an early-sales-based forecasting model.

Despite their close association with the different stages of the new product development, the forecasting procedures used are not purely statistical. Past experience of marketing managers and their subjective estimates are being incorporated with those of the various forecasting models in order to arrive at predictions for each stage of the process. The task is never easy or free of uncertainty.

CURRENT STATE OF NEW PRODUCT OR SERVICE FORECASTING MODELS

Forecasting the potential sales, profit, or market share of new products or services is undertaken at each stage in the new product development process shown in Figure 21-3. In the early stages the forecasts are tentative and broad. As management narrows its product and marketing options, the forecasting task becomes more precise as the range of possibilities narrows down. Forecasting models are designed to assist management in evaluating concept-production options and forecasting their likely performance.

Through a review of the literature a number of conclusions concerning the current status of new product forecasting models can be drawn. These conclusions are summarized below.

1. There are a very large number of new product forecasting models.

2. There is no agreement on the criteria that should be used for evaluating these models.

3. There is no agreement as to the the "best" models within each class of models.

4. Most of the literature evaluates the forecasting models on their statistical characteristics, while little attention is given to their predictive accuracy under various conditions, and their costs and implementation problems.

5. There are no published empirical comparisons of the performance of the various models, except for a very limited comparison of awareness forecasting models provided in the review paper by Mahajan, Muller, and Sharma (1984).

Although the developments of new product forecasting models have occupied much of the attention of the academic marketing researchers, research suppliers, and corporate forecasters, management's acceptance of these models could be improved (*Business Week*, 1987).

In view of the preceding, the following conclusions can be reached concerning new product or service forecasting models.

1. Most of these models are applied under restrictive conditions for specific classes of products or services.

2. Pre-test-market and test-market models are mostly appropriate for frequently purchased products or services in established markets.

3. Early sales models are mostly appropriate for consumer durables.

4. Except for test-market models, all other basic models provide limited information about marketing-mix variables and competitive actions or reactions.

5. Most of the models provide limited assessment of the impact of new products or services on overall profitability.

TRULY NEW PRODUCTS OR SERVICES, OR MAJOR BREAKTHROUGHS

The forecasting process for new products outlined in Figure 21-3 applies mostly to established classes of products or services in stable markets. It cannot be said, however, that it can also be used to forecast truly new products or services or major breakthroughs, which require a different approach (see Nayak and Ketteringham, 1986). Truly new products or services, because they are so new, cannot be known to consumers, who therefore cannot be asked whether or not they will use them. Such products or services create a new market rather than being a response to a market need. Thus it is extremely difficult to evaluate ideas of truly new products or services or breakthroughs. Similarly, it is almost impossible to predict their future sales. Management must, therefore, use more judgment and take decisions based on less concrete or model-based information than in the case of new products or services that provide improvements over existing ones or are aimed at fulfilling existing needs in established markets.

New products or services constitute a sizable portion of total profits in many firms (Booz, Allen and Hamilton, 1982). Rapid technological advances, changing market conditions, and strong market competition have made it imperative for companies to be more focused in their search for and development of new products. Thus, forecasting for new products or services becomes very important as each new product is expected to play a key role in a company's future. Management faces a big challenge to select successful new products or services and predict their sales with a reasonable degree of accuracy. Otherwise, costly mistakes can be made.

SELECTED REFERENCES FOR FURTHER STUDY

Ascher, W., 1978. *Forecasting: An Appraisal for Policy-Makers and Planners*, Johns Hopkins University Press, Baltimore, MD.

Assmus, G., 1984. "New Product Forecasting," *Journal of Forecasting*, 3, April–June, pp. 121–138.

Booz, Allen and Hamilton, 1982. *New Products Management for the 1980s*, 1982, New York.

Burns, A. F., and W. C. Mitchell, 1946. *Measuring Business Cycles*, National Bureau of Economic Research, New York.

"A Case of Malpractice—in Marketing Research," *Business Week*, August 10, 1987, pp. 28–29.

Heeler, R. M., and T. P. Hustad, 1980. "Problems in Predicting New Product Growth for Consumer Durables," *Management Science*, 26, October, 1007–1020.

Kerr, C., 1983. *The Future of Industrial Societies: Convergence or Continuing Diversity?* Harvard University Press, Cambridge, MA.

Kondratieff, N. D., 1935. "The Long Waves in Economic Life," *Review of Economic Statistics*, 17, pp. 105–115.

Kupfer, A., 1987. "Now, Live Experts on a Floppy Disk," *Fortune*, October 12, pp. 69–82.

Lackman, C. L., 1978. "Gompertz Curve Forecasting: A New Product Application," *Journal of Marketing Research Society*, 20, January, pp. 45–47.

Levitt, T., 1983. "The Globalization of Markets," *Harvard Business Review*, May–June.

Mahajan, V., and Y. Wind, 1988. "New Product Forecasting Models: Directions for Research and Implementation," *International Journal of Forecasting*, 4, no. 3, pp. 341–358.

———, 1986. *Innovation Diffusion Models of New Product Acceptance*, Ballinger, Cambridge, MA.

Mahajan, Muller, and Sharma, 1984. "An Empirical Comparison of Awareness Forecasting Models of New Product Introduction," *Marketing Science*, Vol. 3, pp. 179–206.

Makridakis, S., 1988. "Metaforecasting: Ways of Improving Forecasting Accuracy and Usefulness," *International Journal of Forecasting*, 4, no. 3, pp. 467–492.

———, 1987. "The Emerging Long Term: Appraising New Technologies and Their Implications for Management," in S. Makridakis and S. Wheelwright (Eds.), *The Handbook of Forecasting: A Manager's Guide*, 2nd ed., Wiley, New York.

Makridakis, S. and R. L. Winkler, 1983. "Averages of Forecasts: Some Empirical Results," *Management Science*, 29, pp. 987–995.

Meadows, D. H., et al., 1972. *The Limits to Growth*, Universe Books, New York.

Mendell, J. S., 1985. *Nonextrapolative Methods in Business Forecasting: Scenarios, Vision and Issues Management*, Quorum Books, Westport, Conn.

Nayak, P. R., and J. M. Ketteringham, 1986. *Breakthroughs*, Rawson Associates, New York.

Schnaars, S. P., 1986. "When Entering Growth Markets, Are Pioneers Better than Poachers?" *Business Horizons*, March–April, pp. 27–36.

Schnaars, S. P., and C. Bevenson, 1986. "Growth Market Forecasting Revisited: A Look Back at a Look Forward," *California Management Review*, 28, no. 4, pp. 71–88.

Simon, J. L., 1985. "Controversy: Forecasting the Long-Term Trend of Raw Material Availability," *International Journal of Forecasting*, 1, pp. 85–93.

———, 1981. *The Ultimate Resource*, Princeton University Press, Princeton, NJ.

Toffler, A., 1970. *Future Shock*, Random House, New York.

Willis, R. E., 1987. *A Guide to Forecasting for Planners and Managers*, Prentice-Hall, Englewood Cliffs, NJ.

Wind, Y., and V. Mahajan, 1987. "Marketing Hype: A New Perspective for New Product Research and Introduction," *Journal of Product Innovation Management*, 4, March, pp. 43–49.

CHAPTER 22

SUPPORT TOOLS FOR QUANTITATIVE FORECASTING— DATA DEVELOPMENT AND COMPUTERS

Central to any application of a forecasting technique or the development of a forecasting system is the role of data and computers, particularly in repetitive forecasting situations when a large number of items are involved (see Chapters 19 and 23).

Data and computers are necessary, but not sufficient for successful forecasting applications. Considerable effort has to be directed toward effective ways of integrating data, computers, and judgmental knowledge into a system that can carry out the forecasting function within organizations as efficiently and smoothly as possible. Forecasts are useless unless employed in improving planning and decision making. Forecasts must be provided at the right time and place, and managers must be persuaded of their usefulness and accuracy.

This chapter examines forecasting needs for data and computers. In addition it discusses how forecasting systems must exist to provide the right information about the future, when it is needed, to the person that requires it, after the person has incorporated his or her knowledge into the forecasts.

DATA COLLECTION AND DATA SOURCES

There are three sources from which data can be collected: existing accounting records, original data, and published data. We will examine each of them and their characteristics in turn.

Existing accounting records are by far the easiest and least costly source of data. In addition, with internal accounting records the manager can generally determine their accuracy and thus their appropriateness to his or her situation. The major drawback of this data source is that the accounting system may be inflexible, and although it may include data that are similar to those required by the manager for forecasting, it may be nearly impossible, either because of cost or because of resistance to change, to get the data that the manager actually needs. When existing records can be used, however, the only costs are those of accessing the required data, and these costs may be insignificant if the data exist in a computer storage device.

Often when the existing accounting system does not include the data that management requires, the decision will be made to collect new data. The major advantage of choosing to collect original data is that they can be tailored to the specific needs of the manager and that the flexibility that may be desired in the future can be built into the collection procedures. This flexibility and specificity, however, generally incur considerably greater cost than the use of existing accounting records. These costs are generally greater than those of using the third source of data, published records, as well.

During recent years there has been a tremendous increase in the number of published data sources. Accompanying this increase has been a decrease in the cost of obtaining the data. The most important source of published data is governmental. In the United States the *Survey of Current Business* (SCB), published monthly by the Office of Business Economics, Department of Commerce, is the single most important source of economic data.

The data contained in the SCB that corporations generally find to be most useful are the national income and product accounts, which can be grouped into eight basic components: (1) gross national product and national income, (2) personal income and outlay, (3) government receipts and expenditures, (4) foreign transactions, (5) saving and investment, (6) income and employment by industry, (7) supplementary tables, and (8) implicit price deflators. In many cases the national income series are available on both an annual and a quarterly basis. The annual data generally run from 1929 through the current year, and the quarterly series extend from 1946 through the current quarter. Because of the tremendous value of the SCB, we discuss here briefly each of its eight major portions.

Part I of the national income and products accounts includes gross national product and its expenditure components (personal consumption expenditures), gross private domestic investment, net exports of goods and services, inventories, and government purchases of goods and services in both real and current dollars. Consumption investment, net exports, inventories, and government expenditures are broken down further into consumer expenditures on durables, nondurables, and services, nonresidential investment in structures, and producers' durable equipment.

Part II, personal income and outlay, supplies data on three time bases:

personal income by disposition, monthly; personal consumption expenditures by major type, quarterly, seasonally adjusted, and unadjusted; and type of product consumed, annually.

Part III, government receipts and expenditures, presents a detailed breakdown of federal, state, and local government activities. This breakdown is in terms of receipts and expenditures, annually, on a seasonally adjusted quarterly basis, and on an unadjusted quarterly basis.

Part IV, foreign transactions, presents data both annually and quarterly for the various accounts making up these transactions.

Part V, saving and investment, gives the sources and uses of gross savings in the U.S. economy in both real and current dollars and private purchases of producers' durable equipment by type in real and constant dollars. This section also supplies a complete breakdown of annual changes in business inventories and presents an annual comparison of personal savings.

Part VI, income and employment by industry, appears with an SIC two-digit industry breakdown and includes the following series: annual supplement to wages and salaries by industry division; income of unincorporated enterprises by industries division; noncorporate capital consumption and allowances; net interest by industry division; and, both annually and quarterly, before-tax corporate profits and inventory evaluation adjustments by broad industry groups.

Part VII of the national income and product accounts, the supplementary tables, covers annual receipts and expenditures of GNP by major economic groups.

Finally, Part VIII presents implicit price deflators for GNP on both an annual and a quarterly seasonally adjusted basis.

Besides the national income and product accounts, many other types of economic data are published at varying intervals by different government agencies. Some of the most important in these series cover financial and industry data. Although the bulk of the economic data collected is gathered on a national basis, some series are also available at regional levels.

One source of data that is particularly helpful to corporations doing long-range planning is the National Bureau of Economic Research. One of the publications put out by the bureau is a list of business-cycle indicators. These indicators include both leading and lagging series that can be used as the basis for predicting changes in the current business cycle.

A third government source of data that companies have found particularly useful in recent years is the census. For example, both the 1970 and the 1980 censuses supply detailed information for each geographic unit in the United States. For companies interested in forecasting a number of different series that depend on demographic characteristics, the census data can be extremely valuable.

There are also numerous industry sources of data. As one would expect, some industries have much more complete published sources than others, but in almost every major industry some published data are available.

Another source of published information is private organizations. For example, the J. Walter Thompson Company maintains a consumer panel of selected families to check the brands of food products being purchased. The A. C. Nielsen company collects detailed information on consumer purchase patterns at regular intervals. The F. W. Dodge Company collects data on various forms of construction activity. These firms and others often can supply needed data on either a one-time or an ongoing basis.

PROBLEMS OF DATA ACCURACY

In spite of the obvious fact that a forecast can be no more accurate than the data on which it is based, managers very often fail to check the accuracy of the basic data behind the forecast, particularly when published sources are being used. Unfortunately in most instances little information is supplied about the level of accuracy of published data series. At least one author has studied in some detail the importance of accuracy in government data sources. Morgenstern (1963) has found that for the national income and product accounts consumption expenditures have a probable error range of $+10$ to $+15\%$. This means that with consumer expenditures at their current levels this variable could be either over- or understated by well over $100 billion. Yet in the national income and product accounts, consumption is reported to the nearest $0.1 billion. Such reporting can obviously be misleading to the manager who does not examine the accuracy of this data source.

Numerous sources of error can arise in the collection of data for a forecasting situation. Morgenstern has defined *collection error* as ". . . an expression of imperfection and of incompleteness in description." He has found that these errors originate from seven main sources: (1) sampling methods, (2) measurement errors, (3) hidden information, (4) poorly designed questionnaires, (5) data aggregates, (6) classification and definition, and (7) time factors. Since these sources of error can arise in original data collection situations as well as in published data sources, we discuss each one briefly at this point.

1. *Sampling Methods.* In many situations data must be estimated from samples. Optimal sampling methods are fairly well developed in statistics, but these methods have not been used extensively in the collection of most data. Furthermore, they involve errors because only a small part of the total population is used to make sample estimates. When sampling rules are

followed, however, the manager is assured of minimizing the chances of bias and misrepresentation.

2. *Measurement Errors.* Measurement errors occur in the actual collection and processing of data. They are usually human errors that range from collecting the wrong information to data entering errors that result in incorrect information being fed into a computer. Generally speaking, the more automated the measurements and the fewer transformations on data that take place involving humans, the less likely the chances of measurement error.

3. *Hidden Information.* Often information is deliberately hidden or falsified by firms, households, or others reporting in a survey. Managers are well aware that although the accounting profession provides the general guidelines for various accounts within a company, there is still tremendous flexibility in terms of the placement of certain items. Thus the manager must be sure that the data obtained include exactly what he or she wants included. With published sources it is particularly difficult to determine just what the data actually represent and the possibilities that they include hidden information.

4. *Poorly Designed Questionnaires.* Many of the data used in forecasting are collected from respondents who fill in questionnaires. For example, McGraw-Hill uses this approach in collecting data on anticipated investments and production capacity of United States corporations. When such questionnaires are used, errors can creep into the survey for a variety of reasons, which range from the inability of the respondent to understand exactly what is wanted to his or her desire to avoid appearing ignorant by leaving a question blank.

5. *Data Aggregates.* When aggregated data are collected from large populations, errors undoubtedly will occur as the result of omitting part of the population or double-counting elements in the population. Sometimes the periods used in various published sources overlap; thus the task of fitting the data together in a meaningful way is difficult. This problem is particularly significant in the area of financial statistics. For example, national financial data are selected by the Federal Reserve System, the FDIC, and the Comptroller of the Currency. Each of these governmental agencies collects data relevant to a somewhat different population. It is generally impossible for a corporation using these series to sort out the differences in a meaningful way.

6. *Classification and Definition.* As stated in the initial section of this chapter, proper classification and definition are two of the most important areas in the collection of data. This is especially true in the case of multi-

product firms. Suppose, for example, that a firm produces a number of products made from livestock. Although each of the firm's activities may fall into a different industrial category, it may be difficult for the firm to attribute profits, sales, and costs unambiguously to each product. Since the trend in the United States seems to be toward corporations with more joint and diversified production, it is likely that the difficulty of classifying and defining variables to be forecast will become even more important in the future.

7. *Time Factors.* Since data must be collected at discrete intervals, certain time problems can develop. For example, firms that use cash rather than accrual accounting methods will report financial data for a time period that does not accurately reflect their economic activity during that period. Even with an accrual type of accounting method, a problem exists when real transactions are not reported in the same time periods as the corresponding financial transactions. At the corporate level these time problems can generally be minimized by an effort to make all data series consistent with the accounting system. In the use of external published sources, however, this degree of control may be impossible to maintain.

A final source of error in the use of data for forecasting is that the characteristics of a sample or population may change over time, with the result that different observations will be reported than would be the case without these changes. All the forecasting techniques that we have discussed so far are based on the notion that the historical data used with the method come from a homogeneous sample. When the relationships and the patterns of that sample are changing significantly over time, substantial error may be present in the data.

SUPPORT TOOLS FOR QUANTITATIVE FORECASTING

Systems of Forecasting

Almost all work in forecasting assumes that what needs to be forecast is known, that once a forecast is made it will be used, and that adequate data exist—three assumptions that are rarely the case in reality. It takes considerable effort to decide why, when, and what we want to forecast and to determine the benefits of improved forecasting accuracy if a formalized procedure is used. Unless forecasting users are involved *from the very beginning* in determining the questions of why, when, what, and how much improvement is possible, it is unlikely that the forecasts obtained by some staff person utilizing some sophisticated method will be relevant or will ever be used.

Why, When, and What to Forecast.   Are forecasts really necessary? Will they improve decision making? What level of detail is required? When are they needed? These questions must be considered by managers and then discussed with a staff member knowledgeable about forecasting, or an independent consultant, who should not be interested primarily in selling forecasting programs or services. Such a discussion needs to cover at least the feasibility of forecasting in the desired area. For instance, if a manager would like to predict interest or exchange rates, it should be made clear that such forecasts are not possible beyond predicting that today's rate is the best forecast for future ones. Similarly, the limitations and uncertainty of forecasting must be explained in particular as they apply to disaggregate forecasts covering product variations and different geographic areas. Moreover the benefits of forecasting on a continuous basis with many items must be compared with the benefits obtainable from a one-time forecast.

If the manager decides that benefits are possible, the question of what and when to forecast needs to be considered in detail. At this stage it might be preferable that the staff member or consultant spend a few days interviewing the people who are actually involved in planning and operations, as well as the manager himself or herself. A short report should be produced from such interviews and a presentation made to discuss what to forecast and when (or how often) such forecasts are required. The presentation should be followed by a meeting at which specific decisions ought to be made as to what and how often to forecast. Furthermore, a timetable for implementing the decisions taken needs to be established and someone put in charge of supervising such implementation.

Although this procedure applies to new forecasting situations, it might also be necessary to reconsider existing forecasting systems to improve the functioning. In our experience managers are willing to listen and are open-minded when the evidence presented to them shows that they can benefit from using improved forecasting systems. This is particularly true when the methods included are intuitive, the computerized system used is simple and friendly, and, most importantly, when they have control over the quantitative forecasts which they could override judgmentally.

Computer Systems.   Any attempt to forecast many items on a continuous basis is futile without an appropriate computer system. Such a system usually consists of three elements: (1) computer programs that can run one or more of several appropriate and complementary methods and provide forecasts, (2) data management programs that can retrieve the necessary data and can store the forecasts obtained in a way that can be used by other programs (such as production or personnel scheduling) or by people making future-oriented decisions such as planning, (3) an interface allowing forecasting users to introduce their judgmental knowledge about the future by overriding the quantitative forecasts.

At present there exist several such systems, ranging in price from a few thousand to a few hundred thousand dollars. Forecasting users might want to buy one of these systems or buy a computer program that they can incorporate in their own data management system, since most data management systems are extremely expensive. In addition, a procedure for incorporating judgmental inputs needs to be decided upon.

Parallel Run.   Computer systems need to be run in parallel with existing forecasting procedures before they are fully implemented. We have found several failures because a computer system was introduced prematurely. First, people have to learn how the system operates. Second, small bugs will inevitably exist in almost any new computer application, even if a program has been used many times before. Finally, the forecasts of the new system need to be fine-tuned and procedures for making effective judgmental overrides finalized.

Formalizing the Judgmental Overrides.   In Chapter 16 the need for integrating judgmental and qualitative methods was discussed. It was mentioned that the main advantage of quantitative methods is their ability to identify established patterns or relationships and then extrapolate them in an objective manner to forecast. Their biggest disadvantage is their inability to predict changes from established patterns or relationships. Such changes must be figured out judgmentally and introduced into the forecasting system in a consistent, formalized way.

Consider, for example, the start of a recession, the introduction of a new product by a competitor, a big promotional campaign, a machine breakdown, or a sharp increase in raw material prices. How will such factors affect orders, production, sales, revenues, and profits? Obviously their effects need to be considered, because they will have an influence on the future. What is the best way of going about estimating such influence and modifying the quantitative forecasts (see Chapter 19)?

To introduce objectivity, consistency, and learning requires that the effect of changes and their influence on the future be analyzed in a systematic way (see Chapters 16 and 23). This would require the following. (1) An explanatory method (such as regression) should be used to compute the effect of the change, assuming that the relationship is constant. (2) A list of similar past changes, their characteristics (such as a recession lasting 11 months and resulting in an 8% drop in GNP), and their influence (such as a 25% reduction in sales) should be kept. (3) A record of the forecasts of such changes, their characteristics and influence, *as well as* the actual outcome should also be kept, together with an analysis of the forecasting errors and the possible reasons for such errors. (4) Possible important changes from established patterns or relationships need to be considered by more than one person and included in a one-page report outlining such changes. The manager in charge should also write down his or her own changes. (5) The information about forthcoming, important changes should be given to more than one person who should, independently, consider the effects of such changes on the forecasts. These people should also consider the effect of similar past changes and where past forecasts went wrong. (6) The effect of changes should be considered in terms of a percentage (such as the recession will reduce sales 20% during the next six months) so they can override the quantitative forecasts in a way that is easy to apply.

Evaluating changes by ad-hoc procedures based on partial information and affected by optimistic or pessimistic moods often impairs rather than improves quantitative forecasts. Such procedures should not be used. They do not contribute to the accumulation of knowledge or learning. They are one of the major obstacles to accurate forecasting.

Data Adjustments.   Unless the data are collected from original sources and gathering is designed to include all necessary information, data adjustments will probably be required to make the data appropriate.

Data adjustments can take different forms. First, the definition of what is included in the data may change (for example, a division may be divided in two, or three departments merged into one). Second, accounting data may not represent reality adequately. For example, sales is defined as the total revenues (or units) of the goods sold within a given period, but this definition does not include lost sales or delays in fulfilling orders during the period considered. For forecasting purposes, however, lost or delayed sales are as important as goods sold. Third, sales are not the equivalent of "shipments," particularly in manufacturing, where shipments can increase or decrease inventories. Fourth, large orders that cover more than one period should be allocated to *all* periods they cover, rather than be considered as sales (or orders) during the period when they are received. Fifth, sales must be adjusted appropriately for the trading or working days of each period. The number of working or trading days per month can vary from 18 to 23. The difference of 5 days is almost 25% of working or trading days, and it can introduce a sizable fluctuation in sales, which would be considered randomness unless the data are adjusted. (See Chapter 19.)

Data adjustments need to be considered carefully and done in a variety of circumstances. Recipes are not possible inasmuch as the adjustments may differ every time. However, if original data are collected, ways can be included in deciding what to collect in order to minimize the amount of subsequent adjustments required. For example, companies have found it useful to divide a year into 13 months (each month starting on a Monday and consisting of four weeks) or dividing the year into series of 3 months, always starting on a Monday and including 4, 4, and 5 weeks, respectively. Similarly, lost and delayed sales are recorded and included with goods sold to define the sales for a given period.

In the final analysis, what is important is having data that are consistent and represent reality (such as sales) as closely as possible. Unless consistent and representative data are available, forecasting accuracy will suffer, because the accuracy of forecasts *cannot* exceed the adequacy of the data.

COMPUTERS AND FORECASTING

The first commercial computers appeared in the 1950s. They were big enough to fill a large room and were far from simple to operate. In addition, they were slow, expensive, and had very limited storage. By the late 1960s substantial progress had been made. However, even the biggest and most sophisticated business computers of that era did not compare with the powerful microcomputers of today. At present a microcomputer selling for under $1000 is faster, contains more RAM memory, and is more sophisticated than the $1,000,000 + machines of the late 1960s.

There is little reason to believe that present trends in cost, speed, memory capacity, and physical size of computers will not continue. Increasingly, computers will be available to everyone and will be used for a wide range of tasks and functions requiring data handling and computations. The authors believe that forecasting and its practice will be affected greatly by such availability and small cost.

A major advantage of computers is the incredibly high speed with which they can perform calculations. In this respect any forecasting method can be programmed to run on a computer. Today even the most sophisticated and calculation-intensive methods can be run on a microcomputer in a few minutes at most. The simpler methods take but a few hundredths of a nanosecond.

As an example of how a quantitative method can be programmed and run using a computer, Holt's linear exponential smoothing will be described. As presented in Chapter 5, Holt's method uses the following three equations:

$$T_t = \beta(S_t - S_{t-1}) + (1 - \beta)T_{t-1} \tag{22-1}$$

$$S_t = \alpha X_t + (1 - \alpha)(S_{t-1} + T_{t-1}) \tag{22-2}$$

$$F_{t+m} = S_t + T_t m. \tag{22-3}$$

Using BASIC as the computer programming language, these three equations can be programmed as shown in Table 22-1. Assuming that $X_{20} = 240.3$, $X_{21} = 263.2$, $X_{22} = 268.9$, $S_{19} = 230.3$, and $T_{19} = 8.2$, the results obtained from using this program on a data series are shown in Table 22-2.

The program shown in Table 22-1 is of only limited usefulness for management purposes. For example, it requires the user to input values for α and β. This is not necessary, since the computer can be programmed to find the optimal values of these parameters. Similarly, the user is required to input S_{t-1} and T_{t-1}. This is also unnecessary. The computer can be programmed to initialize these at the outset and to store these values on an ongoing basis. Finally, the latest X_t value is needed. This also can be retrieved automatically when stored appropriately in a data base. Thus enhancements and refinements of the program in Table 22-1 can make it quite automatic, requiring

Table 22-1   BASIC Language Computer Program for Holt's Linear exponential Smoothing Method

```
10 REM: ENTER VALUES FOR ALPHA, BETA, AND OTHER INPUTS
20 PRINT "Enter values for alpha and beta";
30 INPUT A,B
40 PRINT "Enter latest actual (X) value";
50 INPUT X
60 PRINT "Enter most recent smoothed (S) value";
70 INPUT S1
80 PRINT "Enter most recent smoothed trend (T) value";
90 INPUT T1
100 REM INPUTS HAVE BEEN COMPLETED
110 REM
120 REM FOLLOWING STATEMENTS ARE THE EQUIVALENT OF HOLT'S
EQUATIONS
130 S = A*X + (1 − A)*(S1 + T1)
140 T = B*(S − S1) + (1 − B)*T1
150 PRINT "Smoothed S value is" ;S; "Smoothed trend (T) value is" ;T;
160 REM
170 REM: ASK FOR NUMBER OF FORECASTS
180 PRINT "Enter number of desired forecasts";
190 INPUT M
200 PRINT "HORIZON          FORECAST"
210 FOR I = 1 TO M
220 F = S + T*I
230 PRINT I,F
240 NEXT I
250 END
```

a minimum of inputs from the user. This is the value of the forecasting systems described in the previous section. Basically, they make it possible to generate automatically forecasts for many thousands of items as often as necessary. The user needs only to be concerned with ways of modifying (overriding) the forecasts when a change in established patterns or relationships has occurred or is about to occur.

Computer Systems for Handling Multiple Quantitative Forecasting Methods

As indicated in several of the preceding chapters, no single forecasting method is appropriate for all situations. Thus the manager generally would find it useful to have a computer program for each of several methods, analogous to that described for Holt's method. In addition, an overall control program that provided a "menu" of alternative methods from which to choose, kept track of the results obtained from various methods, and monitored the data for changes in patterns and relationships would be extremely helpful.

A number of such computer-based forecasting systems have been developed over the past few years. The most widely used of these, compared and evaluated by Mahmoud (1983), are summarized in Table 22-3. In this section we will review a system developed by the authors over the past decade and known as SIBYL. This system has been used widely by universities and business organizations. Currently versions are available that can be run on most large (mainframe) computers, can be used on several major time-sharing networks (for example, General Electric's Mark III, Control Data Cybernet, and Compuserve), can be used on the most popular minicomputers, and can be run on microcomputers (personal computers) such as the IBM and Apple machines. A batch version is also available. (All of these packages are maintained and distributed by Tim Davidson, Temple, Barker and Sloane, 33 Hayden Ave., Lexington, Mass. 02172, USA.)

The SYBYL forecasting system is both a philosophy for systematic forecasting and a computerized package of programs. Essentially, the philosophy is one of building a basic set of forecasting skills, starting with simple applications and straightforward methodologies, and then expanding on those applications by applying a broader range of methods. Since this is an evolutionary approach to learning and applying forecasting skills, the computer programs are set up in such a way that they can be used initially on a tutorial basis by the novice. Once experience with them has been gained, certain features can be suppressed to streamline their application by the more experienced forecaster.

The SYBYL system provides software programs for handling the four

Table 22-2 Results from Applying Holt's Method[a]

run
Enter values for alpha and beta ? .5,.2
Enter latest actual (X) value ? 240.3
Enter most recent smoothed (S) value ? 230.3
Enter most recent smoothed trend (T) value ? 8.2
Smoothed S value is 239.4 Smoothed trend (T) value is 8.379998
Enter number of desired forecasts ? 5

HORIZON	FORECAST
1	247.78
2	256.16
3	264.54
4	272.92
5	281.3

Run
Enter values for alpha and beta ? .5,.2
Enter latest actual (X) value ? 263.2
Enter most recent smoothed (S) value ? 239.4
Enter most recent smoothed trend (T) value ? 8.379998
Smoothed S value is 255.49 Smoothed trend (T) value is 9.922001
Enter number of desired forecasts ? 5

HORIZON	FORECAST
1	265.412
2	275.334
3	285.256
4	295.178
5	305.1

run
Enter values for alpha and beta ? .5,.2
Enter latest actual (X) value ? 268.9
Enter most recent smoothed (S) value ? 255.49
Enter most recent smoothed trend (T) value ? 9.922
Smoothed S value is 267.156 Smoothed trend (T) value is 10.2708
Enter number of desired forecasts ? 5

HORIZON	FORECAST
1	277.4268
2	287.6976
3	297.9684
4	308.2392
5	318.51

[a] See Table 22-1.

Table 22-3 Evaluation of Forecasting Packages for Use at an Educational Institution

	Scores of Packages Evaluated[a]							
Criterion	SPSS	SCSS	BMDP	STATPACK	MINITAB	TSP[b]	SAS/EST	SIBYL
1. Techniques incorporated in package[c]	4	2	3	2	4	2	5	8
2. User-interface language	6	6	5	5	6	5	4	8
3. Hardware compatibility	9	6	7	3	9	3	6	9
4. Special characteristics:								
Documentation	6	5	7	5	9	4	7	10
Ease of use	7	6	5	7	10	4	10	10
5. Data-handling capabilities	8	8	7	4	8	5	10	9
6. Ability to identify data pattern	4	4	5	3	7	3	7	10
7. Interface with other programs or packages	8	6	8	5	6	5	9	8
8. Interpretation of output	3	3	3	2	5	2	4	10
9. Testing opportunities	8	7	8	6	7	5	9	9
10. Maintenance	7	7	8	6	8	6	9	9
11. Multiple modes	0	0	0	0	7	0	0	0
12. Costs	4	4	4	9	6	9	4	6

Source Mahmoud (1983).
[a] Rated from 0 to 10, 10 being best.
[b] TSP, Version 3.5 Time Series Processor, supplied by Concordia University.
[c] Scores have been assigned with respect to the forecasting techniques available.

essential forecasting functions summarized in Table 22-4. The first function is that of data handling—preparation of appropriate historical data files so that the situation can be analyzed systematically and the relevant data used as a basis for preparing forecasts. Several programs for data entry, data updating, transformation of data, and graphing are included in this interactive package. In addition, it can be linked directly to a number of data management systems.

Once the data have been gathered, the second function handled by this system is that of screening alternative forecasting techniques to select those most likely to be appropriate for a given situation. This is done in the SIBYL program through a series of interactive exchanges that provide preliminary analysis of the data. Based on a broad sample of forecasting applications and decision rules reflecting the capabilities of different methods, the program suggests those methods that most closely match the specific situation and its characteristics. Thus, at the conclusion of SIBYL, the user is given a list of methods that are most likely to be appropriate for that situation. In addition, a summary of the characteristics of that situation as they have been identified through the interactive analysis is provided.

The third function is the application of the selected method to the specific forecasting situation. The SIBYL package includes computerized subroutines of two dozen of the most frequently used univariate and multivariate time-series and multiple regression techniques. Thus, forecasting situations that can be tackled with the full range of methods described in Part B are covered by the system.

The final function addressed by SIBYL is that of preparing and combining the results of alternative forecasting methods. As individual techniques are applied to a given situation, the results are automatically stored and recalled during the final stage in the program. Judgmental forecasts also can be input and stored. This provides a comprehensive comparison for determining which methods and which model provide the best results. A schematic of the entire package and its subparts, including each of the quantitative methods covered, is provided in Figure 22-1.

Although the initial focus for application of the SIBYL interactive forecasting package was the teaching of forecasting to business school students,

Table 22-4 Segments of the SIBYL Forecasting System

Phase 1	Data preparation and data handling
Phase 2	Screening of available forecasting methods
Phase 3	Application of selected methods
Phase 4	Comparing, selecting, and combining of forecasts

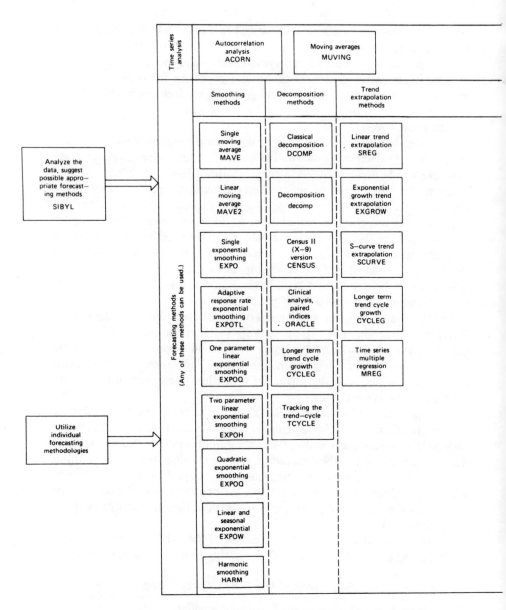

Figure 22-1   Major Subparts of the SIBYL Forecasting Package.

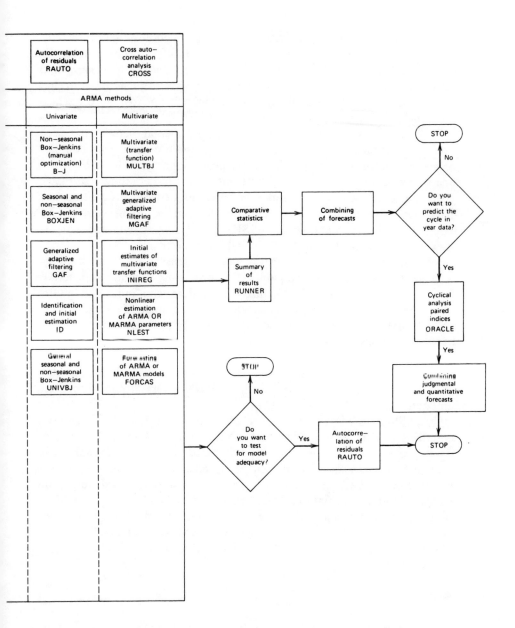

the past years have seen its widespread adoption in corporate, government, and nonprofit institutions seeking to meet their needs for systematic forecasting. In organizations still in the early stages of developing a forecasting and planning process, the package has proved particularly useful as a way to gain access quickly to a number of different methodologies and to have forecasters start applying them.

In several firms where experience in using judgmental methods has been extensive, the package has proved to be very useful in setting up counterbalancing approaches to forecasting and providing a better basis on which one organizational unit can negotiate with another in setting reasonable goals and objectives. For example, negotiations between production and marketing as to capacity allocations and demand requirements might be based on production's application of SIBYL to historical data and marketing's use of a judgmental method like sales force estimates.

A third type of organization that has made extensive use of this package is major utilities. In such companies, the forecasting function is generally centralized with a staff of specialized forecasters who pursue long-term careers in forecasting. Such groups have found the range of methods available in SIBYL and the ability to compare quickly the relative performance of those methods, to be valuable in their work.

Finally, individual managers and researchers using the microcomputer version have found that the package is applicable to a wide range of situations and that its self-help and completeness are very attractive for such autonomous use.

In addition to SIBYL, which includes the major traditional methods described in Part B, a version of SIBYL called METASIBYL has been developed to avoid the problems of many traditional methods. METASIBYL uses the ideas discussed in Chapter 11 and chooses the model of a given method, or the best method among four available ones based on out-of-sample (future) information. METASIBYL is available as a stand-alone program or a subroutine that can be incorporated into an existing forecasting system. (It can be obtained by writing to Tim Davidson, Temple, Barker and Sloan, 33 Hayden Ave., Lexington, Mass. 02172, USA.)

SUMMARY

The computer provides a unique opportunity to make forecasting more relevant and applicable for the manager, the ultimate user. It provides the computational capabilities required for the application of various methods as well as the data-handling and managerial support tasks for forecasting. As computers have become cheaper and more powerful, new computer packages have become available, encouraging even wider use of forecasting as a management tool. Given the relative youth of the fields of forecasting and the computer, such trends in improvement are likely to continue. Furthermore, microcomputers increasingly will be connected to mainframes for data access. This will enable individual users through their microcomputers to gain access to appropriate data, run individual forecasting methods of their choice in their own machines, and then store the resulting forecasts on their microcomputers (and on the mainframes) for subsequent use. This makes the development of forecasting systems even more important. Such systems can facilitate forecasting applications by automating the forecasting process as much as possible and by making the incorporation of judgmental overrides as friendly and efficient as possible.

SELECTED REFERENCES FOR FURTHER STUDY

Mahmoud, E., 1983. "Criteria for Selecting Computer Packages for Forecasting," paper presented at the 3rd International Symposium on Forecasting, Philadelphia, PA.

Makridakis, S., A. Hodgsdon, and S.C. Wheelwright, 1974. "An Interactive Forecasting System," *The American Statistician*, 28, no. 4, pp. 153–158.

Makridakis, S., and R. Winkler, 1983. *ISP: Interactive Statistical Programs*, West Publishing, St. Paul, MN.

Makridakis, S., and S.C. Wheelwright, 1978. *Interactive Forecasting*, 2nd ed., Holden-Day, San Francisco.

Makridakis, S., S.C. Wheelwright, and V.E. McGee, 1989. *Forecasting: Methods and Applications*. 3rd ed., Wiley, New York.

Morgenstern, O., 1963. *On the Accuracy of Economic Observation*, Princeton University Press, Princeton, NJ.

Silk, L.S., and M.L. Curley, 1970. *Business Forecasting: With a Guide to Sources of Business Data*, Random House, New York.

CHAPTER 23

ACHIEVING FORECASTING'S FULL POTENTIAL

Few will argue about the need and importance of forecasting for planning, strategy, and other forms of future-oriented decisions. Questions and problems arise in the way forecasts are made and implemented. In several chapters of this book we have described major forecasting methods and suggested ideas to improve forecasting accuracy and relevance. In this chapter we will go a step further and look at specific ways of achieving forecasting's full potential. Two requirements are necessary: (1) developing a working interface between the forecasting expert and the forecasting user, and (2) developing organizational support for forecasting.

In addressing the ways in which forecasting resources can be used more effectively and the full potential of available methods and experience can be applied, a number of different perspectives can be taken. In this chapter we consider three of those in some detail.

The first approach is to consider the collection or set of forecasting activities in total. This consists of a look at the "forecasting function" within the organization, not so much as a separate organizational unit but as a type of activity that occurs at various levels, within different functions, and for diverse purposes throughout management. Our objective in discussing this perspective is to provide guidelines for directing the range of applications and participants involved.

The second approach recognizes that in the vast majority of situations, some forecasting is already being done, and the challenge is to upgrade its effectiveness. This incremental improvement can be aided through better identification of forecasting problems and pitfalls, appropriate matching of problems and solutions, and taking the position that forecasting is a product or service to be "marketed" to managers (customers). Means to carry out these improvements are described in the second section of this chapter.

The third approach considers the realities of developing a forecasting procedure for a new situation. This is basically a project orientation. It consists of using an overall framework to identify the potential for forecasting, defining a procedure that will tap that potential, and then implementing it. A framework the authors have found useful for guiding the management of such a forecasting project is described and illustrated in the final section of this chapter.

GUIDING THE FORECASTING FUNCTION

A variety of guidance can be given that applies to the aggregate set of forecasting activities in an organization. Much of this will be covered in the next two sections of this chapter, but we want to highlight two aspects here. One has to do with organization structure where a separate forecasting staff group exists. The other concerns the operating procedures and guidelines used to relate forecasting to budgeting and planning systems.

The guiding rule to be used in locating the forecasting function in an organization structure is that the position of this staff group should be consistent with the rest of the firm's organization. Thus, if its staff groups are generally placed under each of the different operating divisions, with only a skeletal staff at the corporate level, a similar approach should be followed in forecasting. In a company in which all the staff support may be completely centralized, that type of organization should be adopted in forecasting too.

One of the problems with forecasting specialists is that they are usually technique oriented rather than management problem oriented. This can become a major problem if staff people are not given thoughtful direction about their responsibilities and where their emphasis should be placed. Forecasting people often select one or two methods of forecasting and then look for situations in which they can be applied, when their prime concern should be with management's problems and their secondary concern the techniques of forecasting (see preceding chapter). The forecasting staff should report to an individual who understands both the technical and the management sides.

In organizing the forecasting function, it is important to make it consistent with the rest of the corporate culture and to establish forecasting procedures that are consistent with other procedures in the firm. Three areas closely related to forecasting are budgeting, planning, and scheduling. Most companies have established procedures in these areas, and it is useful to determine how forecasting procedures can be integrated with these functions.

In the budgeting process followed in most firms an annual cycle is set up that includes the preparation of a budget for each of the next 12 months and perhaps each of the next two years beyond that. (See Chapter 20.) Forecasting generally takes on one of two roles in this budgeting process. In its major role the budget is prepared using an objective forecast based on historical data. This forecast could be reviewed by management and changes made following the guidelines for judgmental forecasts discussed in Chapters 12 and 22. In this role forecasting could save considerable time in the budgeting process, since budgeting is a repetitive task performed each year and often updated midyear. In its alternative role, forecasting would serve as a backup to management's own estimates and would identify any large discrepancies that may need to be justified. One major difference between these two roles of forecasting in budgeting is who actually uses them. In the first case it would be the manager responsible for preparing the budget; in the second it would be the accounting or finance department responsible for checking the appropriateness of the budget. In both cases, however, forecasting can be used to provide objective estimates to avoid judgmental biases and unnecessary swings caused by optimism or pessimism.

The potential application of forecasting to planning tasks can take on one of three major roles. Two are similar to the role identified for forecasting in the budgeting process: the use of forecasts to verify the feasibility and soundness of a plan, and their use as part of the plan itself. Again, in the first case the forecast is used by the corporate planning group; in the second it is used by the manager who is responsible for preparing the plan. A third role of forecasting in formal planning systems, and perhaps the one most often used, is to establish a basic set of assumptions on which plans can be prepared. For example, a company might prepare a set of forecasts relating to the industry in which it operates and then distribute those forecasts at the beginning of the planning cycle. These forecasts would serve as a basis for the development of the operating managers' individual plans.

Setting up a forecasting procedure that will serve as the basis for environmental information in planning is perhaps one of the most difficult types of forecasting applications. The problem is that the forecasts are being prepared for the corporate planning group and a number of different management users. This makes it much more difficult to determine exactly what forecasts are needed and the form in which it would be most useful to report them. In this situation a project team, consisting of someone from the forecasting staff, a member of the corporate planning staff, a member of the management group who will use the forecasts, and possibly a member of the computer systems group, can work effectively in defining those forecasts that would be most useful. However, a single individual must be given responsibility for seeing that the forecasts are prepared and distributed in a timely manner. Many companies have found that a member of the corporate planning staff is the most appropriate person to take on this overall responsibility. This individual can ensure that the forecasting procedure will be consistent with the planning cycle and can obtain feedback from operating managers about its usefulness.

Scheduling activities (personnel, production, and so on) require specific forecasts for a large number of items. As discussed in Chapter 22, it is not possible to obtain such forecasts without an automated procedure that takes into account the planning assumptions and the managerial objectives. This would require a systematic way of incorporating judgmental overrides and objectives into the quantitative forecasts. In addition, uncertainty should be incorporated into the scheduling tasks (in the form of safety stocks, slack capacity, extra personnel, and so on).

In any application of forecasting an evolutionary approach should be taken. The initial application cannot be expected to be perfect in every respect. Trying to second-guess all of the possible problems and considerations in a forecasting situation is impractical, if not impossible. It is much more useful to start with something that is satisfactory and feasible, and then, as managers and forecasters better understand the methods being used and their advantages and limitations, to improve the procedures involved and possibly change the methods employed.

IMPROVING EXISTING APPLICATIONS OF FORECASTING

Much of the authors' work in forecasting has suggested that a good starting point for improving an organization's forecasting is to audit existing problems and opportunities. While there is some literature on performing such reviews, the bulk of it concentrates on accuracy as the key problem and identifies as causes of the problem the use of poor data, the use of the wrong methods, the lack of trained forecasters, and the lack of a systematic procedure to forecast for repetitive situations. Contrary to empirical evidence, there are suggestions that an obvious solution to problems of accuracy would be the use of improved—by which is generally meant more sophisticated—methods. Not surprisingly, such solutions tend to require more sophisticated forecasters or additional training for those already at work.

Thus, the typical solution suggested has been to replace existing methods with those that are more mathematical and to replace and upgrade existing forecasters so that they can handle those more mathematical methods. As pointed out previously, empirical evidence does not support the assumption that sophisticated methods outperform simple ones (see Chapter 15).

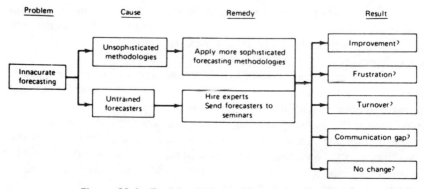

Figure 23-1 Traditional Views of Forecasting Problems.

The results of such actions range from no improvements to management frustration. Even organizations with trained statisticians and sophisticated methods are frequently disappointed with the performance and impact of their complex forecasting methods. This interaction of problem–causes–remedies–results often leads to the undesired scenario summarized in Figure 23-1. It fails to recognize that applying a specific method and obtaining a numerical output are only two steps, albeit important ones, in the process of forecasting. Concentrating on accuracy is like trying to melt an iceberg by heating the tip: when forecasting accuracy is slightly improved, other managerial problems of implementation rise to the surface to prevent the realization of forecasting's full potential. It is preferable, therefore, to use a simple method that management understands rather than a sophisticated method that is a black box, even if such a method could produce more accurate forecasts in an ideal environment.

Characterizing Forecasting Problems and Possible Improvements

One framework the authors have found useful places forecasting problems, as seen by management, in one of four categories: bias, credibility and impact, lack of recent improvement, and lack of a firm base on which to build the forecasting function (see Table 23-1). These will be discussed below.

Bias.   In many situations there is an incentive for the forecast to represent personal, political, or self-serving organizational goals. This incentive may be systematic, such as might be caused by a reward system, or some overt manipulation by those in control of forecasting. It may also be benign, such as sales force optimism or a narrow view of the goals of a business. Whatever

Table 23-1   A Framework for Matching Forecasting Problems and Solutions

Major Classes of Problems	Major Elements of Solutions
Bias, gaming, negotiating, politics	Incentives for forecasters, rewards, punishments
Credibility, impact	Relevance of forecasts, when, where, and how: Interpersonal, users and preparers, organizational positioning
Lack of improvement, plateaued, stale	Resource commitment, development plan, periodic reviews
Base of experience, data knowledge	Getting started, good practice, forecasting strategy
Major weaknesses, opportunities to improve	Response to change, environment, completeness

Source: S. Makridakis and S. C. Wheelwright (1987). Reprinted by permission.

the cause, forecasting is often caught up in an organizational whirlwind that biases its representation of future outcomes and decreases its accuracy considerably (see Chapters 12, 13, and 16). It is therefore imperative to establish a procedure for an objective assessment of forecasts (see Chapters 16 and 22).

Credibility and Impact.   Forecasting often has little impact on decision making because the forecast lacks relevance in terms of what, when, how, and in what form such forecasts are provided (see Chapter 22). The problem may be interpersonal—for example, when those who prepare the forecasts and those who use them fail to communicate effectively—or it may be one of organizational structure, that is, forecasting may be unlikely to have much impact on decision making because of the level at which it is performed. Forecasters also tend to concentrate on well-behaved situations that can be forecast with standard methods and ignore the more dynamic (and often more interesting) situations that involve changes from established patterns or relationships. Managers must establish and formalize systems designed to avoid the problems of credibility and impact.

Lack of Recent Improvements in Forecasting.   Forecasting problems arise when forecasting is no longer improving. Sometimes it is no longer improving simply because the resources committed to it have become so stretched in maintaining ongoing forecasting procedures that no new development is possible. At other times forecasting may not be improving because there is not enough commitment to attain the next level of substantial progress or because organizational change and managerial interface problems are not recognized. The remedies prescribed in Figure 23-1 are blocked by barriers that they cannot overcome. Furthermore, these remedies probably would not be helpful, even if they were accepted by the organization. Thus, it would be necessary to reexamine the forecasting function within the organization at recurrent intervals (say, once every two or three years) to determine possible changes and improvements.

Lack of a Firm Base on Which to Build.   This type of problem is generally one of getting started. Resources or emphasis committed to forecasting may be insufficient for it to make substantial impact. Even when the resources have been committed, knowledge of good forecasting practice and available methods may be lacking during startup. Finally, a sufficient data base usually is not available to start an effective forecasting function. Such a data base must be built slowly. Management should not expect miracles. Improvements in forecasting come slowly as experience and a larger data base are calculated.

Weaknesses and Major Opportunities for Improvement.   Organizations frequently describe their forecasting problems in terms of opportunities for substantial improvements. They may be quite satisfied with what is being done, but feel that more could be done. This would be the case if certain areas were not being handled systematically as part of the forecasting system or if performance was not yet at the expected level. Organizations may also feel this way when they think their forecasting approach is extremely vulnerable to changes in the environment or when changes in their strategy may require (be contingent on) significant improvements in forecasting performance.

Additional Perspectives on Improving Forecasting

Other authors who have tackled the issues we have summarized in Table 23-1 have come up with different approaches. Two that seem to have been particularly effective in practice deserve mention at this point. One is that outlined by Armstrong (1985, 1987). Armstrong's approach starts with a basic audit of the existing forecasting situation. Table 23-2 summarizes the checklist that he suggests.

Underlying Armstrong's audit checklist is the notion that both the forecasters and the decision makers who use their forecasts tend to do a number of

Table 23-2 Armstrong's Forecasting Audit Checklist

1. *Assess the methods without the forecasts.* Most of the discussion should focus on the methods. Which forecasting methods were considered, and which ones were used? The auditor is in a good position, as an outside observer, to say whether the methods are reasonable. (See checklist items 1 through 8.)

2. Given that the methods are judged reasonable, *what assumptions and data were used in the forecast?* (This step may be difficult to separate from the previous step.) One role of the auditor is to judge whether all relevant factors have been examined. In particular, the auditors might help to ensure that key environmental factors have been assessed. (See items 9 through 11.)

3. *An assessment should be made of uncertainty.* This should include upper and lower bounds for each forecast, contingency forecasts, previous accuracy, and the arguments *against* each forecast. Interestingly, in a study on long-range metals forecasts, Rush and Page found that while 22 percent of the 27 forecasts published from 1910 to 1940 made explicit references to uncertainties, only 8 percent of the 63 studies from 1940 to 1964 did so. In other words, the concern over uncertainty *decreased* over time. (See items 12 through 15.)

4. Finally, an *assessment should be made of costs.* (See item 16.)

Forecasting Methods	No	?	Yes
1. Forecast independent of top management?	—	—	—
2. Forecast used objective methods?	—	—	—
3. Structured techniques used to obtain judgments?	—	—	—
4. Least expensive experts used?	—	—	—
5. More than one method used to obtain forecasts?	—	—	—
6. Users understand the forecasting methods?	—	—	—
7. Forecasts free of judgmental revisions?	—	—	—
8. Separate documents prepared for plans and forecasts?	—	—	—
Assumptions and Data			
9. Ample budget for analysis and presentation of data?	—	—	—
10. Central data bank exists?	—	—	—
11. Least expensive macroeconomic forecasts used?	—	—	—
Uncertainty			
12. Upper and lower bounds provided?	—	—	—
13. Quantitative analysis of previous accuracy?	—	—	—
14. Forecasts prepared for alternative futures?	—	—	—
15. Arguments listed *against* each forecast?	—	—	—
Costs			
16. Amount spent on forecasting reasonable?	—	—	—

Source: J. S. Armstrong (1987). Reprinted by permission.

things "wrong." Because of these errors, forecasting cannot realize its full potential for their organization. As suggested in Table 23-2, Armstrong had identified 16 pitfalls commonly found in practice. Table 23-2 also presents a suggestion to help the forecaster avoid each of those pitfalls. As indicated in this checklist, a firm that can answer yes to each one of those questions is doing an outstanding job of avoiding the mistakes and getting the most out of its forecasting applications. The larger the percentage of negative responses for a given situation, the higher the number that are being done incorrectly and the greater the opportunity to improve significantly the way the forecasting situation is being handled.

Another author who has suggested a checklist to guide the realization of forecasting's full potential is Hoffman (1975). His checklist, originally developed to deal with a range of operations research applications, is particularly applicable to forecasting situations. Unlike Armstrong's approach, which starts with an audit of the existing situation, Hoffman's approach is aimed at directing a major new application of forecasting and guiding its marketing and selling as a project activity. The steps suggested by Hoffman are summarized in Table 23-3.

The first step in Hoffman's approach is that of *market research*, determining what is wanted so it can be coordinated with what it is possible to deliver. Since the literature is replete with applications of technical problem-solving techniques in which either the wrong problem was solved or a problem was solved that was of little or no value to the potential user, this first step of marketing research is particularly critical. Part of this step might well be an audit of existing forecasting procedures along the lines suggested by Armstrong.

The second step is that of *product design*, developing a forecasting product that will meet the customer's (decision maker's) wants. Central to this step is reaching agreement between the forecaster and the user as to the product to be delivered, its specifications, and the performance standards that will be used to evaluate it. It is also important to avoid what might be termed technological overkill. As Woolsey (Woolsey and Swanson, 1975, p. 169) has hypothesized: "A manager would rather live with a problem that he cannot tolerate than use a solution he cannot understand."

The third step is that of *selling*, convincing the customer that the product will satisfy his or her needs and wants. As suggested in Table 23-3, in order to qualify the prospect, the forecaster must determine whether the customer has (1) the authority to buy the product and (2) the inclination to buy it. If the latter requirement is not met, it may not be worth the effort to try to change the customer's mind, and it may be better to seek initial applications elsewhere. To establish credibility, the forecaster must rely on past successes, establish a history of fulfilling promises, and acknowledge incidents of failure when they occur.

Table 23-3 Basic Elements of a New Forecasting Application

Market Research—Determining what the decision maker (customer) wants.
1. The customer's goal is *not* to keep the forecaster in business.
2. The customer doesn't always know what he or she wants. The customer who does know may be willing to tell the forecaster what it is.
3. What the customer says is wanted and what is actually wanted may be two different things.
4. What the customer wants may not be what the customer needs.

Product Design—Developing a product that will satisfy the customer's wants. In addition to the product itself, product design includes:

1. Price
2. Delivery
3. Convenience
4. Style

Selling—Convincing the customer that the product will satisfy his or her wants at acceptable cost. The important steps in selling include:
1. Qualifying the prospective customer.
2. Establishing the forecaster's credibility.
3. Knowing the customer.
4. Knowing the product.
5. Selling benefits not features. (It should be noted that features usually increase cost, while benefits increase value.)
6. Taking the order. (One of the most prevalent failings of salespersons is not asking for the order.)

Product Creation
1. Develop the product as agreed upon.
2. Get customer input on major options identified during product development.
3. Continue to market the product actually being developed.

Delivery—Delivering a product that meets the customer's wants:
1. As specified and as expected.
2. On time.
3. At quoted cost.

Service—Ensuring that the product continues to meet the customer's wants.
1. Maintenance.
2. Postaudit of costs and benefits.
3. Identification of new wants and opportunities arising from use of product. (Repeat the entire cycle.)

Source: G. M. Hoffman (1975). Reprinted by permission.

One important aspect of selling a product is selling benefits, not features. Features include such things as the sophistication and intricacies of the model to be used in forecasting. Benefits (the manager's real concern) include the impact of the forecast in that particular decision-making situation, the kinds of risks that improved forecasting will be able to reduce, and the time that accurate forecasts may save the decision maker. Other benefits might include helping the decision maker to identify a broader range of options and to implement specific decisions.

The final stage of the selling—one that is usually done badly, particularly by forecasters—is taking the order, which requires getting the specifications down in writing before the product is built. The forecaster must know when to stop selling (rather than forcing the manager to listen to a complete presentation) and when to take no for an answer.

The fourth step suggested by Hoffman is *developing a product to be delivered.* In many management science applications, the product development is fairly far removed from the management user. In most forecasting situations, that is not practical. A series of interactions between the forecaster and the manager is required to complete the definition of the product and ensure that the manager understands the product, its use, and its benefits by the time this step is completed.

The fifth step, *delivering the product*, involves being certain that it has been tested adequately and validated before it is turned over to the manager. Like any product, the forecasting application must be delivered on time and within budget if the manager is to be fully satisfied.

The final step, of *ongoing service*, involves maintaining (including debugging and making minor modifications) and performing postaudits of the application's costs and benefits. Two important aspects of this step are that the user must have solid reinforcement to support the changes in behavior required for its application and that the forecasting group must recognize the additional opportunities and needs that exist once an initial application has been made. This final step of service often becomes the first step of market research for the next forecasting application.

DEVELOPING NEW FORECASTING APPLICATIONS*

Like any other management task, forecasting can benefit significantly from the development of an effective plan of action. Nowhere is this more true than

*Parts of this section are adapted from R. A. Leone and S. C. Wheelwright (1980). Reprinted by permission.

Forecasting System

Decision Area	Labor	Fleet Requirements	Construction
1. Focus and purpose	Determined explicitly by previous study	Potential users defined purpose and provided focus	Lacking
2. Choosing forecast variables:			
Level of detail	←——————————— No explicit rationale ———————————→		
Time span	10-year intervals	5-year intervals	Annual forecast
Supply/demand interaction	←———————————— Ignored ————————————→		
3. Performance criteria	Sensitivity testing Forecast ranges No comparison of actual vs forecast	Experts determined "reasonableness"	Only criterion was technical sophistication
4. Forecasting methodology	←———————————— Econometric ————————————→		
5. Data requirements	←——————— Little systematic attention ———————→		
	←——————— Few qualitative inputs ———————→		
6. Organizational strategy:	←——————— Little systematic attention ———————→		
Start-up	←———————————— Ignored ————————————→		
Ongoing maintenance	←———————————— Ignored ————————————→		Needs narrowly defined
Authority and responsiblity	←———————————— Diffused ————————————→		
Evolution	Ignored	Diffused User involvement in preparation	Allowance for input/output changes, not methodology

Figure 23-2   Major Decision Areas in Developing a Forecasting System: Three Examples.

in the development of a new forecasting application. The authors' experience indicates six major decision areas to be addressed in such a plan of action for forecasting. The range of options available is illustrated in Figure 23-2, where three forecasting systems—one for labor requirements in the state of Michigan, one for ocean shipping requirements, and one for construction activity in the Kansas City region—are contrasted in terms of their decisions regarding key dimensions of a forecasting system. In this section, we will explore these six decision areas.

Focus and Purpose

The first question confronting designers of a forecasting system relates to the focus and purpose of that system. All too often this question is addressed after the system has been designed. The difficulty—and the necessity—of answering this question initially results from the fact that trade-offs must always be made in system design and development.

As Figure 23-2 shows, in the examples outlined, very different approaches were taken in defining the focus and purpose. In the labor forecasting system, focus was determined by a previous study. In the fleet requirements forecasting system, the preparers of the system were also potential users; thus the preliminary definition of focus and purpose was not as important, since they could let that definition evolve as they developed the system. In the construction forecasting system, system design and system use were completely separate. Only general guidelines were developed as to purpose and focus. Lack of focus, it is worth noting, did not hinder the development of a methodologically sophisticated forecasting system. In this third case, it appears that the sacrifice of a specific decision focus was the price paid to obtain a system that was ostensibly general in purpose.

The failure to understand the purpose and focus of a forecasting system may be the most common pitfall confronted by systems designers. This danger may be compounded in "general-purpose" or "integrated" forecasting systems. This assertion is based on the simple premise that it is difficult for a single forecasting system to be all (or even many) things for all users. Indeed, where there are such scale economies in forecasting, the private sector often responds by providing a marketable service. Macroeconomic forecasts and some industry-specific forecasts fit this model. Firm-specific forecasting systems, virtually by definition, ought to reflect the unique competitive and economic situation of the firm, whether this uniqueness stems from geography, market niche, or some other firm attribute.

The interest in all-purpose systems may well result from the technical allure of such systems, not their economy or usefulness. To yield to such temptations is to acknowledge the dysfunctional division between users and forecasters. This is not to condemn large and complex forecasting models, but merely to stress that the demand for such systems should be predicated on usefulness, not availability.

Choosing the Forecast Variables

One of the most important and crucial decisions in the articulation of a sound forecasting strategy concerns the choice of the variables to be forecast. The level of detail that can be forecast usefully must be considered too.

Closely related to the choice of variables to be forecast is the choice of time span of the forecast. In this regard, a period (for example, year-by-year) forecasting strategy, a long-term time horizon forecast (for example, for 10 years out, using a simple rule to split that forecast among intervening years), and a cumulative forecasting strategy are all important alternatives. Cumulative forecasts can often simplify the problem of modifying forecasts on the basis of recent experience. Thus, it may be possible to forecast a long-term trend with some degree of accuracy and then examine cumulative deviations from that trend to identify potential short-term problems or cyclical deviations (see Chapters 14 and 20).

As Figure 23-2 shows, all three systems described forecast demand directly and then disaggregate the results as needed. In terms of time span for the forecast, the labor forecasting system predicted demand at 10-year intervals. Forecasts for intervening years were simply interpolations of each 10-year forecast. In the fleet requirements system, the forecast period was five years. The construction forecasting system developed and updated an annual forecast on a periodic basis. In all three instances some forecasts were based on a top-down approach and others were based on a bottom-up approach. There was no explicit rationale for any of these choices.

In choosing forecast variables, system designers often ignore important interactions of key factors. Indeed, there is a common tendency to focus attention solely on issues of demand to the neglect of issues of supply. It is interesting to note, for example, that none of the three systems we examined considered supply or the interaction between that supply and demand. It is not at all clear to us that these two factors are completely separable. Rather, it might be more useful to consider, as a subpart of the system, the way in which they interact and how that might be incorporated to affect the demand forecasts that are developed.

Specification of Performance Criteria

To be of full value, the credibility of a forecast must be determinable. Thus, a forecasting strategy must consider the set of criteria that will be used to measure the performance of the forecasting system. Important strategic issues in this area include the kinds of accuracy that are sought and the ways in which accuracy will be measured. There must be some built-in cross-checks and some redundancy so that users can calibrate the credibility of the forecast for their own purposes. A range of criteria was used in the three case examples to determine the reliability of the forecasts provided by each system, as Figure 23-2 shows.

When identifying performance criteria, it is important to recognize, as outlined in Chapter 18, that there are major differences between the criteria employed by users of a forecasting system and the criteria designers and developers (preparers) of such a system attempt to satisfy. Recognition of these differences is important in forecasting system design. On one hand, the final product should complement the reasonable expectations of both preparer and user; on the other hand, efforts should be made to alter unreasonable expectations before they destroy the system's credibility. Direct user involvement in the design and development of a forecasting system and its performance criteria would be one way to do this.

Among the three forecasting systems described previously, the labor and fleet requirements systems attempted to accommodate some user perceptions, but the construction system took no account of user perceptions at all. In practice the accommodation of user and preparer perceptions may require little more than an explicit consideration of the intended uses of the forecasts before the system is constructed. Or, to put it another way, there is a need for some overlap between what the preparers consider their role in developing the forecast and the forecasting system, and the users' view of their role as users of that system in decision making and planning.

In addition, our three examples demonstrate that there is a real danger that system performance evaluations will be based on process and methodology criteria, not on the forecasting results. The exception was the fleet requirements system, where designers did use expert opinion to evaluate the reasonableness of their results and procedures.

When specifying performance criteria, it is important to recognize that checks and balances are helpful to a forecasting system. They not only validate and challenge the resulting forecasts but also serve as the basis for user discussions of the strengths and weaknesses of the forecasts. Such checks and balances might be thought of as built-in system redundancy.

These checks and balances can be in the form of different methodological approaches to the same forecasting problem, for example, different cuts at the problem, as in the case of both a top-down and a bottom-up approach to disaggregated forecasts. Alternatively, redundancy might come in the form of judgmental inputs that augment quantitative inputs, or it might involve the application of a similar methodology to different sets of survey data.

Choice of Forecasting Methodologies

In evaluating a forecasting strategy, important questions must be asked regarding the appropriateness of econometric forecasting techniques and the potential of alternative methods. For example, a cumulative forecasting strategy, if deemed desirable, might rest on time-series projections, with deviations amenable to analysis using more mechanistic techniques, such as exponential smoothing and tracking signals. Similarly, if the long-term strategy dictates the forecasting of conversion factors, one might address this problem by examining trends using a time-series approach, estimating production relationships using an econometric approach, or examining emerging technological changes using a qualitative (technological) approach.

In all three of the forecasting systems presented, Figure 23-2 shows that the starting point was an econometric model that would provide forecasts of demand. On the basis of that econometric methodology and its results, all three of the systems made some use of time-series analysis, and two of the three also made extensive use of judgmental techniques. Only the third system failed to make extensive use of more qualitative techniques and relied completely on quantitative methods.

Identification of Data Requirements

Because data collection is costly, there are often pressures to economize in this area. For example, it would seem an obvious economy to use short-term forecasting information as the basis for a long-term forecasting model. From a strategic viewpoint, it is essential to evaluate the extent to which it is productive to apply long-term forecasting methodologies to short-term data. In this regard, it is important to restate the obvious: a long-run forecast is not merely a serial repetition of a short-run model. The ability to forecast short-run movements is different from the ability to make long-term forecasts, which are influenced mostly by trend factors, whereas shorter term forecasts are influenced by seasonal and cyclical fluctuations. Like any system, a forecasting process is only as strong as its weakest link, so care must be taken to ensure that data quality is matched with the need of the forecast methodology.

A data base designed to satisfy immediate needs may make compromises in quality and coverage not necessary—or even destructive—to a long-run forecast. Thus someone developing a short-run forecasting model in the construction industry might opt for F. W. Dodge data, as was the case in the construction system, because they are available quickly. On the other hand, a model might opt to utilize Census data, which may be acquired only with some time lag, but with offsetting advantages in detail, consistency, and coverage.

Similarly, even if data on current (and past) projections were used as the data base for the long-term forecast, a number of questions remain regarding the level of aggregation appropriate when using such data and the length of history that is necessary. Also important are questions concerning the identification and use of external data sources that can complement an existing data base.

In all three systems described, the designers say very little as to the amount of historical data necessary to validate their forecast (see Figure 23-2). In fact, it would appear in each instance that the designers simply obtained as many data as they could without asking whether those data were sufficient.

Development of an Organizational Strategy

The five preceding questions relate to specific forecasting techniques and data requirements. We feel strongly that a forecasting strategy should also address the organizational issues that will arise in the development of the forecasting capability. For example, important decisions must be made regarding the system start-up. Since credibility is essential to any forecasting system, a superb system can be rendered valueless by a troubled start-up.

Similarly, the sophistication of any system is often limited more by the technical capabilities of those using it than by the boundaries of forecasting science. Forecasting problems are complex and entail considerable subtlety. Trade-offs must be made between a simple system and one that may capture this complexity and subtlety but may sacrifice practical application. In the case of the third system, for example, was it really appropriate to leave the addition of judgmental information to the discretion of individual users?

Finally, since it appears that the ultimate objective is to develop an ongoing system, it is essential to consider the resource requirements of alternative forecasts. It is important to distinguish the operating resources required for maintenance and the resources initially required for system design and development.

In all three forecasting systems described, Figure 23-2 shows that the question of organizational strategy does not appear to have been addressed in any systematic fashion. Only in the instance of the construction system was consideration given to ongoing maintenance of the forecasting system. However, even there the maintenance function was defined very narrowly and addressed only the acquisition of data and not the ongoing use of the system by potential decision makers.

Throughout this section we have stressed the need for focus. An important benefit of focus is that authority and responsibility for maintaining the system and ensuring that its results will be comparable with the desired objectives can be more easily assigned to individuals in the organization.

When developing an organizational strategy, forecasting system designers often ignore the potential of evolutionary approaches to complex systems. Such an evolutionary approach allows the users and preparers to exchange information and experiences effectively and to interact while upgrading the system over time.

An evolutionary approach should encompass technical features of the forecasting system as well as data base and report generation features. It will be recalled that our examples demonstrated that evolutionary changes are often limited to data inputs. In the construction forecasting system, the technical aspects of the system were designed at the current level of knowledge of the preparers, and allowance for evolution of the system related mainly to features of output format and to data inputs, not to technical evolution. This problem was largely overcome in the fleet requirements system because preparers and users were involved in the design and development of the system; as a consequence, much technical evolution took place as the system was developing.

SUMMARY

This chapter has outlined a number of steps that can be taken by the manager and by individuals responsible for forecasting to improve the likelihood that the forecast will be useful in a particular situation. A number of more general situation attributes are associated with the successful application of forecasting, such as the type of manager involved, the general level of support within the firm, and the forecasting situation itself.

The level of success in applying formalized forecasting methods is closely related to the type of manager involved in the forecasting situation. Three things generally characterize a manager who successfully implements forecasting. First, he or she understands the situation for which the forecast is being prepared and knows what is required for successful decision making in that area. This ensures that the forecast is in a meaningful area and that the manager will feel comfortable about using it in that type of situation. Second, the manager must be interested in real improvements in decision making. A manager who simply implements a forecasting procedure because the boss thought it would be a good idea will never be as successful as the manager who adopts forecasting because he or she really wants to improve decision making. Third, the manager must understand the forecasting technique and its value. Even in a large firm in which adequate staff support is available, it is only when the manager takes the time to become familiar with the forecasting technique and its strengths and weaknesses that the forecast has significant value.

The second aspect of a successful forecasting application is the environment within the company. There are severeal things that a company can do to support formalized applications, such as communicating successful applications to others in the company, which indicates that the company is concerned with forecasting and takes note of those who are successful in using it. Another is training its managers in various forecasting techniques and the general procedures for adapting them to their own situations. Top management in the company also needs to give its support and encouragement to such applications. Finally, the company must give the manager access to those resources that are required to utilize forecasting. These resources include historical data (and the personnel to update the data), specialists in the area of formal forecasting techniques, and computer support to help in the preparation of the forecasts.

Finally, the situation itself is important to ensure the success of forecasting. Situations must be chosen that are helpful to the manager and in which the values of improvements in decision making is substantial. Although it may be easier to use forecasting on well-established problems for which historical data are available, the firm's decision-making procedures in such areas are often also well developed, so there is little room for improvement even with formal forecasting. Situations are needed in which the opportunity for improvement exists and in which the manager involved would like to improve the decision making.

In this chapter, we have raised a number of issues, considerations, and choices that must be made in first designing and then managing any forecasting system. Our analysis leads us to make several specific recommendations to management:

1.   Management should identify the users of the "ultimate" system and their needs and interests. We believe strongly that user involvement throughout the entire process is essential. Our experience suggests that the user's viewpoint is most often underrepresented.

2.   Management should distinguish the preparation of the forecast from data analysis and research. In the instance of short-run forecasts, the limiting factor is often timely, accurate, and detailed information. In contrast, the major limitation to a truly sophisticated long-range forecasting system is often a poor understanding of important dynamic elements being forecast. In a market situation, for example, how geographically mobile are labor or other input resources in the long run? Does supply analysis require the same degree of geographic detail as demand analysis? How price-elastic is demand over time? Answers to these kinds of questions are important to the design of a useful forecasting system, but the answers themselves are necessarily the product of independent data analysis and research efforts. Indeed, the commitment to a forecasting system requires a parallel—and often more significant—commitment to a research program that will develop the understanding and knowledge needed for the forecasting capability to become more sophisticated and more useful over time.

3.   Management should consider the development of an evolutionary forecasting system. If a research program is to be of any use, interim findings must be reflected in adaptations of the forecasting system. Indeed, the primitive nature of forecasting knowledge suggests that many firms may still be at a stage of development where ostensibly redundant, parallel systems are in order. Parallel efforts would simultaneously permit individual systems to

maintain focus and not deny the advantages of multiple coordinated efforts. Indeed, we suspect that redundant forecasting efforts might be usefully paralleled by research programs that would yield important economies of scale and simultaneously guarantee the maintenance of communications channels on the individual forecasting efforts.

4.   Management should develop explicit forecasting system performance criteria for the system users and the system designers. The existence of crosschecks would lend credibility to the forecasts from the perspective of users and identify areas of methodological improvement from the perspective of system designers. Furthermore, they would aid in maintaining the appropriate focus for the system.

These actions would go a long way toward satisfying the criteria for a good forecasting system and realizing forecasting's full potential.

SELECTED REFERENCES FOR FURTHER STUDY

Armstrong, J. S., 1987, "The Forecasting Audit", in Makridaki, S. and S. Wheelwright, *The Handbook of Forecasting: A Manager's Guide*, 2nd ed., Wiley, New York.

———, 1985. *Long-Range Forecasting. From Crystal Ball to Computer*, 2nd ed., Wiley, New York.

Hammond, J. S., III, 1974, "The Roles of the Manager and Management Scientists in Successful Implementation," *Sloan Management Review*, 15, no. 2, pp. 1–24.

Hoffman, G. M., 1975 "Selling Operations Research to Management, " working paper, Standard Oil Company of Indiana.

Leone, R. A. and S. C. Wheelwright, 1980. "Managing a Forecasting System," in *Applications of Management Science*, JAI Press, Greenwhich CT.

Makridakis, S., and S. C. Wheelwright (Eds.), 1987. *The Handbook of Forecasting: A Manager's Guide*, 2nd ed., Wiley, New York.

———., 1981. "Forecasting an Organization's Futures," in P. C. Nystrom and W. H. Starbuck (Eds.), *Handbook of Organizational Design*, vol. I, Oxford University Press, New York, chap. 6.

Woolsey, R. E. D., and H. F. Swanson, 1975. *Operations Research for Immediate Application: A Quick and Dirty Manual*, Harper & Row, New York.

INDEX

461